Wolverine

Hiking & Biking in

New River Gorge

A Trail User's Guide

R. Bryan Simon

HIKING AND BIKING IN THE NEW RIVER GORGE: A Trail User's Guide

Author: R. Bryan Simon
Photographs: R. Bryan Simon, unless otherwise credited.
Design: McKenzie Long
Editor: Matt Samet

Published and distributed by Wolverine Publishing, LLC.

International Standard Book Number: 978-1938393-07-5

Cover photo: Fog rising after an autumn rain. R. Bryan Simon.

Opening photo: A summer rainstorm washes over the New River Gorge Bridge. R. Bryan Simon.

For more information about other books from Wolverine Publishing and a free color catalog, please contact us:
970-876-0269
email sales@wolverinepublishing.com
www.wolverinepublishing.com

Please Note: Risk is always a factor in backcountry and mountain travel. Many of the activities described in this book can be dangerous, especially when weather is adverse or unpredictable, and when unforeseen events or conditions create a hazardous situation. The author has done his best to provide the reader with accurate information about backcountry travel, as well as to point out some of its potential hazards. It is the responsibility of the users of this guide to learn the necessary skills for safe backcountry travel, and to exercise caution in potentially hazardous areas.

Printed in China

Discover world-class ROCK CLIMBING
in the NEW RIVER GORGE
climber: Elaina Arenz-Smith of New River Mountain Guides. photo: Michael Turner.
The NEW RIVER GORGE ROCK CLIMBS guidebook
www.wolverinepublishing.com
WOLVERINE

ACKNOWLEDGEMENTS

I would like to take a moment to thank all the people who assisted me with this project. A special thanks to Mike Williams for helping me get the ball rolling. Thanks to Gene and Maura Kistler, Kenny Parker, and Gigi Craig for their faith in and support for the book and for me. Thanks to the men and women at the National Park Service, and especially to Robin Snider, Jodi French-Burr, and Jamie Fields for their time and effort helping me make this guide as useful as possible. I owe thanks to Dan McCarthy and Gary Hartley at the Boy Scouts of America Summit Bechtel Reserve for their input and support. A very special thanks goes to Andy Forron and Adam Stephens for sharing their time and mountain biking expertise — without them, the mountain biking chapter could not have happened.

Charles Jeffries: Teachers don't get enough credit, but you should. Your passion for writing and instruction in the art has made all the difference for me. All teachers should be like you. Thank you, Linda Laskowski-Jones and Seth Hawkins: Your friendship, editorial expertise, and encouragement mean so much to me. I am a better writer and person because of you two.

Thank you to the team at Wolverine...Dave for your confidence that I could pull this off, Matt Samet for keeping me on track and making this whole project better, and McKenzie Long for wrapping my text in such a beautiful design.

Thanks to the Harrison, Simon, and Vander Kant families for their support while I hiked more than 350 miles and huddled endlessly over the computer these past months. Your support, encouragement, and love have made me who I am, and I appreciate everything you have done for me over the years. Thanks, Wayne: I saved the longest day of hiking for your visit! And a very special thanks to my grandmother, who allowed me to take over a room and fill it with maps, notes, and scraps of paper without batting an eye.

Last and certainly not least, a loving thank you to my wife and best friend, Deb. Without you, all of this would have little meaning. Our time together has been a wonderful adventure. Your selflessness and hard work allowed this book to come to fruition. Team Simon, as always...

The Thurmond Depot: remembering the vibrant past of this rail and coal town.

CONTENTS

ADVERTISERS

The classic Skyline Trail (Trail 70) vista at 0.8 miles.

FOREWORD

For more than 30 years the New River Gorge has quietly been developing into a world-class outdoor-recreation mecca, presenting paddlers, climbers, bikers, and hikers with a scenic playground that offers tremendous diversity and exceptional quality. This playground serves as powerful bait for outdoor enthusiasts. Our story is common: We came here to climb and paddle, fell in love with the area, and figured out a way to stay. In our case this involved starting a specialty outdoor-retail business called Water Stone Outdoors, located on a corner in downtown Fayetteville.

For almost twenty years we and our staff have had the pleasure of sharing our outdoor resources with visitors from around the world. The number-one question visitors ask is, "Where can I find a good hike?" We wish we had a dollar for every time we drew a rough map with sketchy directions on a Post-it note and sent folks out the door to tangle with West Virginia's notoriously windy roads, confusing geography, and confounding lack of signage. We knew that we had great trails, but getting folks to the trailhead was killing us!

Enter Bryan Simon. A climber, ex-Army Ranger, and well-rounded outdoorsman, Bryan brought considerable skills to the table, including the all-important one for any guidebook author: attention to detail. He teamed up with Wolverine Publishing, one of the premiere outdoor-industry publishing houses, which was responsible for publishing Mike Williams' terrific NRG climbing guide. For his guidebook research, Bryan spent five months hiking more than 350 miles, always with an eye to discerning the details that distinguish each particular trail. The result is this comprehensive, carefully researched, and beautifully presented book, which will meet the need of all trail users, be they walking, riding, or running. With almost 200 photos and state-of-the art maps, this guide becomes a critical tool to empower locals and visitors alike to explore this remarkable area. We offer Bryan a huge Thank You for filling this void!

Our trail offering is extensive, with new development continuing apace. From short-and-sweet strolls to technical, lung-busting marathons, people can find a hike that suits their mood. Expect lush forests, constantly changing vistas, and fascinating glimpses into the socioeconomic and cultural history of the regions. After two decades spent logging hundreds and hundreds of miles running, biking, and hiking on these trails, we can attest to their power to keep you fit, make you happy, and fix whatever ails you. We are convinced that our community's collective mental health depends on these trails!

The timing of this guide is serendipitous, coinciding as it does with an exciting phase in our local history. The New River Gorge is arriving on a much bigger stage, finally shedding its long-term status as a well-kept secret. The Boy Scouts of America's Summit Bechtel Reserve project is bringing intense national interest to our area, as well as thousands of new visitors. The climbing and bouldering scenes are surging. Mountain bikers, standup paddle boarders, birders, and a growing number of people who are simply looking for R & R are all discovering that the combination of outdoor activities and small-town charm is hard to beat. And local entrepreneurs have been steadily building a stellar assortment of restaurants and accommodations that have attracted regional attention. In short, we are ready to soar, and this top-notch guide will enable us to fly higher. So, Welcome to the New River Gorge! Now get out there, get moving, and have fun!

—Maura and Gene Kistler

View of the New River Gorge from the Grandview Rim Trail.

1 INTRODUCTION TO THE NEW RIVER GORGE

The New River Gorge National River and surrounding state parks encompass more than 80,000 acres of beautiful Appalachian forest and river habitat. This area is an outdoor lover's paradise, with a plethora of adventure sports and opportunities to keep a person busy for a lifetime. Unfortunately, we can't play in the hills all the time — family, friends, and work are also essential components of life! So, with the idea of our limited free time, the purpose of this guide is to introduce you to this wonderful area, inform you about the wide range of opportunities, and get you on the trails as quickly as possible. The text, photos, maps, and elevation charts will keep you on track and help you experience the hidden wonders available along each trail, all 114 of them in this guide.

The New River Gorge offers a wonderful combination of natural beauty, areas of historical and cultural significance, and a healthy dose of adventure sports. Few places in the United States offer such a mix, and it's one of the reasons I've made the New River my home. Be it the simple pleasure of a light breeze rustling the vivid red, brown, and orange leaves in autumn or a swift descent along a switchback by mountain bike, moments spent here are special. Enjoy!

HOW TO USE THIS GUIDE

Organization

This guide is organized into four major sections: The first includes chapters 1 through 4 — this intro, planning your visit, natural history, and regional history. The second comprises chapters 5 through 11 and describes the seven major regions within the New River Gorge National River, geographically from northwest to southeast. Each chapter introduction identifies area highlights, gives general directions, and details the area's historical and cultural significance. Within each chapter/region, the trails are organized from shortest to longest.

The third section (chapters 12 through 18) describes the New River region's West Virginia state parks, again arranged geographically from northwest to southeast. Each chapter features an introduction, with highlights, directions, and other useful park information. The trails are again arranged from shortest to longest, with the intention of making it easier to identify a hike length to your liking.

The final section includes chapters 19 and 20, plus seven appendices. Chapter 19 describes other local trails not part of the national river or a state park, descriptions of other significant area state parks, and a discussion of the exciting future of trail growth in the area. Chapter 20 focuses on the visiting mountain biker, providing supplemental details for experiencing any of the 57 trails open to riding within the region (and described in this book). Respectively, the seven appendices help you find a place to rest after a long day on the trail, refuel with outstanding local cuisine, find gear and further adventures, purchase a map, find contact info for the area's parks, read more about the region, and find the trails listed alphabetically.

Each chapter head is color coded in one of four schemes to make identification easier. The overall regional map included in Chapter 2 (page 16) is meant to orient the visitor to the regions, while the road map on the same page will assist in reaching the trailheads. You can also find detailed driving directions to each trailhead within its respective hike.

Trail Information

The hikes have been numbered from 1 through 114, allowing for easy reference in connecting multiple trails for longer link-ups. Within each trail description you'll find a large amount of information to keep you on the right track and focused on enjoying the trail, including:

Overview: The page header includes the hike's number and name as well a brief description of trail highlights.

Information Panel: Your "one-stop shop" for a large amount of information to assist in selecting a trail.

• **Trail Difficulty:** Trails are rated from 1–5, with the easiest rated as 1 and the most difficult as 5. Very few regional trails allow for one-way travel, which often compels the hiker to complete an "out and back." Difficulty levels take this "mileage doubling" into account, and the trails are graded as such. If you design a combination that allows for an easy ascent, based upon the trail elevation chart and description, many out-and-back trails will be easier than the assigned grade — see the "Trail Difficulty Grading System" (page 14) for more.

• **Ascent/Descent:** The first triangle shows the elevation gain, while the second triangle shows the elevation loss. If returning by the same trail, the two triangles switch places. Ascent and descent triangles are color coded to graphically indicate the severity of the climb or steepness of decline:

- •Green: An elevation change of 500 feet or less.
- •Orange: 500–1,000 feet of elevation change.
- •Red: 1,000-plus feet of elevation change.

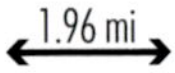

• **Length and Trail Type:** The next symbol indicates whether the trail is an out-and-back trail or a loop trail. In both cases, the one-way distance is cited above the icon — you should effectively double this distance for all out-and-back hikes.

• **Trail Activities:** The following icons describe which activities can occur on an individual trail. These symbols include:

Climber Access
Cross-Country Skiing
Handicap Access
Hiking
Mountain Biking
Horseback Riding
Trail Running

Upper-Left Sidebar/Trail Information: This panel details the general location of the trail, which USGS maps cover the area, options and combinations, facilities, and a short synopsis of highlights.

• **Location:** Using major roads and towns, this section orients the reader to the trail's general location.

• **Maps:** All topo maps within the guide are United States Geological Survey (USGS) maps, which are available for free download from the USGS, or you can purchase hard copies locally at Waterstone Outdoors in Fayetteville, WV. These maps are scaled at 1:24,000, with the particular quads pertaining to each hike also listed.

• **Trail Options:** A brief description of trail options and combinations that allow for a longer adventure.

• **Facilities:** Availability of facilities both at the trailhead and on the route.

• **Highlights:** A brief description of trail highlights.

Lower-Left Sidebar/Trail Milestones: This panel lists significant milestones along the trail in the following format:

Distance from trailhead - Point of Interest
(GPS Coordinates)

Text: Discussion of each trail is divided into the following sections:

• **Finding the Trailhead:** Grid coordinates are given for each trailhead. The description that follows includes detailed directions from major roads, usually US Route 19, Interstate 64, or Interstate 77, the three major four-lane roads in the region; or from Fayetteville, WV, the region's adventure center and home to the New River Gorge Bridge.

• **Trail Description:** The hike description begins at the trailhead. If a trail has multiple trailheads, I've used the most popular/easily accessible one and noted this fact. All major turns or changes in the trail are noted, along with a special emphasis on interesting details, fauna, flora, and areas of cultural or historical significance. A description of trail intersections is included, along with the character of the trail and any significant dangers. The description synchs up with the Trail Milestones sidebar as well as the elevation chart.

• **Trail Combinations/Options:** This section gives a detailed description of opportunities to lengthen or shorten a hike, or to connect with a nearby trail to create a longer excursion. Particular emphasis is paid to combinations, and distance calculations have been included.

• **Additional Notes (and sometimes Caution):** Includes a discussion of important cultural or historical sites or any areas where caution is required.

Photos: The photos were chosen to reflect the character and nature of each hike, with a special emphasis on highlights. Each photo includes a caption detailing its location or significance.

Maps: Individual maps are provided for many trails, and/or many trails also appear in overview maps in the chapter intros showing the trails' relation to each other, for combining hikes. All maps feature the trailheads in numbered yellow circles that correspond to each hike's given number. The overview maps are also color-coded by trail, with a map key provided on the same page. All maps are based upon the USGS 1:24,000 maps but are not meant for compass work. They do, however, offer important insights into the nature of the terrain and are extremely effective in terrain orientation. The shortest trails do not include maps, as these offer no value to trail users.

Elevation Charts: Elevation charts have been provided for most trails, with trail milestones marked on the graph. The elevation scale changes for each trail to show the minor nuances in elevation gain and loss — this detail is another tool to help keep you on course. Elevation charts are for one-way travel: If returning by the same trail, re-read the elevation chart from right to left to gain an understanding of the elevation changes involved.

Trail Difficulty Grading System

The trails are graded on a system of 1 through 5. The grade assigned is the subjective opinion of the author in consultation with other local hikers. All trail ratings are based upon the completion of the hike and return via the same route to the initial trailhead. This is important to remember, especially on trails that lead from the New River Gorge rim to the bottom. Obviously, traveling one-way, from top to bottom, would not be as strenuous as a return uphill. Thus, trails are rated as round-trips to prevent any surprises!

In addition, ratings do not take into account a hike's length, but rather focus on trail condition, steepness of ascent and descent, and the technical nature of the trail (i.e., rocky, uneven terrain, difficult stream crossings, and surrounding terrain).

1. Easy: Generally flat in nature, with very few, if any, sections of uneven terrain. These trails include boardwalks and wide trails along former well-graded access roads.

2. Easy-Moderate: Maintains a generally flat course, with some areas of ascent and descent. These trails gain or lose elevation over a long distance. You'll encounter some uneven terrain, but in small doses.

3. Moderate: Includes areas of ascent and descent along shorter distances. These trails may include ascending a short, steep bank or negotiating around boulders or other natural barriers. Expect uneven terrain.

4. Moderate-Difficult: Will test your stamina and fitness. These trails include longer, steep sections of ascent and descent along uneven terrain as well as the ability to negotiate natural barriers and obstacles.

5. Difficult: Requires a high level of fitness as well as the ability to climb steep grades for long periods along uneven terrain and to negotiate natural obstacles. Often, these trails are less used and may require route-finding in autumn after the leaves have fallen.

Special Note: While flipping through this guide or reading this chapter you may have noticed I haven't used any "Must See" or "Best Hike in the Region"–type designations. Why is that? The reason is because the New River area has so many overall-amazing trails and highlights. One person may value historical significance in a hike, while another just wants to see wildlife. Each hike included offers an experience that is ever changing and individual in nature. Choose your own path and enjoy the adventure!

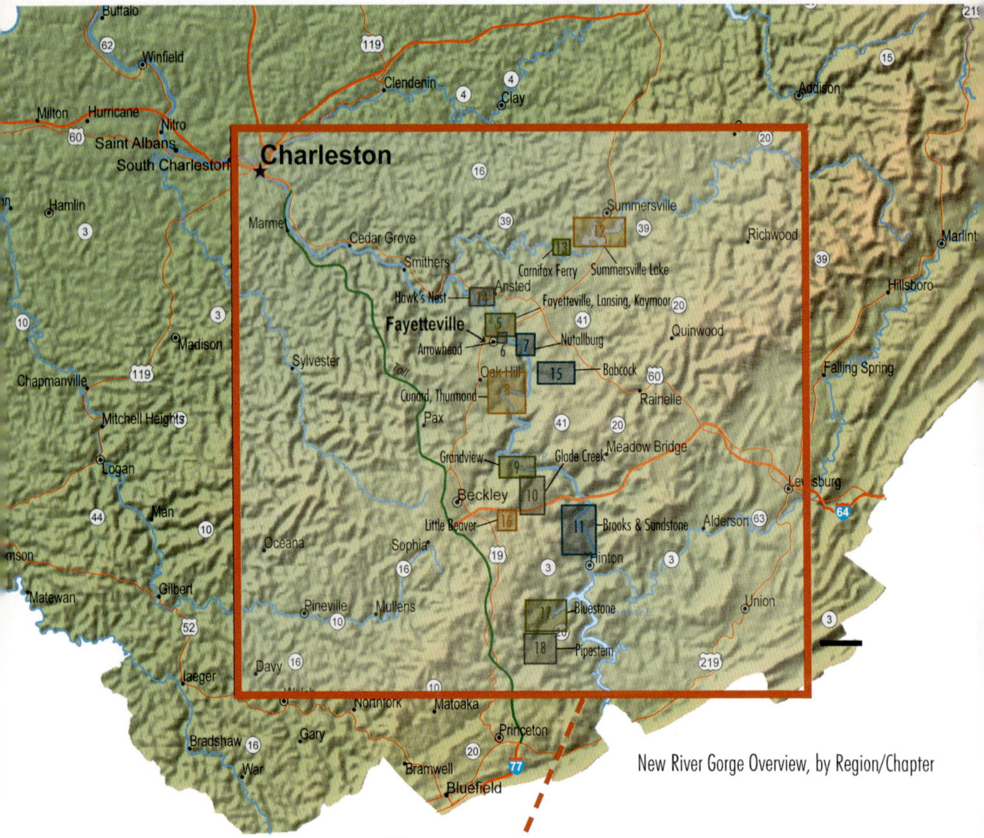

New River Gorge Overview, by Region/Chapter

West Virginia Road Map

2 PLANNING YOUR VISIT

TRAVELING TO THE NEW RIVER GORGE

The New River Gorge is located in southern West Virginia, a region within an easy day's drive of much of the eastern United States. The roads leading here are outstanding, with two major Interstates (64/77) connecting in the southern portion of the region and a scenic four-lane highway, US Route 19, coming from the north.

Arriving by Car?

From the North: Two major interstates bring visitors to the New River Gorge. From northern West Virginia, Pennsylvania, New York, and beyond, visitors use Interstate 79 and connect with US-19, continuing south along this four-lane road to the New River area. Interstate 77 brings vacationers from Ohio and parts northwest.

From the East: Interstate 64 links to this region by way of central Virginia with a connection, just across the state line, to the major north-south corridor of Interstate 81.

From the South: Travel along Interstate 77 north from Wytheville, Virginia. Once across the West Virginia state line, portions of the interstate require tolls. At the time of publication, this stretch required payment of $2 at one toll plaza and 40¢ at a second.

From the West: Interstate 64 is the major roadway bringing travelers from Ohio, Kentucky, and farther afield.

If using Google, MapQuest, or GPS, use either the address provided in this guide for your selected lodging or enter the address for the Fayetteville Convention and Visitor's Bureau (at right). The fine staff there will assist you in learning about all the local tourist opportunities, and this location makes a great central starting point for exploring Fayetteville and the gorge.

Fayetteville Convention and Visitor's Bureau
310 North Court Street
Fayetteville, WV 25840
(304) 574-1500
(888) 574-1500
visitfayettevillewv.com
facebook.com/visitfayettevillewv

Arriving by Air?

The closest airport with connections to major eastern cities is Yeager Airport (CRW) in Charleston, WV. The drive to Fayetteville from Charleston takes around 70 minutes and follows a beautiful route along the Kanawha and New rivers.

Arriving by Train?

Yes, you can! Thanks to Amtrak service you can visit by train. The Amtrak Cardinal line runs from New York's Penn Station to Chicago, and offers stops within the New River Gorge at Hinton, Prince, and Thurmond.

Best Times to Visit

Spring
Advantages: wildflower blooms, moderate temperatures
Disadvantages: rain, insects

Summer
Advantages: long days, more activities
Disadvantages: heat, humidity, thunderstorms, busier

Autumn
Advantages: brilliantly colorful trees, low humidity, moderate temperatures
Disadvantages: sometimes cold

Winter
Advantages: more views through trees, ability to see along sides of trails, less busy
Disadvantages: cold weather, short days

Weather: A common local saying is, "If you don't like the weather, wait 10 minutes and you will get another chance." The weather in the New River Gorge is variable throughout the seasons. As an example, in the last 48 hours — late January — while I wrote this, we've seen torrential rain with 60° F temperatures, high winds with 50 mph gusts, and now it is currently 28° F with three inches of snow on the ground. How is that for variable?

Spring and autumn tend to be the most pleasant for hitting the trails, and offer vivid colors from blooms or changing leaves. The temperatures are moderate during each period (60–80° F), but in spring you should expect more rain. Summer can be extremely hot, usually topping out in the mid-90° F range. Winter offers lower temperatures, with daytime highs around the mid-40s. The wettest months for the region are May and July, with the driest, by far, being October. The hottest months are July and August, while January and February bring out the down jackets on a regular basis.

Each season offers different advantages/disadvantages along the trail. See chart at left.

Events: In addition to the area's scenic locale and history, the residents of the New River Gorge know how to put together a good, fun-filled festival.

The most well-known event is Bridge Day, held on the third Saturday of every October. This is the one day when the New River Gorge Bridge closes to vehicles and it is legal to walk on and jump off the bridge — a draw for BASE jumpers from around the world. You can also rappel from the bridge or stroll out and enjoy the view. Vendors

Month	Location	What
May		
New River Nature & Birding Festival	NRG	bird watching
New River Rendezvous	NRG	climbing event
June		
Hometown Mountain Heritage Festival	Ansted, WV	local heritage
July		
2013/2017/2019 BSA Jamboree	Mount Hope, WV	Boy Scout event
August		
Oak Leaf Festival	Oak Hill, WV	local heritage
WV State Water Festival	Hinton, WV	local heritage
September		
GauleyFest	Summersville, WV	rafting event
Country Roads Festival	Ansted, WV	local heritage
October		
Bridge Day (third Saturday)	NRG Bridge	BASE jumping
Hinton Railroad Days	Hinton, WV	local heritage

from all over West Virginia gather to sell their wares to the roughly 100,000 spectators that flood Fayetteville. And do not forget to walk on into downtown Fayetteville and experience the Chili Cook-off, a superb way to end the day.

The Boy Scouts of America will be hosting their 2013 National Jamboree at their new Summit Bechtel Reserve facility on July 15-24, 2013. This same facility will host many other Boy Scout events throughout the year, and is slated to host the 2017 National Scout Jamboree and the 2019 World Scout Jamboree.

In addition to Bridge Day and the Jamboree, the New River area hosts a variety of other events. The list above includes local festivals and events, with a particular emphasis on outdoor activities.

For more information on these and other events, contact the New River Gorge Convention and Visitors Bureau.

New River Gorge Convention and Visitors Bureau
310 Oyler Avenue
Oak Hill, WV 25901
(800) 927-0263
newrivergorgecvb.com

The iconic New River Gorge Bridge, home of Bridge Day each October. Photo: Dawn Green

Hospitals

If it is not an emergency but you need urgent medical care, these are the closest hospitals:

Plateau Medical Center
Oak Hill, WV
(304) 469-8600

Princeton Community Hospital
Princeton, WV
(304) 487-7000

Raleigh General Hospital
Beckley, WV
(304) 256-4100

Summersville Memorial Hospital
Summersville, WV
(304) 872-2891

Enjoying the New River Gorge

Safety: No matter how careful you are or how much you know, accidents happen. The following information is included to help you prepare for a day trip into the New River Gorge and to respond correctly in case of an accident.

IN CASE OF EMERGENCY
Call 911.
What to do:
1) Tell them the *type* of incident/injury.
2) Tell them *where* you are.
3) Be *calm* and answer their questions.

National Park Service – New River Gorge National River
Report any violations of park regulations, dangerous actions, or concerns that are non-life-threatening:
Glen Jean, WV
(304) 465-0508

Prepare and Prevent

The "Ten Essentials": You can bring along any number of variations on the Ten Essentials for an outdoor adventure. Below is a list suited for the New River Gorge and surrounding state parks:

1. **Water** – Heavy, but worth it.
2. **Extra food** – You never know when you'll need extra calories.
3. **Another layer (extra clothing)** – The weather changes fast in the New River Gorge.
4. **First-aid kit** – You never know…
5. **Sunscreen/sunglasses** – Especially down by the river.
6. **Headlamp** – The steep gorge walls block the sun early in places; night falls quickly in the forest.
7. **Knife** – Doesn't need to be something Rambo would carry — just a good, useful trail knife.
8. **Matches or firestarter** – Just in case, but only if you have to.
9. **Cell phone** – Reception is pretty good in most areas.
10. **This guide, and/or a map and compass** – To avoid getting lost.

Many simple preventative actions help keep you out of trouble on the trail. The first, and most important, is to thoroughly educate yourself about the area you're visiting. Another is to let someone back home know where you're headed. If out with others, find out if they have any ailments that might be of concern. The final thing is to take a wilderness first aid or CPR course — a little knowledge goes a long way in the field.

Leave No Trace

The New River Gorge National River and surrounding state parks are a treasure to preserve now and for future generations. The area's beauty, history, and culture must be protected, and each of us has a role in this endeavor. When you see a flower, don't pick it, but instead take a picture and leave it for the next hiker. If you find a relic near the ruins of a coal-mining town, leave it in place and think about what life was like back in those days. When you finish your lunch, put the packaging back in your backpack, so that an animal does not ingest the plastic wrapper.

If you're unfamiliar with the Leave No Trace organization (LNT.org), I encourage you to read about their mission and incorporate their teachings into your outdoor activities. Below are the Leave No Trace Seven Principles:

1. **Plan Ahead and Prepare**
2. **Travel and Camp on Durable Surfaces**
3. **Dispose of Waste Properly**
4. **Leave What You Find**
5. **Minimize Campfire Impacts**
6. **Respect Wildlife**
7. **Be Considerate of Other Visitors**

leave no trace™
CENTER FOR OUTDOOR ETHICS

The member-driven Leave No Trace Center for Outdoor Ethics teaches people how to enjoy the outdoors responsibly. This copyrighted information has been reprinted with permission from the Leave No Trace Center for Outdoor Ethics: LNT.org

Trail Etiquette

In addition to the Leave No Trace principles mentioned above, you can also practice other trail "niceties" to improve the experience for yourself and for everyone else. Below are the Top 10 trail-etiquette tips, in no particular order:

1) Bikers yield to hikers and horses; hikers yield to horses.
2) Keep to the established trail. Do not cut switchbacks or take shortcuts through the forest.
3) Do not destroy cairns or trail markers. Do not gather stones to make new ones.
4) If traveling on wide trails, keep to the right; if you want to pass, do so on the left.
5) Don't harass or disturb wildlife.
6) Turn off the phone and the music. When in nature, *be* in nature.
7) If you encounter another hiker on a steep section, the person descending should step aside and allow the ascending person to pass (unless, of course, the latter is looking for a handy excuse to take a quick break!).
8) When nature calls, get well off the trail and at least 200 feet from any water sources.
9) Keep your dog leashed.
10) Say "Hello" — this is just what hikers do!

Jason Marshall climbing on Endless Wall. Photo: Mike Williams

Other Activities

Not only does the region offer amazing trails, it's also home to a variety of adventure sports. The list below speaks to just a few of them:

- **Climbing:** The New River Gorge is home to more than 1,500 climbing routes. Don't know how? No worries: Two local climbing outfits, New River Mountain Guides and Hard Rock Climbing, can get you up and cranking.
- **White Water Rafting and Kayaking:** The New and Gauley rivers are two of the best whitewater rivers in the United States. Take a ride on the river!
- **Zip Lining:** One of the newest adventures is the treetop canopy tour offered by many local resorts. Fly between trees and experience the forest from above.

Rules and Regulations

Rules and Regulations for the New River Gorge National River

The New River Gorge National River has a number of rules and regulations governing park usage. These rules are in place to allow all user groups to enjoy the gorge and to protect this amazing and unique national treasure. Two key documents include the "Code of Federal Regulations" and the "Superintendent's Compendium," the definitive rules for all National Park Service (NPS) lands in the region, including the Gauley River National Recreation Area and the Bluestone National Scenic River. To review these documents and for more information, visit nps.gov/neri/parkmgmt/lawsandpolicies.htm or speak with NPS personnel. They will provide the latest information to help you safely enjoy the gorge.

Overall Park Regulations:

- **Visiting Hours:** Visiting hours are limited from sunrise to sunset in the following areas: Canyon Rim Visitor Center and grounds, Sandstone Visitor Center and grounds, park headquarters in Glen Jean, WV, the Dunglen Day Use area (except the parking lot and group campsite), and a portion of Beauty Mountain.
- **Commercial Trips:** Certain regulations pertain to commercial trips. These regulations involve overall group size and group-to-guide ratios. Please refer to the "Superintendent's Compendium" for additional details.
- **Road Access and Usage:** Off-road vehicles/ATVs are prohibited within the park and on all park roads.
- **Firewood Transportation:** Due to infestation by the emerald ash borer beetle, transporting firewood into the New River Gorge National River or the Gauley River National Recreation Area is prohibited. (See "Fauna" in Chapter 3 for additional details on the beetle.)
- **Alcohol Use:** Alcoholic beverages are permitted within the park except in the following areas: park headquarters, Dunglen Day Use area, Grandview Top, Bluestone National Scenic River, Stone Cliff visitor use area, and Thayer public areas.

• **Historic Buildings and Mines:** Entering any mine opening is prohibited, not to mention extremely dangerous. Do not enter mine buildings or other structures!

Trail Regulations:

1) Pack it in, pack it out. No littering. Carry out all trash.
2) Do not disturb, destroy, or remove any natural or cultural objects found within the park.
3) No motorized vehicles are permitted on park trails. No off-road vehicles or ATVs.
4) Bicycles are only permitted on designated trails. See Chapter 20: New River Gorge Mountain Biking for more information.
5) All pets must be kept on a leash no longer than six feet.

Paddlers digging hard through rapids near Nuttallburg.

Biking Regulations:

1) Ride only on permitted trails.
2) Stay in control at all times and remember your abilities.
3) Yield the right of way to pedestrians; be considerate of other users.
4) Wear a helmet at all times.
5) Do not scare animals or birds.

Other User-Group Regulations:

• **Camping:** Camping is permitted within the park at established campsites along riverfront land. You'll find primitive *drive-in campsites* at: Army Camp, Grandview Sandbar, Glade Creek, Hellems Beach, and Gauley Tailwaters. The primitive *walk-in campsites* include: Glade Creek, Grandview Sandbar, Thayer, Stone Cliff, and Brooklyn. All sites are first-come, first-served. Camping is prohibited within 25 feet of all main roads within the park and within 100 feet of any developed area, trail, trailheads, park structures, historical ruins, water source, or improved area. Additionally, camping is prohibited in certain named areas. Please see the "Superintendent's Compendium" for the latest information. You may use deadwood found on the ground in campfires; however, under no circumstances may you fell standing trees (dead or alive) for firewood. Please speak with NPS personnel for additional details.

• **Climbing:** Climbing is permitted throughout the park with the exception of the Grandview Region. The climbing ban in Grandview includes any type of climbing, rappelling, or bouldering. A permit is necessary for group commercial climbing anywhere within NPS boundaries. The maximum size for a commercial climbing group is 15 persons per group in the Bridge area and 10 persons per group at any other crag. The client-to-guide ratio must be at least 4:1 in all climbing areas. The cutting or removal of vegetation is also prohibited.

• **Fishing:** Fishing is permitted throughout the park except within 100 feet of boat launch/take-out areas. Permits from the West Virginia Division of Natural Resources (WVDNR) are required. Some areas require catch and release. Speak with NPS personnel for additional details.

• **Hunting/Trapping:** Hunting is permitted in the park with a valid West Virginia hunting license and during the seasons regulated by the WVDNR. Trapping is prohibited throughout the entire park. The following areas do not allow hunting at any time:
• **Burnwood environmental education area:** This is the location of Burnwood Trail (Trail 9; Fayetteville, Lansing, and Kaymoor Region). For more information about the boundaries of this no-hunting area, refer to the "Superintendent's Compendium."
• **Grandview:** The area of the former Grandview State Park is off-limits to hunting and includes Grandview Top, home to the majority of the Grandview Region trails.
• **Park Loop Trail (Trail 8; Fayetteville, Lansing, and Kaymoor Region):** Hunting is prohibited along this trail and in the surrounding area.

• **Pets:** Pets are allowed but must be kept on a leash no greater than six feet long. Pets may be secured to objects for up to four hours, but cannot be secured to trees, woody plants, or garbage receptacles. At any of the visitor centers, pets may only be secured to objects for one hour. Pets left unattended must have access to shade, water, and fresh air. Pet owners must pick up and discard any pet excrement.

Rules and Regulations for West Virginia State Parks

The West Virginia state-park system has a number of rules and regulations governing public use of the lands and park facilities. The chief governing document is Title 58, Series 31: "Public use of West Virginia State Parks, State Forests, and State Wildlife Management Areas under the Division of Natural Resources." This document is an active link — "WV State Park Regulations" — along the left-hand column at any of the state-park home pages.

Overall Park Regulations:

• **Visiting Hours:** Unless otherwise posted, all state parks, forests, and wildlife management areas are closed from 10 p.m. to 6 a.m.
• **Road Access and Usage:** Off-road vehicles/ATVs, trail bikes, snowmobiles, and motorbikes are prohibited on any trail.
• **Alcohol Use:** Alcoholic beverages are not permitted unless served by a state park–owned facility or by authorized exception from the Director.
• **Fires:** Fires may only be lit in designated areas: fire pits, fire rings, and fireplaces.
• **Swimming:** Swimming is prohibited except where designated.

Trail Regulations:

1) Pack it in, pack it out. No littering. Carry out all trash.
2) Do not disturb, destroy, or remove any natural or cultural objects found within the park.
3) No motorized vehicles are permitted on park trails. No off-road vehicles or ATVs.
4) Bicycles are only permitted on designated trails. See Chapter 20: New River Gorge Mountain Biking for more information.
5) All pets must be kept on a leash no longer than ten feet.

Biking Regulations:

1) Ride only on permitted trails.

2) Do not ride on trails designated for horseback only.

3) Mountain bikes may be ridden on logging, oil, or gas-well roads.

Other User-Group Regulations:

Adventure Activities: Rock climbing, rappelling, hang gliding, parachuting, parasailing, skydiving, spelunking, and other "like or similar activities that require a high degree of specialized training and equipment" are permitted.

Camping: Camping is permitted at established campsites.

Fishing: Fishing is not permitted unless specified within an individual park. See park employees for additional information.

Hunting/Trapping: Hunting is prohibited in state parks, but allowed in state forests and wildlife management areas. Hunters must have a valid West Virginia hunting license and hunt only during a valid WVDNR season.

Pets: Only dogs and cats are allowed, and must be kept on a leash no longer than ten feet. Owners must pick up and discard any pet excrement and must keep their pet from disturbing other guests. Pets are allowed in selected pet-friendly lodging, but not in lodges or at swimming pools or beaches.

An amphibious resident of Nuttallburg.

3 NATURAL HISTORY OF THE NEW RIVER GORGE

The New River Gorge and surrounding region are blessed with a variety of plants and animals that populate a diverse landscape of river bottoms and mountaintops. From large mammals to the smallest wildflower, any trail in this area will reward you with a glimpse of the Mother Nature at her finest. The following section gives a brief overview of the region's many natural wonders.

Flora

Diversity best describes the New River Gorge when speaking of plants. With well over 1,800 flora species within the national river and surrounding state parks, there is hardly a time throughout spring and summer when the area is devoid of blooms. Within West Virginia, 2,500 different species of plants have been identified, of which 74 percent are considered native to the area (the Appalachian Mountains), while the other 26 percent comprise some form of non-native/invasive plant.

The forests of the New River Gorge are mixed mesophytic, which translated from biology-speak means a forest that receives a moderate amount of moisture. Here, you'll find a number of different species of hardwood tree, including maple, oak, beech, sycamore, ash, and birch. The Sugar Maple, the West Virginia state tree, is also commonly found here. Among the local evergreens, none is more abundant than the rhododendron, which predominates around area streams. (Rhododendron blooms are the West Virginia state flower.) You will also find groves of Eastern hemlock and various species of pine, as well as mountain laurel in the forest undergrowth.

The Appalachian Mountains are known for their hundreds of perennial and annual wildflowers and herbs. Spring and summer are a wonderful time to visit and experience the vivid colors of an Appalachian forest. Among unique plants in the area, the American ginseng is highly valued around the world for its medicinal benefits, but do not pick any, as it is a protected species. Other regional medicinal plants include goldenseal, bloodroot, and black cohosh.

A discussion on New River flora would not be complete without mentioning a significant loss to the region: The New River Gorge forests were once predominately populated by the American chestnut (*Castanea dentata*). The chestnut blight of the early twentieth century eliminated this species, leaving only small sprouts that are immune to the fungus.

The National Park Service has developed handouts listing many of the area's trees, shrubs, vines, and wildflowers. As always, remember your Leave No Trace Seven Principles (page 21) when observing the diverse flora.

Fauna

The New River Gorge and surrounding region are blessed with an abundance of wildlife. The New River Gorge National River hosts no less than 54 different species of mammals, 233 species of birds, 38 species of reptiles, and 48 different species of amphibians, a wildlife boon for any curious visitor!

Mammals

So what will you see during your visit? The most common mammals you'll encounter on a trip into the gorge are white-tailed deer, gray squirrels, and chipmunks. That said, you never know what you might run into on the trail. The black bear population is growing in West Virginia, and most rapidly within this region. Ask locals if they have seen a bear in the park, and the most likely answer will be *Yes!*.

Other mammals that also call this area home include multiple species of small mammals like moles, shrews, and mice. Skunks, raccoons, bobcats, coyotes, and red and gray foxes are seen on occasion, and river animals such as muskrat, beaver, river otter, and mink populate the streams.

Two gorge-dwelling mammals are on the Endangered Species List: the Indiana bat and the Virginia big-eared bat. These bats, along with the other nine bat species identified within the area, use abandoned mines to roost. Another important regional species that is threatened and may soon be added to the endangered list is the Allegheny woodrat. This brownish-gray rat makes its home under boulders, along rock walls, and in caves or mines, making the New River Gorge a perfect environment.

Birds

An amazing 233 different bird species have been identified locally. From wild turkey to bald eagles and many species in between, the area is a bird watcher's wonderland. The wild turkey population is large and thriving — visitors often see them running through the forest. While researching this guide, I saw well over 100 different gobblers and hens.

Bird watchers have identified 13 different species of raptors. A bald eagle nest is perched upon a high branch of a sycamore tree on the northern end of Brooks Island; learn more about this nest in the Sandstone Falls Overlook Trail (Trail 44). On a recent winter eagle survey (January 2013) conducted at multiple locations, watchers identified 27 bald eagles, five golden eagles, and two undetermined eagle species. In addition to eagles, peregrine falcons and a number of hawk species live in the area.

Waterfowl and other migratory birds make up the remainder of the bird population and account for the greatest number of species. For anyone interested, the National Park Service has developed a "Bird Checklist" that exemplifies the region's diversity.

Reptiles

Amongst the many reptile species that live here, pay special attention to poisonous snakes. The timber rattlesnake and copperhead are both common. As with any snake, give them wide birth. Both are of the pit viper family; their venom is toxic, but they are not naturally aggressive. If given a choice, they will retreat — as should you!

If you are bitten, call 911, evacuate as quickly as possible, and get to a local hospital. Hospitals in this area carry CroFab, an antivenin for pit viper bites. Do not cut, suck, or squeeze the bite location.

Timber rattlesnake. Photo: Larry Jones

Copperhead. Photo: Larry Jones

Amphibians

A great number of frogs, toads, and salamanders live within the park. It is not uncommon to see salamanders while hiking, particularly near rock walls.

Geology

The New River Gorge National River offers an interesting view into the forces that have shaped our world over the eons. The New River, thought to be among the oldest in the world, has carved a 900-foot gorge within one of the oldest mountain ranges in the world, the Appalachian Mountains (no spring chickens themselves at 480 million years old).

The River

The New River originates in western North Carolina and flows north through Virginia and into West Virginia for 320 total miles, 53 of which lie within the New River Gorge National River. The New River is actually thought to be part of an ancient river system called the Teays River that dates back to around 320 million years ago. The terminus of this older New River is at the junction with the Gauley River, where these two rivers combine to form the Kanawha River. The water that flows through the gorge eventually makes its way out of the mountains, into the Ohio River and to Illinois, and finally down the mighty Mississippi to the Gulf of Mexico.

The Rock

The rock formations in the New River Gorge and surrounding areas are mainly from the Pennsylvanian and Mississippian periods (320–330 million years ago). These formations are composed of various types of sandstone, including the quartz-rich Nuttall sandstone loved by climbers, shale, and coal. The coal seams found in the gorge walls had an enormous impact on the area in the late 1800s and early 1900s, and still play an enormous role in the regional economy today. See Chapter 4: Regional History of the New River Gorge (page 30) for more.

The Emerald Ash Borer

The emerald ash borer is an exotic beetle whose larvae feed on the inner bark of ash trees, disrupting the trees' ability to transport water and nutrients, and eventually killing them. Discovered in Michigan in 2002 and in West Virginia in 2007, this beetle is the reason for the local firewood quarantine. *Do not transport any firewood into or out of the area, as this is a common transmission vector.* You may see green or purple triangular traps hanging in various trees — these are meant to trap the emerald ash borer.

Emerald ash borer trap.

4 REGIONAL HISTORY OF THE NEW RIVER GORGE

The New River Gorge and the surrounding area have a unique and interesting history, dating from prehistoric times, up through the pioneer days and Civil War, and continuing into the Industrial Revolution and present. The following chapter gives a short synopsis of this history. For additional information regarding regional lore, please see Appendix F: Recommended Reading (page 350) for outstanding titles on the subjects below.

Native Americans

The Adena people were a prehistoric Native American culture that populated the New River Gorge area from roughly 800 BC to 1 AD. These people populated a large region of the Mid-Atlantic and Midwest, including West Virginia, Ohio, Kentucky, and Indiana. The Adena were one of the first cultures that transitioned from a purely hunter-gatherer society into one that incorporated farming into their way of life.

Documented Adena sites have been found within the gorge. This culture notoriously built mounds to bury their dead, hence their moniker the "mound builders." Some of these mounds measured up to 300 feet in diameter, and one of the largest is located at the Grave Creek Mound State Park in the northern panhandle of West Virginia. The closest mound to the New River Gorge region is the Criel Mound in South Charleston, WV.

Just west of the gorge, along the Kanawha River and in present-day Mount Carbon, WV, engineers of the Chesapeake and Ohio Railway (C&O) discovered an enormous rock wall measuring almost ten miles in length in the late 1800s. Although many guesses have been made regarding the wall's purpose, none are for sure. Dating suggests that the Hopewell people, a culture that post-dates the Adena, built this wall.

Pioneers

Surveyors began to move into southern West Virginia (then Virginia) in the mid-1700s. Conflict with Native Americans was common during that period, and real settlement did not begin until the late 1700s and early 1800s. See the Additional Notes for the Bluestone Turnpike Trail (Trail 98) to learn about Mary Draper Ingles and an interesting event from this era.

Travel by haulage to the Kaymoor mines.
Photo: National Park Service

Civil War

You'll find many Civil War–related sites in the area, as it changed hands between Confederate and Union forces on multiple occasions throughout the conflict. The first battle of note took place to the west at Gauley Bridge in 1861 when General Wise, former governor of Virginia and Confederate commander of Wise's Legion, burned the covered bridge here during a retreat down-valley.

Near Summersville, WV, two important early engagements, the Battle of Kessler's Crossroads and the Battle of Carnifex Ferry, were fought in the late summer and early fall of 1861. General John B. Floyd routed a Union force at Kessler's Crossroads on August 15, 1861, and rather than continue to press the defeated enemy, he stayed put with his command in defensive positions within today's Carnifex Ferry Battlefield State Park. On this ground he was defeated less than a month later, and was himself forced to retreat toward Lewisburg, WV.

The town of Ansted, near Hawk's Nest State Park, is also a site of Civil War importance and has three listings on the Civil War Trails of West Virginia: Contentment is the home of Colonel George Imboden, who served with the 18th Virginia Cavalry during the Gettysburg Campaign and who settled here after the war; his home now serves as a museum. Another site, the Tyree Tavern, served as headquarters for units of both armies on multiple occasions during the war. And the Westlake Cemetery is the burial site of Julia Jackson, mother of the famous West Virginia native and Confederate commander General Thomas J. "Stonewall" Jackson.

One year after the Confederate defeat at Carnifex Ferry, the war returned here in full force with the Battle of Fayetteville on September 10, 1862. General William Loring defeated Union forces and controlled this area into the winter of 1862.

The most historically significant local Civil War event, and one that has had a lasting effect on military tactics worldwide, occurred on May 19, 1863, in Fayetteville, WV. On that day, a young Confederate sergeant named Milton Wylie Humphreys revolutionized the use of artillery by employing the concept of "indirect fire": firing a weapon at an opposing force without a direct line of sight to the target. This idea forms the foundation from which all modern artillery principles have developed.

One last item of note related to the Civil War and a future president: During the campaigns in West Virginia, President Rutherford B. Hayes (the nineteenth president of the United States) served in the 23rd Ohio and attained the rank of Major General in the Union Army. He fought at the Battle of Carnifex Ferry and served for a great portion of the war in West Virginia, and specifically this area.

Mining/Timber

Kaymoor Bottom tipple.
Photo: National Park Service

The industrial revolution and discovery of coal in the New River Gorge changed the region forever. The need for fuel to power the factories of a growing nation brought attention to the gorge not long after the Civil War; this boom blossomed in the valley after the C&O Railway completed its tracks into the gorge in 1873. Entrepreneurs such as George Nuttall identified the need for high-quality coal and purchased large tracts of land. The New River Gorge coal boom lasted around 80 years, with untold millions of tons of coal mined from the seams, fueling American industry through the early twentieth century.

The towns of Thurmond, Kaymoor, Nuttallburg, and Royal thrived and flourished, and just as quickly died out and turned to the ruins you see today from the boom and bust as the coal seams yielded their last ton.

At the same time, the timber industry here grew, and rail cars, when not loaded with coal, shipped out with timber. Look at any old photograph from that period and you'll see the steep banks of the New River Gorge almost devoid of trees.

New River Gorge Bridge

Can you imagine the New River Gorge without the bridge? Well, that was the reality until the late 1970s. The New River Gorge Bridge, once the largest single-span bridge in the world, was completed on October 22, 1977, marking the final phase in the Corridor L plan developed by the Appalachian Development Highway Authority. Before the bridge, it routinely took 45 minutes to drive from one side of the gorge to the other. It now takes less than a minute to cross the 3,030-foot-long structure. Construction began in June 1974 by the Michael Baker Company and cost $37 million dollars.

To commemorate the construction of the bridge and its benefits to the region, the area celebrates on the third Saturday of every October with an event aptly named Bridge Day. Around 100,000 visitors flock to Fayetteville to enjoy the festival and watch BASE jumpers fling themselves off the span.

New River Gorge National River

On November 10, 1978, just over a year after the dedication of the newly constructed New River Gorge Bridge, President Jimmy Carter signed Public Law 95-625, which created the New River Gorge National River for the "purpose of conserving and interpreting outstanding natural, scenic, and historic values and objects in and around the New River Gorge and preserving as a free-flowing stream an important segment of the New River in West Virginia for the benefit and enjoyment of present and future generations…"

Kaymoor Bottom. Photo: National Park Service

This new law allocated $20 million to make the park a reality and preserve 53 miles and more than 70,000 acres of the New River Gorge from the Bluestone Dam to the Hawk's Nest Dam. Since that time, National Park Service staff have worked diligently not only to preserve the area's scenic vistas and cultural heritage, but also to open these treasures to the public. They have worked to protect endangered species such as the Virginia big-eared bat and Allegheny woodrat, reintroduce peregrine falcons, and uncover and restore areas such as the Nuttallburg mine complex.

Part 1:

Hiking in the New River Gorge National River

Aerial view of the New River Gorge Bridge, with Fayette Station and the New River below. Photo: Dawn Green

5 FAYETTEVILLE, LANSING, & KAYMOOR REGION

View looking upriver from the Fayette Station Bridge.

Overview and Highlights

The Fayetteville, Lansing, and Kaymoor Region is the adventure capital of the New River Gorge area. This zone has an abundance of hiking, climbing, rafting, and other outdoor opportunities and makes for a perfect base to plan excursions. It is also home to the legendary New River Gorge Bridge and the National Park Service's Canyon Rim Visitor Center.

The area has a wonderful array of restaurants for every taste as well as lodging options that range from primitive camping to wonderfully appointed bed and breakfasts.

How to Get There

The region is centered on the New River Gorge Bridge, with hikes on both sides of the river. All trailhead directions are given from the intersection of US Route 19 and WV Route 16, the main intersection just west of the town of Fayetteville. Please see individual trail descriptions for in-depth directions to the trailheads.

Rules and Regulations

Please see "Rules and Regulations for the New River Gorge National River" (page 22) for rules and regulations governing the area.

History and Culture

Much of this area was once home to coal mines and logging operations, but today it plays host to one of the most distinctive transportation structures in West Virginia and the United States, the New River Gorge Bridge. The bridge, completed on October 22, 1977, took three years to erect and was the centerpiece of the "Corridor L" project to link interstates 77 and 79. This 3,030-foot span reduced travel time across the New River from 45 minutes to 45 seconds and transformed travel in the region. (See Chapter 4: Regional History of the New River Gorge for additional details about the bridge, and Chapter 2: Planning Your Visit for information regarding the annual Bridge Day celebration, which features BASE jumping.)

FAYETTEVILLE, LANSING, & KAYMOOR REGION HIKES

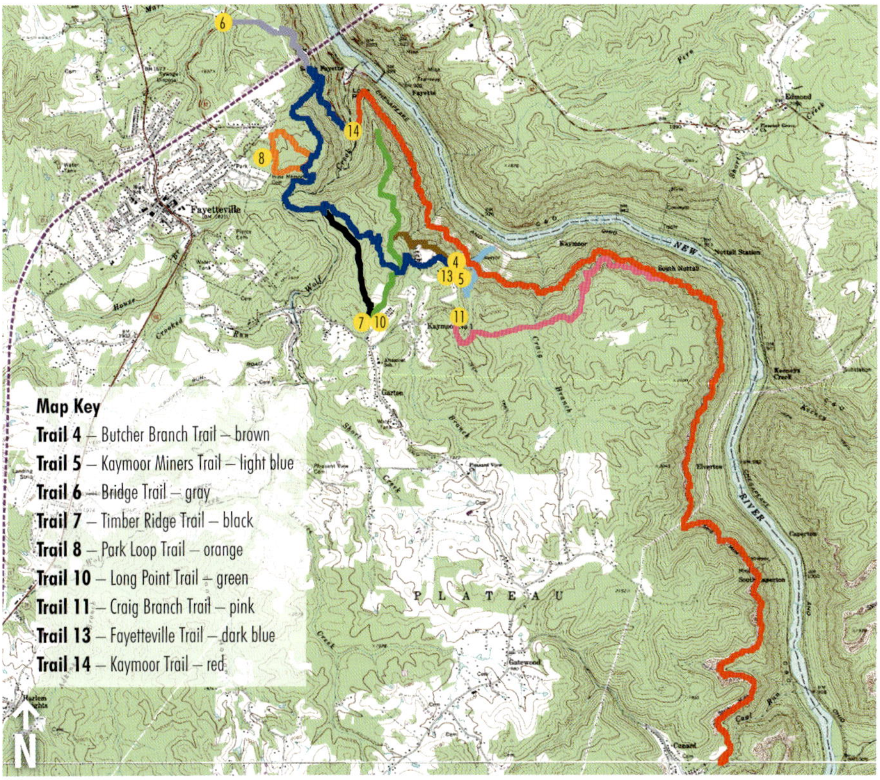

Fayetteville: Abraham Vandal, a Revolutionary War veteran and local farmer, founded the town of Fayetteville in 1837. It was originally called Vandalia, but the name was changed to Fayetteville to honor Marquis de Lafayette, the Revolutionary War hero who earned fame as a leading general under George Washington.

During the Civil War, Fayetteville changed hands between Union and Confederate forces on multiple occasions and is notably the birthplace of the military tactic of "indirect fire": firing a weapon at an opposing force without a direct line of sight to the target. This concept, developed and deployed for the first time by Sergeant Milton Wylie Humphreys, of Bryan's Battery, 13th Virginia Light Artillery, against Union Cavalry, revolutionized the use of artillery. This idea forms the foundation from which all modern artillery principles have developed.

Kaymoor: Kaymoor, listed on the National Register of Historic Places, is named after James Kay, of the Low Moor Iron Company; Kay is also the builder of the Kaymoor mining complex. This complex has three distinct areas: Kaymoor Top, Kaymoor No. 1 Mine, and Kaymoor Bottom.

Kaymoor Top housed the majority of the miners and their families. In 1923, the community had 131 homes, with around 560 residents. Some of these homes had electricity, and some running water. Homes and facilities in this town were segregated, and schooling was available for the children.

Kaymoor No. 1 Mine operated from 1900 until 1962. Located midway down the gorge, it's accessible via the Kaymoor Miners Trail (Trail 5) and the Kaymoor Trail (Trail 14). Extensive ruins remain in this area, and the No. 1 Mine entrance is still visible.

Kaymoor Bottom served as the loading area for mined coal onto railway cars. You'll see remains of coke furnaces, the company store, and other mine buildings and equipment here. This area was abandoned in 1952, and many of the structures were destroyed by fire in 1960.

1 CANYON RIM BOARDWALK

A short wooden boardwalk with fabulous viewpoints over the gorge and the New River Gorge Bridge.

1 | 5 ft | 118 ft | 0.11 mi

Location: Northeast of Fayetteville, WV, adjacent to the New River Gorge Bridge at Canyon Rim Visitor Center
Maps: USGS Fayetteville quad 1:24,000
Trail Options: No hiking options, but there's a wonderful scenic drive available.
Facilities: Canyon Rim Visitor Center, ample paved parking, toilet and picnic facilities.
Highlights: Up-close views of the New River Gorge Bridge, expansive views of the gorge, Canyon Rim Visitor Center and museum.

Trail Milestones:

0.11 mi – Overlook
(38°04.201 N, 081°04.703 W)

Finding the Trailhead

(38°04.241 N, 081°04.597 W)
If traveling south along US Route 19 from Summersville, WV, or any points to the north, access the Canyon Rim Visitor Center and this boardwalk by taking a left onto Fayette Mine Road (CR 85/9), the last exit to the left prior to crossing the New River Gorge Bridge. The trailhead is located on the bridge side of the visitor center near the lot. NPS signage both along the exit and at the visitor center assist in reaching the trailhead.

If traveling from Fayetteville, WV, drive north along US Route 19, cross the New River Gorge Bridge, turn right onto Fayette Mine Road (CR 85/9), and park at the Canyon Rim Visitor Center. The trailhead is located on the bridge side of the visitor center near the lot. NPS signage both along the exit and at the visitor center assist in reaching the trailhead.

Trail Description

Begin along a sidewalk roughly 60 meters from the Canyon Rim Visitor Center entrance. The upper portion of the boardwalk to the first overlook is wheelchair accessible — walk along a wide boardwalk to the overlook for your first view of the gorge. This area has benches and numerous information boards that describe the bridge-building process and other interesting facts about the area.

From this point you must navigate 176 stairs to the bottom of the boardwalk to reach the lower viewpoint. While mellow going down, the climb back out gives many people trouble, as it's quite steep. Please take care when deciding to continue. The lower viewpoint offers a spectacular view of the New River Gorge Bridge and the astounding depth (876 feet from bridge to river) of the gorge in this area. The platform here, while large, can get busy in summer or during events. Please be cognizant of your fellow visitors and allow everyone a chance to take in the amazing views.

New River Gorge Bridge from the lower overlook.

Trail Combinations/Options

There are no hiking combinations from this boardwalk, though a scenic drive that starts here is well worth your time. This drive takes you along a winding and unevenly paved road to the bottom of the gorge, across a lower bridge over the New River, and back up along the opposite side of the gorge. It passes the trailheads for Kaymoor Trail (Trail 14), Fayetteville Trail (Trail 13), and Bridge Trail (Trail 6). From the visitor-center lot, turn right along Fayette Mine Road until intersecting Fayette Station Road; turn sharply and steeply right at this intersection.

Now continue along Fayette Station Road 1.0 miles and turn sharply left, staying on Fayette Station Road. Continue to the bottom of the gorge, crossing active railroad tracks and the Fayette Station Bridge across the New River. At the end of the bridge turn right, passing a large gravel parking area on the right, and begin ascending along the gorge. Pass the trailhead for Kaymoor Trail and the waterfalls of Wolf Creek on your left, followed by the trailhead for Fayetteville Trail. Wind ever upward along this one-way road, passing waterfalls along the Marr Branch just right of the road. Pass ACE Adventure Center to your right and the trailhead parking for Bridge Trail to the left, and then ascend the remaining 0.8 miles to intersect US Route 19 and continue your journey.

2 BUTCHER BRANCH CLIMBER ACCESS SPUR TRAIL

A short access trail from Butcher Branch Trail that leads to a spectacular waterfall and the Butcher's Branch and Seven-Eleven walls (climbing areas).

3 | 3 ft 127 ft | 0.16 mi

Location: Southeast of Fayetteville, WV, along Gatewood Road
Maps: USGS Fayetteville quad 1:24,000
Trail Options: Connect from Butcher Branch Trail (Trail 4).
Facilities: Gravel parking for 15 vehicles, close access to toilet and picnic facilities at Arrowhead Trail System parking.
Highlights: Beautiful waterfall and cascades, cliff.

Trail Milestones:

0.16 mi – Waterfall (38°02.998 N, 081°04.379 W)

Finding the Trailhead

(38°02.956 N, 081°04.333 W)
From US Route 19, follow WV 16 through Fayetteville 0.7 miles to the intersection with Gatewood Road. Bear left and follow Gatewood Road 2.0 miles before turning left onto Kaymoor No. 1 Road — National Park Service "brown" signs point the way toward Kaymoor at this intersection. Follow this road 0.9 miles to a T intersection; turn left here and follow the gravel road to the parking area at 0.15 miles. The trailhead is located 0.4 miles down the Butcher Branch Trail (see Butcher Branch Trail [Trail 4] for a detailed description of the route).

Trail Description

From the intersection with Butcher Branch Trail (Trail 4) descend steeply amongst rhododendron. Multiple smaller trails lead off the main climber-access path — stay on the well-worn switchbacks. At 100 meters encounter a rock wall. Break away from this wall and move along a boulder field until reaching Butcher Branch Creek at 0.16 miles. Above the crossing note a beautiful waterfall with lower cascades. It is possible to continue along this trail to the climbing areas of Butcher's Branch or Seven-Eleven walls, frequented by climbers throughout the year. Return by the same path.

Butcher Branch Falls and cascades.

Trail Combinations/Options

After viewing the waterfall, return to the intersection with Butcher Branch Trail and retrace the 0.4 miles back to its trailhead by staying left. Alternatively, turn right on Butcher Branch Trail and complete that hike. For in-depth info on this trail and other options, refer to the Butcher Branch Trail (Trail 4) description.

3 THE "FACE" LOOP TRAIL

The highlight of this short and easily accessible trail is a boulder with a meticulously carved face etched into the stone.

2 | 181 ft | 140 ft | 0.25 mi

Location: Just east of the Canyon Rim Visitor Center and New River Gorge Bridge
Maps: USGS Fayetteville quad 1:24,000
Trail Options: The trail is a branch of a climber-access trail for Endless Wall.
Facilities: Gravel parking at pulloff for five vehicles.
Highlights: An intricate carving and pretty waterfall.

Trail Milestones:

0.1 mi – The "Face"
(38°04.063 N, 081°04.158 W)
0.18 mi – Waterfall and right turn
(38°04.029 N, 081°04.158 W)

Additional Notes

The climber trails are not sign-posted and are not recommended unless you're familiar with the area. See Mike Williams' *New River Gorge Rock Climbs* for more information regarding this and other unmaintained climber-access trails.

Finding the Trailhead

(38°04.060 N, 081°04.257 W)
Drive north along US Route 19 from Fayetteville, WV, crossing the bridge. Turn right onto Lansing-Edmond Road (County Route 5/82). Continue 0.3 miles and turn right onto Fayette Station Road (CR Route 82). Travel 0.1 miles, reaching a Y intersection. Keep left here and travel an additional 0.6 miles to a pulloff with an NPS informational board describing scenic drives in the region.

Trail Description

From the informational board, walk 40 meters uphill along the road until reaching a doublewide trail that veers to the right. "No Hunting" signs are posted to the left as you descend and reach a paved path with stone. Turn right along this path and cross a small stream by way of a stone bridge. Rounding a bend in the trail, begin to watch for the moss-covered face to the left at 0.1 miles. Take a moment here and examine the detail of the carving in the boulder. Why here? Why just a face? The story is unknown, but the etching's quality is impressive.

Continue along the trail another 0.08 miles, arriving atop a 20-foot waterfall. At this point and just above the falls turn right, crossing the stream and climbing steeply through rhododendron to return to the trailhead and parking area. Take caution in this area with children or in wet and icy conditions, as the trail crosses this stream above a 20-foot drop on the left.

Trail Combinations/Options

This trail is a short branch from an unmaintained climber-access trail that serves the Fern Buttress climbing area. To explore this area, at 0.2 miles continue straight rather than turning right (and returning to the trailhead). This trail meanders for miles along the base of the cliff, accessing ladders and cliff breaks to reach the rim of the gorge.

A brave "Face" in any weather.

THE "FACE" LOOP TRAIL

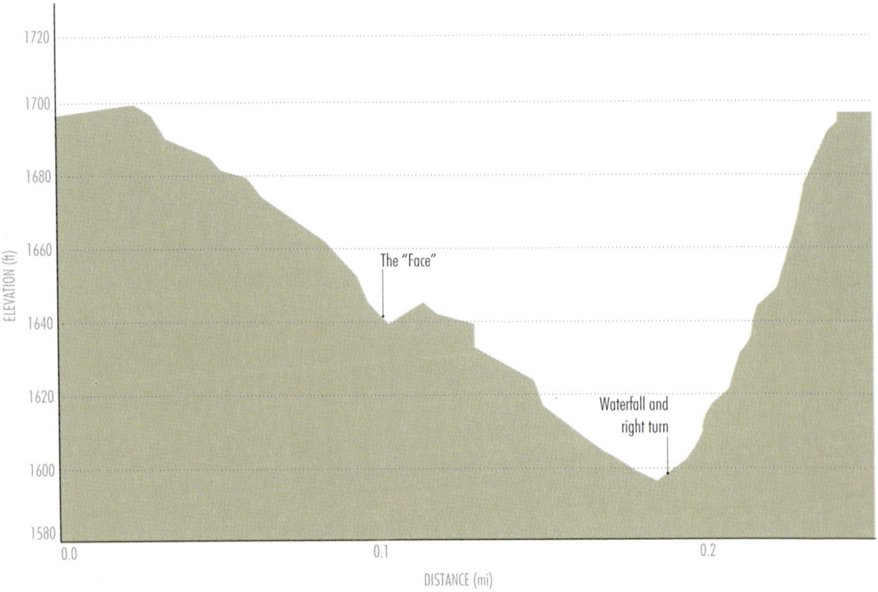

4 BUTCHER BRANCH TRAIL

This trail runs along the gorge rim and through thick rhododendron before crossing Butcher Branch Creek and ending at the intersection with Long Point Trail (Trail 10).

2 152 ft 208 ft 0.66 mi

Location: Southeast of Fayetteville, WV, along Gatewood Road
Maps: USGS Fayetteville quad 1:24,000
Trail Options: Connect with Butcher Branch Climber Access Spur Trail (Trail 2), Long Point Trail (Trail 10), and Fayetteville Trail (Trail 13).
Facilities: Gravel parking for 15 vehicles, close access to toilet and picnic facilities at Arrowhead Trail System parking.
Highlights: Butcher Branch Creek, remnants of mining operations, beautiful rhododendron.

Trail Milestones:

0.2 mi – Buried cable (38°02.929 N, 081°04.188 W)
0.4 mi – Intersection with BB Climber Access Trail (38°02.956 N, 081°04.333 W)
0.43 mi – Butcher Branch Creek (38°02.929 N, 081°04.393 W)
0.66 mi – Trail's end/intersection with Long Point Trail (38°02.973 N, 081°04.543 W)

Finding the Trailhead

(38°02.768 N, 081°04.101 W)
From US Route 19, follow WV 16 through Fayetteville 0.7 miles to the intersection with Gatewood Road. Bear left and follow Gatewood Road 2.0 miles before turning left onto Kaymoor No. 1 Road — National Park Service "brown" signs point the way toward Kaymoor at this intersection. Follow this road 0.9 miles to a T intersection; turn left here and follow the gravel road to the parking area at 0.15 miles. The trailhead is located at the far end of the lot.

Trail Description

From the shared trailhead (with Fayetteville Trail) move into the forest, encountering a small viewpoint to the right of the trail at 150 meters. At 0.2 miles keep your eyes on the trail to see a partially buried large cable, part of a system used to transport equipment to and from the mines below. Descend, and at 0.4 miles the trail splits in a stand of rhododendron. Stay left to remain on the main Butcher Branch Trail, or move right for the Butcher Branch Climber Access Spur Trail (Trail 2).

Keeping left, move up a small incline before dropping toward Butcher Branch Creek. Cross the stream using rocks (if the water's high, you might get a little wet!). Continue through rhododendron and emerge at 0.66 miles at the intersection with Long Point Trail (Trail 10). This is the trail's end — either return by the same route, or follow the directions below to reach the viewpoint on Long Point Trail or return to the trailhead via the Long Point Trail and Fayetteville Trail (Trail 13).

Overlooking the New River from Butcher Branch Trail.

Trail Combinations/Options

At the end of the trail and intersection with Long Point Trail, you can reach the viewpoint on Long Point Trail by turning right and traveling 0.6 miles (see Long Point Trail [Trail 10] for details).

To return to the trailhead, turn left on Long Point Trail and follow it 0.2 miles until intersecting the Fayetteville Trail (Trail 13). Turn left at this intersection and continue 0.7 miles to the trailhead for Fayetteville Trail (the same trailhead as Butcher Branch Trail); for details on this 0.7-mile section, see the Fayetteville Trail description. This forms a 1.56-mile loop, which increases to 2.76 miles if you include a jaunt out to the Long Point viewpoint.

BUTCHER BRANCH TRAIL

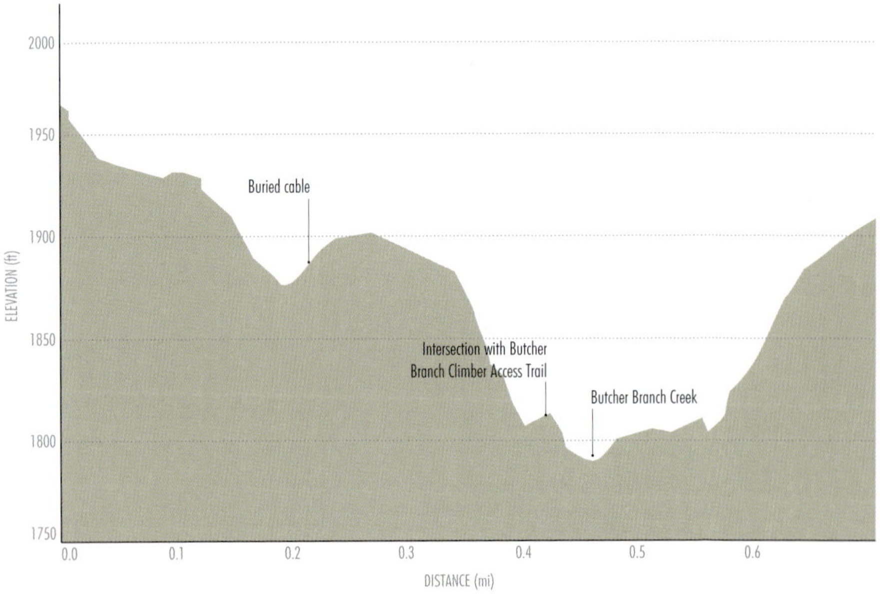

5 KAYMOOR MINERS TRAIL

One of the most strenuous hikes in the New River Gorge. Those that dare are rewarded with some of the most interesting and best-preserved ruins of the region's coal-mining industry.

5 | 0 ft 937 ft | 0.68 mi

Location: Southeast of Fayetteville, WV, along Gatewood Road
Maps: USGS Fayetteville quad 1:24,000
Trail Options: Connect with the Kaymoor Trail (Trail 14).
Facilities: Gravel parking for 15 vehicles; close access to toilet and picnic facilities at Arrowhead Trail System parking.
Highlights: Ruins of mine operations, views of gorge.

Trail Milestones:

0.2 mi – Waterfall
(38°02.700 N, 081°03.961 W)
0.5 mi – Intersection with Kaymoor Trail/Kaymoor No. 1 Mine ruins
(38°02.843 N, 081°03.797 W)
0.68 mi – Ruins of Kaymoor Bottom
(38°02.917 N, 081°03.797 W)

Finding the Trailhead

(38°02.715 N, 081°04.057 W)
From US 19, follow WV 16 through Fayetteville 0.7 miles to the intersection with Gatewood Road. Bear left and follow Gatewood Road 2.0 miles before turning left onto Kaymoor No. 1 Road — National Park Service "brown" signs point the way toward Kaymoor at this intersection. Follow this road 0.9 miles to a T intersection; turn left here and follow the gravel road to the parking area at 0.15 miles. The trailhead is located along the road to the right (gorge side), just before reaching the parking lot.

Trail Description

From the trailhead move along an easy portion of trail to 0.1 miles where you begin a long and continuous descent. Climbers frequently use the first 0.2 miles of trail to access the cliff faces visible to either side of the path. This area is also often damp, so take care with each step along this rocky segment of the hike. The trail passes beneath a wide waterfall to the right that often is but a trickle during the hot summer months at 0.2 miles. Continue downhill along a winding path until reaching the intersection with Kaymoor Trail (Trail 14) at 0.5 miles; an I-beam stating "Your Family wants you to work Safely" greets you at this point. Before rushing headlong onto the stairs immediately below this sign, take a moment to absorb the view across the gorge to Endless Wall, visit the surrounding ruins associated with the Kaymoor Mine complex (including the No. 1 Mine entrance), and learn the history of this area.

The next portion of the trail consists of a wooden staircase featuring 820 steps. Do not underestimate the effort that will be required to ascend these stairs back to the trailhead! Few platforms allow you to rest on the return, and there are no other trail options available at the ruins below.

Continue down the stairs, making sure to look under them and to the side to spot an old rail line. These tracks were used as haulage for the mines and as the chief transportation for miners to and from work. The line could carry 15 workers in multiple small carriages at any one time, and utilized a cable to lower the cars down the gorge. Mining was a dangerous profession, and that included just getting to

KAYMOOR MINERS TRAIL

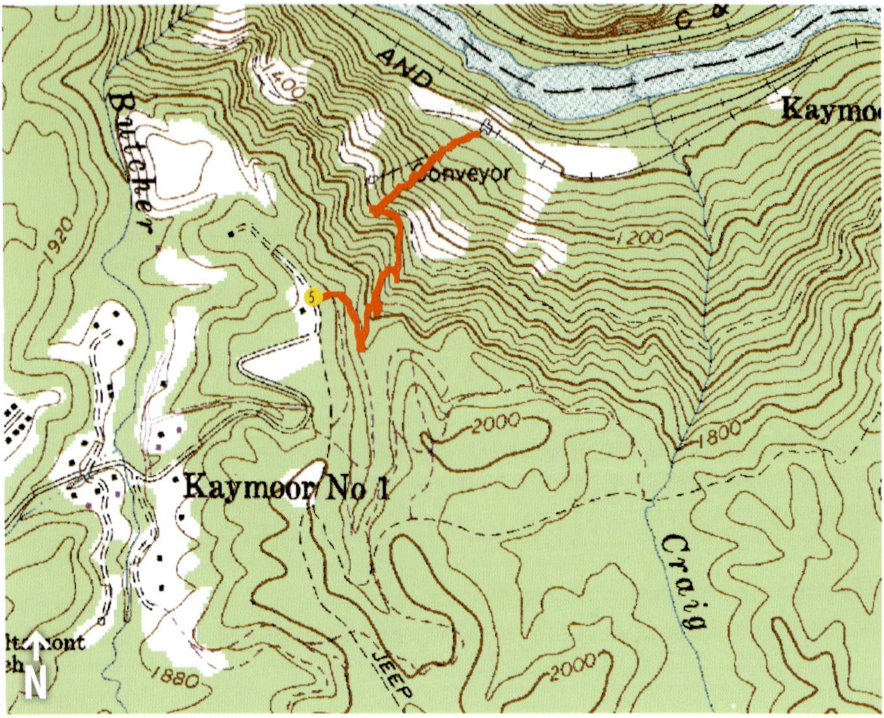

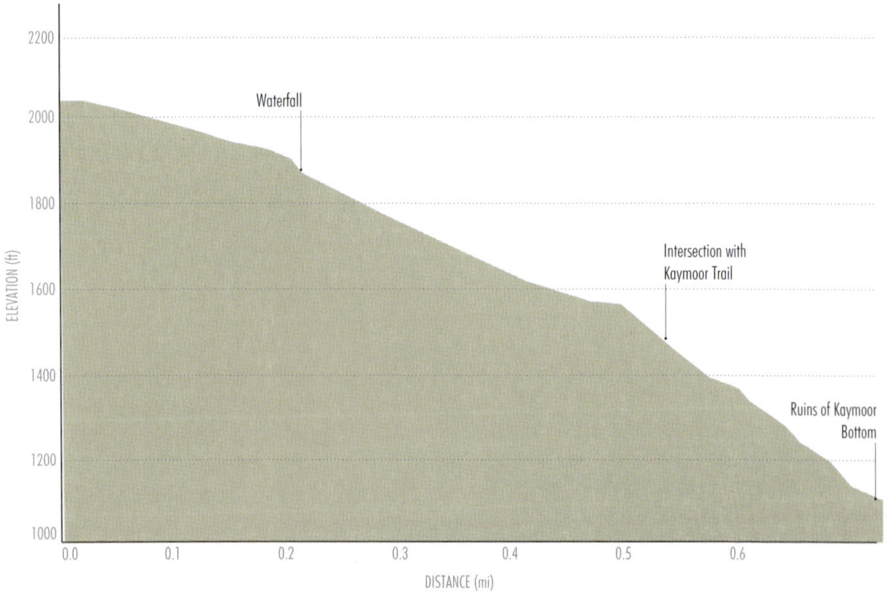

Industrial remains at the base of the Kaymoor Miners Trail.

the jobsite: In 1913, an accident on this haulage track killed two men when the cable snapped at the Kaymoor Top station.

Once at the bottom, the trail ends at a platform and an information board discusses the ruined complex. It is possible to explore on your own, but take great care — this is a former industrial site. The buildings are unstable, there are numerous holes throughout the area (many of them hidden by leaves), and various species of poisonous snakes are known to nest in the area.

The many steps down to Kaymoor Bottom.

Trail Combinations/Options:

After completing the Kaymoor Miners Trail and returning by the stairs to the 0.5-mile mark (the Kaymoor Mine opening), turn left along the Kaymoor Trail (Trail 14). Hike 1.8 miles to the intersection with Craig Branch Trail (Trail 11) and hike that trail's 2.19 miles to Kaymoor Top. This creates a strenuous 4.85-mile-total loop.

Turning left at the intersection will result in reaching the Kaymoor Trail's Fayette Station Road trailhead after 2.1 miles. From there you can connect to the Fayetteville Trail (Trail 13) and return to the Kaymoor Miners trailhead. This round-trip (Kaymoor Miners – Kaymoor – Fayetteville) results in a 6.89-mile loop.

6 BRIDGE TRAIL

This hike encompasses all the natural features of the New River Gorge: deciduous forest along the high ground, a small hill meadow, and then a descent along rock walls amongst rhododendron until arriving at the trail's namesake, the New River Gorge Bridge.

2 | 224 ft 266 ft | 0.83 mi

Location: West of New River Gorge Bridge, north of Fayetteville, WV
Maps: USGS Fayetteville quad 1:24,000
Trail Options: Connect with Fayetteville Trail (Trail 13) to access it and other trails in the region.
Facilities: Gravel parking for 20-plus vehicles.
Highlights: Boulders galore and close-up views of the NRG Bridge.

Trail Milestones:

0.22 mi – Hill meadow
(38°04.199 N, 081°05.526 W)
0.35 mi – Power-line cut
(38°04.140 N, 081°05.402 W)
0.55 mi – NRG Bridge
(38°04.129 N, 081°05.273 W)
0.83 mi – Intersection with Fayetteville Trail
(38°03.935 N, 081°05.173 W)

Finding the Trailhead

(38°04.191 N, 081°05.758 W)
From the intersection of US Route 19 and WV Route 16 in Fayetteville, WV, drive north along US Route 19 for 0.4 miles to Fayette Station Road (CR 82). Turn left here and follow Fayette Station Road steadily downhill 0.8 miles until reaching the trailhead and gravel parking area.

An alternative approach is via the Canyon Rim Visitor Center by way of a scenic drive to the bottom of the gorge. *Note: While paved, this is a one-way road with uneven surfaces and tight turns. Large vehicles, like RVs, are highly discouraged from attempting to negotiate this road.* From the Canyon Rim Visitor Center, turn right out of the parking area and travel 0.1 miles to Lansing Loop Road. At the intersection turn (very!) sharply right and continue 0.2 miles. Reaching a second intersection, turn right, following the sign for CR 82. Travel 1.0 miles to the intersection with Burma Road; turn left here. A good rule of thumb when making a decision on this road is to always take the turn that leads downhill! Continue 1.3 miles, passing many streams to the left, and reach the Fayette Station Bridge. At the end of the bridge, turn sharply right and at 0.2 miles stay left and cross under a railway trestle to continue toward Bridge Trail trailhead. Travel uphill 2.9 miles to the trailhead on the left.

Trail Description

From the trailhead parking area, ascend a straight path along a 20-degree slope for 0.22 miles before emerging from the forest into a small hill meadow. This area is popular with turkey and deer. Reenter a younger forest before reaching a power-line cut at 0.35 miles. Just beyond, at roughly 0.4 miles, begin descending into the gorge along a rock path and stairs. This portion of the path uses a break in the cliff line to access the base of the sandstone walls. To the left notice the sheer cliff as you move downward. (Heads-up in this area if hiking with children or it's wet or icy!) In fall and winter, it is possible to glimpse the New River Gorge Bridge as you move along this portion of the trail.

BRIDGE TRAIL

After reaching the base of the cliff, the trail meanders amongst boulders until at 0.55 miles you arrive underneath the bridge. The trail moves just to the right of one of the concrete-and-steel bases for this enormous bridge — for many visitors, this view first highlights the sheer size of the structure. (Please see Chapter 4: Regional History of the New River Gorge for an in-depth description of the building of the bridge.) From this point, many visitors return to the trailhead, but the official trail continues to 0.83 miles and ends at the intersection with Fayetteville Trail at a section of wooden stairs. This intersection allows you to access many of the other trails in the Fayetteville, Lansing, and Kaymoor Region.

Trail Combinations/Options

Using the connection at 0.83 miles with the Fayetteville Trail is a great way to continue to explore, and the potential combinations easily allow for a day of adventure with a stop for lunch at one of the many restaurants in Fayetteville before returning to the trailhead.

Using the left branch of the intersection with Fayetteville Trail, descend for 0.64 miles, crossing numerous streams and drainages and arriving at Fayette Station Road. Turn right along this road for 0.1 miles to the trailhead for Kaymoor Trail (Trail 14) and the bridge across Wolf Creek. From here you can connect with the Kaymoor Miners Trail (Trail 5) or Craig Branch Trail (Trail 11) to reach the gorge rim at Kaymoor Top before returning along Fayetteville Trail to the Bridge Trail. This large loop is strenuous, with many options.

Taking the right fork at the intersection with Fayetteville Trail allows access to eight additional hikes within the region, all described within this chapter, to create numerous interesting longer hikes. One interesting option, and a favorite running route of mine, is to follow the Fayetteville Trail to the Park Loop Trail (Trail 8) at 1.0 miles. From this point follow Park Loop Trail to its trailhead and into Fayetteville for a cup of coffee or lunch.

7 TIMBER RIDGE TRAIL

Timber Ridge Trail meanders through deciduous and rhododendron forest until connecting to the Fayetteville Trail (Trail 13). It is a great introductory trail for beginning or young mountain bikers.

2 | 20 ft | 186 ft | 0.87 mi

Location: Southeast of New River Gorge Bridge, east of Fayetteville, WV
Maps: USGS Fayetteville quad 1:24,000
Trail Options: Connect with Fayetteville Trail (Trail 13) to access other trails within the region.
Facilities: Parking for approx. 20 vehicles, toilet facilities.
Highlights: A peaceful hike through the woods.

Trail Milestones:

0.1 mi – Cross stream twice (38°02.561 N, 081°04.696 W)
0.6 mi – Enter rhododendron stand (38°02.953 N, 081°04.816 W)
0.87 mi – Trail junction with Fayetteville Trail (38°03.124 N, 081°05.037 W)

Finding the Trailhead

(38°02.503 N, 081°04.682 W)
From US Route 19, follow WV Route 16 through Fayetteville 0.7 miles to the intersection with Gatewood Road. Bear left and follow Gatewood Road 1.9 miles, and then turn left on Newton Road. Trailhead parking is available on the left at 50 yards. (NPS "brown" signage available throughout the route.)

Trail Description

Timber Ridge Trail has a large gravel parking lot at the trailhead that is shared with the Long Point Trail (Trail 10). Begin on the left side of the parking lot and proceed into the wood line almost immediately along single-track. At 0.1 miles cross a stream twice, using small wooden bridges. Continue along the trail until reaching a stand of rhododendrons at 0.6 miles that continues for roughly 0.1 miles. At 0.87 miles reach the trail's end as it intersects with the Fayetteville Trail (Trail 13). Either backtrack along the Timber Ridge Trail or use the Fayetteville Trail to continue your adventure. This trail is a wonderful introduction to trail riding for new mountain bikers, with very little technical difficulty.

Trail Combinations/Options

You can combine the Timber Ridge Trail with the Fayetteville Trail in two ways: First, at the intersection at 0.87 miles, take the left-hand trail and continue 0.3 miles until reaching a bridge over Wolf Creek. This additional distance is well worth the time. The Fayetteville Trail then continues past Fayetteville and links to a multitude of trails (see its trail description for details). Second, take the right-hand fork at the intersection to visit Long Point Trail (Trail 10) or create a loop that returns to the trailhead. Hike 1.0 miles to the intersection with Long Point Trail. To visit the viewpoint, turn left and travel 0.8 miles. Finally, to return to the trailhead for Timber Ridge Trail, turn right and travel 0.7 miles.

TIMBER RIDGE TRAIL

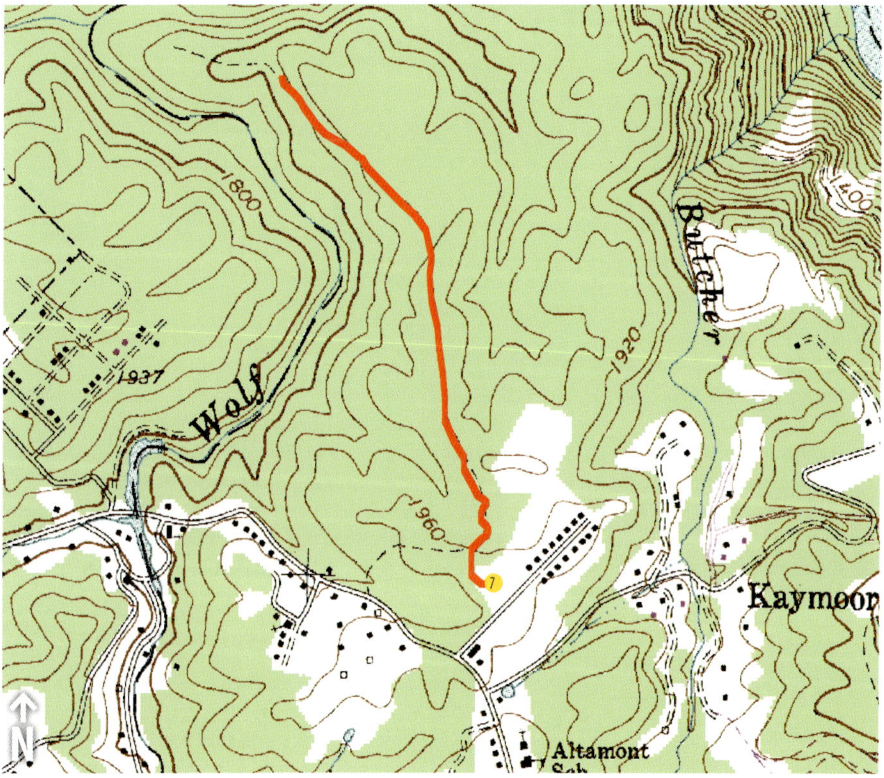

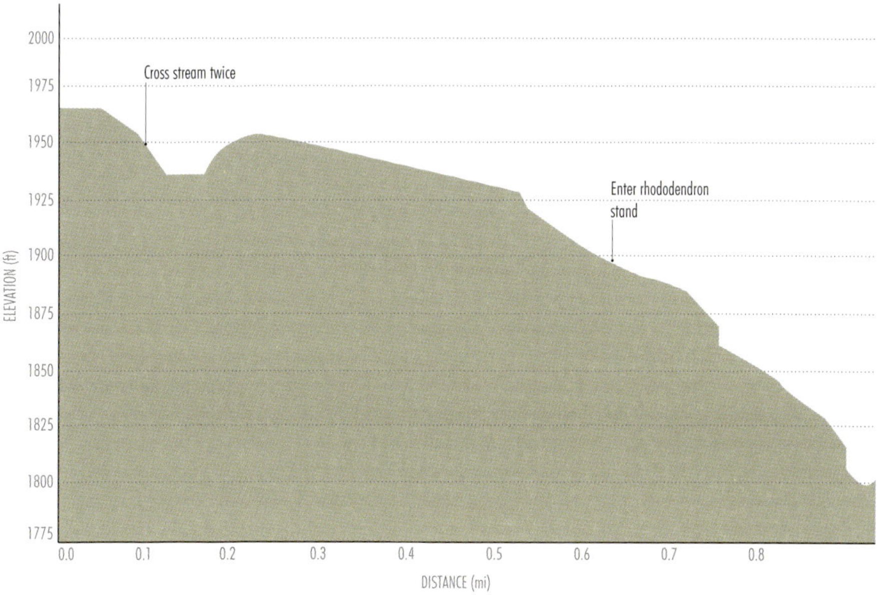

8 PARK LOOP TRAIL

A pretty loop through the woods that is easily accessible from anywhere in Fayetteville, WV.

1 | 181 ft 140 ft | 1.09 mi

Location: Fayetteville, WV
Maps: USGS Fayetteville quad 1:24,000
Trail Options: Connect with Fayetteville Trail (Trail 13).
Facilities: Parking for 20–25 vehicles near Fayetteville Town Park, with additional parking, playground, and toilet facilities.
Highlights: Easily accessible forest-walk.

Trail Milestones:

0.2 mi – Bridge over stream (38°03.559 N, 081°05.422 W)
0.5 mi – Intersection with Fayetteville Trail (38°03.449 N, 081°05.137 W)
0.6 mi – Fayetteville Trail moves to left (38°03.371 N, 081°05.200 W)

Finding the Trailhead

(38°03.425 N, 081°05.473 W)
From US Route 19, turn onto WV Route 16 (N. Court Street) and proceed through Fayetteville (through one stoplight) for 0.4 miles. Turn left on Fayette Avenue and travel 0.3 miles. At the stop sign, turn right onto Park Drive and after 40 meters turn left again on Academy Drive. Fayetteville Town Park will be visible to your right. Drive 0.2 miles, passing the playground and courts to the right; just beyond, turn onto a gravel road for the Park Loop trailhead.

Trail Description

From the gravel parking area, the trailhead is located nearest the forest and is marked by an NPS sign. Descend slightly as you reach the forest and within 60 meters reach a Y intersection. Stay left here and continue close to homes until reaching a bridge that crosses a small stream at 0.2 miles. Meander through the forest along even terrain until reaching an intersection with Fayetteville Trail (Trail 13) at 0.5 miles — stay right here. The two trails run along the same track for 0.1 miles; at this point, again stay right (Fayetteville Trail moves sharply left). You'll begin to see a wooden fence to the right that parallels the trail for almost 0.4 miles. Now cross a small stream using a wooden bridge and turn left. Climb slightly at 1.0 miles, passing the Y intersection, to arrive back at the trailhead.

Trail Combinations/Options

Park Loop Trail intersects the Fayetteville Trail, allowing numerous longer hikes and connection possibilities. From the intersection of the two trails at the 0.5-mile mark, it is best to head west along Fayetteville Trail to connect with Bridge Trail (Trail 6), or farther along, with Kaymoor Trail (Trail 14) at the end of the Fayetteville Trail. From the intersection with Fayetteville Trail at the 0.6-mile mark, it is easiest to connect to the trails farther east, such as Timber Ridge Trail (Trail 7), Long Point Trail (Trail 10), or Butcher Branch Trail (Trail 4).

PARK LOOP TRAIL

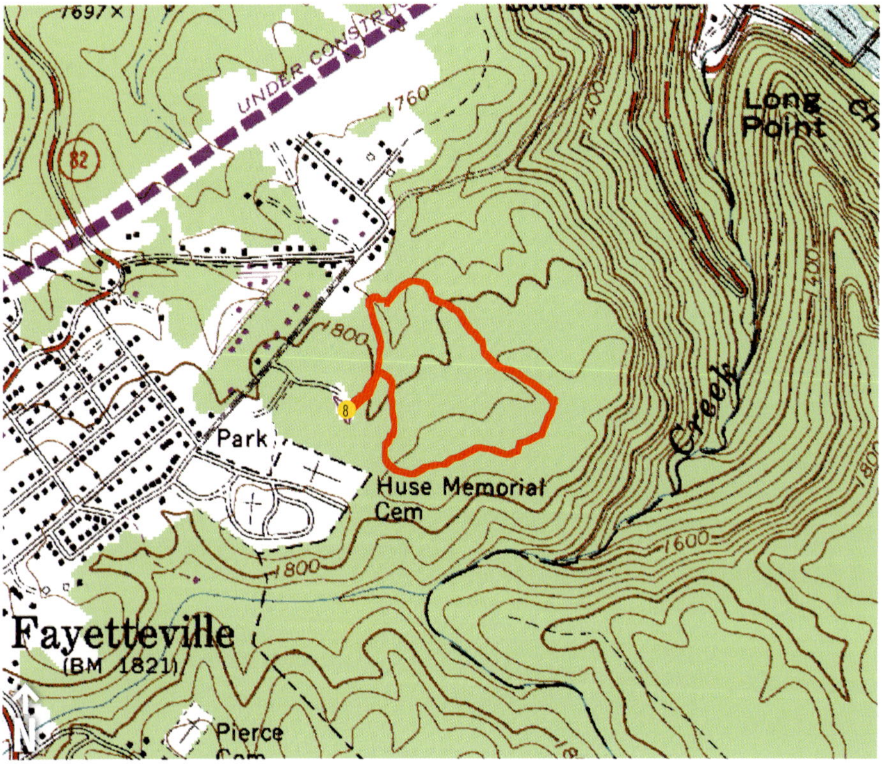

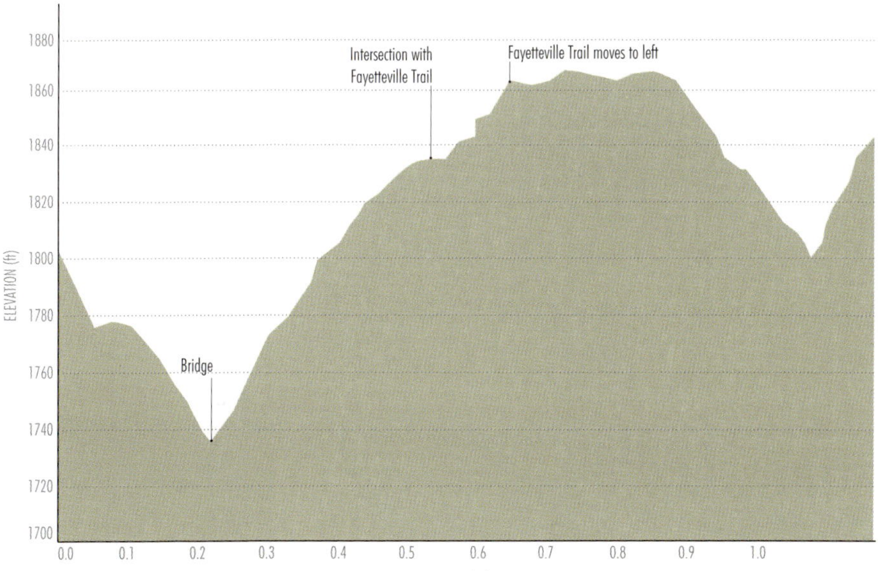

9 BURNWOOD TRAIL

This loop trail ventures through the former Laing family farm, along the gorge rim, and past a particularly old beech tree before returning to the Burnwood day-use area.

2 | 274 ft 167 ft | 1.24 mi

Location: North of the New River Gorge Bridge, northeast of Fayetteville, WV
Maps: USGS Fayetteville quad 1:24,000
Facilities: Gravel parking for 30-plus vehicles, toilet facilities, picnic facilities and shelters.
Highlights: Laing Homestead, gorge rim, and an enormous beech tree.

Trail Milestones:

0.35 mi – Turn left (38°04.638 N, 081°04.501 W)
0.4 mi – Loop intersection (38°04.639 N, 081°04.558 W)
0.55 mi – Beech tree (38°04.662 N, 081°04.695 W)
0.9 mi – Loop intersection (38°04.639 N, 081°04.558 W)

Finding the Trailhead

(38°04.451 N, 081°04.660 W)

If traveling south along US Route 19 from Summersville, WV, or any points to the north, access the trailhead by turning right just prior to the New River Gorge into the Burnwood day-use area.

If traveling from Fayetteville, WV, drive north along US Route 19, cross the New River Gorge Bridge, and then turn left at the first available road into the Burnwood day-use area.

Follow the gravel road straight past a few NPS buildings and park at the end of a large gravel lot. To the right you will see a toilet facility. The trailhead is just beyond, tucked into the wood line.

Trail Description

Also known as Laing Loop Trail

From the trailhead immediately descend and move into a thick stand of mature Eastern hemlock with rhododendron tucked beneath. At 0.2 miles cross a wooden bridge over a rocky stream and keep your eyes peeled for evidence of the Laing Homestead in the trees to either side. At 0.3 miles emerge from the forest into a meadow that is slowly being reclaimed, as evidenced by the thicket of saplings now growing to the right. Continue straight in this area, with mature forest to the left and the meadow to your right, until turning sharply left and reentering forest. Not far into the woods come upon the trail-loop sign. Take the left branch at this intersection (proceed in a clockwise direction).

Burnwood Trail.

Continue straight for 0.1 miles along a relatively flat section before the trail moves right and begins to parallel the gorge rim. At 0.55 miles the trail passes an extremely old and large beech tree. Take a moment to check out

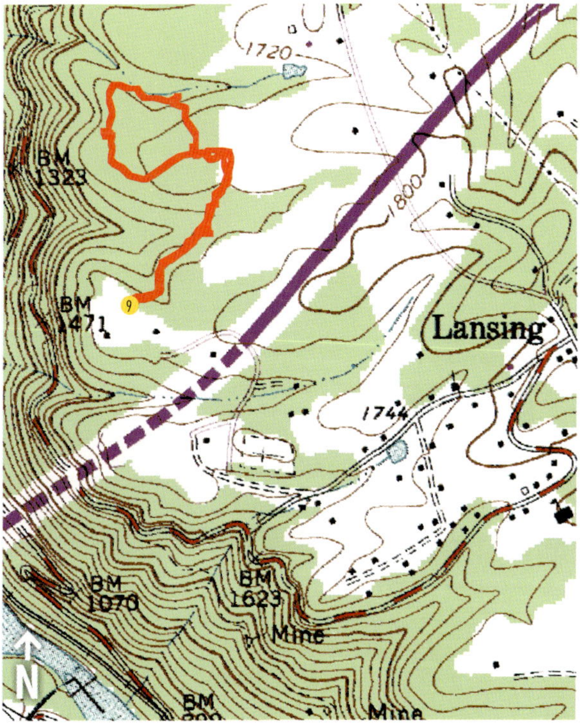

one of the gorge's elder arboreal statesmen, easily accessible by trail. In another 0.15 miles the trail begins to move right and descends into a low area near a stream. A path branches to the left near this stream and leads toward the American Alpine Club's new campground. Do not cross the stream, but instead move right and uphill. At 0.9 miles reach the original loop intersection, this time from the right branch. Turn left at this intersection, follow it to the field, and turn sharply right, again paralleling the forest. Continue to retrace your steps back toward the trailhead, regaining it at 1.24 miles.

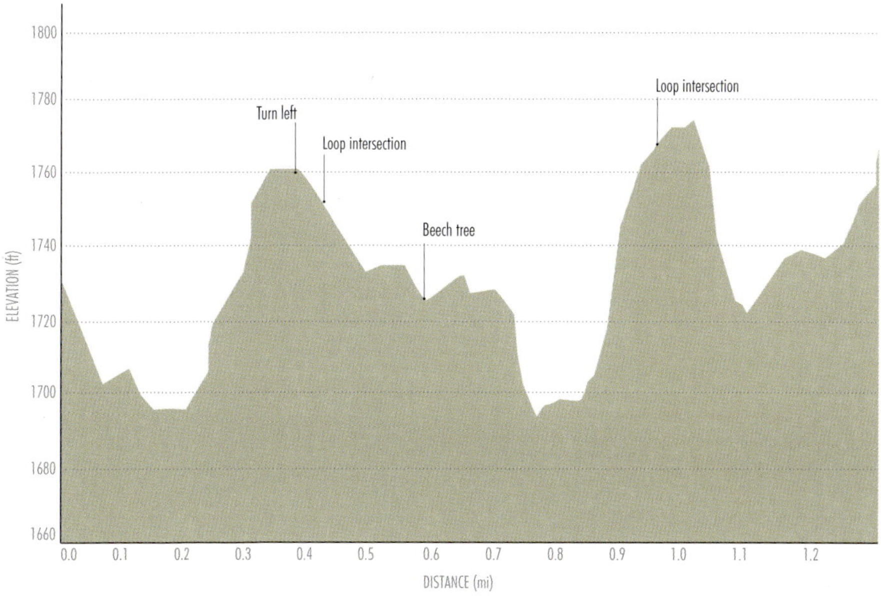

10 LONG POINT TRAIL

Long Point Trail is the perfect introduction to the New River Gorge, with a panoramic view that exemplifies the natural beauty of the area.

2 | 91 ft | 347 ft | 1.5 mi

Location: Southeast of New River Gorge Bridge, east of Fayetteville, WV
Maps: USGS Fayetteville quad 1:24,000
Trail Options: Connects to Butcher Branch Trail (Trail 4) or Fayetteville Trail (Trail 13).
Facilities: Parking for approx. 20 vehicles, toilet facilities.
Highlights: Spectacular views of the New River Gorge, the NRG bridge, and multiple distant waterfalls.

Trail Milestones:

0.3 mi – Enter forest
(38°02.700 N, 081°04.568 W)
0.7 mi – Intersection with Fayetteville Trail
(38°02.785 N, 081°04.502 W)
0.9 mi – Intersection with Butcher Branch Trail
(38°02.973 N, 081°04.543 W)
1.4 mi – Enter rhododendron grove
(38°03.406 N, 081°04.552 W)
1.5 mi – Long Point view of New River Gorge
(38°03.582 N, 081°04.645 W)

Finding the Trailhead

(38°02.503 N, 081°04.682 W)
From US Route 19, follow WV Route 16 through Fayetteville 0.7 miles to the intersection with Gatewood Road. Bear left and follow Gatewood Road 1.9 miles. Turn left on Newton Road. Trailhead parking is available on the left at 50 yards. (NPS "brown" signage available throughout the route.)

Trail Description

Long Point Trail has a large gravel lot at the trailhead shared with the Timber Ridge Trail (Trail 7). Begin on the right side of the lot and proceed onto a well-developed trail that quickly enters a small copse of trees. Emerge from the trees onto a wooden walkway that leads you through a mountain meadow. You'll see many native wildflowers here at various times throughout the spring and summer.

After a short distance, reenter the tree line for the remainder of the hike. Continue along the trail, enjoying close-in views of the deciduous forest. At 0.7 miles the trail intersects the Fayetteville Trail — you can access Fayetteville or the top of Kaymoor Trail from here. At 0.9 miles into the hike, you'll intersect the Butcher Branch Trail.

Continue along Long Point Trail as it meanders without significant elevation gain or loss until you reach a rhododendron grove that creates a "foliage tunnel." This area is spectacular in the spring during flowering or in the winter after a wet snow. The trail begins to descend, and the terrain on either side begins to close in. Listen to your left for Wolf Creek, a rapidly flowing stream with an abundance of waterfalls. The rhododendron grove gradually gives way to scraggly, windblown Virginia pines clinging precariously along the increasingly narrow path. Meanwhile, you'll catch views of the bridge and gorge through the trees until the trail emerges onto a grouping of flat boulders that look north along the gorge. One of the most-photographed views in the gorge, this rock outcropping — Long Point — is famed for its beautiful vistas of morning fog lifting off the river.

Take caution in this area, as tall cliffs border Long Point to three sides; additionally, snakes often sun themselves just off the trail. After enjoying the view, return to the trailhead via the same route.

LONG POINT TRAIL

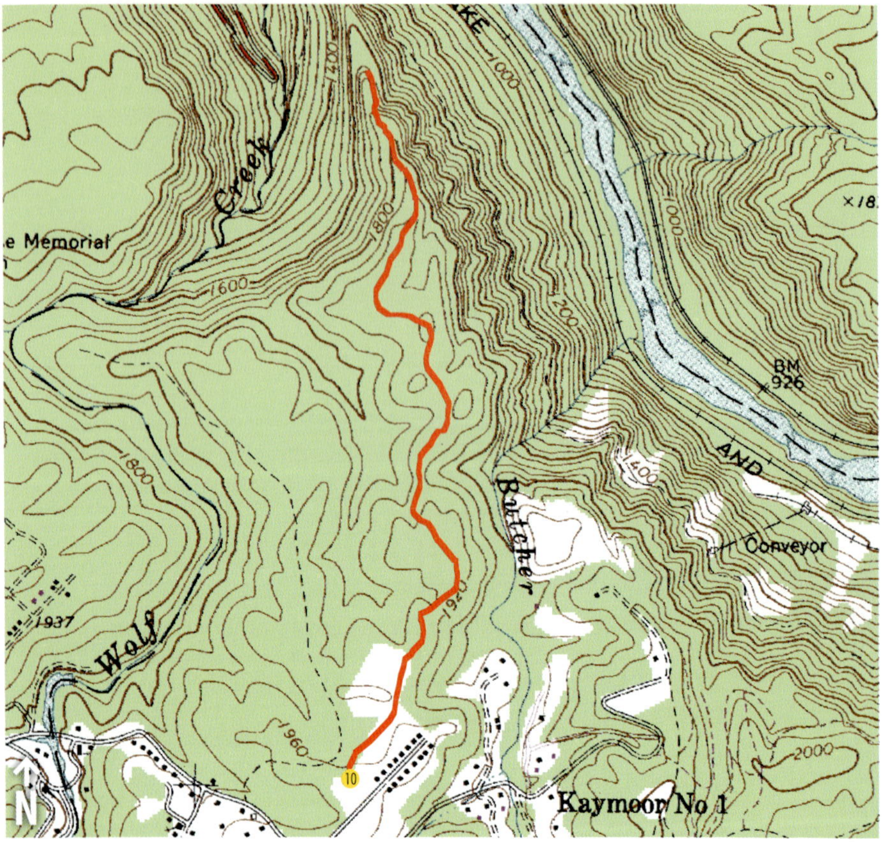

Trail Combinations/Options

Combine this trail with Fayetteville Trail for access toward Fayetteville, the New River Gorge Bridge, or Fayette Station Road near the Kaymoor Trail (Trail 14) trailhead. Combine with Butcher Branch Trail (Trail 4) at 0.6 miles into your return trip to reach Kaymoor Top (trailhead for Kaymoor Miners Trail [Trail 5]). From Kaymoor Top, visit the wonderful viewpoint and then reconnect to the Long Point Trail using Fayetteville Trail, turning left and hiking the remaining 0.7 miles back to your original trailhead.

Additional Notes

Mountain biking is permitted along this trail with the exception of the final 0.2 miles, due to the narrow and precipitous nature of the terrain there.

The trail ends on a rocky point with cliffs to three sides. Be heads-up, especially in wet or icy conditions or with children.

LONG POINT TRAIL

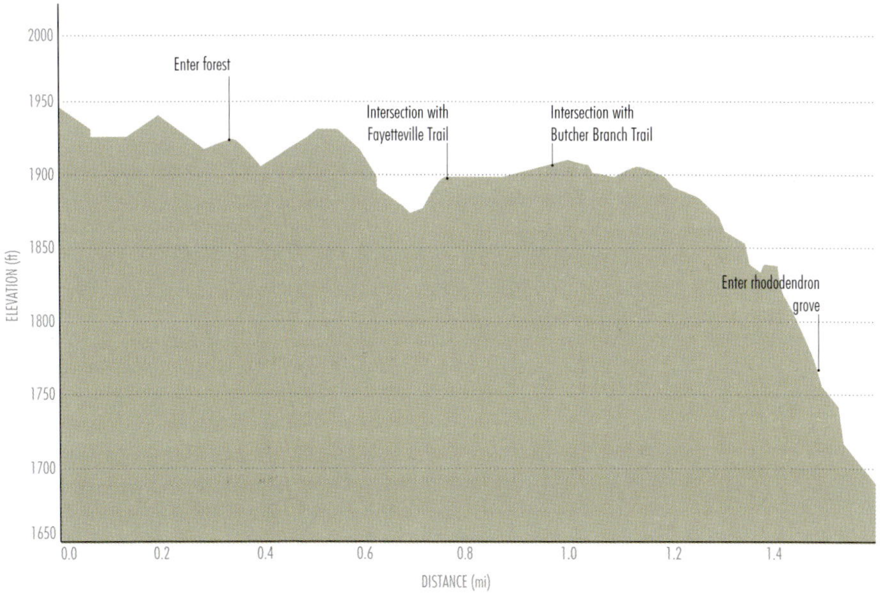

11 CRAIG BRANCH TRAIL

Descend to the Kaymoor Trail via this wide and enjoyable trail that passes along a break in the cliff and weaves between boulders the size of homes.

3 | 142 ft | 537 ft | 2.19 mi

Location: Southeast of Fayetteville, WV, along Gatewood Road
Maps: USGS Fayetteville quad 1:24,000
Trail Options: Connect with Arrowhead Trail System paths; connect to Kaymoor Trail (Trail 14).
Facilities: Shares parking area with the Arrowhead Trail System; gravel parking for 20 vehicles, toilet facilities, picnic facilities.
Highlights: Boulder field, gorge views.

Trail Milestones:

0.2 mi – Intersection with Dalton and Adena trails (H)
(38°02.425 N, 081°03.880 W)
0.9 mi – Dalton Trail splits from Craig Branch (N)
(38°02.532 N, 081°03.323 W)
1.3 mi – Boulder field
(38°02.697 N, 081°03.143 W)
2.19 mi – Intersection with Kaymoor Trail
(38°02.741 N, 081°02.484 W)

Finding the Trailhead

(38°02.488 N, 081°04.053 W)
From US Route 19, follow WV 16 through Fayetteville 0.7 miles to the intersection with Gatewood Road. Bear left and follow Gatewood Road 2.0 miles before turning left onto Kaymoor No. 1 Road — National Park Service "brown" signs point the way toward Kaymoor at this intersection. Follow this road 0.9 miles to a T intersection; turn right here and follow the gravel road toward the Arrowhead Trail System parking at 0.25 miles. The trailhead is to the left, just as you enter the lot, and is marked by a large gate that prevents vehicle access to the trail.

Trail Description

From the trailhead, begin descending along a wide and well-maintained road. At 0.2 miles intersect the Adena Trail (Trail 17) on the right and a connector trail for the Dalton Trail (Trail 18) on the left. This is intersection H within the Arrowhead System. Continue along the Craig Branch Trail and connect with Dalton Trail shortly thereafter. Dalton Trail shares its path with Craig Branch for the next 0.7 miles until moving right at 0.9 miles at intersection N. Before these trails diverge they cross a rocky stream enveloped by rhododendrons, making for a pretty stop in late May when they are in bloom.

Begin to catch glimpses of the gorge at 1.0 miles, and then the trail begins to steepen at 1.2 miles, with rhododendron to either side and a steep drop-off to the left. At 1.3 miles begin to negotiate several switchbacks and see massive boulders, some the size of homes, strewn throughout the forest. At roughly 1.4 miles during fall and winter, you'll catch good views of the gorge. Just 0.2 miles farther along, keep your eyes peeled to the right to see an outstanding example of the effect of rain and weather on rock. Continue downhill and arrive at the intersection with Kaymoor Trail (Trail 14) at 2.19 miles. At this intersection a nice flat stone makes for a great seat, but before you plop down to rest sneak a peek over the back of the stone to spot the wreckage of an old automobile just over the bank.

Giant boulders along Craig Branch Trail.

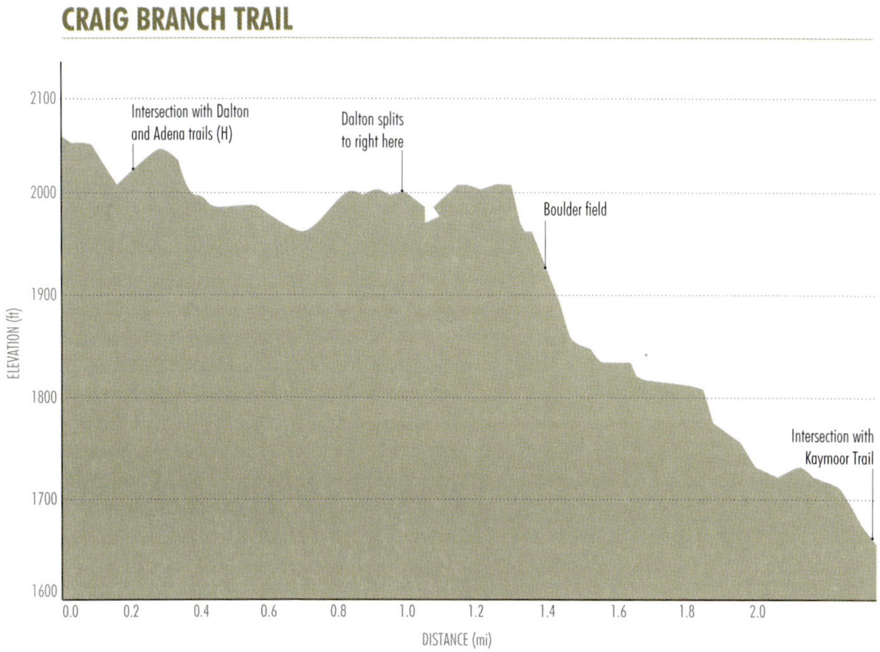

CRAIG BRANCH TRAIL

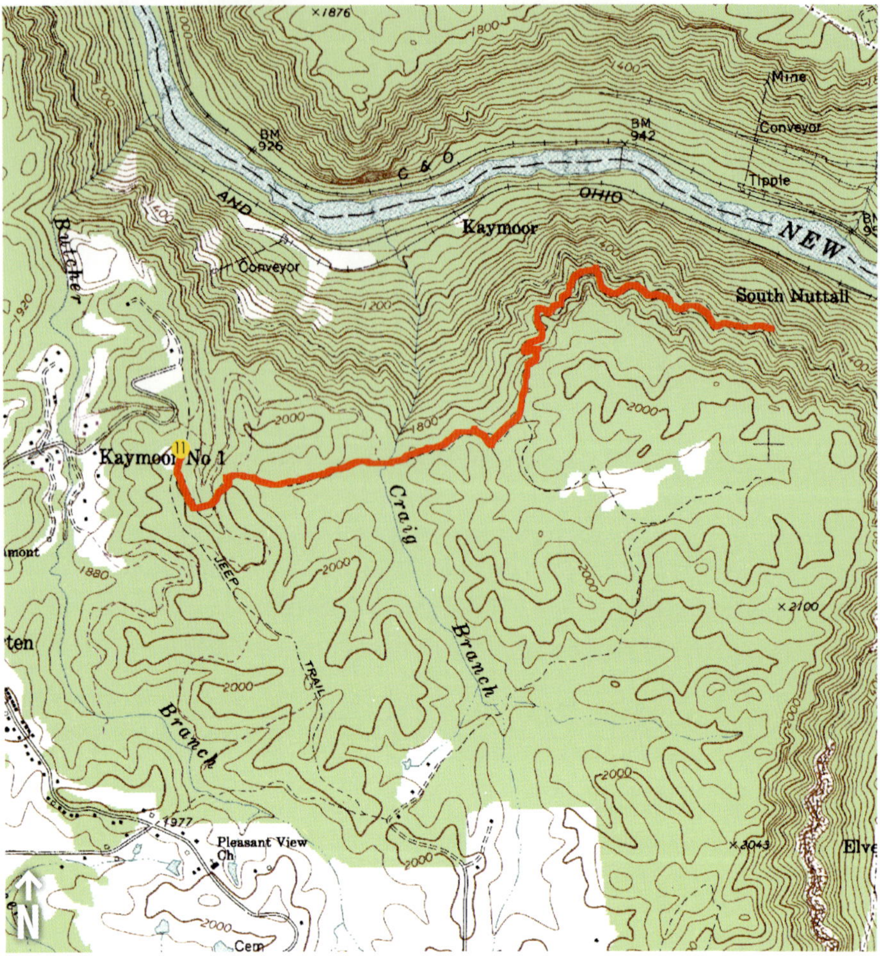

Trail Combinations/Options

Trail combinations that are available via the Dalton and Adena trails let you create an alternate route through the Arrowhead Trail System. Meanwhile, connecting with and turning left on the Kaymoor Trail (Trail 14) allows access to the historical site of Kaymoor and the potential for a strenuous 4.49-mile loop using the Kaymoor Miners Trail (Trail 5) to return to the Kaymoor Top area, only 0.35 miles from the Arrowhead lot.

12 ENDLESS WALL TRAIL

Reach one of the most fabulous viewpoints in the New River Gorge, Diamond Point, during this sunny and engaging hike.

2 | 363 ft 271 ft | 2.37 mi

Location: East of Fayetteville, WV, on the northeast side of New River

Maps: USGS Fayetteville quad 1:24,000

Facilities: Two gravel parking areas for approximately 15 vehicles each; both have toilet facilities.

Highlights: Diamond Point, other viewpoints.

Finding the Trailhead

Fern Creek trailhead: (38°03.784 N, 081°03.413 W)
Nuttall trailhead: (38°03.581 N, 081°02.946 W)
Endless Wall Trail has two trailheads: one at Fern Creek parking area, the other at Nuttall parking area. To reach the Endless Wall trailheads drive north along US 19 from Fayetteville, WV, crossing the bridge. Turn right onto Lansing-Edmond Road (County Route 5/82). Continue 1.3 miles and turn right into the Fern Creek parking area, or reach the Nuttall parking area at 1.8 miles.

Trail Milestones:

0.0 mi – Fern Creek parking area (38°03.784 N, 081°03.413 W)
0.4 mi – Fern Creek (38°03.475 N, 081°03.663 W)
0.57 mi – Fern Creek Ladder intersection (38°03.460 N, 081°03.684 W)
1.0 mi – Diamond Point (38°03.241 N, 081°03.612 W)
2.0 mi – Cirque Ladder intersection (38°03.411 N, 081°02.736 W)
2.37 mi – Nuttall parking area (38°03.581 N, 081°02.946 W)

Trail Description

Note: Hike described from Fern Creek trailhead. From the Fern Creek parking area, move into a mixed-forest canopy of hemlocks and deciduous trees, with rhododendrons in the understory. Ferns, moss-covered rocks, and downed trees covering the ground here make for a beautiful walk. At 0.4 miles cross a wooden bridge over Fern Creek. After the crossing, the forest changes character and is heavily populated by chestnut oaks. At 0.57 miles reach a branch trail to the right that leads to the Fern Creek Ladder, an access route to the cliff bottom frequently used by climbers.

Continue on the trail and begin to encounter many smaller branch trails to the right that lead to the gorge rim. These vantage points afford views of large portions of the gorge as well as of intrepid climbers tackling routes on the cliff face. Continue along the trail as it parallels the cliff edge and at 1.0 miles arrive at the highlight of the trail, and one of the most visited spots in the New River Gorge, Diamond Point. From this outcropping you can see the bridge to the west and a long expanse of gorge to the east. This is also a great spot to take a break, as it is shady and often blessed with a cool breeze.

From here, many hikers return to the Fern Creek parking area via the same route. You can, however, continue along the trail to complete your hike. You'll first encounter another branch trail, this time leading to the Honeymooners Ladder on the right. At 2.0 miles encounter the last branch trail leading straight and to the right: This ladder leads to an area that climbers call "The Cirque." Keep left at this intersection and begin to move away from the gorge. At 2.1 miles encounter the first of three bridges in a rhododendron thicket.

ENDLESS WALL TRAIL

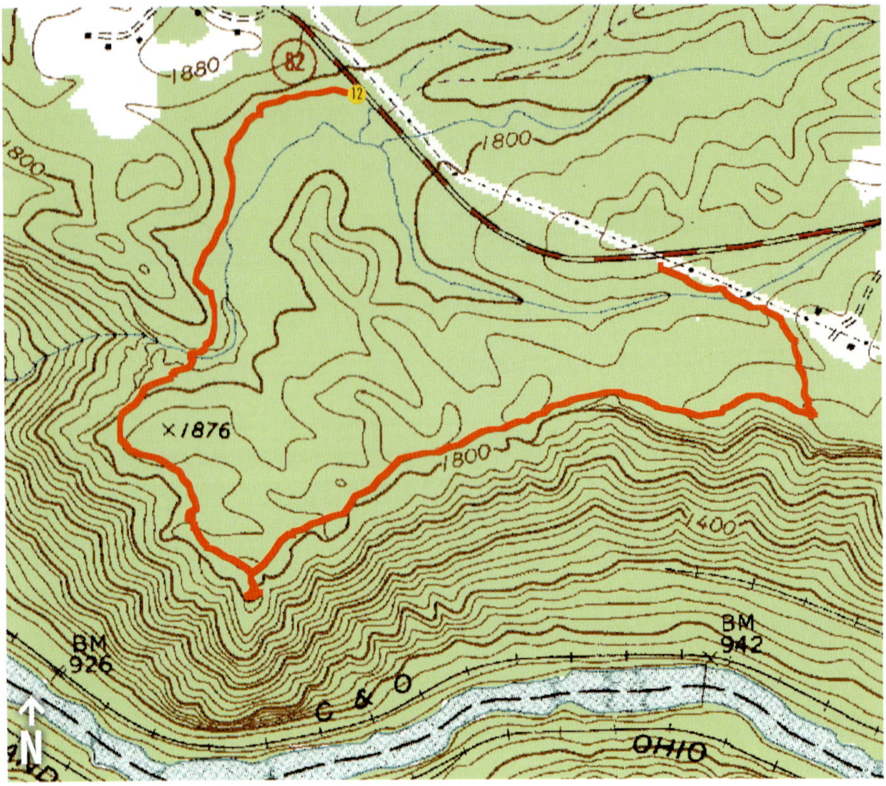

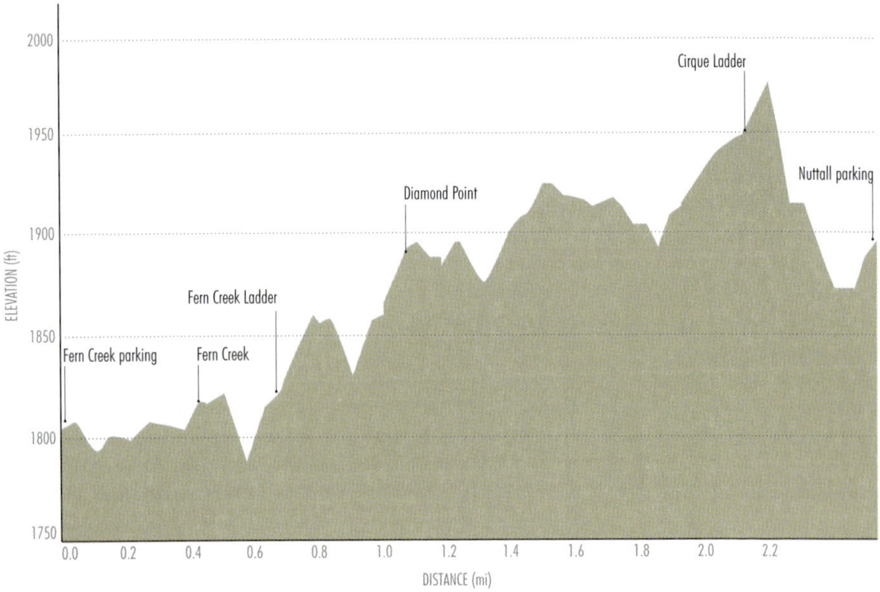

The aptly named Endless Wall.

Crossing the last bridge, parallel the stream until arriving at 2.37 miles at the Nuttall parking area. To complete the loop and return to the Fern Creek parking area, hike down the paved road (Lansing-Edmond Road) for 0.5 miles.

Additional Notes

This hike parallels the gorge rim for a majority of its length. Proceed with caution when approaching the cliff edge along the main or smaller branch trails. Special attention should be paid with children and when conditions are wet or icy.

Do not throw any objects over the cliff edge. Climbers frequent this area, and any dropped rock or object has the potential to provoke disastrous consequences.

A bridge along the Endless Wall Trail.

13 FAYETTEVILLE TRAIL

Want it all? You can have it all on the Fayetteville Trail. From single-track to old roadbed, and from natural wonders to scenic delights, this trail brings it and also connects to five other trails in the region.

4 | 384 ft | 1192 ft | 3.93 mi

Location: Southeast of Fayetteville, WV, along Gatewood Road
Maps: USGS Fayetteville quad 1:24,000
Trail Options: Connects to Bridge, Kaymoor, Long Point, Park Loop, and Timber Ridge trails.
Facilities: Gravel parking for 15 vehicles; close access to toilet and picnic facilities at Arrowhead Trail System parking.
Highlights: Wolf Creek, multiple trail intersections, NRG Bridge, waterfalls and cascades.

Trail Milestones:

0.6 mi – Intersection with Long Point Trail (38°02.785 N, 081°04.502 W)
1.6 mi – Intersection with Timber Ridge Trail (38°03.124 N, 081°05.037 W)
1.9 mi – Wolf Creek (38°03.195 N, 081°05.329 W)
2.3 mi – Intersection with Park Loop Trail (38°03.371 N, 081°05.200 W)
3.3 mi – Intersection with Bridge Trail (38°03.935 N, 081°05.173 W)
3.94 mi – Trail's end/Kaymoor Trail trailhead nearby (38°03.590 N, 081°04.859 W)

Finding the Trailhead

Kaymoor Top trailhead: (38°02.762 N, 081°04.107 W)
From US 19, follow WV 16 through Fayetteville 0.7 miles to its intersection with Gatewood Road. Bear left and follow Gatewood Road 2.0 miles before turning left onto Kaymoor No. 1 Road — National Park Service "brown" signs point the way toward Kaymoor at this intersection. Follow this road 0.9 miles to a T intersection; turn left here and follow the gravel road to the parking area at 0.15 miles. The trailhead is located at the far end of the lot.

Fayette Station trailhead: (38°03.590 N, 081°04.859 W)
Note: While paved, this is a one-way road with uneven surfaces and tight turns. Large vehicles, like RVs, are highly discouraged from attempting to negotiate this road. From the Canyon Rim Visitor Center, turn right out of the parking area and travel 0.1 miles to Lansing Loop Road. At the intersection turn (very!) sharply right and continue 0.2 miles. Reaching a second intersection, turn right, following the sign for CR 82. Travel 1.0 miles to the intersection with Burma Road; turn left here. A good rule of thumb when making a decision on this road is to always take the turn that leads downhill! Continue 1.3 miles, passing many streams to the left, and reach the Fayette Station Bridge. If no one is behind you, take a moment to appreciate the roughly 250-million-year-old river flowing beneath. At the end of the bridge, turn sharply right and at 0.2 miles stay left and cross under a railway trestle to continue toward the Fayette Station trailhead. Travel uphill 1.0 miles until reaching a deep bend in the road that marks the Kaymoor Trail trailhead and Wolf Creek. Park along the road uphill of this bend — the Fayette Station trailhead is on the left-hand side of the road.

FAYETTEVILLE TRAIL

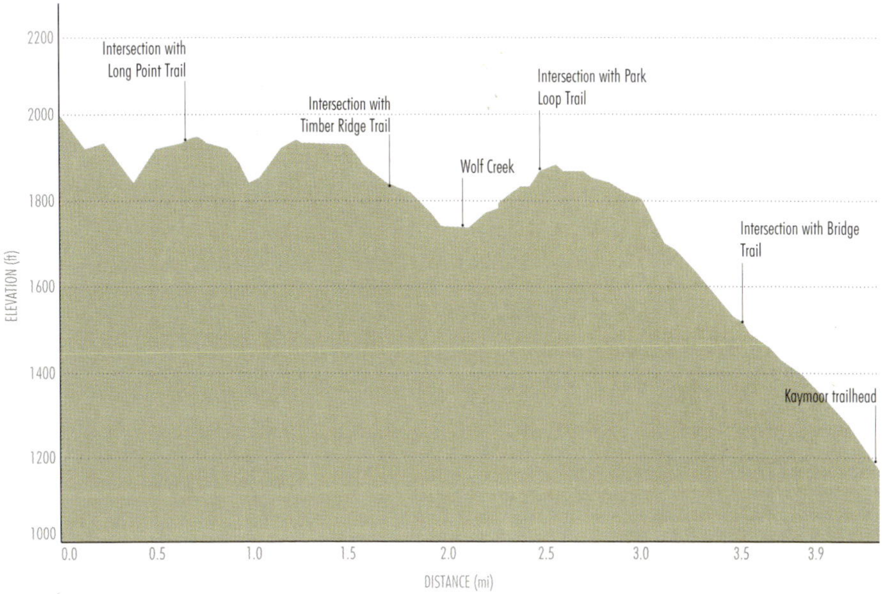

Trail Description

Note: Hike described from Kaymoor Top trailhead. From the shared trailhead with Butcher Branch Trail move into the forest and begin to descend. At 0.3 miles move into a stand of Virginia pine with an open meadow to your right before reaching Butcher Branch. Cross over the wooden bridge (slippery when wet!) and gradually move uphill through rhododendron and hemlock. At 0.6 miles intersect with Long Point Trail (Trail 10).

The trail remains relatively flat for the next 0.3 miles and then descends to a small stream with some impressive boulders to the right (downstream). Ascend out of this small valley for 0.2 miles, moving over a ridge, and then move gradually downhill to the intersection with Timber Ridge Trail (Trail 7). Turn sharply right here and continue 0.3 miles until reaching a large bridge crossing high above Wolf Creek, a highlight of this trail. Just upstream from the bridge and within view, Wolf Creek combines with House Branch.

After crossing the bridge stay right along the trail and climb out of the low point created by Wolf Creek. Atop this rise a moss-covered boulder to the left offers a place to rest. The next 0.2 miles is flat, but it's worth stopping to listen to the roar of Wolf Creek as it begins its tumble down the mountain toward the New River. At 2.3 miles intersect the Park Loop Trail (Trail 8). The two trails combine for 0.1 miles: At that point, stay on the Fayetteville Trail by moving right at the split toward Fayette Station Road (a sign marks this split).

Wolf Creek.

FAYETTEVILLE TRAIL

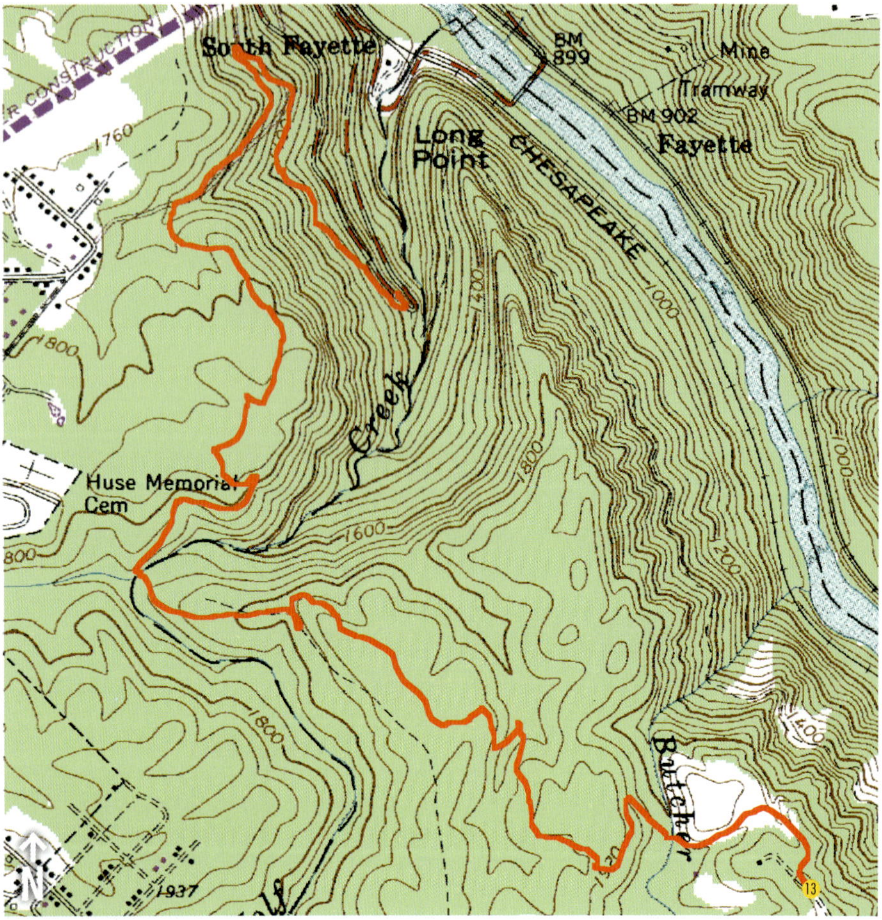

In another 0.3 miles you'll catch glimpses of the bridge and far ridgeline, especially in winter. Begin to move steadily downward, passing spur trails that lead to nearby homes on the left, until reaching a stream and wooden bridge at 2.9 miles. Ascend steeply out of this creekbed and turn right along a wide former road. Rock walls begin to tower higher to the left as you gradually descend into the gorge.

At 3.3 miles intersect the Bridge Trail (Trail 6) and turn right to descend stairs. *Note: Continuing straight along the Bridge Trail for 0.28 miles allows views from beneath the New River Gorge Bridge and is a highly recommended extension.* Descend the stairs and continue along a well-graded descent for the final 0.64 miles, crossing numerous streams and drainages until arriving at the lower trailhead, on Fayette Station Road. This trailhead is located just 100 meters uphill from the trailhead for Kaymoor Trail (Trail 14) and a large collection of waterfalls and cascades on Wolf Creek.

Trail Combinations/Options:

Trail combinations for all five trails that intersect Fayetteville Trail are described in each of the individual trail sections (Bridge, Kaymoor, Long Point, Park Loop, and Timber Ridge trails). Fayetteville Trail is heavily used due to its connectivity and the ability to vary and create myriad loops.

14 KAYMOOR TRAIL

The longest trail in the region, the Kaymoor Trail offers visitors insight into the mining operations of the early twentieth century, and a brilliant array of natural beauty.

1 981 ft 577ft 8.34 mi

Location: Southeast of Fayetteville, WV, along Fayette Station Road
Maps: USGS Fayetteville quad 1:24,000
Trail Options: Connect with Fayetteville Trail (Trail 13), Kaymoor Miners Trail (Trail 5), Craig Branch Trail (Trail 11), Brooklyn Mine Trail (Trail 28), and Southside Trail (Trail 31).
Facilities: Gravel parking for 10 vehicles.
Highlights: Wolf Creek, waterfalls, Kaymoor ruins, views.

Trail Milestones:

1.5 mi – Mine openings (38°03.568 N, 081°04.824 W)
2.1 mi — Kaymoor Mine/Kaymoor Miners Trail (38°02.843 N, 081°03.797 W)
3.9 mi – Intersection with Craig Branch Trail (38°02.741 N, 081°02.484 W)
4.2 mi – Kudzu "jungle" (38°02.466 N, 081°02.122 W)
5.8 mi – Picnic spot and views (38°01.354 N, 081°02.320 W)
8.3 mi – Bridge over Coal Run Creek (38°00.006 N, 081°02.089 W)

Finding the Trailhead

Fayette Station trailhead: (38°03.568 N, 081°04.824 W)
Note: While paved, this is a one-way road with uneven surfaces and tight turns. Large vehicles, like RVs, are highly discouraged from attempting to negotiate this road. From the Canyon Rim Visitor Center, turn right out of the parking area and travel 0.1 miles to Lansing Loop Road. At the intersection turn (very!) sharply right and continue 0.2 miles. Reaching a second intersection, turn right, following the sign for CR 82. Travel 1.0 miles to the intersection with Burma Road; turn left here. A good rule of thumb when making a decision on this road is to always take the turn that leads downhill! Continue 1.3 miles, passing many streams to the left, and reach the Fayette Station Bridge. If no one is behind you, take a moment to appreciate the roughly 250-million-year-old river flowing beneath. At the end of the bridge, turn sharply right and at 0.2 miles stay left and cross under a railway trestle to continue toward the trailhead. Travel uphill 1.0 miles until reaching a deep bend in the road that marks the Kaymoor Trail trailhead and Wolf Creek. Park along the road uphill of this bend — the Fayette Station trailhead is on the left-hand side of the road.

Cunard trailhead: (38°00.017 N, 081°02.061 W)
From US Route 19, follow WV 16 through Fayetteville 0.7 miles to the intersection with Gatewood Road. Bear left and follow Gatewood Road 4.5 miles before turning left onto Cunard Road. Follow this road 1.8 miles to Cunard. Take a left toward the Cunard River Access area; after traveling 0.5 miles arrive at the parking lot for the trail. The trailhead is located across the road and 100 meters uphill.

Trail Description

Also known as Kaymoor-Cunard Trail
Note: Hike described from Fayette Station trailhead. Begin by hiking toward the steel bridge over Wolf Creek. Pause a moment to view the cascades and pool above the bridge. There is also a difficult-to-see waterfall below the bridge. Continue uphill slightly and at 200 meters encounter a beautiful waterfall that flows right beside (and under) the trail. Continue to 0.4 miles, making a sharp turn to the

A small waterfall along Kaymoor Trail.

right. This trail segment lies directly below the overlook on Long Point Trail, hundreds of feet above. Continue along this wide and well-maintained trail, with occasional views of the gorge and river below. At 0.6 miles watch for a small spring that burbles from under a rock to the right.

This area is beautiful in the fall, with myriad brilliant colors from the various oak, maple, and hickory trees that populate the area. At 1.5 miles come upon the first evidence of mining, in the area to the right. These openings were used as utility entrances and allowed for drainage, ventilation, and power for the Kaymoor Mine complex.

Continue along the trail and at 1.6 miles cross a steel bridge over Butcher Branch Creek. At 2.0 miles begin to see the remnants of buildings for the main mine complex. The large and relatively intact building on the right once housed a ventilation fan for the mines. Around the curve in the trail arrive at the mine entrance and associated Kaymoor Mine building. It's worth spending some time here, as the area is packed with historical significance and is listed on the National Register of Historic Places. This point also marks the intersection with the Kaymoor Miners Trail, which leads down along 820 steps to the bottom portion of the mine complex, or up to Kaymoor Top where the miners and their families lived.

Hidden mine portal.

The next segment offers an abundance of historical treats for those with a keen eye. Reentering the forest, continue along the trail and at 2.3 miles watch for the partially buried remains of mine cars and tracks to the right. A little farther along (at 2.7 miles) look for the remnants of a block building that connects to a boulder above and right of the trail. What was the purpose of this small shed? Perhaps a moonshine still? Its actual purpose is not known. At 2.8 miles stay to the left of the trail to catch a glimpse of the wreckage of an old truck, partially buried in the hillside. After another 0.1 miles come upon a large boulder perched to the

KAYMOOR TRAIL

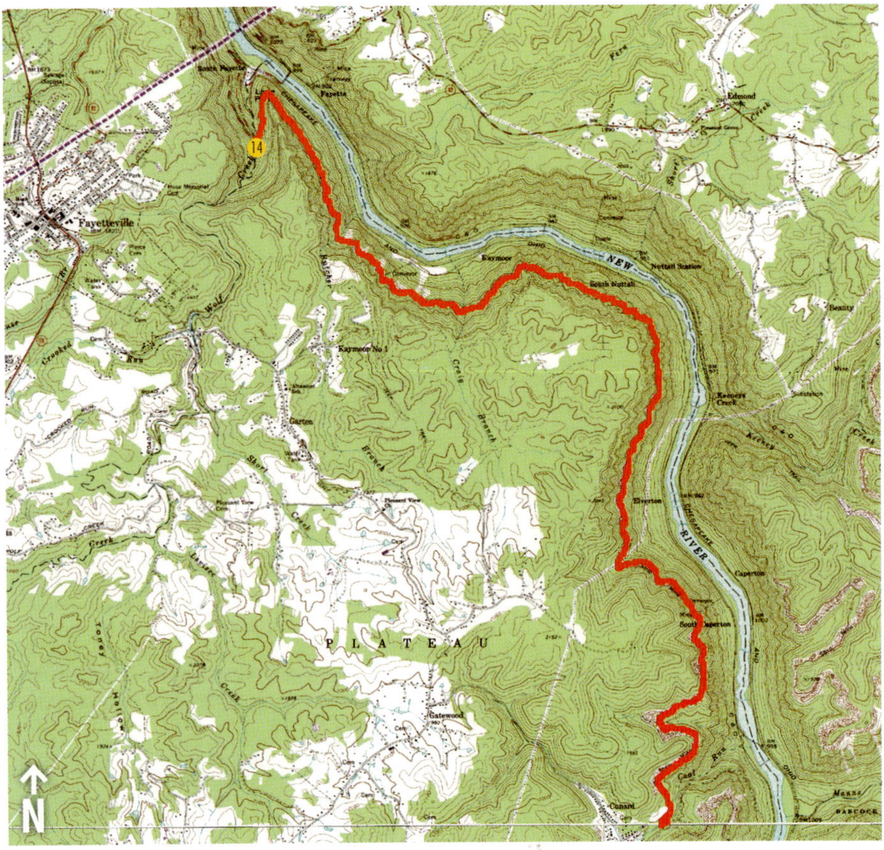

left side of the trail. Over the next 1.0 miles wind along a flat path until reaching the intersection with Craig Branch Trail at 3.9 miles. A nice rock here offers a place to sit and take a break; just over the bank is the remnants of an old car. Craig Branch Trail moves uphill and right of the Kaymoor Trail at this point; Kaymoor Trail, meanwhile, continues straight and narrows considerably.

At 4.2 miles, the trail breaks into the open and then enters an area that more closely resembles a steamy jungle than an Appalachian forest. This is due to the kudzu vine, first introduced to the United States in 1876 and now prevalent throughout the Southeast. This plant, native to southern Japan and southeastern China, is an invasive species that "outcompetes" other plants. Move through this jungle-like setting along single-track before entering the forest and continuing along the trail.

At 5.3 miles the trail steepens along the ruins of a building, with steps and old bricks visible, before leveling out again. In 0.5 miles you'll catch nice views looking upstream along the New River. This is a great spot to rest in the sun, just off the trail, and have a picnic lunch. Continuing around a bend and slightly uphill, come across a trail intersecting to the right; stay straight here. Continue along the path into a younger forest and into an area that was strip-mined in the past. The trail widens here, with a large, flat expanse to the right. At 7.6 miles move into a young pine forest. At 8.3 miles cross Coal Run Creek by way of a metal bridge before arriving at the Cunard trailhead and the trail's end.

Looking upstream along Coal Run.

Trail Combinations/Options

Amongst the kudzu (*Pueraria lobata*).

Kaymoor Trail connects with multiple trails throughout the region, allowing for daylong hikes and multiple loop variations. Two of the most popular loops are:

1) Kaymoor – Craig Branch – Fayetteville Trail: This creates a loop of 10.02 miles and returns to the Fayette Station trailhead. This is a moderately strenuous hike due to the length of the ascent along Craig Branch Trail (2.19 miles).

2) Kaymoor – Kaymoor Miners – Fayetteville Trail: This creates a loop of 6.69 miles and is considered strenuous due to the steep ascent of the Kaymoor Miners Trail.

3) Kaymoor – Cunard Road – Southside – Arbuckle – Rend Trail: For longer, two-day hikes, you can link up with the Southside Trail (Trail 31), and farther along, the Arbuckle Connector (Trail 26) and Rend (Trail 30) trails. This adventure can be completed either as an out-and-back or by car shuttle. Camping facilities are available along this route — ask NPS staff for more information. The complete hike involves one section of paved road heavily used by rafting companies and kayakers to reach a popular put-in on the river. Use caution if hiking this portion of the route. The one-way distance for this connection is 18.42 miles. A proposed trail called the Brooklyn Miners Trail would eliminate the need for the Cunard road portion of this connection. No completion date is set for this trail.

You'll find numerous other variations for loop and connector hikes in this area due to the close proximity of multiple regions. With road connections, you can even hike from Fayette Station Road through the New River Gorge south to Little Beaver State Park.

KAYMOOR TRAIL

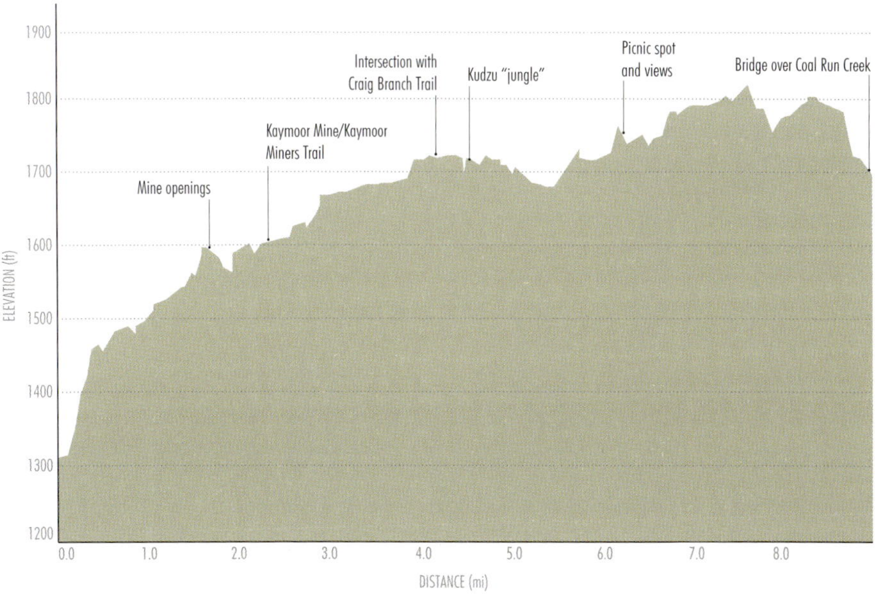

6 ARROWHEAD TRAIL SYSTEM

Overview and Highlights

The Arrowhead Trail System, located southeast of Fayetteville, WV, and bordering many of the trails in the Fayetteville, Lansing, and Kaymoor Region, comprises the newest group of trails in the New River Gorge National River. Developed in conjunction with the Boy Scouts of America's honor society, the Order of the Arrowhead, these trails present almost 13 miles of outstanding single-track for the hiker or biker.

How to Get There

From US Route 19, follow WV 16 through Fayetteville 0.7 miles to the intersection with Gatewood Road. Bear left and follow Gatewood Road for 2.0 miles before turning left onto Kaymoor No. 1 Road — National Park Service "brown" signs point the way toward Kaymoor at this intersection. Follow this road 0.9 miles to a T intersection; turn right here and follow the gravel road to the Arrowhead Trail System parking area at 0.25 miles.

Rules and Regulations

Please see "Rules and Regulations for the New River Gorge National River" (page 22) for rules and regulations governing the area.

General Trail Information

The Arrowhead Trail System, while made up of four paths of varying lengths, is unique in that it creates a "stacked loop" system, offering myriad possible routes. To help navigate these trails, each intersection has been assigned a letter from A through O. I've described each trail from its trailhead to trail's end, though the possible combinations are almost endless, allowing for a unique experience with every visit. See the Grid References for Arrowhead Trail Intersections (facing page) to plan your adventure!

History and Culture

The area shares its history and cultural heritage with the Fayetteville, Lansing, and Kaymoor Region. Much of this area was once home to coal mines and logging operations.

Additional Notes

Boy Scouts of America: The Boy Scouts of America is currently in the process of making its regional base a permanent home for scouts to visit, explore, and develop into responsible and ethical citizens and leaders. The Boy Scouts of America Summit Bechtel Reserve will serve as a High Adventure Base and permanent home to the Boy Scout Jamboree, an event held every four years with tens of thousands of scouts and scout leaders attending.

ARROWHEAD TRAIL SYSTEM HIKES

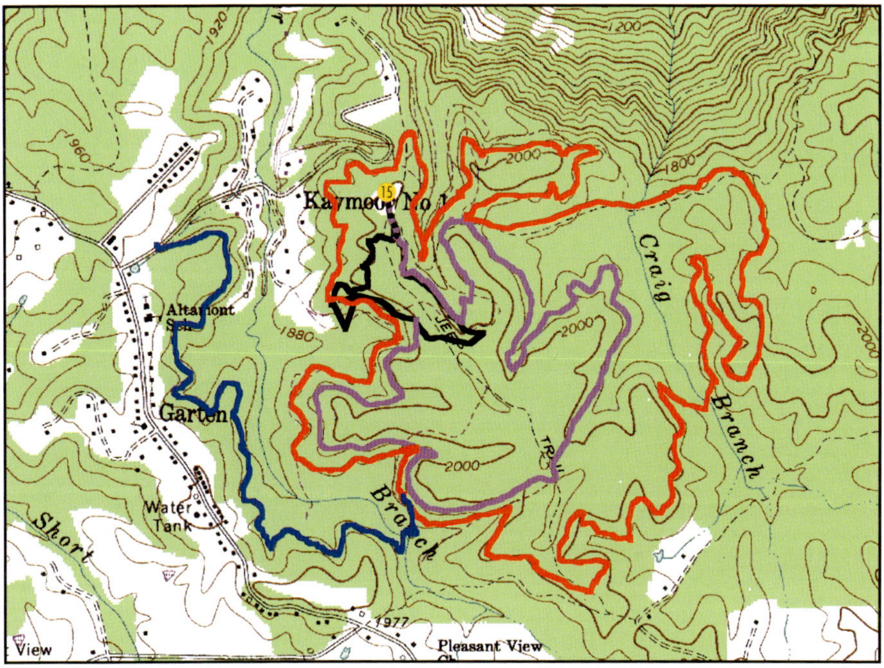

Building the Arrowhead Trail System

This trail system, built in 2011, offers the perfect mix of trails for all users. Members of the Scouts' Order of the Arrow donated almost 79,000 volunteer hours to make these trails a reality. The paths, aptly named for types of arrowheads and spear tips used by prehistoric Native American cultures, offer hours of enjoyment.

Grid References for Arrowhead Trail Intersections

A – (38°02.586 N, 081°04.015 W)
B – (38°02.428 N, 081°04.065 W)
C – (38°02.266 N, 081°04.185 W)
D – (38°02.267 N, 081°04.014 W)
E – (38°02.265 N, 081°03.918 W)
F – (38°02.050 N, 081°04.046 W)
G – (38°02.032 N, 081°03.686 W)
H – (38°02.425 N, 081°03.880 W)
I – (38°02.459 N, 081°03.956 W)
J – (38°02.061 N, 081°04.277 W)
K – (38°02.041 N, 081°04.418 W)
L – (38°01.928 N, 081°04.018 W)
M – (38°02.154 N, 081°03.453 W)
N – (38°02.532 N, 081°03.323 W)
O – (38°02.400 N, 081°04.615 W)

Fall color along the trail.

15 CLOVIS TRAIL

The shortest of the Arrowhead Trails, this trail lets you link into the Adena and Dalton trails for longer adventures.

3 | 152 ft | 71 ft | 1.19 mi

Location: Southeast of Fayetteville, WV, along Gatewood Road
Maps: USGS Fayetteville quad 1:24,000
Trail Options: Connect with Adena Trail (Trail 17) and Dalton Trail (Trail 18).
Facilities: Ample gravel parking, toilets, picnic facilities.
Highlights: A winding trail through the forest.

Trail Milestones:

0.3 mi – Intersection with Dalton Trail (C)
(38°02.266 N, 081°04.185 W)
0.5 mi – Intersection with Adena Trail (D)
(38°02.267 N, 081°04.014 W)
0.8 mi – Intersection with Adena Trail (E)
(38°02.265 N, 081°03.918 W)
1.19 mi – Return to Arrowhead parking area (B)
(38°02.428 N, 081°04.065 W)

Finding the Trailhead

(38°02.428 N, 081°04.065 W)
From US Route 19, follow WV 16 through Fayetteville 0.7 miles to the intersection with Gatewood Road. Bear left and follow Gatewood Road for 2.0 miles before turning left onto Kaymoor No. 1 Road — National Park Service "brown" signs point the way toward Kaymoor at this intersection. Follow this road 0.9 miles to a T intersection. Turn right here and follow the gravel road to the Arrowhead Trail System parking area at 0.25 miles.

Trail Description

Once at the Arrowhead lot, find the Clovis trailhead between the large sign with the trail map and the toilet facilities — it's designated with the letter B. Begin along a gravel single-track that quickly moves into the forest and transitions to a normal trail surface of soil and leaves. Wind through 0.3 miles of mixed deciduous forest until reaching the trailhead for the Dalton Trail (Trail 18) at intersection C. Continue straight through this intersection and in another 0.2 miles reach the trailhead for Adena Trail (Trail 17) at the D intersection. The Clovis Trail continues to wind through the forest until reaching the second intersection (E) with the Adena Trail, at 0.8 miles. Continue along a gradual ascent until regaining the Arrowhead parking area at 1.19 miles.

Using the intersection lettering to track your hike, the Clovis Trail would be:

B-C-D-E-B

Trail Combinations/Options

The Clovis Trail connects with the Adena Trail (Trail 17) at intersections D (0.5 miles) and E (0.8 miles). The trail also connects with the Dalton Trail (Trail 18) at intersection C (0.3 miles).

Additional Notes

Why Clovis? The Clovis Trail is named for a prehistoric Native American culture whose existence has been dated back to around 11,500 to 13,500 years ago. One of the first finds, near Clovis, New Mexico, consisted of a variety of artifacts, most significantly distinctive fluted stone spear points. These projectile points, known as Clovis Points, have been found throughout North America.

CLOVIS TRAIL

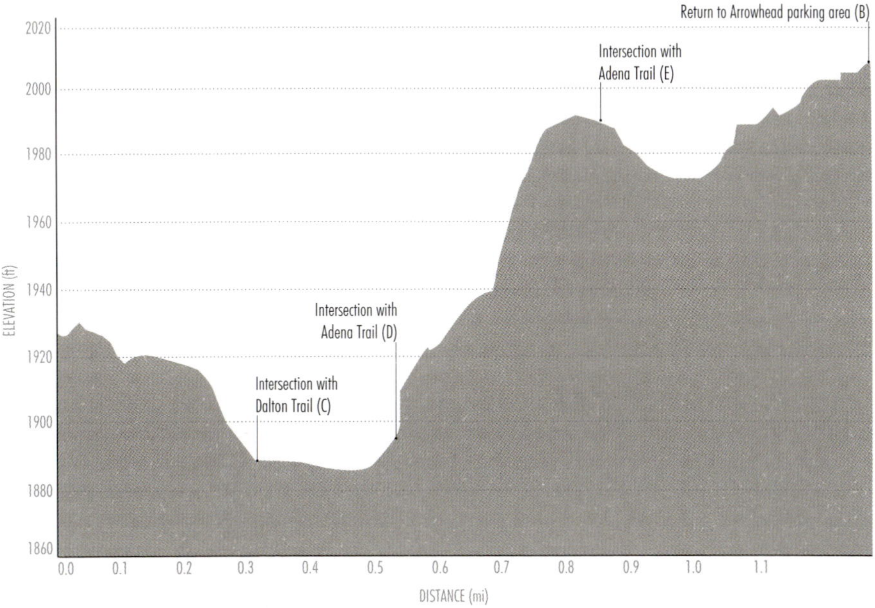

16 LECROY TRAIL

A fun 1.78-mile out-and-back trail that winds through mature forest and over a stone bridge before leading down to Kaymoor No. 1 Road.

3 | 211 ft 204 ft | 1.78 mi

Location: Southeast of Fayetteville, WV, along Gatewood Road
Maps: USGS Fayetteville quad 1:24,000
Trail Options: Connect with Dalton Trail (Trail 18).
Facilities: Ample gravel parking, toilets, picnic facilities. At point O, parking for six vehicles.
Highlights: Mature forest, streambed with stone bridge, rhododendron.

Trail Milestones:

0.1 mi – Cross stream
(38°01.887 N, 081°04.042 W)
0.6 mi – Trail art
(38°01.884 N, 081°04.362 W)
0.8 mi – Intersection with connector trail (K)
(38°02.041 N, 081°04.418 W)
1.78 mi – Trail's end (O)
(38°02.400 N, 081°04.615 W)

Finding the Trailhead

(38°01.928 N, 081°04.018 W)
From US Route 19, follow WV 16 through Fayetteville 0.7 miles to the intersection with Gatewood Road. Bear left and follow Gatewood Road for 2.0 miles before turning left onto Kaymoor No. 1 Road — National Park Service "brown" signs point the way toward Kaymoor at this intersection. Follow this road 0.9 miles to a T intersection. Turn right here and follow the gravel road to the Arrowhead Trail System parking area at 0.25 miles.

To reach the trailhead at intersection L from the parking area, follow the Clovis Trail (Trail 15) 0.3 miles until it intersects with the Dalton Trail (Trail 18) at intersection C. At this point turn left and follow the Dalton Trail 1.12 miles, passing intersection J until reaching intersection L, the LeCroy trailhead.

Trail Description

From the trailhead (L), quickly cross a stream at 0.1 miles and begin ascending. At 0.4 miles begin to see some homes above and left of the trail along the visible ridgeline. The trail curves at 0.6 miles just before an interesting bit of "trail art." Continuing for 0.2 miles, reach intersection K, which links LeCroy and Dalton trails by a 0.3-mile connector. Stay straight, and at 1.6 miles begin to see Kaymoor No. 1 Road to your front and right. Reach the end of the trail by crossing a wide, rocky stream and arriving at point O.

Using the intersection lettering to track your hike, the LeCroy Trail would be:

B-C-J-L (trailhead)**-K-O**

Trail Combinations/Options

The LeCroy Trail connects with the Dalton Trail (Trail 18) at intersections L (trailhead) and K (via 0.3-mile connector). The trail ends at point O (Kaymoor No. 1 Road). Turn left on this road and climb to Gatewood Road. At Gatewood Road turn right and then right again on Newton Road to access the trailhead for Long Point Trail (Trail 10) and Timber Ridge Trail (Trail 7).

Additional Notes

Why LeCroy? This trail's name is related to another early American people who lived between 6,500 and 5,800 BC and whose fine spear points are today known as LeCroy bifurcated spear points. These points are small and thin but distinctive in appearance due to their bifurcated stem. The range of the LeCroy culture included all of West Virginia, and eventually spread throughout the Mid-Atlantic States.

LECROY TRAIL

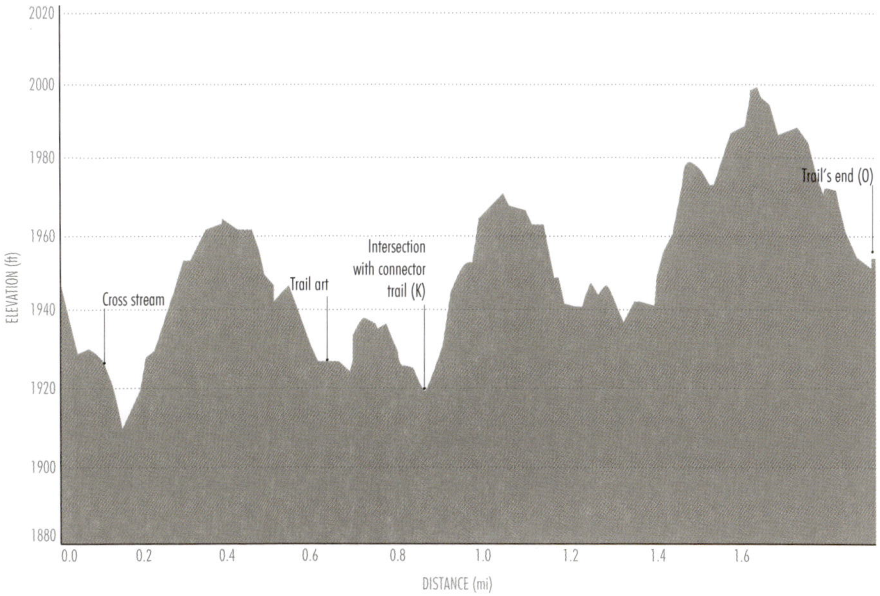

17 ADENA TRAIL

A fun hike — but a brilliant trail run or bike ride — along a forested track that encounters boulders, a stream, and numerous intersections to vary your route.

3 | 386 ft | 357 ft | 3.18 mi

Location: Southeast of Fayetteville, WV, along Gatewood Road
Maps: USGS Fayetteville quad 1:24,000
Trail Options: Both trailheads located off Clovis Trail (Trail 15); connects to Dalton Trail (Trail 18) and, briefly, to Craig Branch Trail (Trail 11).
Facilities: Ample gravel parking, toilets, picnic facilities at Arrowhead parking area.
Highlights: Forest trail with potential for wildlife.

Trail Milestones:

0.7 mi – Intersection with Dalton Trail (F)
(38°02.050 N, 081°04.046 W)
1.3 mi – Intersection with connector (G)
(38°02.032 N, 081°03.686 W)
2.2 mi – Enter thick rhododendron
(38°02.228 N, 081°04.787 W)
2.5 mi – Intersection with Dalton and Craig Branch trails (H)
(38°02.425 N, 081°03.880 W)
2.8 mi – Intersection with Clovis Trail (E)
(38°02.265 N, 081°03.918 W)

Finding the Trailhead

(38°02.267 N, 081°04.014 W)
From US Route 19, follow WV 16 through Fayetteville 0.7 miles to the intersection with Gatewood Road. Bear left and follow Gatewood Road for 2.0 miles before turning left onto Kaymoor No. 1 Road — National Park Service "brown" signs point the way toward Kaymoor at this intersection. Follow this road 0.9 miles to a T intersection. Turn right here and follow the gravel road to the Arrowhead Trail System parking area at 0.25 miles.

Starting at the Arrowhead lot at point B between the trail map and toilet facilities, hike 0.5 miles down the Clovis Trail (Trail 15), passing intersection C en route to the Adena trailhead at intersection D.

Trail Description

From the Adena trailhead, hike along the forested trail 0.7 miles to the intersection/trailhead for Dalton Trail at point F. Cross a small stream and keep left at the stone cairn, paralleling the stream toward its source. Continue along this twisting portion of trail to a group of interesting moss-covered boulders. At 1.3 miles reach intersection G; stay straight here. *Note: Turning right along this short trail (0.3 miles) connects you to intersection M on the Dalton Trail.*

The trail now breaks into an open area and begins to take on a hard-packed-clay consistency. Continue along this open area for 0.3 miles until reentering the forest. At 2.2 miles the trail moves again into an open area before reentering the clutches of a thick rhododendron forest.

At 2.5 miles reach the intersection with Craig Branch Trail (Trail 11) and Dalton Trail (Trail 18). Turn left along Craig Branch Trail for 25 meters and reach point H. Three trails intersect here — stay left on the Adena Trail. *Note: Continuing straight at this intersection will return you to the Arrowhead parking via the Craig Branch Trail. Turning right connects to the Dalton Trail in 0.1 miles.* At 2.8 miles intersect the Clovis Trail (Trail 15) at point E. Keep right for 0.38 miles, arriving at the Arrowhead parking area just to the right of the toilet facilities.

Using the lettering of intersections to track your hike, the Adena Trail would be:

B-C-D (trailhead)**-F-G-H-E-**Arrowhead parking

Trail Combinations/Options

To reach Adena Trail's western trailhead (as described on the preceding pages), it is essential to follow Clovis Trail (Trail 15) for its first 0.5 miles. Adena Trail also connects to Dalton Trail (Trail 18) either directly or via short connectors at three intersections: F, G, and H. Adena Trail also links with Craig Branch Trail (Trail 11) at 2.5 miles (near intersection H); this connection allows access to a great number of trails, including Kaymoor Trail (Trail 14). Numerous options let you create a longer or shorter hike using these connections.

Additional Notes

Why Adena? The Adena were an early Native American culture that populated areas of West Virginia, Ohio, Kentucky, and Indiana between roughly 800 BC and 1 AD. This culture was among the first in the Americas to transition from a solely hunter/gatherer society to a society that incorporated farming into their way of life. Adena burial mounds are still in evidence today throughout the region. The closest mound to the New River Gorge area is the Criel Mound in South Charleston, WV. Evidence of the Adena culture has been identified in multiple locations within the park.

Point F, along the Adena Trail.

ADENA TRAIL

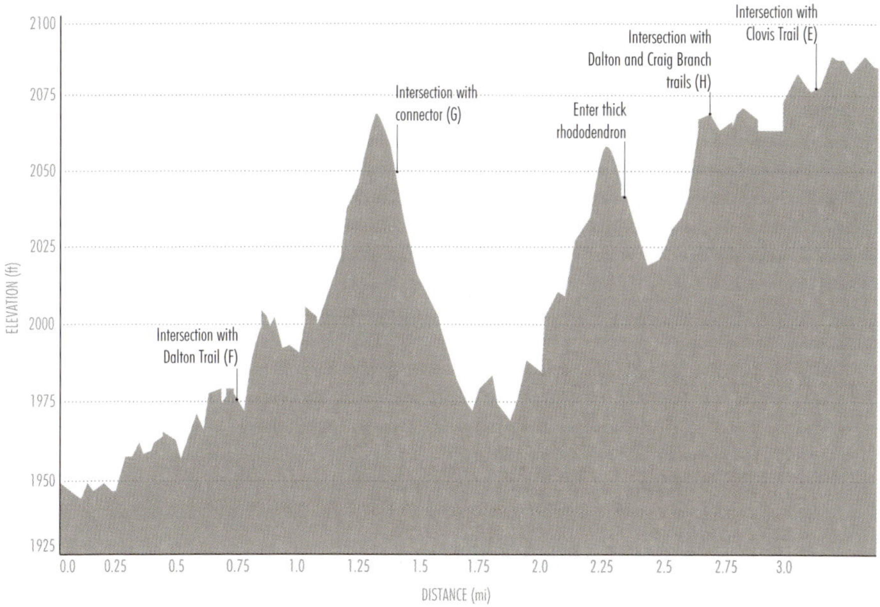

18 DALTON TRAIL

The longest trail in the Arrowhead Trail System, the Dalton Trail takes you on a wild ride through mature forests, rhododendron and mountain laurel thickets, and along the rim of the New River Gorge.

3 152 ft 71 ft 6.51 mi

Location: Southeast of Fayetteville, WV, along Gatewood Road
Maps: USGS Fayetteville quad 1:24,000
Trail Options: Connect to the Clovis Trail (Trail 15), Adena Trail (Trail 17), Craig Branch Trail (Trail 11), and the LeCroy Trail (Trail 16).
Facilities: Ample gravel parking, toilets, picnic facilities.
Highlights: Winding trail, views of New River, rhododendron and mountain laurel thickets.

Trail Milestones:

0.6 mi – Intersection with access road (A)
(38°02.586 N, 081°04.015 W)
1.0 mi – Intersection with connector trail (I)
(38°02.459 N, 081°03.956 W)
1.9 mi – Intersection with Craig Branch Trail
(38°02.463 N, 081°03.882 W)
2.5 mi – Trail splits from Craig Branch Trail (N)
(38°02.532 N, 081°03.323 W)
3.7 mi – Stream with bridge
(38°02.158 N, 081°03.315 W)
3.9 mi – Intersection with connector trail (M)
(38°02.154 N, 081°03.453 W)
5.4 mi – Intersection with LeCroy Trail (L)
(38°01.928 N, 081°04.018 W)
5.5 mi – Intersection with Adena Trail (F)
(38°02.050 N, 081°04.046 W)
5.9 mi – Intersection with connector trail (J)
(38°02.061 N, 081°04.277 W)
6.52 mi – Intersection with Clovis Trail/ trailhead (C)
(38°02.266 N, 081°04.185 W)

Finding the Trailhead

(38°02.266 N, 081°04.185 W)
From US Route 19, follow WV 16 through Fayetteville 0.7 miles to the intersection with Gatewood Road. Bear left and follow Gatewood Road for 2.0 miles before turning left onto Kaymoor No. 1 Road — National Park Service "brown" signs point the way toward Kaymoor at this intersection. Follow this road 0.9 miles to a T intersection. Turn right here and follow the gravel road to the Arrowhead Trail System parking area at 0.25 miles.

Starting at the Arrowhead lot at point B between the trail map and toilet facilities, hike 0.3 miles down the Clovis Trail (Trail 15) to the Dalton trailhead at intersection C.

Trail Description

The trail, as described, runs clockwise along narrow single-track. Move steadily upward to 0.2 miles and cross a small drainage area. The trail is edged here with stones to prevent erosion. Continue, and at 0.5 miles cross an old forest access road; in the distance and to the left you'll see a paved road. At 0.6 miles cross a gravel road — this access road and intersection are 0.15 miles from the Arrowhead Trail parking area and are designated as point A.

Picking up the trail on the other side of the road, begin to descend on the gorge side of the trail system. At 1.0 miles reach intersection I (it's possible to turn right here to connect to the Adena Trail). Stay straight, and in 0.4 miles the trail moves along the gorge rim where in autumn and winter you can view a large expanse of the gorge and ridgeline on the opposite side. At 1.9 miles the trail intersects the Adena Trail (briefly) and Craig Branch Trail. Keep left, and the trail transforms from single-track to a wide access road (as part of the Craig Branch Trail). Slightly uphill from this point, you'll spot intersection H. Continuing downhill along this well-graded portion of trail, cross a rocky stream surrounded by a lush rhododendron grove. This spot is a must-see in the spring when the grove is blooming.

Just 0.2 miles farther along, Dalton Trail breaks right away from Craig Branch Trail over large boulders — this intersection is marked as N. At 3.4 miles move through a rhododendron grove and proceed through stands of mountain laurel until reaching a stream. Cross

DALTON TRAIL

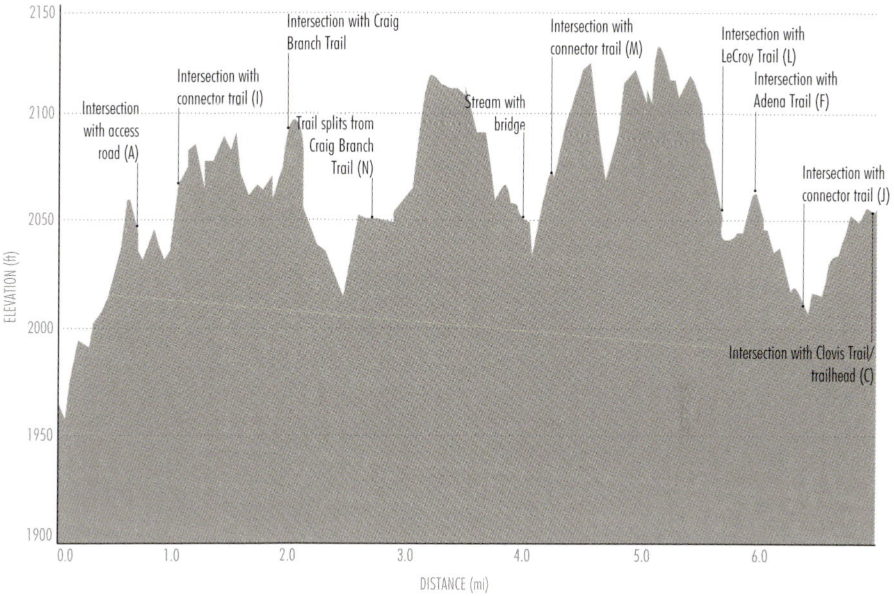

using a wooden bridge at 3.7 miles and reach intersection M at 3.9 miles. This intersection provides a connector to the Adena Trail (0.3 miles); keep sharply left here to stay on the Dalton Trail. Continue through the forest and at 4.8 miles pass a private home to the left. At 5.0 miles cross over a rocky point with a small rock wall to the right, and shortly thereafter see Gatewood Road in the distance to the left. A short 0.4 miles later reach intersection L, the trailhead for the LeCroy Trail, followed quickly by point F, a junction with the Adena Trail where you must keep left through this more intricate intersection. At 5.9 miles reach intersection J, which allows you to connect to the LeCroy Trail or stay straight and at 6.52 miles reach intersection C, Dalton Trail's original starting point. To regain the Arrowhead lot, retrace the Clovis Trail 0.3 miles along the same route you used at the beginning.

Using intersection lettering to track your hike, the Dalton Trail would be:

B-C (trailhead)**-A-I-**Craig Branch Trail**-N-M-L-F-J-C-B**

Trail Combinations/Options

Hike the Clovis Trail (Trail 15) 0.3 miles to reach the Dalton trailhead. Dalton intersects with all the other trails in the Arrowhead Trail System, including the Adena Trail (Trail 17) at intersection I (1.0 miles), briefly near intersection H (1.9 miles), at intersection M (3.9 miles), and finally at intersection F (5.5 miles). Dalton connects with and runs along the Craig Branch Trail (Trail 11) from near intersection H (1.9 miles) to intersection N (2.5 miles). Dalton also connects with the LeCroy Trail (Trail 16) at two locations: intersection L (5.4 miles) and intersection J (5.9 miles). These intersections allow for any number of combos utilizing portions of all four trails.

Additional Notes

Why Dalton? Dalton Trail is named for the Dalton culture of ancient Native American hunter/gatherers who lived between 9,900 and 10,500 years ago, generally in the middle of the modern-day United States. One distinctive feature of their culture is the often-found Dalton Point, a distinctive leaf-shaped spear point, examples of which have been unearthed in the New River Gorge.

Mountain Laurel (*Kalmia latifolia*).

7 NUTTALLBURG REGION

Overview and Highlights

The town of Nuttallburg, founded in 1870 by John Nuttall, became one of the leading towns in the region during the coal-mining boom of the late 1800s and early 1900s. Mr. Nuttall, born in England, identified the demand for the coal as well as the rich deposits located in the New River Gorge, and began buying up thousands of acres of land. His foresight resulted in the town and mines of Nuttallburg.

Among the highlights of a visit are the well-preserved mining complex, both at the level of the mine and headhouse, and at the bottom of the gorge, as well as the tipple buildings. These, along with the remnants and relics of the town, are a reminder of the New River Gorge's industrial past.

How to Get There

The majority of the hikes in this region are accessed from the Keeneys Creek Road and Nuttallburg parking area. The Headhouse Trail (Trail 24) and the upper trailhead of the Conveyor Trail (Trail 21) are most easily reached from Lansing-Edmond Road (County Route 5/82). See trail descriptions for directions to these trailheads.

To reach the Nuttallburg Region parking area and associated trails, drive north along US Route 19 from Fayetteville, WV, crossing the bridge. Turn right onto Lansing-Edmond Road (County Route 5/82). This road is a narrow, curvy byway, with some areas that are extremely rough; be prepared to meet vehicles and move to the berm in order to pass. Continue 6.0 miles and turn right onto Keeneys Creek Road (County Route 85/2). This road is also very narrow and alternates between pavement and gravel. Follow Keeneys Creek Road 4.1 miles to the parking area at Nuttallburg. The drive is gorgeous, as it descends into a narrow valley and features numerous cascades along the route — take your time and enjoy the views. Additionally, you'll pass numerous points of historical interest such as the remains of a pedestrian bridge across the New River.

Nuttallburg and the area trailheads are also accessible from US Route 60 (Midland Trail). From the intersection of US Route 60 and US Route 19, take US Route 60 east for 4.2 miles and turn right onto Lansing-Edmond Road (County Route 5/82). Travel this road 2.1 miles, staying straight and intersecting Keeneys Creek Road (County Route 85/2). Follow Keeneys Creek Road 4.1 miles to the Nuttallburg parking.

Rules and Regulations

Please see "Rules and Regulations for the New River Gorge National River" (page 22) for rules and regulations governing the area.

History and Culture

The mines of Nuttallburg operated over a span of 85 years, from 1873–1958 delivering untold tons of coal to America's industrial cities. John Nuttall's death in 1897 did not slow production, and the mines continued operating under the direction of the family. In the 1920s, Henry Ford purchased the mines and improved the mining and delivery systems in an effort to increase production and supply coal to the Ford

NUTTALBURG REGION HIKES

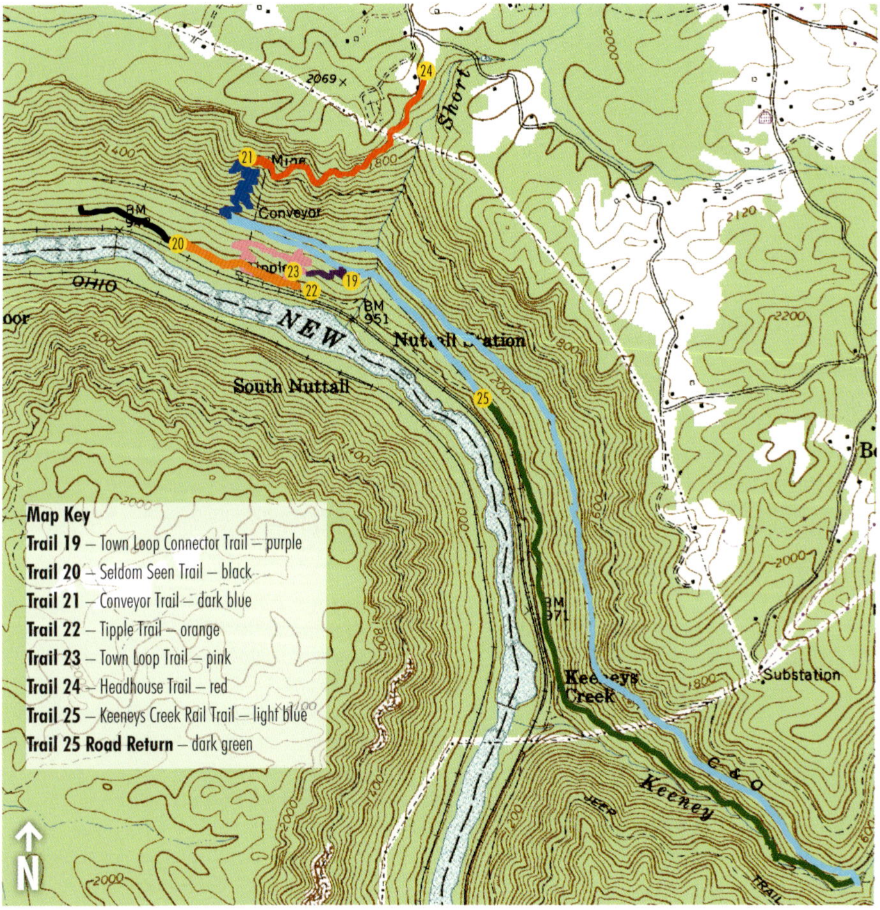

Motor Company plants in Dearborn, Michigan. His plan was unsuccessful, and Ford sold his shares of the property in 1928.

The town of Nuttallburg was once racially segregated; this past has been preserved, allowing visitors to learn about this different era through the thoroughly researched informational boards the National Park Service has placed throughout the site. The Nuttalls organized the town using the readily identifiable stream, Short Creek, to effect this segregation: African Americans lived, worshipped, and attended school on the east side of the stream, while white workers did the same on the west side.

With production declining over the years, the mine finally closed in 1958. The Nuttall family continued to own the property until 1998 when the National Park Service acquired the land and incorporated it into the New River Gorge National River. After years of work to open the area to the public, Nuttallburg in 2005 was added to the National Register of Historic Places.

Note: Please leave artifacts alone. These items, as well as the remnants of buildings that surround them, are part of our cultural heritage. Remember the Leave No Trace Seven Principles.

19 TOWN LOOP CONNECTOR TRAIL

This short trail connects the Keeneys Creek Rail Trail to the Town Loop Trail and the other Nuttallburg trails.

2 | 0 ft 113 ft | 0.13 mi

Location: East of Fayetteville, WV, US Route 19, and on the banks of the New River
Maps: USGS Fayetteville quad 1:24,000
Trail Options: A connector trail from Keeneys Creek Rail Trail (Trail 25) to the Town Loop Trail (Trail 23).
Facilities: No facilities at either trailhead. Gravel parking available at Keeneys Creek trailhead. Additional facilities nearby at Nuttallburg parking area.
Highlights: Ruins of a large house.

Trail Milestones:

0.03 mi – Intersection with rough trail (38°03.051 N, 081°02.377 W)
0.07mi – Ruins of large house (38°03.051 N, 081°02.377 W)
0.13 mi – Intersection with Town Loop Trail (38°03.033 N, 081°02.390 W)

Finding the Trailhead

Upper trailhead: (38°03.040 N, 081°02.296 W)
Drive north along US Route 19 from Fayetteville, WV, crossing the bridge. Turn right onto Lansing-Edmond Road (County Route 5/82). This road is a narrow, curvy byway, with some areas that are extremely rough; be prepared to meet vehicles and move to the berm in order to pass. Continue 6.0 miles and turn right onto Keeneys Creek Road (County Route 85/2). This road is also very narrow and alternates between pavement and gravel. The drive is gorgeous, as it descends into a narrow valley and features numerous cascades along the route — take your time and enjoy the views. Additionally, you'll pass numerous points of historical interest such as the remains of a pedestrian bridge across the New River. Drive this road 3.5 miles to the Keeneys Creek Rail Trail parking, and then hike the Keeneys Creek Rail Trail for 0.4 miles, passing the trestle bridge across Short Creek, to the trailhead.

Nuttallburg and the area trailheads are also accessible from US Route 60 (Midland Trail). From the intersection of US Route 60 and US Route 19, take US Route 60 east for 4.2 miles and turn right onto Lansing-Edmond Road (County Route 5/82). Follow this road 2.1 miles, staying straight and intersecting Keeneys Creek Road (County Route 85/2). Follow Keeneys Creek Road 3.5 miles to the Keeneys Creek Rail Trail (Trail 25) parking area. Proceed 0.4 miles along Keeneys Creek Rail Trail to reach the trailhead.

Lower trailhead: (38°03.033 N, 081°02.390 W)
Access the lower trailhead from the Nuttallburg parking area and Town Loop Trail (Trail 23). Follow the above directions to Keeneys Creek Road and then follow this road 4.1 miles to the Nuttallburg parking area. Hike the Town Loop Trail 0.06 miles to the intersection and lower trailhead for the Town Loop Connector Trail.

Ruins of the large home.

Wildflowers abound within Nuttallburg.

Trail Description

Note: Hike described from upper trailhead. From the upper trailhead, located 0.4 miles along Keeneys Creek Rail Trail, descend 0.03 miles to an intersection with a rougher trail that leads back to Keeneys Creek Rail Trail. Stay right here and descend to view the ruins of a large home at 0.07 miles. Continue along the trail and reach the lower trailhead at 0.13 miles. Take the left-hand branch of the Town Loop Trail to access the parking area and other facilities at Nuttallburg, or turn right to continue exploring along the remaining 0.61 miles of the Town Loop Trail.

Trail Combinations/Options

This trail is a connector between the Keeneys Creek Rail Trail (Trail 25) and the Town Loop Trail (Trail 23). Please see their respective trail descriptions for more information.

20 SELDOM SEEN TRAIL

Visit the ruins of the town of Seldom Seen, hidden amongst boulders and the forest that has reclaimed the area.

1 | 44 ft 12 ft | 0.26 mi

Location: East of Fayetteville, WV, US Route 19, and on the banks of the New River
Maps: USGS Fayetteville quad 1:24,000
Trail Options: Must use Tipple Trail (Trail 22) to reach the trailhead.
Facilities: Benches at trailhead, additional facilities at Nuttallburg parking area.
Highlights: Relics and ruins of the town of Seldom Seen.

Trail Milestones:

0.20 mi – Seldom Seen (38°03.159 N, 081°02.916 W)

Trail Combinations/Options

This trail is best done as part of a combination with Tipple Trail (Trail 22). At the 0.3-mile mark on the Tipple Trail branch onto Seldom Seen Trail, check out the ruins, and then return to the Tipple Trail to hike it in its entirety. This creates a 1.01-mile hike encompassing a great portion of the ruins in this area.

Finding the Trailhead

(38°03.095 N, 081°02.723 W)

Drive north along US Route 19 from Fayetteville, WV, crossing the bridge. Turn right onto Lansing-Edmond Road (County Route 5/82). This road is a narrow, curvy byway, with some areas that are extremely rough; be prepared to meet vehicles and move to the berm in order to pass. Continue 6.0 miles and turn right onto Keeneys Creek Road (County Route 85/2). This road is also very narrow and alternates between pavement and gravel. Follow this road 4.1 miles to the parking area at Nuttallburg. The drive is gorgeous, as it descends into a narrow valley and features numerous cascades along the route — take your time and enjoy the views. Additionally, you'll pass numerous points of historical interest such as the remains of a pedestrian bridge across the New River.

Nuttallburg and the area trailheads are also accessible from US Route 60 (Midland Trail). From the intersection of US Route 60 and US Route 19, take US Route 60 east for 4.2 miles and turn right onto Lansing-Edmond Road (County Route 5/82). Follow this road 2.1 miles, staying straight and intersecting Keeneys Creek Road (County Route 85/2). Follow Keeneys Creek Road 4.1 miles to the Nuttallburg parking.

The trailhead is located 0.3 miles along the Tipple Trail (Trail 22) — follow the trail description for Tipple Trail to arrive.

Trail Description

Beginning from the 0.3-mile mark of the Tipple Trail, move into the forest, paralleling the river and weaving amongst boulders. The trail quickly narrows to single-track. Keep your eyes peeled to either side for relics of the former inhabitants, as bottles, washbasins, and various items remain half-buried in the woods. At 0.20 miles begin to see rock pillars above the foliage to the left and right — the foundational structure of the homes that once stood in Seldom Seen. At 0.23 miles the trail comes close to one former home where past visitors have collected artifacts. Please leave any artifacts in place and do not remove anything further from the site. After exploring the town, return by the same trail and, once reaching the Tipple Trail, reverse it back to its trailhead.

21 CONVEYOR TRAIL

A rough and strenuous trail that leads down the gorge. This trail allows visitors to follow in the footsteps of the Nuttall coal miners who used the path to travel from the tipple to the mine and back.

4 | 5 ft 400 ft | 0.59 mi

Location: Northeast of Fayetteville, WV; on the east side of the New River, not far from the Canyon Rim Visitor Center
Maps: USGS Fayetteville quad 1:24,000
Trail Options: Use Headhouse Trail (Trail 24) to reach the trailhead as well as connect with multiple trails below that reach the river.
Facilities: No facilities.
Highlights: Walk in the footsteps of miners; find chunks of coal and artifacts spread throughout the trail.

Trail Milestones:

0.00 mi – Intersection with Headhouse Trail/trailhead (38°03.260 N, 081°02.549 W)
0.06 mi – Landslide (38°03.237 N, 081°02.579 W)
0.59 mi – Keeneys Creek Rail Trail (38°03.151 N, 081°02.592 W)

Finding the Trailhead

(38°03.260 N, 081°02.549 W)
The trailhead is located at the 0.64-mile mark of the Headhouse Trail. To reach the Headhouse trailhead, drive north along US Route 19 from Fayetteville, WV, crossing the bridge. Turn right onto Lansing-Edmond Road (County Route 5/82). Continue 2.5 miles and turn right onto Beauty Mountain Road (County Route 85/5). Travel 0.1 miles and park below the Nuttall Cemetery sign.

Trail Description

Depart from the trailhead at the 0.64-mile mark of the Headhouse Trail and follow single-track 0.06 miles until reaching a landslide blocking the trail. Footing here is poor, though you can move downhill and rejoin the trail without crossing the landslide. (The landslide is unstable in many areas — keep off the loose rocks.) Once reconnected to the main path, follow a series of 12 switchbacks toward the bottom of the gorge. Along the eastern portion of these switchbacks, you can see the conveyor structure suspended amongst the treetops. The trail throughout this area is of poor quality so pay attention to your footing as you descend. There is also wildlife around, and since the Conveyor Trail is less traveled than many other trails, you might even see larger animals such as the bear (!) I encountered on one recent outing.

As you move through these switchbacks watch for relics of the coal-mining operation. Small bits of coal lost from the conveyor are scattered about, as are larger chunks up to basketball size. With a keen eye, you might even spot bits of equipment half-buried in the leaves of the many autumns (55 at press time) that have passed since the mine closed, in 1958. The trail ends at a turn in the Keeneys Creek Rail Trail — the upper branch of this trail (on the left) leads to the remainder of the rail trail, while the lower branch (on the right) leads to the Town Loop Connector Trail and eventually to the Town Loop Trail and the Nuttallburg parking area.

Trail Combinations/Options

From the trail's end and connection to the Keeneys Creek Rail Trail (Trail 25), follow the lower branch of the latter 0.3 miles to access the Town Loop Connector Trail (Trail 19). Follow this to the Town Loop Trail (Trail 23) and the Nuttallburg parking area. This results in a 1.69-mile one-way hike. For a longer, 5.17-mile one-way hike, take the upper portion of the Keeneys Creek Rail Trail to its terminus and then follow the Keeneys Creek Road Return/Keeneys Creek Road back to the Nuttallburg parking.

CONVEYOR TRAIL

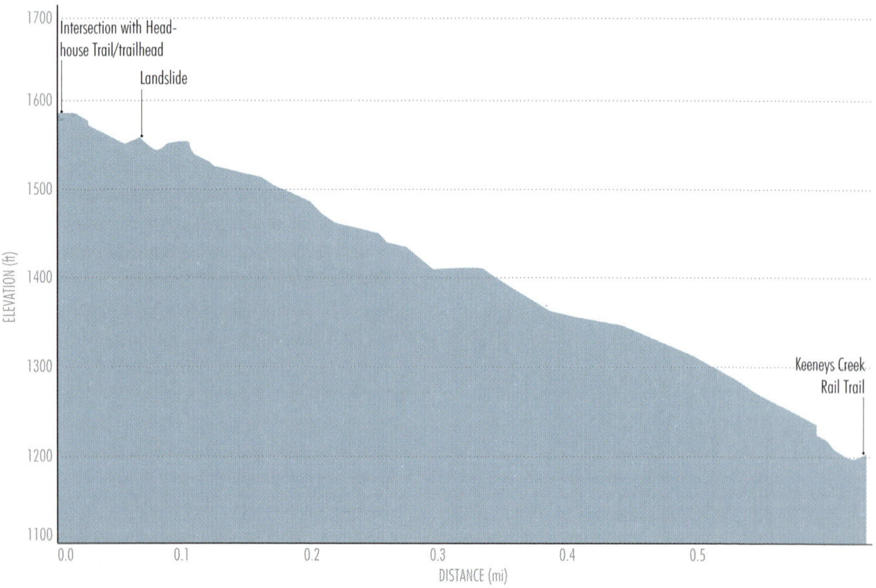

22 TIPPLE TRAIL

Walk back in time along the Tipple Trail as you move through one of the best-preserved coal-mining complexes in the New River Gorge.

1 | 35 ft 112 ft | 0.64 mi

Location: East of Fayetteville, WV, US Route 19, and on the banks of the New River
Maps: USGS Fayetteville quad 1:24,000
Trail Options: Multiple trailheads in vicinity; connect with Seldom Seen Trail (Trail 20) at 0.3 miles.
Facilities: Toilets, gravel parking, benches.
Highlights: Historic mining structures, company store, views of rapids.

Trail Milestones:

0.15 mi – Coal tipple and conveyor (38°03.051 N, 081°02.551 W)
0.23 mi – Open field on right (38°03.051 N, 081°02.551 W)
0.3 mi – Company store/Seldom Seen Trail (38°03.093 N, 081°02.714 W)
0.31 mi – Coke ovens (38°03.097 N, 081°02.200 W)
0.49 mi – Coal tipple and railroad tracks (38°03.051 N, 081°02.551 W)

Finding the Trailhead

(38°03.006 N, 081°02.406 W)
Drive north along US Route 19 from Fayetteville, WV, crossing the bridge. Turn right onto Lansing-Edmond Road (County Route 5/82). This road is a narrow, curvy byway, with some areas that are extremely rough; be prepared to meet vehicles and move to the berm in order to pass. Continue 6.0 miles and turn right onto Keeneys Creek Road (County Route 85/2). This road is also very narrow and alternates between pavement and gravel. Follow this road 4.1 miles to the parking area at Nuttallburg. The drive is gorgeous, as it descends into a narrow valley and features numerous cascades along the route — take your time and enjoy the views. Additionally, you'll pass numerous points of historical interest such as the remains of a pedestrian bridge across the New River.

Nuttallburg and the area trailheads are also accessible from US Route 60 (Midland Trail). From the intersection of US Route 60 and US Route 19, take US Route 60 east for 4.2 miles and turn right onto Lansing-Edmond Road (County Route 5/82). Follow this road 2.1 miles, staying straight and intersecting Keeneys Creek Road (County Route 85/2). Follow Keeneys Creek Road 4.1 miles to the Nuttallburg parking.

The trailhead is co-located with that of the Town Loop Trail (Trail 23), 10 meters west of the parking lot toward visible mine buildings.

Trail Description

From the trailhead begin walking west along a wide trail/road with a ruined building on the left side. A small spring flows from the trail's right side, and in the spring and summer months this area is covered in wildflowers. Continue past wheelchair-accessible parking and arrive at the coal tipple at 0.15 miles. To the right a series of informational boards detail the history of Nuttallburg and the area's buildings. Take a moment to learn about Nuttallburg, listed on the National Register of Historic Places in 2005. Now pass beneath the conveyor that once transported coal to the tipple for decades. At 0.23 miles pass an open field to the right and continue 0.07 miles until you can peer into a structure from above — this stone remnant of a building was once Nuttallburg's company store. Around to the side

TIPPLE TRAIL

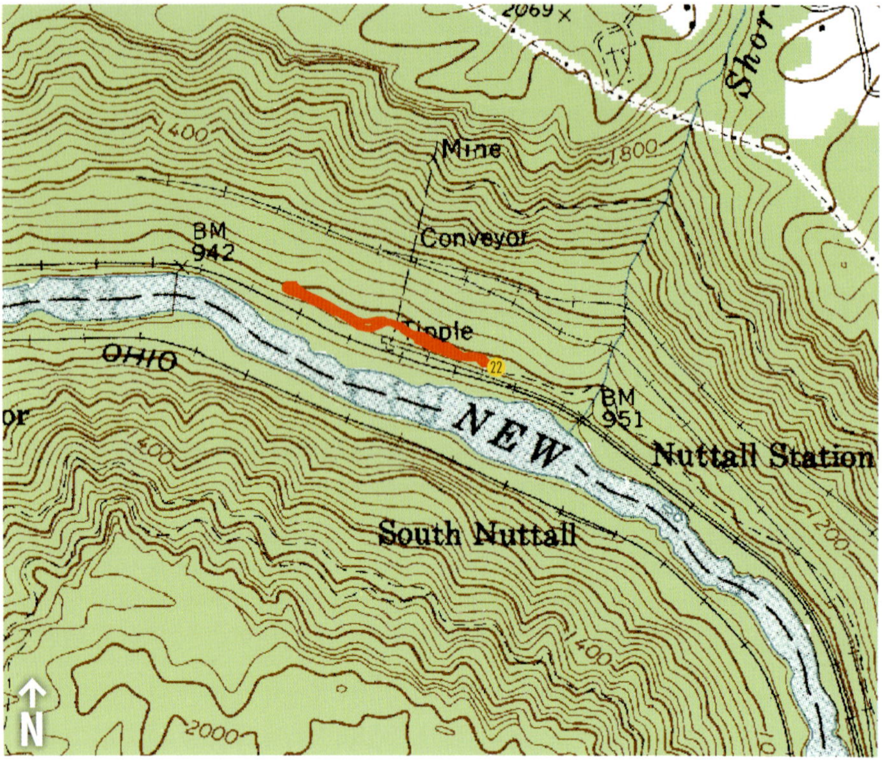

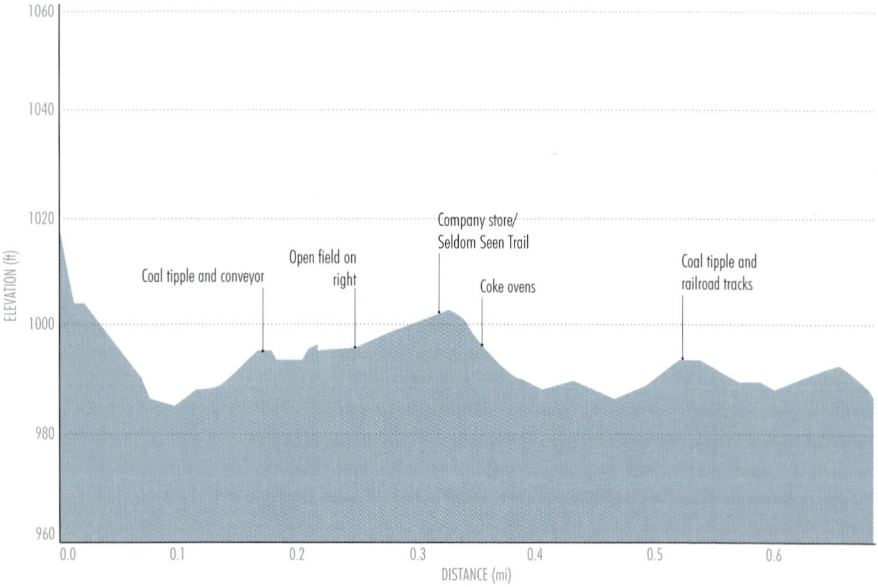

The Nuttallburg tipple and rail track.

of the building you'll find the trailhead for Seldom Seen Trail (Trail 20).

Continue around the company store and at 0.31 miles see the first of a series of coke ovens. Walk below and examine these ovens as you begin to make your way back toward the tipple. Look to the right here to see the old rail lines that once transported mined coal from the gorge. Notice the trees growing through these tracks as evidence of the 55 (and counting) years since this mine was last active. Pass under the conveyor and continue to the trailhead and trail's end.

A well-preserved coke oven.

Trail Combinations/Options

This trail shares a trailhead with the Town Loop Trail (Trail 23). Also, at the 0.3-mile mark, it intersects the Seldom Seen Trail (Trail 20). For a longer hike of 1.01 miles, walk to the ruins of the town of Seldom Seen and then return to complete the Tipple Trail loop.

Additional Notes

Mountain biking is only permitted on the first 0.3 miles of trail, until reaching the company store.

23 TOWN LOOP TRAIL

Walk along what was once the main thoroughfare of the town of Nuttallburg and visit ruins of this formerly thriving community on the banks of the New River.

2 | 0 ft 113 ft | 0.67 mi

Location: East of Fayetteville, WV, US Route 19, and on the banks of the New River
Maps: USGS Fayetteville quad 1:24,000
Trail Options: Connect with Town Loop Connector Trail (Trail 19) to reach the Keeneys Creek Rail Trail (Trail 25).
Facilities: Toilets, gravel parking, benches.
Highlights: Ruins and relics of a bygone era.

Trail Milestones:

0.06 mi – Intersect with Town Loop Connector Trail (38°03.033 N, 081°02.390 W)
0.14 mi – Branch trail to "white" school (38°03.058 N, 081°02.420 W)
0.21 mi – "White" school (38°03.051 N, 081°02.377 W)
0.30 mi – Branch trail to "white" church (38°03.082 N, 081°02.470 W)
0.40 mi – Conveyor overhead (38°03.051 N, 081°02.377 W)

Finding the Trailhead

(38°03.006 N, 081°02.406 W)
Drive north along US Route 19 from Fayetteville, WV, crossing the bridge. Turn right onto Lansing-Edmond Road (County Route 5/82). This road is a narrow, curvy byway, with some areas that are extremely rough; be prepared to meet vehicles and move to the berm in order to pass. Continue 6.0 miles and turn right onto Keeneys Creek Road (County Route 85/2). This road is also very narrow and alternates between pavement and gravel. Follow this road 4.1 miles to the parking area at Nuttallburg. The drive is gorgeous, as it descends into a narrow valley and features numerous cascades along the route — take your time and enjoy the views. Additionally, you'll pass numerous points of historical interest such as the remains of a pedestrian bridge across the New River.

Nuttallburg and the area trailheads are also accessible from US Route 60 (Midland Trail). From the intersection of US Route 60 and US Route 19, take US Route 60 east for 4.2 miles and turn right onto Lansing-Edmond Road (County Route 5/82). Follow this road 2.1 miles, staying straight and intersecting Keeneys Creek Road (County Route 85/2). Follow Keeneys Creek Road 4.1 miles to the Nuttallburg parking.

The trailhead is co-located with the trailhead for the Tipple Trail (Trail 22), 10 meters west of the parking lot toward visible mine buildings.

Trail Description

From the trailhead climb up and right, coming to a cut sandstone wall below an old foundation. Continue along this path until reaching the intersection with the Town Loop Connector Trail at 0.06 miles. Continue leftward from this intersection until you come to a second intersection at 0.14 miles; turn right here and visit the ruins of the "white" school at 0.21 miles before returning to the main trail. Upon returning to the intersection, turn right and continue along the main trail to a second branch trail, which leads to the "white" church. Explore this area and return to the main trail, turning right and crossing a small stream over a wooden bridge. At 0.4 miles cross under the conveyor and meander along the final 0.27 miles, exploring the ruins of Nuttallburg.

Sandstone walls along the Town Loop Trail.

Trail Combinations/Options

Connect with the Town Loop Connector Trail (Trail 19) and the Keeneys Creek Rail Trail (Trail 25).

Reminders of Nuttallburg's past.

TOWN LOOP TRAIL

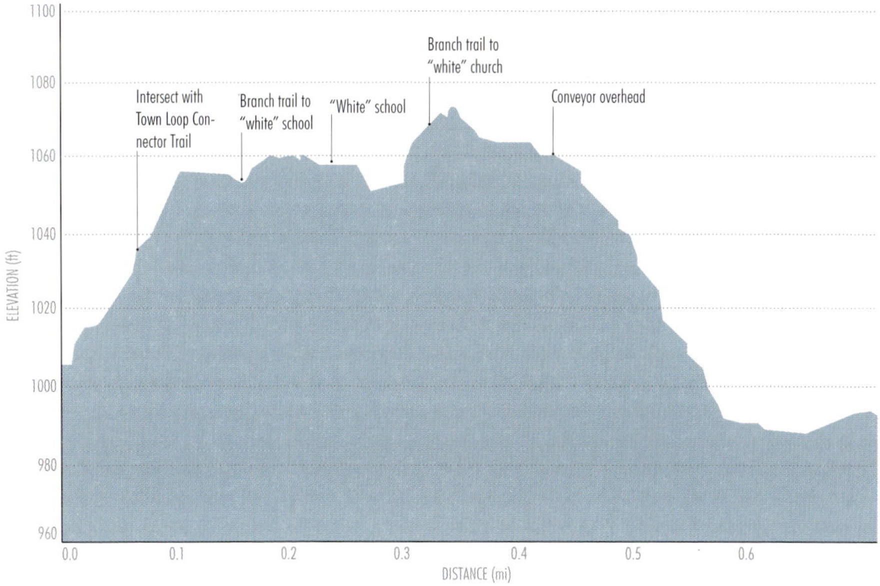

24 HEADHOUSE TRAIL

An outstanding short trail that leads to the Nuttall mining complex and features some of the best-preserved remains of the New River Gorge's coal-mining past.

3 24 ft 396 ft 0.70 mi

Location: East of Fayetteville, WV; on the east side of the New River, not far from the Canyon Rim Visitor Center
Maps: USGS Fayetteville quad 1:24,000
Trail Options: Connect with the Conveyor Trail (Trail 21) for access to Nuttallburg, other trails, and the New River.
Facilities: Gravel parking for six vehicles, benches available at mine site.
Highlights: Well-preserved mine building, the Nuttall Mine, access to cliffs.

Trail Milestones:

0.00 mi – Parking (38°03.417 N, 081°02.079 W)
0.15 mi – Middle-road trailhead (38°03.318 N, 081°02.153 W)
0.29 mi – Cliff line (38°03.320 N, 081°02.149 W)
0.37 mi – Rock shaped like "ship's prow" (38°03.229 N, 081°02.326 W)
0.64 mi – Conveyor Trail trailhead (38°03.260 N, 081°02.549 W)
0.7 mi – Mine entrance/trail's end (38°03.245 N, 081°02.485 W)

Finding the Trailhead

(38°03.417 N, 081°02.079 W)
Drive north along US Route 19 from Fayetteville, WV, crossing the bridge. Turn right onto Lansing-Edmond Road (County Route 5/82). Continue 2.5 miles and turn right onto Beauty Mountain Road (County Route 85/5). Travel 0.1 miles and park below the Nuttall Cemetery sign.

Trail Description

Note: Three small gravel roads converge at the parking area and sometimes cause confusion. The hike as described takes off from the middle road — see below. Three gravel roads intersect at the parking area: a road to the right, with a sign pointing to the Nuttall Cemetery; a road in the middle, which continues straight; and a well-used road to the left, which travels downhill. The trailhead is located 0.15 miles down the *middle* road, and is indicated by a brown gate and sign on the left. *Note: In summer, foliage can obscure the sign.* From the trailhead walk along a wide path and at 0.29 miles pass a cliff line on the left and boulders on the right. This is a popular climber-access route, and smaller trails lead into the woods from both sides of the main trail. Stay straight along the path and at 0.37 miles walk beneath a boulder on the right that resembles a "ship's prow."

Continuing down the trail, which becomes less well graded due to storm runoff, pass a rock formation on the left that tells the story of how time and weather can erode even the hardest of stone (0.45 miles). At 0.64 miles the trail intersects the trailhead for the Conveyor Trail (Trail 21) and turns sharply left to the mine entrance and headhouse area. At 0.7 miles reach the entrance to the mine and the trail's end. Enjoy the cool air that emanates from the mine entrance as you explore. A great example of a mine car sits unused and abandoned between the mine and the headhouse. Meanwhile, stairs to the right of the headhouse allow a closer look at the conveyor complex. Informational boards scattered throughout this zone tell the unique stories of the miners and their work.

Nuttallburg mine entrance and car.

Trail Combinations/Options

Combine this trail with the Conveyor Trail (Trail 21), Keeneys Creek Rail Trail (Trail 25), Town Loop Connector Trail (Trail 19), and Town Loop Trail (Trail 23) to reach the bottom of the gorge. *Note: The Conveyor Trail is a rough trail that drops steeply down the gorge. As of January 2013, the upper portion of this trail is somewhat obscured due to a rockslide.*

The "ship's prow."

Additional Notes

Nuttall Headhouse Information: The Nuttall mine complex operated from 1873 to 1958. Among the ruins in this area you will find the following structures:

Headhouse: Workers dumped coal from cars onto the conveyor belt for transport to the tipple at the bottom of the gorge.

Hoist House: This building contained the machinery used to transport equipment back and forth between the headhouse and tipple.

Electric Substation: This building controlled electricity throughout the entire complex.

Sand House: Miners stored sand here for use on the mine-car tracks during icy weather.

HEADHOUSE TRAIL

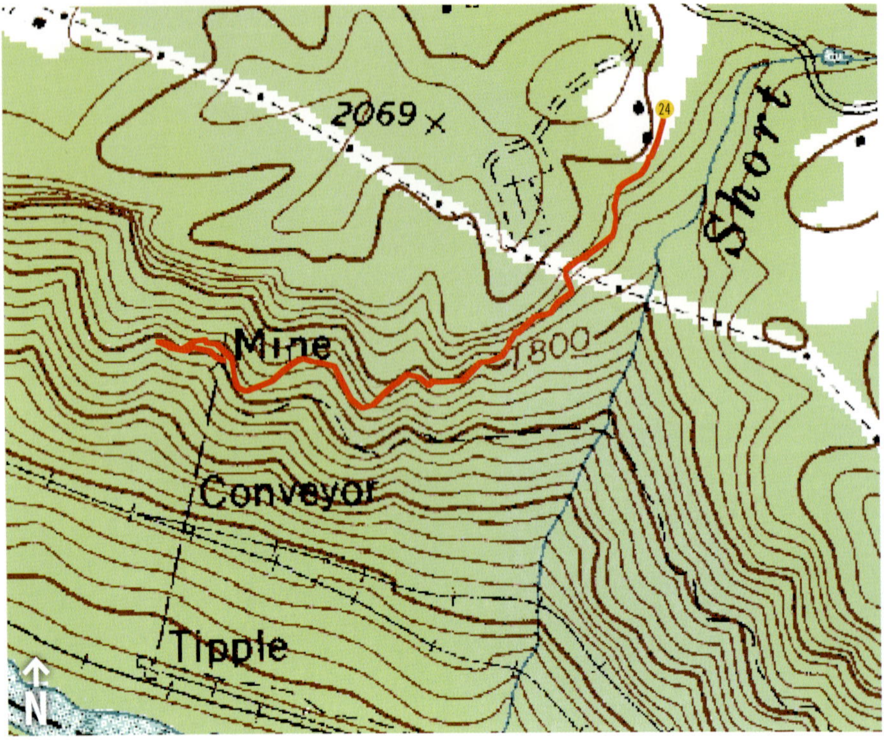

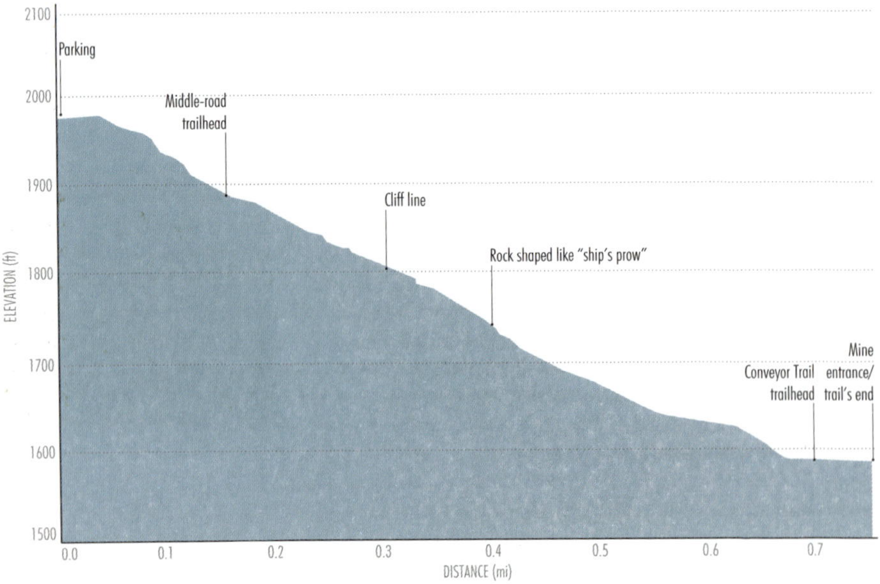

25 KEENEYS CREEK RAIL TRAIL

This well-graded trail through a quiet forest runs along an abandoned rail line, crosses over numerous streams, and offers connections to Nuttallburg.

1 | 462 ft | 52 ft | 3.18 mi

Location: East of Fayetteville, WV, US Route 19, and on the banks of the New River

Maps: USGS Fayetteville quad 1:24,000

Trail Options: Connect with Town Loop Connector Trail (Trail 19) and the Conveyor Trail (21).

Facilities: Gravel parking for seven vehicles, additional facilities available in Nuttallburg area.

Highlights: Mountain streams, view of the Nuttallburg conveyor.

Trail Milestones:

0.4 mi – Trestle bridge across Short Creek (38°03.032 N, 081°02.217 W)

0.7 mi – Pass under conveyor (38°03.090 N, 081°02.407 W)

0.8 mi – Intersect Conveyor Trail (38°03.151 N, 081°02.592 W)

1.1 mi – Trestle bridge across Short Creek (38°03.079 N, 081°02.216 W)

1.6 mi – Railroad spur (38°02.822 N, 081°01.848 W)

2.0 mi – Rock wall (38°02.533 N, 081°01.683 W)

2.3 mi – Cross stream on bridge (38°02.286 N, 081°01.645 W)

2.4 mi – Cut in hillside with two manmade towers (38°02.212 N, 081°01.585 W)

3.1 mi – Intersection and steep descent (38°01.847 N, 081°01.011 W)

Finding the Trailhead

(38°02.788 N, 081°01.933 W)

Drive north along US Route 19 from Fayetteville, WV, crossing the bridge. Turn right onto Lansing-Edmond Road (County Route 5/82). This road is a narrow, curvy byway, with some areas that are extremely rough; be prepared to meet vehicles and move to the berm in order to pass. Continue 6.0 miles and turn right onto Keeneys Creek Road (County Route 85/2). This road is also very narrow and alternates between pavement and gravel. Follow this road 3.5 miles to the parking area along the right. (This parking area is located 0.6 miles prior to the main parking area for the other Nuttallburg trails.)

Nuttallburg and the trailheads in this location are also accessible from US Route 60 (Midland Trail). From the intersection of US Route 60 and US Route 19, take US Route 60 east for 4.2 miles and turn right onto Lansing-Edmond Road (County Route 5/82). Travel this road 2.1 miles, staying straight and intersecting Keeneys Creek Road (County Route 85/2). Follow Keeneys Creek Road 3.5 miles to the parking area along the right.

The trailhead is at the end of the parking area and is marked by a gate.

Trail Description

From the trailhead parking move into the wood line, bypassing a metal gate that impedes vehicular traffic along the trail. The trail is wide, with two well-worn paths for the majority of its length. As you get started keep an eye open for moss-covered railroad cross-ties just to your left. At 0.4 miles cross a trestle bridge over Short Creek where the waters plummet to an eventual meeting with the New River. Just beyond the bridge find the first of two connections to the Town Loop Trail (Trail 23) on your left. If you are interested in seeing the town of Nuttallburg, bypass this first trail and use the next trail on the left — this second option is the better-maintained trailhead for the Town Loop Connector Trail (Trail 19). To continue on the Keeneys Creek Rail Trail, keep straight along the much larger and well-defined path.

Continue along the 4 percent grade and reach an area with a rock wall and a pretty stream to the right. At 0.7 miles cross under the rusting (but safe!) hulk of the Nuttallburg conveyor system. Here,

Trestle bridge along Keeneys Creek Rail Trail.

One of the area's many varieties of mushroom.

take in nice views of the gorge and ridge opposite from either side of the conveyor. In another 0.1 miles connect with the Conveyor Trail (Trail 21) and make a sharp turn to the right. At 0.9 miles again cross under the conveyor and continue another 0.2 miles before again crossing Short Creek along a tall trestle bridge. Encounter an old spur rail line at 1.6 miles that is easy to miss, as Mother Nature has almost completely reclaimed the area. At 2.0 miles pass a tall rock wall on the left, and at 2.3 miles cross the tallest trestle bridge in the area, roughly 65 feet in height. The sheer size of this trestle brings to focus the difficulties that the railroad builders encountered in this steep environment. Just beyond, hike through a cut in the hillside where two manmade sandstone towers stand guard.

The trail continues gently over the next 0.7 miles until reaching an intersection with multiple trails at 3.1 miles. Take the trail to the right, which descends steeply among small rocks and arrives at a small turnoff on Keeneys Creek Road. Follow Keeneys Creek Road Return (described on following spread) back to the original trailhead.

Trail Combinations/Options

Combine this trail with the Keeneys Creek Road Return for a combined mileage of 4.78 miles, or combine with the Town Loop Connector Trail (Trail 19) to reach the lower Nuttallburg mine complex and surrounding trails. You can also connect with the Conveyor Trail (Trail 21) and hike this trail from bottom to top before linking into the Headhouse Trail (Trail 24).

KEENEYS CREEK RAIL TRAIL

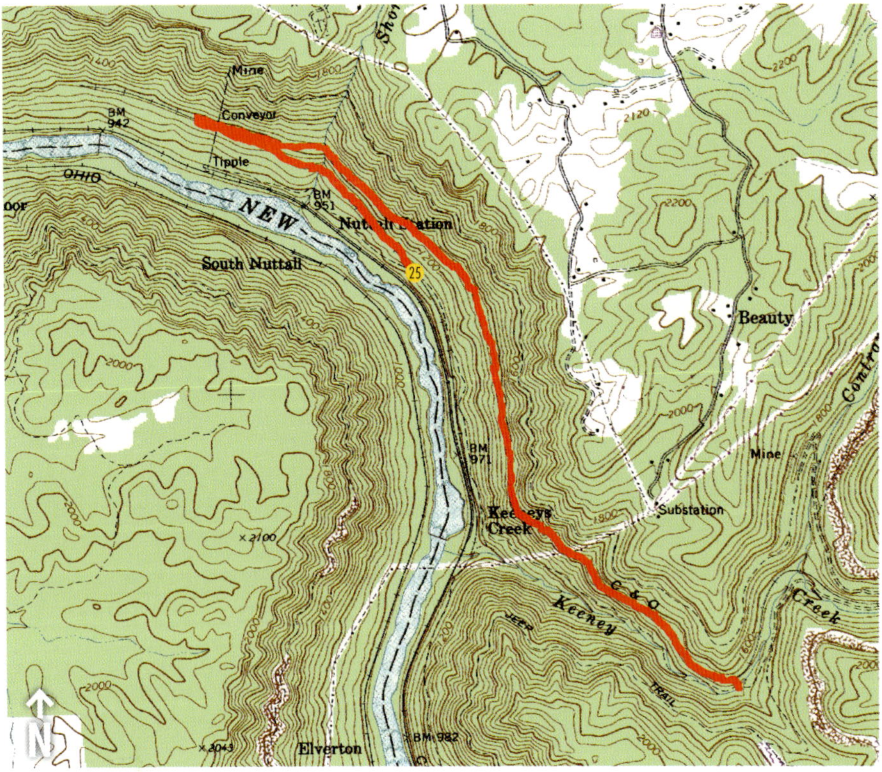

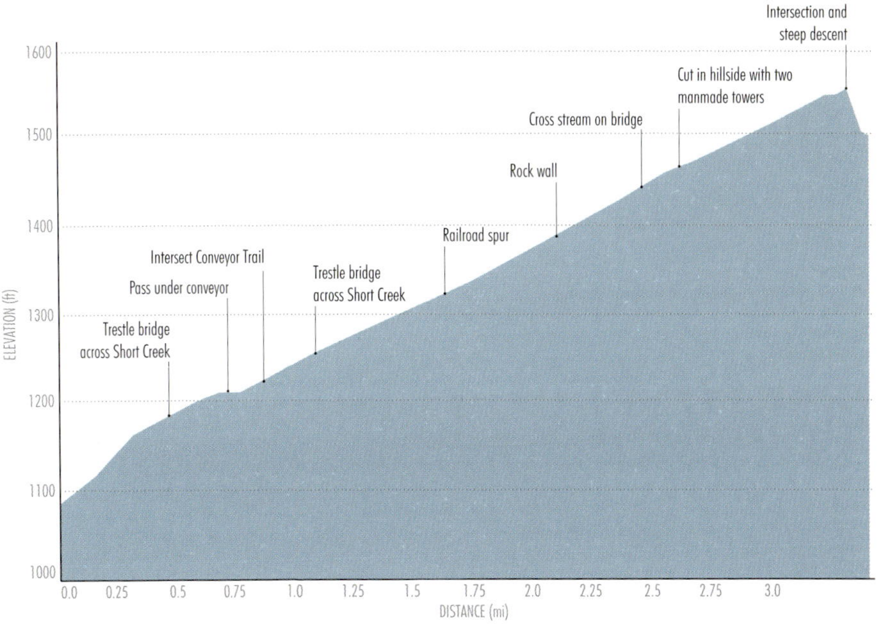

KEENEYS CREEK ROAD RETURN

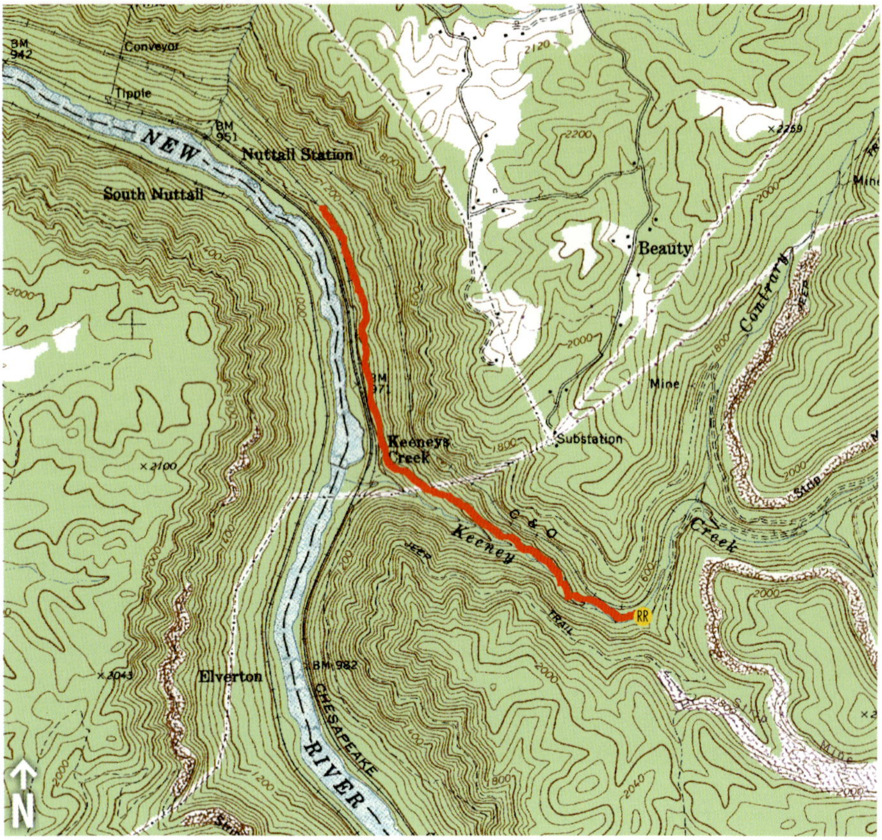

2 | 75 ft | 511 ft | 1.6 mi

Trail Description

The Keeneys Creek Road Return is a beautiful track paralleling Keeneys Creek and its wonderful collection of cascades and falls. The road is straightforward, with no intersections along its 1.6 miles. At the 1.0-mile mark begin to hear the roar of the Keeneys Rapids below on the New River. At 1.6 miles arrive at the trailhead — the rapids you hear below are called "Dudley's Dip."

Additional Notes

Watch for vehicle traffic along Keeneys Creek Road.

One of the myriad falls and cascades along Keeneys Creek.

KEENEYS CREEK ROAD RETURN

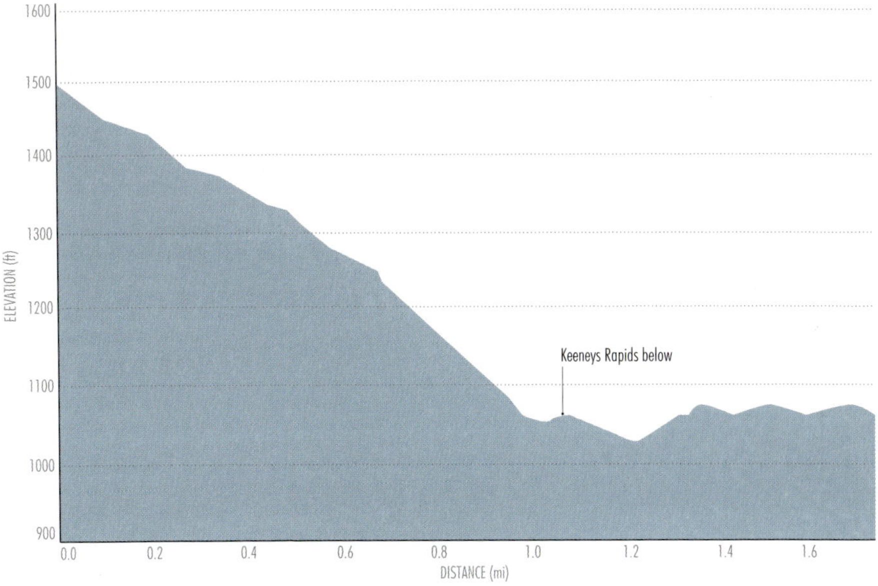

Road-rail bridge to Thurmond, WV.

8 CUNARD & THURMOND REGION

Overview and Highlights

Saturated with railroad and coal history, the Cunard and Thurmond Region hosts a collection of great trails that allow an exploration of this past. The historic town of Thurmond is the region's historical and cultural center, and is not to be missed. The trails here are easy to moderate in difficulty, and offer the visitor wonderful views into the past, as most are built along old rail lines and pass through the ruins of former coal communities.

The Thurmond Depot Visitor Center is open in summer from June through August. You'll find a small museum here along with a gift shop and Amtrak passenger station. While here, visit the remaining buildings of the once-lively town of Thurmond.

How to Get There

The Cunard and Thurmond Region is located in the center of the New River Gorge National River. To reach the Thurmond Depot Visitor Center, take the Glen Jean exit off US Route 19. Encounter a stop sign almost immediately and turn left. Travel 0.5 miles along WV 61/16. Turn right onto Main Street and then immediately turn left at the Glen Jean Bank building. Travel 6.1 miles along Thurmond Road (WV Route 25) to a three-way intersection; stay straight and cross the combination road and rail bridge to the depot on the far side. This bridge is single lane — be aware of oncoming traffic. See individual trail descriptions for directions to each trailhead.

Rules and Regulations

Please see "Rules and Regulations for the New River Gorge National River" (page 22) for rules and regulations governing the area.

History and Culture

Thurmond, the once-bustling center of the region's coal and timber industry, is but a shadow of its former self. Starting in 1873 when Captain W.D. Thurmond purchased this land and continuing through its peak importance in 1910, and through the early twentieth century, this town played an important role in the development of the New River Gorge.

In 1910, Thurmond became one of the most important centers for the Chesapeake and Ohio Railway, producing more freight than many large cities and serving tens of thousands of passengers that year. This railway boom continued until the 1930s when the Great Depression took its toll on the area. The National Bank of Thurmond failed like so many other American banks at the time, and fires, a plague for Thurmond throughout the years, destroyed structures within the town.

A number of historically significant buildings remain at this site, and each is worth a visit. Stop by the visitor center for more information.

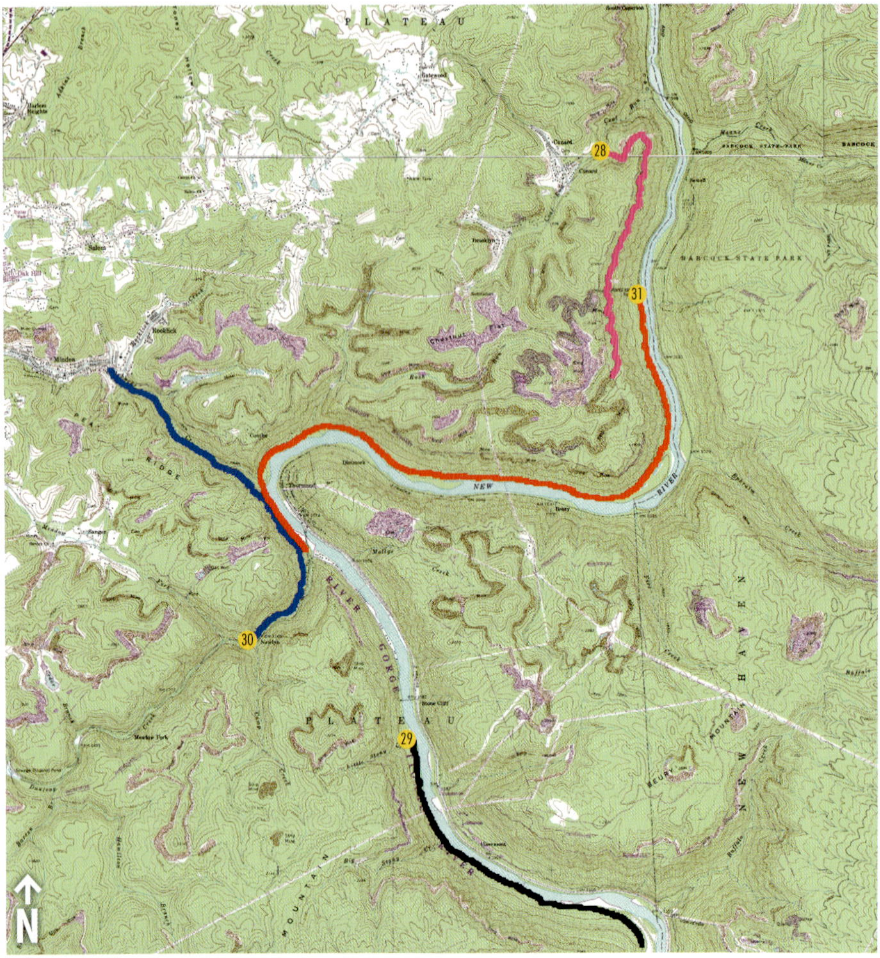

Town of Thurmond.

Map Key

Trail 28 – Brooklyn Mine Trail – pink

Trail 29 – Stone Cliff Trail – black

Trail 30 – Rend Trail – blue

Trail 31 – Southside Trail – red

26 ARBUCKLE CONNECTOR TRAIL

Arbuckle Connector Trail is a beautiful trail that allows access between Rend and Southside trails, crossing a small stream with a waterfall on the way.

2 | 32 ft | 0.25 mi

Location: Access this trail via either the Rend Trail or Southside Trail; access to the Rend Trail is available at its 1.7-mile mark

Maps: USGS Thurmond quad 1:24,000

Trail Options: Connector trail between Rend and Southside trails.

Facilities: No Facilities.

Highlights: This short connector trail could pack a highlight reel, with stone stairs, a small waterfall, and a bit of railroad/coal-mining history.

Trail Milestones:

0.1 mi – Cross-stream over stones (37°57.694 N, 081°05.183 W)

0.2 mi – Cross wooden bridge (37°57.748 N, 081°05.178 W)

0.25 mi – Trailhead at Southside Trail (37°57.739 N, 081°05.139 W)

Finding the Trailhead

(37°57.654 N, 081°05.198 W)

Locate this path's upper trailhead 1.7 miles down the Rend Trail (Trail 30) from the Thurmond side; it is clearly marked by a sign on the right side of the Rend Trail. The lower trailhead (Southside Trail) is found at the end of Southside Trail. *Note: While Southside Trail continues toward Thurmond, as of January 2013 it is closed beyond the Arbuckle Connector Trail. Please see the Southside Trail description (page 116) for more details.*

Trail Description

From Rend Trail drop steeply down before leveling off and crossing a gorgeous stream at 0.1 miles. Be sure to look back after crossing to appreciate the waterfall. Continue 0.1 miles to a wooden bridge where the trail makes a right turn. Cross the bridge and after traveling 15 meters along an old rail line turn sharply left toward Southside Trail — the trail will terminate at a long trestle bridge that signals the intersection with Southside Trail. Keep your eyes peeled for the remnants of Wee Win, one of many small coal-mining towns in the area.

Trail Combinations/Options

This trail, while beautiful on its own account, exists to connect the Rend Trail (Trail 30) and Southside Trail (Trail 31).

Additional Notes

The Arbuckle Connector Trail is often also used to portage bikes between the Southside and Rend trails.

27 CHURCH LOOP TRAIL

A short loop hike off Rend Trail that descends to the First Baptist Church of Thurmond, WV.

2 | 78 ft | 133 ft | 0.26 mi

Location: Near Thurmond, WV, on the west bank of the New River; it is accessible from the Glen Jean exit off US Route 19
Maps: USGS Thurmond quad 1:24,000
Trail Options: Add this short trail onto the longer Rend Trail.
Facilities: Gravel parking for twelve vehicles, toilet facilities.
Highlights: A short loop trail easily accessed from the Rend Trail that adds a little history to your hike.

Trail Milestones:

0.1 mi – Church
(37°57.136 N, 081°04.727 W)
0.26 mi – Trailhead and intersection with Rend Trail
(37°57.173 N, 081°04.774 W)

Finding the Trailhead

(37°57.101 N, 081°04.751 W)
The trailhead is located 0.8 miles down the Rend Trail (Trail 30; Thurmond side). To reach the Rend trailhead, take the Glen Jean exit off US Route 19. Encounter a stop sign almost immediately and turn left. Travel 0.5 miles along WV 61/16. Turn right onto Main Street and then immediately turn left at the Glen Jean Bank building. Travel 5.1 miles along Thurmond Road (WV Route 25) to the Rend Trail on the left (signage states: "Thurmond-Minden Trail"). From the Rend Trail trailhead, it is necessary to hike 0.8 miles to reach the Church Loop trailhead — there is no access to this trail from the Thurmond historic area.

Trail Description

Hike 0.8 miles along Rend Trail to reach the trailhead for Church Loop Trail, as marked by a sign. Begin along single-track and at 30 meters turn sharply left. If you miss this turn you will eventually run into a large downed tree. After turning left, continue to the church. While there, venture to the back of the building: From the porch you can look in and see the pews. Continue along the trail another 0.16 miles to regain Rend Trail approximately 100 meters from the original trailhead.

Trail Combinations/Options

The Church Loop Trail is a nice addition to the Rend Trail (Trail 30). If biking along the Rend Trail, leave your bikes at the trailhead and enjoy a quick turn through the forest on foot.

First Baptist Church of Thurmond.

28 BROOKLYN MINE TRAIL

A moderate hike or horseback ride along an old access road to the former Brooklyn Mine complex.

2 | 438 ft | 69 ft | 2.83 mi

Location: West side of the New River; this area is most easily accessed from US Route 19
Maps: USGS Fayetteville quad 1:24,000, USGS Thurmond quad 1:24,000
Trail Options: The trailhead for the Kaymoor Trail is located 100 meters from the Brooklyn Mine trailhead.
Facilities: Paved parking for nine vehicles and horse trailers.
Highlights: A beautiful waterfall at the trailhead followed by a nice hike to the Brooklyn Mine complex, with stone stairs, a small waterfall, and a bit of railroad/coal-mining history.

Trail Milestones:

0.0 mi – Trailhead (38°00.032 N, 081°01.983 W)
0.5 mi – Views of New River (37°57.694 N, 081°05.183 W)
1.1 mi – Views of New River (37°59.677 N, 081°01.674 W)
1.9 mi – Mine complex (37°59.107 N, 081°01.958 W)
2.5 mi – Large boulder (37°58.697 N, 081°01.895 W)
2.83 mi – Trail's end (37°58.459 N, 081°01.915 W)

Finding the Trailhead

(38°00.032 N, 081°01.983 W)
From US Route 19, follow WV 16 through Fayetteville 0.7 miles to the intersection with Gatewood Road. Bear left and follow Gatewood Road 4.5 miles before turning left onto Cunard Road. Follow this road 1.8 miles until reaching Cunard. Take a left toward the Cunard River Access area. After traveling 0.5 miles arrive at the parking lot — the trailhead is at the top of this lot.

Trail Description

Before starting out, cross the paved road and take in the gorgeous waterfall of Coal Run. Return to the trailhead, at the upper end of the lot, and slowly ascend along an old access road. The trail curves left, where the forest temporarily opens up, before reentering the forest and veering to the right at 0.5 miles. This area offers winter views of the New River, while you can hear the rapids below year-round. At this point the trail intersects a game trail — keep right. Continue along a well-graded area until at 1.1 miles you reach a bend that offers long views up the New River, with additional views along the next 0.2 miles. The Brooklyn Mine is located at 1.9 miles. The first indication of the area will be a series of hitching posts for horses to the left. You can look into the mineshaft on the right and see the rotting wooden beams that support the mine roof. Take a break here on a nicely built stone bench and consider the area's history: The trail and mine take their name from the Brooklyn Coal Company, the original operators of the mine back in 1896. Having passed through several owners over the years, the mine closed in 1953. The trail continues 0.6 miles, reaching a large boulder on the right, and ends at 2.83 miles, with private-property signs along a more developed road.

Trail Combinations/Options

You can connect the Kaymoor Trail (Trail 14) with the Brooklyn Mine Trail. After completing the Kaymoor Trail from Fayette Station to Cunard, travel downhill 100 meters to the Brooklyn Mine trailhead.

A "peek-a-boo" view of the New River from Brooklyn Mine Trail.

BROOKLYN MINE TRAIL

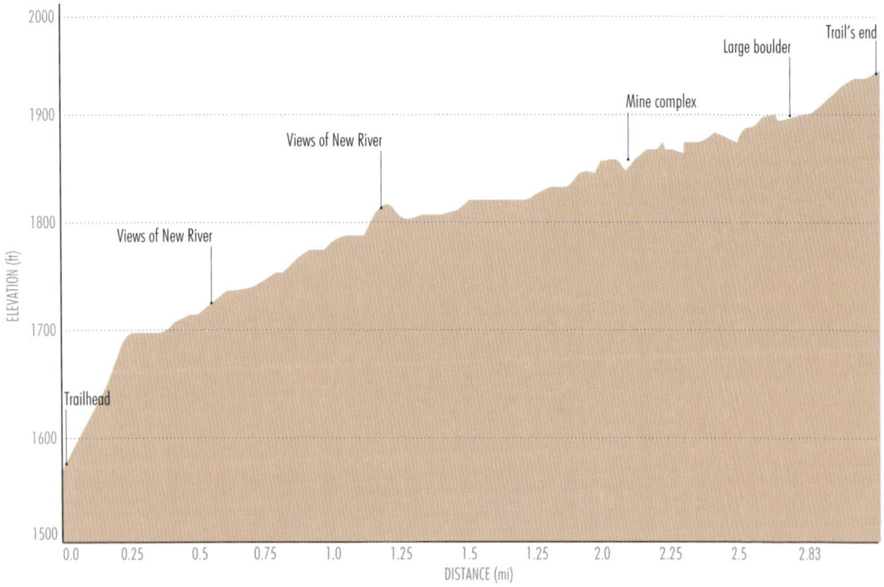

29 STONE CLIFF TRAIL

Stone Cliff Trail parallels the New River, with beautiful views upstream.

2

327 ft 225 ft

3.01 mi

Location: Near Thurmond, WV, on the west bank of the New River; it is accessible from the Glen Jean exit off US Route 19
Maps: USGS Thurmond quad 1:24,000
Trail Options: None at present.
Facilities: Toilets, changing rooms, large gravel parking area, picnic facilities that include grills, and camping facilities.
Highlights: Beautiful views of the New River.

Trail Milestones:

0.0 mi – Trailhead
(37°55.932 N, 081°03.792 W)
0.4 mi – View upstream
(37°55.619 N, 081°03.690 W)
0.8 mi – Close view of river
(37°55.344 N, 081°03.581 W)
1.8 mi – Silo Rapids
(37°54.875 N, 081°02.767 W)
3.01 mi – Trail's end
(37°54.454 N, 081°01.662 W)

Finding the Trailhead

(37°55.932 N, 081°03.792 W)
Take the Glen Jean exit off US Route 19. Encounter a stop sign almost immediately and turn left. Travel 0.5 miles along WV 61/16. Turn right on Main Street and immediately turn left at the Glen Jean Bank building. Travel 6.1 miles along Thurmond Road (WV Route 25) to a three-way intersection. Turn right and continue down a paved road for 1.5 miles. Just before the bridge, turn right at the "Stone Cliff" sign.

Trail Description

From the trailhead ascend slowly for 0.4 miles, reaching a high point with views looking upstream along the New River. From this point descend; at 0.8 miles the trail comes very close to the river, offering great opportunities for photos. Continue 0.2 miles, crossing an intermittent stream, and begin to see silos across the river. At 1.8 miles you'll catch views of "Silo Rapids." On the far side of the gorge, the rapids' namesakes sit nestled within the trees. Continue along the trail until at 2.5 miles you begin a slow ascent to the trail's end at 3.01 miles, as marked by a large "No Trespassing" sign. Return to the trailhead via the same route.

Trail Combinations/Options

There are no options available at this time. A proposed stacked-loop trail system in the area of Garden Ground might someday link to the end of Stone Cliff Trail.

A train rumbles along the New River.

STONE CLIFF TRAIL

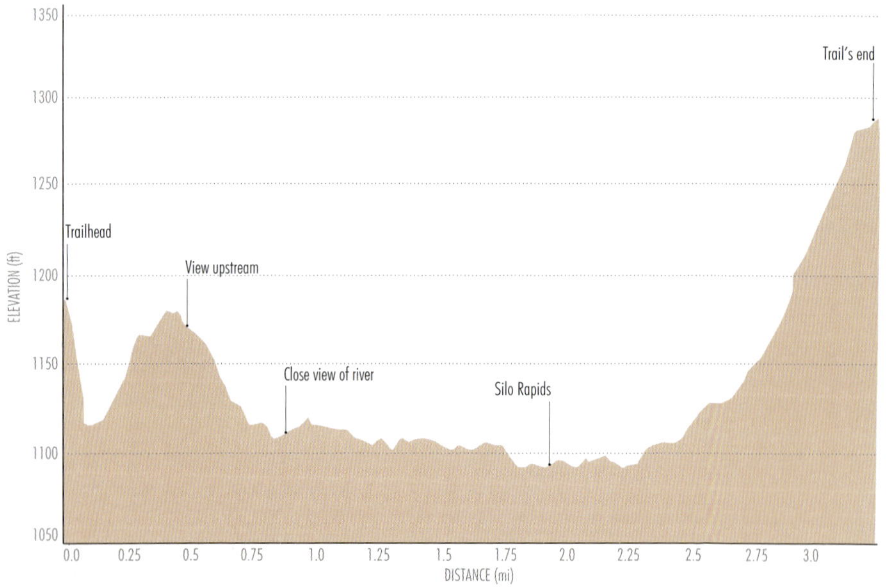

30 REND TRAIL

An easy yet scenic trail that overlooks the historic town of Thurmond and the New River, and parallels two mountain streams.

1 | 469 ft | 30 ft | 3.44 mi

Location: Near Thurmond, WV, on the west bank of the New River; accessible from the Glen Jean or Main Street/Oak Hill exits off US Route 19

Maps: USGS Thurmond quad 1:24,000

Trail Options: Add Church Loop Trail or use Arbuckle Connector Trail to access Southside Trail for a longer adventure.

Facilities: Thurmond trailhead: Gravel parking for twelve vehicles, toilet facilities. Minden trailhead: Gravel parking for twenty vehicles.

Highlights: Ride in the path of coal on this former Chesapeake and Ohio (C&O) rail line that overlooks the New River and the town of Thurmond. Don't miss the sandstone spire!

Trail Milestones:

0.0 mi – Thurmond trailhead (37°56.613 N, 081°05.266 W)

0.8 mi – Church Loop trailhead No. 1 (37°57.136 N, 081°04.727 W)

0.9 mi – Church Loop trailhead No. 2 (37°57.173 N, 081°04.774 W)

1.5 mi – Sandstone spire (37°57.527 N, 081°05.053 W)

1.6 mi – Overlook at bend in river (37°57.615 N, 081°05.137 W)

1.7 mi – Arbuckle Connector Trail (37°57.654 N, 081°05.198 W)

3.3 mi – Waterfall (37°58.435 N, 081°06.415 W)

3.44 mi – Minden trailhead (37°58.521 N, 081°06.511 W)

Finding the Trailhead

Thurmond trailhead: (37°56.613 N, 081°05.266 W)

Take the Glen Jean exit off US Route 19. Encounter a stop sign almost immediately and turn left. Travel 0.5 miles along WV 61/16. Turn right onto Main Street and then immediately turn left at the Glen Jean Bank building. Travel 5.1 miles along Thurmond Road (WV Route 25) to the Rend Trail on the left (signage states: "Thurmond-Minden Trail").

Minden trailhead: (37°58.521 N, 081°06.511 W)

Take the Main Street (Oak Hill) exit off US Route 19 — if approaching from the Fayetteville area, take this exit and turn left at the stop sign. Travel 0.2 miles and turn right onto Minden Road. If traveling from Beckley on US Route 19, exit at Main Street (Oak Hill), and at the stop sign turn right. Travel 0.1 miles and take a right on Minden Road. Travel 2.1 miles, cross a small bridge, and turn right into the trailhead parking.

Trail Description

Also known as Thurmond-Minden Trail

Note: Hike described starting at Thurmond trailhead. This trail, formerly known as the Thurmond-Minden Trail, begins on the east side of the parking lot near the toilet facilities. Paralleling Dunloup Creek to the right, continue along this wide and flat trail until you reach a Y intersection with a lesser-used and unmaintained trail. Keep left at this intersection and continue hiking 0.4 miles until reaching the trailhead for the Church Loop Trail. The First Baptist Church of Thurmond is nestled in the hillside below, and you can see the Dunloup Day Use area parking beyond. Continuing along the Rend Trail, you'll soon pass a "Trail Closed" sign to the right — this trail is not maintained and is not recommended. (It connects the Rend Trail to Thurmond but passes over private property and heavily used train tracks.) There are also a series of wooden benches along this stretch where you can rest and enjoy the forest.

Continue along the trail, with close-up views of cliff line to the left and distant views of the New River and historic Thurmond to your right through the trees. At 1.1 miles cross the first of a series

REND TRAIL

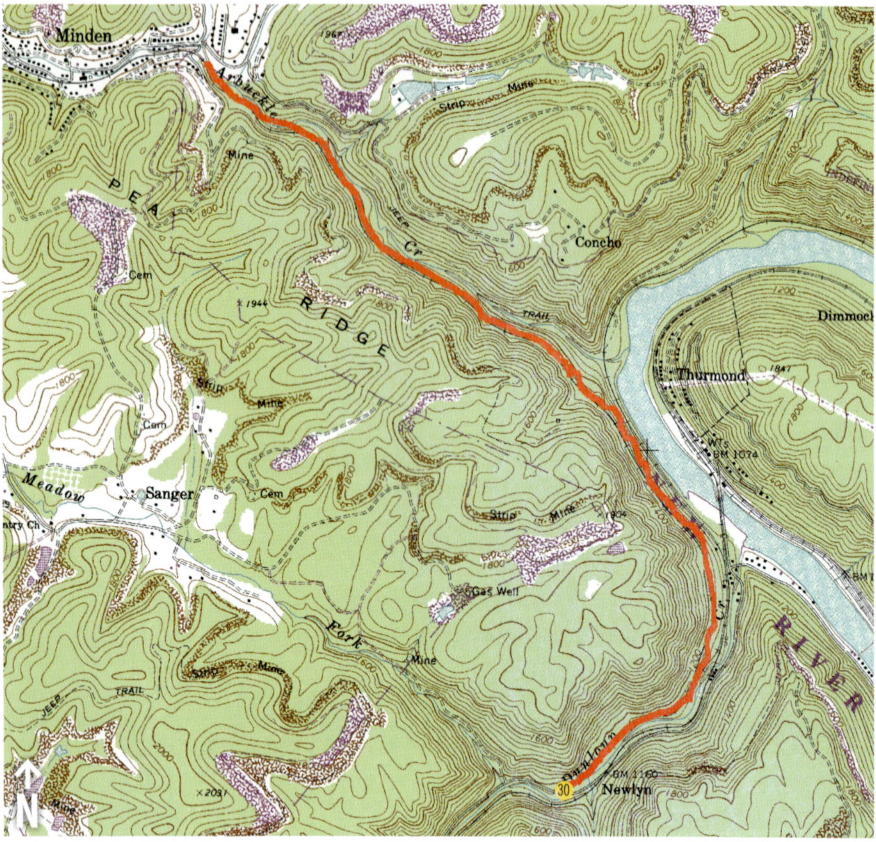

of trestle bridges. If biking, it's best to walk your bikes across these wooden bridges, as they're quite slippery when wet. At 1.5 miles come upon one of the main highlights, a sandstone spire that has detached from the surrounding cliff and now blocks the old railroad. Here, you'll also spot old train tracks and moss-covered crosstie beams. Navigate around the spire by climbing stairs to the left (30 steps) and descending stairs (20 steps) back to the trail. In this area the trail narrows to single-track but quickly widens. Continue 0.1 miles to an outstanding overlook that allows views of a deep bend in the New River and vistas of the railroad and ridgelines. Cross another bridge after 0.1 miles and reach the intersection with Arbuckle Connector Trail. From this point the trail parallels another stream, Arbuckle Creek. At 1.9 miles, 2.2 miles, and 2.6 miles cross trestles as you venture closer to the Minden trailhead. Continue 0.7 miles to distant views of a large waterfall that is, unfortunately, partially obstructed by a pipeline. Continue another 0.14 miles to the Minden trailhead and the trail's end.

Trail Combinations/Options

The Church Loop Trail (Trail 27) is a nice addition to the Rend Trail that allows close-up views of the First Baptist Church of Thurmond and adds 0.3 miles to the total distance. Visit Arbuckle Connector Trail (Trail 26) to see the beautiful falls that parallel this trail, or use it to connect to the southern terminus of the Southside Trail (Trail 31). Tacking on the Arbuckle and Southside trails will add an additional 6.44 miles to the hike or ride.

The deep-bend overlook at 1.6 miles.

REND TRAIL

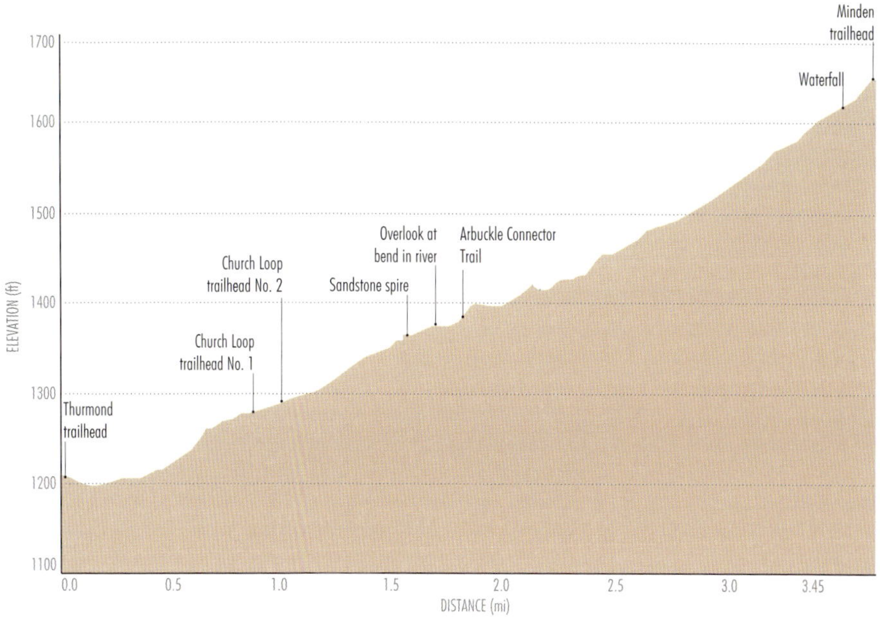

31 SOUTHSIDE TRAIL

An enjoyable hike or ride along the west bank of the New River, passing the ruins of multiple old coal towns.

1 | 380 ft 213 ft | 6.39 mi

Location: Cunard, WV, on the west bank of the New River; accessible from Fayetteville or the Main Street (Oak Hill) exit off US Route 19
Maps: USGS Thurmond quad 1:24,000
Trail Options: Combinations with the Rend and Kaymoor trails.
Facilities: Cunard/Brooklyn trailhead has toilets, picnic facilities, and ample parking; camping also available here.
Highlights: Parallels the New River and ruins of the bustling coal towns that populated this region in the early twentieth century. Well-preserved coke furnaces and close-up views of rapids.

Trail Milestones:

0.6 mi – Cunard/Brooklyn trailhead (37°59.031 N, 081°01.690 W)
0.6 mi – Sunrise Rapids (37°58.582 N, 081°01.598 W)
2.0 mi – Red Ash (37°57.625 N, 081°01.882 W)
2.9 mi – Well-preserved coke furnaces (37°57.740 N, 081°02.767 W)
3.6 mi – Rush Run (37°57.765 N, 081°03.448 W)
3.9 mi – Berms to left of trail (37°57.793 N, 081°03.668 W)
5.1 mi – Erskine/trail intersection (37°58.052 N, 081°04.765 W)
5.5 mi – Intersection with gravel road (37°57.899 N, 081°05.091 W)
5.7 mi – Arbuckle Connector Trail/trail closed (37°57.741 N, 081°05.142 W)
6.39 mi – Trail's end (37°57.257 N, 081°04.736 W)

Finding the Trailhead

(37°59.031 N, 081°01.690 W)
From US Route 19, follow WV 16 through Fayetteville 0.7 miles to the intersection with Gatewood Road. Bear left and follow Gatewood Road 4.5 miles before turning left onto Cunard Road. If traveling from the south, you can also reach Cunard by taking the Main Street (Oak Hill) exit off US Route 19, turning right at the stop sign, and traveling 0.4 miles to Gatewood Road — turn right at the stoplight and travel 5.4 miles to Cunard Road. From either direction, follow this road 1.8 miles until reaching Cunard. Take a left toward Cunard River Access area. Travel down this paved, winding road to the access area, a "put in" for rafters on the New River. You can park here and walk 1.0 miles to the trailhead via a gravel road, or drive this same stretch and park in a gravel lot. This gravel road is well maintained and accessible to most vehicles.

Trail Description

Also known as Southside Junction Trail/Southside Junction-Brooklyn Trail
The trailhead is the site of a coal town named Brooklyn, but is often referred to as Finlow as well. Higher in the gorge sits the mine entrance for Brooklyn Mine, which can be accessed via the Brooklyn Mine Trail (Trail 28). Above the trailhead you'll find ruins, and below, closer to the New River, established campsites. The trail parallels the New River for the hike's entirety, with great views of rapids and across the river to active rail lines that service freight trains loaded with coal, as well as the occasional New York–Chicago Amtrak passenger service. Travel 0.2 miles along this flat and wide trail and watch for additional ruins to the right hidden amongst the trees. At 0.6 miles keep your eyes open for a narrow access trail on the left that allows a close view downstream of Sunrise Rapids. Continue along the trail until at 1.4 miles it veers inland and away from the New River as the river makes a deep bend within the gorge. Look to your left to see many pools of water from channels the river cuts during high water. At 2.0 miles you'll start noticing ruins of the town of Red Ash on either side of the trail. Take a moment to explore the area, but remember not to disturb any artifacts. Rejoining the river shortly thereafter, the trail narrows and crosses an intermittent stream at 2.5 miles.

Hidden coke ovens alongside Southside Trail.

After a short walk of 0.3 miles encounter a large display of rails and ties. The mature trees growing within these old rails are a testament to the age of this former railway and the time that's passed since it was abandoned. At 2.9 miles come upon a highlight of both the trail and the region: a well-built hand-cut sandstone wall above and right of the trail. Leave the trail and walk toward this wall to see some of the region's best-preserved coke furnaces. (Visitors often miss these, as they are hidden from view.) These furnaces stretch along the trail for the next 0.2 miles. Please take care in this area, as it is a former industrial site.

At 3.6 miles arrive at ruins on the left and a rock wall to the right. This marks the beginning of the Rush Run community and mines. Continue 0.3 miles and arrive at extensive ruins to either side of the trail. Notice a "berm" on the left beside the trail. Do not walk on this berm, as it is actually the roof of coke furnaces, many of which have caved in over the years. For a better view of the furnaces, walk around either end of the berm. The ruins continue intermittently for another 0.3 miles whereupon it becomes necessary to climb a small rise and cross a stream. At 5.0 miles cross Rush Run creek using an old trestle and pass a small building on the right. Encounter a split in the trail at 5.1 miles and keep left. This area is the former location of a town named Erskine. The trail intersects a gravel road at 5.5 miles. Move straight across and resume the trail on the road's left side. In 0.2 miles reach a trestle bridge and the lower trailhead for the Arbuckle Connector Trail. As of 2013, the Southside Trail ends here — the remaining 0.69 miles are closed due to an active railway at the trail's former southern terminus. (The National Park Service is, however, in negotiations with RJ Corman and CSX to reopen this portion of the trail.)

Southside Trail.

SOUTHSIDE TRAIL

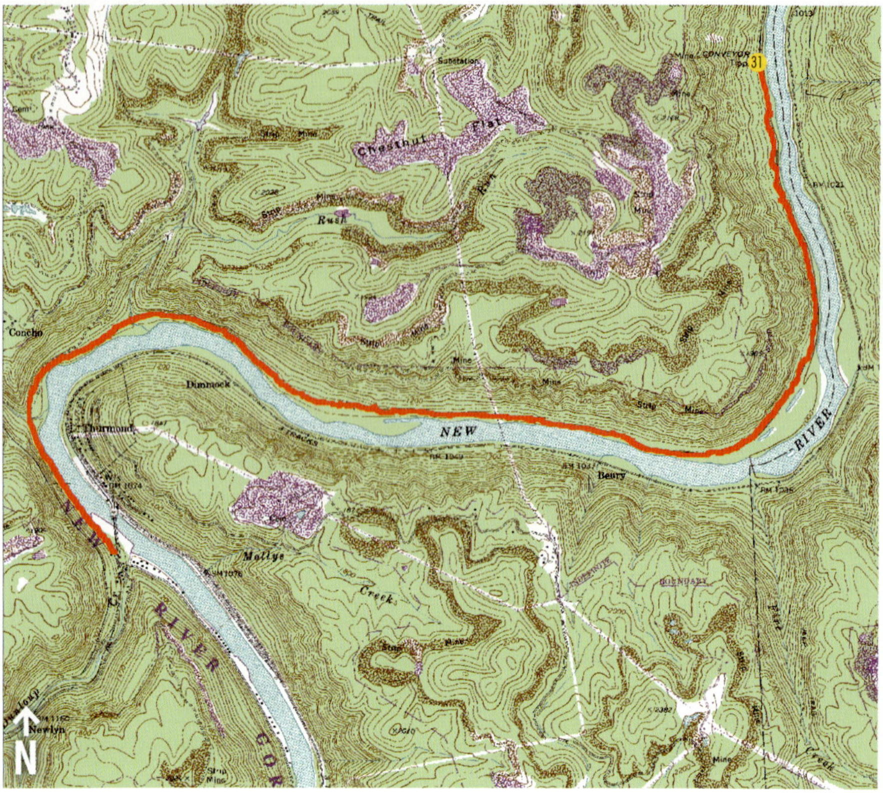

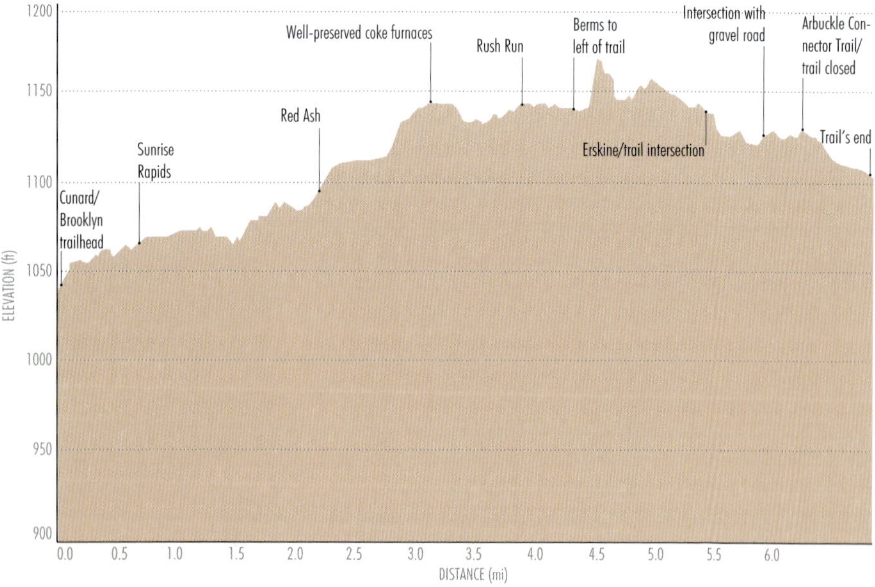

Calm before the fury: the New River before a set of rapids.

Trail Combinations/Options

Southside-Rend Trail: Utilizing the Arbuckle Connector Trail (Trail 26), you can create a 7.6-mile hike or bike. Travel down the Southside Trail 5.7 miles to the Arbuckle Connector Trail. Using this trail (0.25 miles), arrive at the Rend Trail (Trail 30) and turn left, for 1.7 miles to the trailhead.

Kaymoor-Southside-Rend Trail: You can also connect the Kaymoor Trail (Trail 14) with the Southside Trail by riding 1.3 miles along the Cunard River Access Road to join the gravel road/Southside Trail; this connection creates a 17.29-mile journey. Start at the Fayette Station trailhead of the Kaymoor Trail and arrive at the Cunard trailhead after 8.34 miles. Travel along a paved road 1.3 miles to the Cunard River Access area and a further 1.0 miles to the Brooklyn trailhead of the Southside Trail. Use the Arbuckle Connector Trail (Trail 26; at 5.7 miles) to connect with the Rend Trail (Trail 30). Turn left on the Rend Trail and continue to the trailhead (1.7 miles).

A proposed trail, tentatively called the Brooklyn Miner's Connector Trail, will connect the Brooklyn Mine Trail (Trail 28) to the Southside Trail in the future.

Vista from the Grandview Overlook.

9 GRANDVIEW REGION

Overview and Highlights

The Grandview Region of the New River Gorge National River is a newer portion of the park. In 1939, the State of West Virginia protected this area and created Grandview State Park. One of the most popular state parks for years, Grandview in 1990 was incorporated by the National Park Service into the greater national river area.

A highlight of any trip here is a visit to the main Grandview and Turkey Spur overlooks. These overlooks are easily accessible and provide panoramic vistas of the New River Gorge and the mountains beyond. While beautiful in any season, in autumn these overlooks reward visitors with bursts of yellow, red, and orange as leaves fade and fall before the coming winter. The area is also home to a variety of wildlife, including deer, turkey, and various other birds.

Grandview Visitor Center.

The Grandview Visitor Center is open in summer from June through August (12 p.m.–5 p.m.).

How to Get There

The area is located north of Interstate 64, just outside Beckley, WV. If traveling from Beckley or Interstate 77, take exit 129B (Grandview Road) off Interstate 64; if traveling west on Interstate 64, take exit 129. Follow Grandview Road (WV Route 9) north 4.8 miles to the national-park entrance.

Rules and Regulations

Please see "Rules and Regulations for the New River Gorge National River" (page 22) for rules and regulations governing the area.

History and Culture

Grandview, protected since the 1930s, offers many opportunities beyond hiking its trails and enjoying the overlooks. Among them are the shows that Theatre West Virginia (theatrewestvirginia.com) performs each summer in the amphitheater here. Founded in 1955, this organization has as its mission to present the unique culture of West Virginia through theater productions. Among their most popular productions are *The Hatfields and McCoys* and *Honey in the Rock*. The troupe performs from June through August every summer. An evening spent enjoying a performance here is well worth your time.

GRANDVIEW REGION HIKES

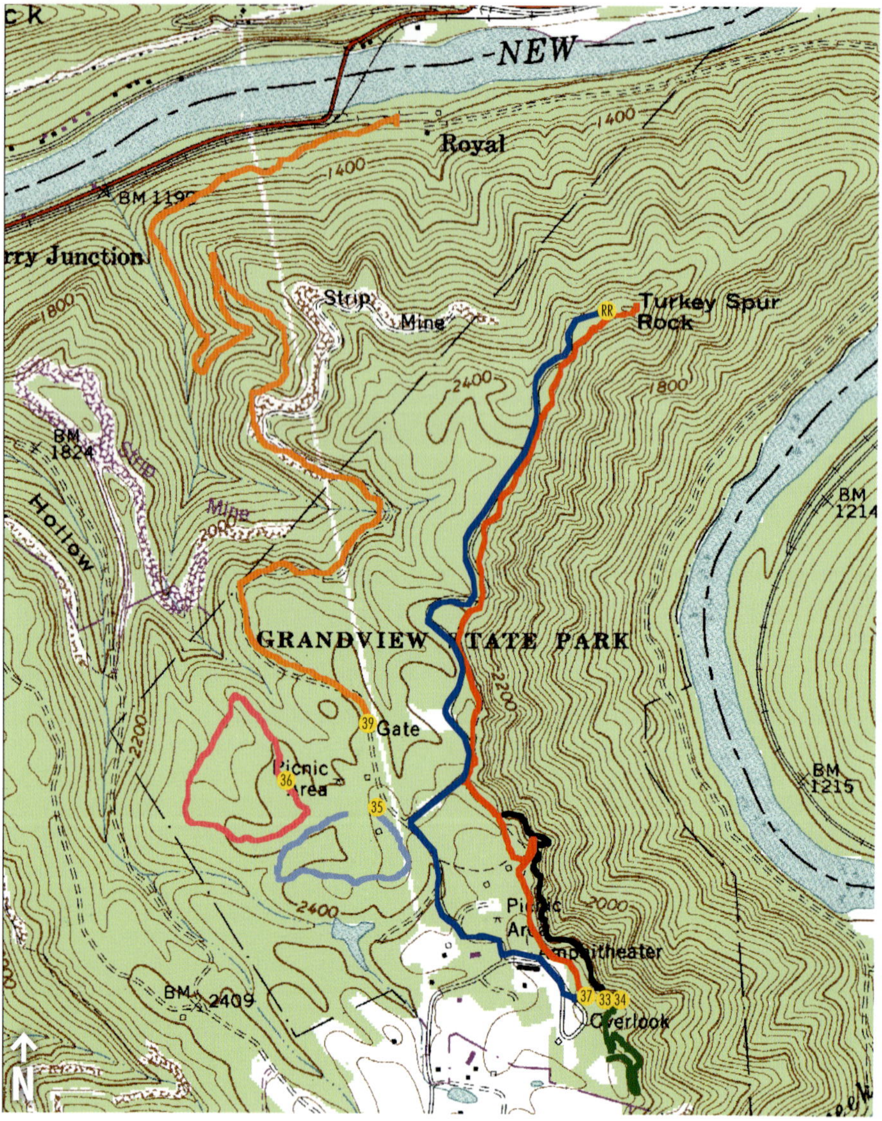

Map Key

Trail 33 – Tunnel Trail – green

Trail 34 – Castle Rock Trail – black

Trail 35 – Woodland Loop Trail – light blue

Trail 36 – Big Buck Trail – pink

Trail 37 – Grandview Rim Trail – red

Trail 37 Road Return – dark blue

Trail 39 – Little Laurel Trail – orange

32 TURKEY SPUR OVERLOOK WALKWAY

Turkey Spur Overlook Walkway is a short, developed trail that consists of wooden and stone stairs leading to a fabulous 360-degree view of the area.

2 | 79 ft 10 ft | 0.12 mi

Location: North of Interstate 64, Grandview Road exit 129
Maps: USGS Prince quad 1:24,000
Trail Options: Easily combined with Grandview Rim Trail and Road Return.
Facilities: Paved parking (eight spaces), benches at various points, trash receptacles.
Highlights: The "Air Conditioner" Crack and beautiful 360-degree views of the Grandview portion of the New River Gorge.

Trail Milestones:

0.06 mi – Viewing platform No.1 (37°50.905N, 81°03.683)
0.08 mi – Viewing platform No. 2 37°50.909 N, 81°03.670)
0.10 mi – Viewing platform No. 3 (37°50.902 N, 81°03.692)

Finding the Trailhead

(37°50.888 N, 81°03.736)
Take exit 129 (Grandview Road) from Interstate 64 and travel 4.8 miles to the national-park entrance. Once in the Grandview Region of the park, follow signs to Turkey Spur Overlook. The trail begins at the parking lot.

Trail Description

This is a very short trail that requires the ability to climb stairs, featuring a grand total of 128 mostly wooden steps leading to the various overlooks. From the parking lot continue along a rock wall where you will encounter the "Air Conditioner" Crack, a large vertical fissure in the sandstone that provides visitors with a dose of cool air, quite welcome on a hot summer day. Continue to the base of the stairs and climb to the viewpoints. On a clear day you can, as they say, see for miles! From the viewpoints, note the extreme bend the New River makes as it journeys northward — this is the so-called Stretcher Neck. Below the second, easternmost overlook you can also spot the railroad near the towns of Prince and Quinnimont. After enjoying the view, return down the stairs and back to the trailhead.

Trail Combinations/Options

At the end of the walkway, it's possible to link into the Grandview Rim Trail (Trail 37); combining the Grandview Rim Trail, the Turkey Spur Overlook Walkway (Trail 32), and the Grandview Rim Road Return (Trail 37A) yields a fun 3.42-mile loop. See Grandview Rim Trail and Grandview Rim Road Return for further details.

33 TUNNEL TRAIL

Well-developed trail near the Grandview Overlook that passes through a rock "tunnel."

2 | 82 ft 127 ft | 0.38 mi

Location: North of Interstate 64, Grandview Road exit 129
Maps: USGS Prince quad 1:24,000
Trail Options: No combinations, but multiple trailheads are found nearby.
Facilities: Large paved parking, toilets, visitor center, picnic facilities, open-air theater.
Highlights: A short hike into a tunnel and rhododendron grove that are always cooler than the surrounding area on a hot summer day.

Trail Milestones:

0.0 mi – Trailhead
(37°49.848 N, 081°03.714 W)
0.1 mi – Tunnel entrance
(37°49.774 N, 081°03.721 W)
0.2 mi – Tunnel exit
(37°49.788 N, 081°03.700 W)
0.38 mi – Trail's end
(37°49.762 N, 081°03.727 W)

Finding the Trailhead

(37°49.848 N, 081°03.714 W)
Take exit 129 (Grandview Road) from Interstate 64 and travel 4.8 miles to the national-park entrance. Once in the Grandview Region of the park, stay on the main road leading to the Grandview Overlook. Park in the main lot between the visitor center and gorge rim; the trailhead is located along the path leading to the main overlook at Grandview.

Trail Description

From the trailhead descend stone stairs to a level rock trail that leads to an intersection at 120 meters. An enormous boulder dominates this area and is worth the time to explore. Take the right fork, reaching the tunnel entrance at 0.1 miles. (If the tunnel is closed, return to the intersection and take the left fork, which circles around the boulders that form the tunnel.) At 0.2 miles arrive at the tunnel exit on the right. Continue along the trail, noting tall rock walls and overhangs to your right. When the rock walls end, climb stairs to the cliff top and keep right. Take care here, especially with children — there are no guardrails at the cliff's edge. You can see the baseball field from this point, as well as the trail's end. Cross the field to return to the parking lot.

As of 2013, the tunnel is closed. Please consult with NPS rangers before attempting to navigate the tunnel.

Trail Combinations/Options

While there are no combinations for this specific trail, you'll find the trailheads for Castle Rock Trail (Trail 34) and Grandview Rim Trail (Trail 37) nearby.

The rock tunnel.

TUNNEL TRAIL

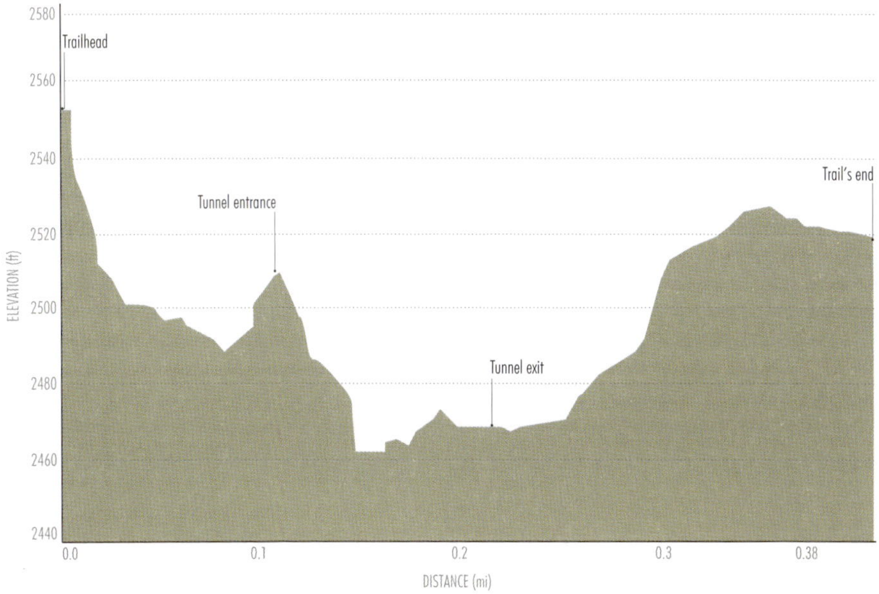

34 CASTLE ROCK TRAIL

A rocky and uneven trail that runs at the base of a cliff, above steep ground, and offers nice views of the New River Gorge.

3 | 105 ft 141 ft | 0.53 mi

Location: North of Interstate 64, Grandview Road exit 129
Maps: USGS Prince quad 1:24,000
Trail Options: Combine with Grandview Rim Trail for a longer, more adventurous hike.
Facilities: Large paved parking, toilets, visitor center, picnic facilities, open-air theater.
Highlights: This technically challenging trail offers views of the gorge. Not recommended for children due to the steep nature of the terrain below the trail.

Trail Milestones:

0.0 mi – Trailhead
(37°49.853 N, 081°03.712 W)
0.4 mi – Viewpoint
(37°50.087 N, 081°03.871 W)
0.53 mi – Intersection with Grandview Rim Trail
(37°50.130 N, 081°03.948 W)

Finding the Trailhead

(37°49.853 N, 081°03.712 W)
Take exit 129 (Grandview Road) from Interstate 64 and travel 4.8 miles to the national-park entrance. Once in the Grandview Region of the park, stay on the main road leading to the Grandview Overlook; park in the main lot between the visitor center and gorge rim. The trailhead is located along the path leading to the main Grandview Overlook.

Trail Description

The trailhead is located left of the path that leads to the main overlook at Grandview. From the trailhead, descend along a rocky, uneven path shaded by a rhododendron grove. As you continue, watch the rock wall to the left grow in height, eventually coming to tower above the trail like a medieval castle wall. Take the opportunity to examine the layers of rock exposed along the cliff — note a small coal seam integrated within the sandstone. At 0.4 miles reach an opening in the trees to the right that offers an expansive view of the New River Gorge. At 0.5 miles begin to ascend to the cliff top and intersect the Grandview Rim Trail (Trail 37) at 0.53 miles.

Caution

This trail, while not physically demanding, is technically quite challenging, with an uneven base that runs above steep ground. This trail is not recommended for children.

Trail Combinations/Options

After completing this hike, two different options let you combine with the Grandview Rim Trail (Trail 37). At the trail's end (intersection with Grandview) turn right and return to the trailhead, creating a 1.03-mile loop. This loop combines the thrill of the challenging Castle Rock Trail with the amazing viewpoints of the Grandview Rim Trail. (This combination is the best link-up for visitors with limited time in the Grandview area.) The other option is to turn right at the trail's end and continue along the Grandview Rim Trail for its final 1.13 miles, yielding a total distance of 1.66 miles.

CASTLE ROCK TRAIL

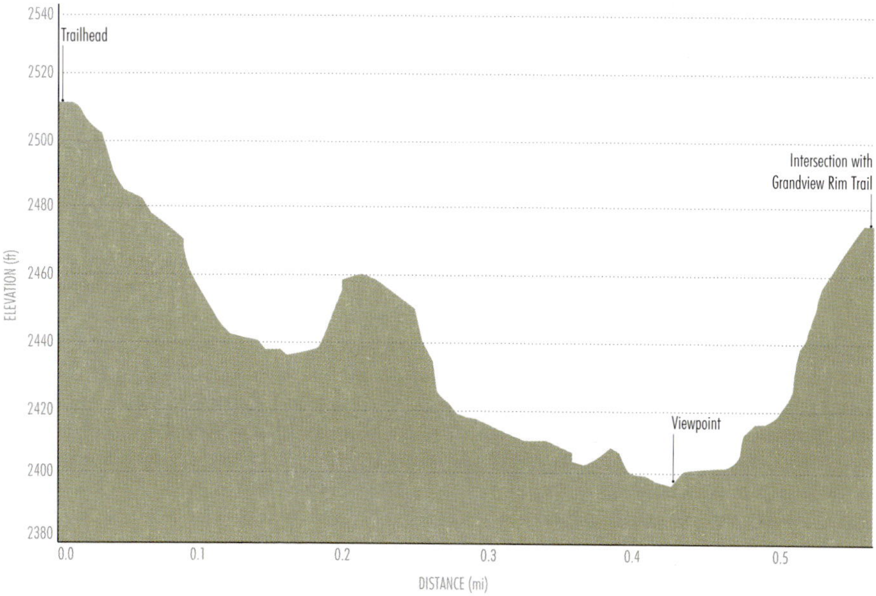

35 WOODLAND LOOP TRAIL

A short, easy stroll through a forest that explodes with color from wildflowers in spring and the lush foliage change in autumn.

1 | 79 ft 292 ft | 0.57 mi

Location: North of Interstate 64, Grandview Road exit 129
Maps: USGS Prince quad 1:24,000
Facilities: Large parking area, toilets, picnic facilities, playground, group shelters.
Highlights: A gentle hike through the forest that exemplifies the natural beauty of the area throughout the year.

Trail Milestones:

0.0 mi – Trailhead
(37°50.135 N, 081°04.186 W)
0.4 mi – Stream
(37°50.100 N, 081°04.326 W)
0.5 mi – Picnic area
(37°50.045 N, 081°04.380 W)
0.53 mi – Trail's end/parking area
(37°50.132 N, 081°04.247 W)

Finding the Trailhead

(37°50.135 N, 081°04.186 W)
Take exit 129 (Grandview Road) and travel 4.8 miles to the national-park entrance. Once in the Grandview Region of the park, follow signs leading to Shelter No. 2. The trailhead is located left of the entrance road about 20 meters before the parking area.

Trail Description

Descend gradually along a winding trail, taking in the open and mature forest. This trail is less frequented than many others in the area and offers a great opportunity to see wildlife, including squirrels, deer, and various birds. At 0.4 miles cross a stream over a small wooden bridge and begin to ascend. At 0.5 miles begin to see picnic facilities to the left and above the trail. At 0.57 miles emerge from the forest, with a playground to the left and the parking area straight ahead.

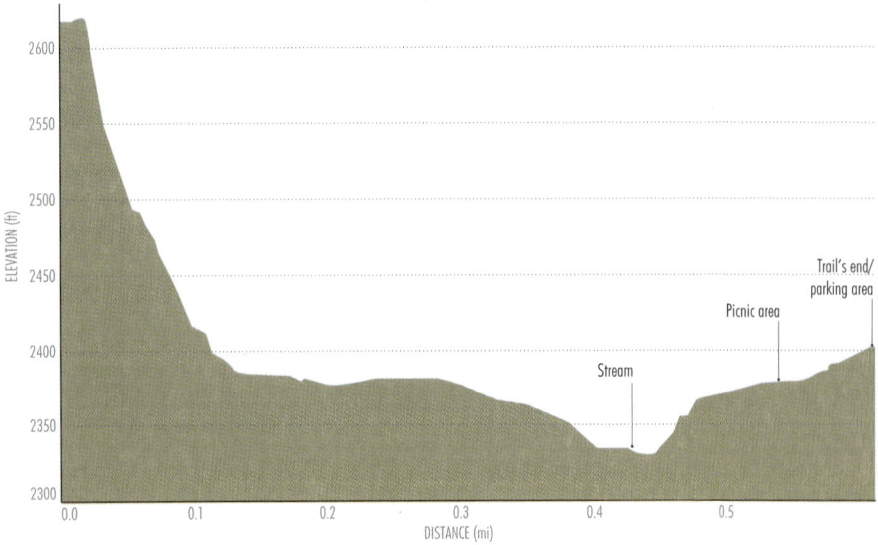

36 BIG BUCK TRAIL

This short but beautiful trail offers an outstanding teaching opportunity for kids and adults alike to learn about the trees that make up Appalachian forests.

2 | 144 ft 108 ft | 0.75 mi

Location: North of Interstate 64, Grandview Road exit 129
Maps: USGS Prince quad 1:24,000
Trail Options: Other nearby trailheads — Little Laurel Trail (Trail 39) and Woodland Loop Trail (Trail 35).
Facilities: Large parking area, toilets, picnic facilities, playground, & group shelters.
Highlights: Educational signboards for trees commonly found in an Appalachian forest. Deer and turkey frequent this area.

Trail Milestones:

0.00 mi – Trailhead
(37°50.138 N, 081°04.325 W)
0.75 mi – Trail's end
(37°50.135 N, 081°04.324 W)

Finding the Trailhead

(37°50.138 N, 081°04.325 W)
Take exit 129 (Grandview Road) and travel 4.8 miles to the national-park entrance. Once in the Grandview Region of the park, follow signs to Shelter No. 2. The trailhead is located just beyond Shelter No. 2.

Trail Description

Set out by taking the right-hand branch of the loop trail. The trail meanders through mature and open forest, leading hikers from one educational opportunity to another — take the time to read the informational boards located beside numerous trailside trees. These boards describe the characteristics of each tree and various facts related to how each fits into the eastern woodland ecosystem. The trail gradually descends along the initial 0.3 miles and then begins to ascend for the final 0.45 miles before returning to the trailhead. Keep a watchful eye throughout for deer, turkey, and squirrels.

Trail Combinations/Options

No combinations/options available, though you'll find trailheads for Little Laurel Trail (Trail 39) and Woodland Loop Trail (Trail 35) nearby.

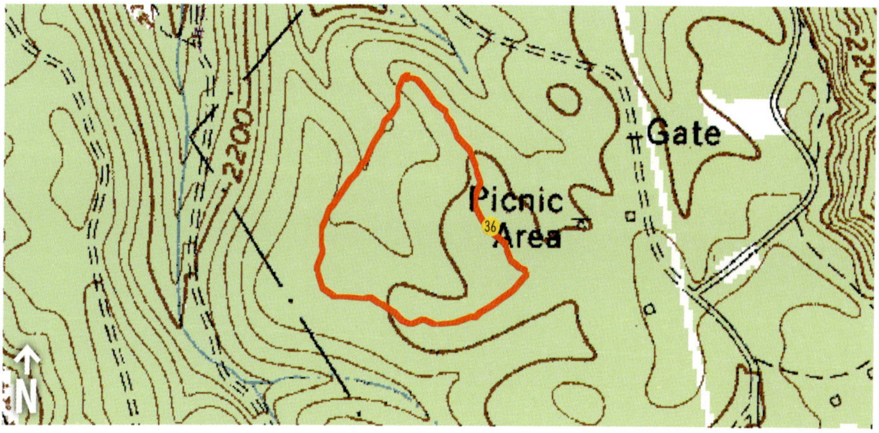

Fall brilliance along Big Buck Trail.

BIG BUCK TRAIL

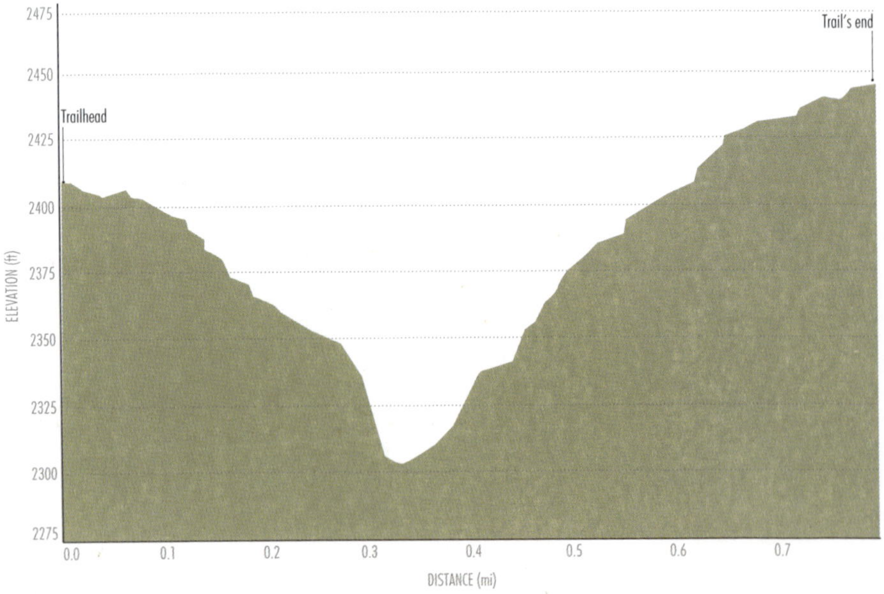

37 GRANDVIEW RIM TRAIL

Offering multiple scenic viewpoints along the way, this trail is the longest on the Grandview Rim.

2 | 237 ft | 351 ft | 1.63 mi

Location: North of Interstate 64, Grandview Road exit 129
Maps: USGS Prince quad 1:24,000
Trail Options: Combine with Turkey Spur Overlook Walkway and/or Grandview Rim Road Return; connection with Castle Rock Trail.
Facilities: The Grandview facilities include an abundance of parking, toilets, picnic facilities, and an amphitheater for special events.
Highlights: Amazing viewpoints over the gorge.

Trail Milestones:

0.0 mi – Trailhead
(37°49.862 N, 081°03.772 W)
0.2 mi – First overlook
(37°50.002 N, 081°03.885 W)
0.35 mi – "North Overlook"
(37°50.094 N, 081°03.875 W)
0.5 mi – Intersection with Castle Rock Trail
(37°50.130 N, 081°03.948 W)
1.4 mi – Steep descent
(37°50.805 N, 081°03.827 W)
1.63 mi – Turkey Spur parking
(37°50.888 N, 081°03.736 W)

Finding the Trailhead

(37°49.862 N, 081°03.772 W)
Take exit 129 (Grandview Road) from Interstate 64 and travel 4.8 miles to the national-park entrance. Once in the Grandview Region of the park, stay on the main road leading to the Grandview Overlook. Park in the main parking area between the visitor center and the gorge rim; the trailhead is located along the path that leads to the main Grandview Overlook.

Trail Description

Also known as Canyon Rim Trail
The trailhead is located along the short path leading to the main overlook in Grandview, and left of the trailheads for the Castle Rock and Tunnel trails. Begin by hiking along flat ground amongst lower rhododendron and taller deciduous trees. You'll find picnic facilities scattered along the left-hand side of the trail, while the cliff line above the New River Gorge dominates to your right. At 0.2 miles reach the first overlook, offering dramatic views east and up river. Continue to the "North Overlook" at 0.35 miles — accessed by following the right-hand branch of the Y intersection for 25 meters. After soaking up views of the gorge, return to the intersection and take the left branch to continue along Grandview Rim Trail. Continue to 0.5 miles and intersect with Castle Rock Trail to the right.

Following the trail another 0.1 miles, turn right just before intersecting a paved road. The next 0.8 miles of trail swing in and out of Virginia pines and rhododendron forest, always within sight of the gorge rim, but occasionally winding close to the park road. At 1.4 miles begin a steep descent along half-sunken wooden stairs that are very slippery when wet, and cross a wooden bridge. Continue 0.23 miles to the Turkey Spur parking area and trailhead for the Turkey Spur Overlook Walkway, a highly recommended 0.12-mile hike that offers a 360-degree panorama of the New River Gorge.

Wooden footbridge.

GRANDVIEW RIM TRAIL AND ROAD RETURN

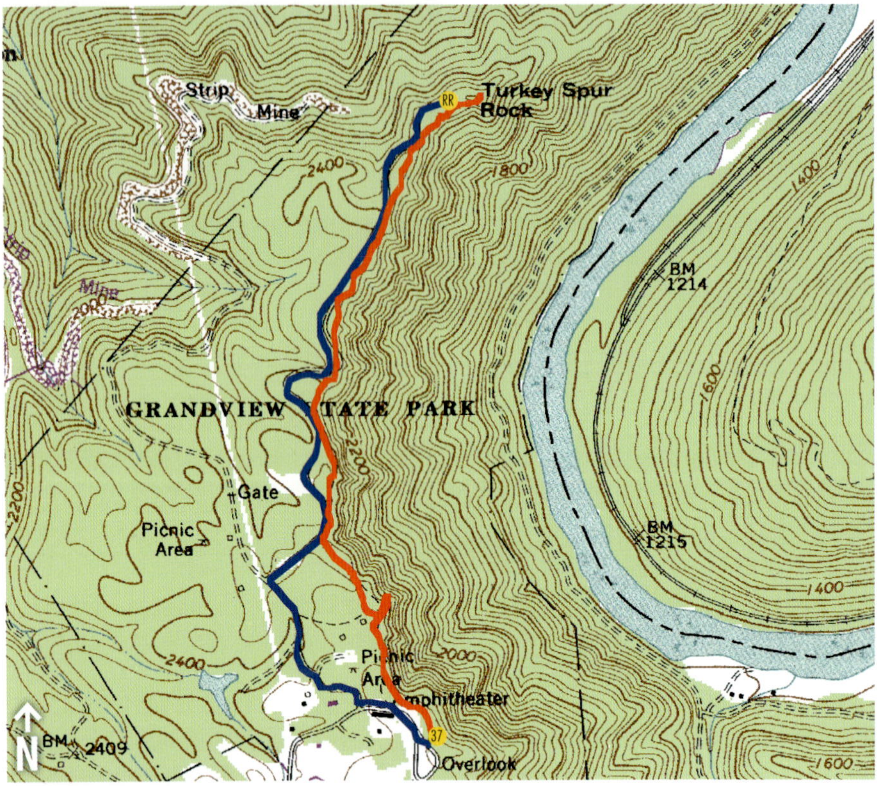

Amongst rhododendrons on the Grandview Rim Trail.

Trail Combinations/Options

Castle Rock Trail (Trail 34): After hiking the initial Grandview Rim Trail, connect with Castle Rock Trail's terminus at the intersection at 0.5 miles. Turn right and descend along rocky and uneven ground, following the Castle Rock Trail in reverse. Total distance: 1.03 miles.

Turkey Spur Overlook Walkway (Trail 32): You can easily combine Grandview Rim Trail with a trip to the overlook. At trail's end, cross the Turkey Spur Overlook Walkway parking area to reach its trailhead. Total link-up distance: 1.75 miles.

Far-off gorge views along the Grandview Rim Trail.

GRANDVIEW RIM TRAIL

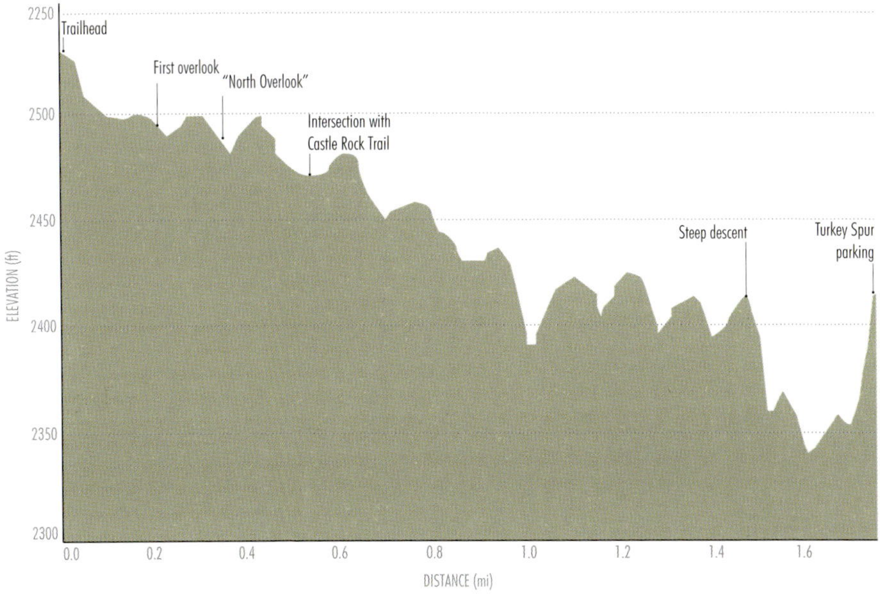

GRANDVIEW RIM ROAD RETURN

2 | 273 ft | 237 ft | 1.67 mi

Trail Milestones:

0.0 mi – Turkey Spur Overlook Walkway trailhead (37°50.888 N, 081°03.736 W)
1.1 mi – Turn left (37°50.125 N, 081°04.127 W)
1.4 mi – Turn left (37°49.970 N, 081°04.035 W)
1.67 mi – Main Grandview lot (37°49.852 N, 081°03.793 W)

Trail Description

From the Turkey Spur Overlook Walkway (Trail 32) parking, set out along the road to the right of the rock outcropping. While not directly on the gorge rim, this road offers visitors an alternative and pretty route back to the trailhead and main parking area. The road curves though the forest and on multiple occasions veers close to the Grandview Rim Trail. Continue along the road 1.1 miles to an intersection. Turn left here and continue another 0.3 miles until reaching a second intersection. Again turn left, and follow the road toward the main lot at the Grandview Visitor Center. Signage posted throughout this road makes it easy to follow. Keep watch for some of the many deer that call this high ground home. This road is well used due to the popularity of the Turkey Spur Overlook, so stay heads-up for traffic.

Additional Notes

The National Park Service offers a brochure detailing the first 0.5 miles of the Grandview Rim Trail. This guide discusses many native trees and plants, including various species of rhododendrons, oaks, maples, and Eastern hemlocks. You can pick up a brochure at the visitor center or trailhead signboard.

GRANDVIEW RIM ROAD RETURN

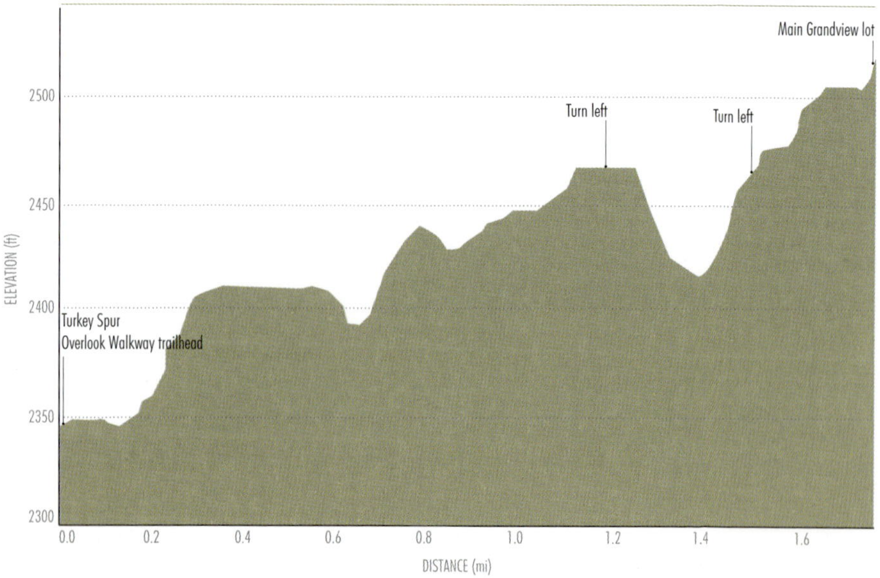

38 TERRY TOP TRAIL

A well-defined trail that leads through older forest to an open ridgeline and an old family cemetery dating back to the 1800s.

3 | 97 ft | 477 ft | 1.91 mi

Location: Just south of the BSA Summit Bechtel National Scout Reserve, west bank of the New River
Maps: USGS Prince quad 1:24,000
Trail Options: None at present.
Facilities: Gravel parking for six vehicles.
Highlights: A nice walk through forest and hill meadows leading to a family cemetery dating back to the 1800s.

Trail Milestones:

0.0 mi – Trailhead
(37°52.452 N, 081°06.032 W)
0.7 mi – Viewpoint
(37°52.138 N, 081°05.603 W)
1.1 mi – Open ridgeline
(37°52.049 N, 081°05.372 W)
1.91 mi – Martin Graveyard
(37°52.201 N, 081°04.922 W)

Martin Graveyard.

Finding the Trailhead

(37°52.452 N, 081°06.032 W)
Terry Top Trail is located close to the Boy Scouts of America Summit Bechtel National Scout Reserve. From US Route 19 take the Glen Jean exit. The exit leads immediately to a stop sign. Turn right here and travel on WV Route 16/61 for 2.8 miles. Turn left onto WV 61 and drive 1.8 miles. Turn left onto Garden Grounds Road (this area is undergoing construction related to the Summit Bechtel Reserve). Drive 1.1 miles along this road and take the first right (Mill Creek Road), then climb steadily for 1.6 miles, passing the National Park Service boundary sign on the left. Drive another 0.4 miles to the trailhead on the right; you'll be able to see the Terry Top Trail sign and gate from the road. *Note: As of 2013, this is a gravel road and well maintained. It is not, however, recommended for low-clearance vehicles.*

Trail Description

From the trailhead walk along a wide, gentle path that descends gradually. At 0.7 miles the trail bends right, with a nice view of the gorge through the trees just off the trail. Continue descending and at 0.8 miles pass a pool of water to the left at a bend in the trail. At 1.1 miles emerge from the forest into an open ridgeline ringed with evergreens. This open terrain continues for 0.6 miles and offers numerous gorgeous spots for a picnic. At this point (1.7 miles) reach a group of boulders on the right that allows views into the gorge. The trail continues through hemlocks and pines until turning sharply right and descending steeply at 1.8 miles. Arrive at the Martin Graveyard and the trail's end at 1.91 miles.

The Martin Graveyard has headstones that date back to the 1800s, and many of the sandstone markers are now blank, their etching effaced after years of rain and wind weathering. May those buried here rest in peace on this quiet point in the New River Gorge. Please do not disturb this burial site.

Trail Combinations/Options

No trail combinations available at present. A proposed stacked-loop trail system may open nearby, allowing numerous new options.

TERRY TOP TRAIL

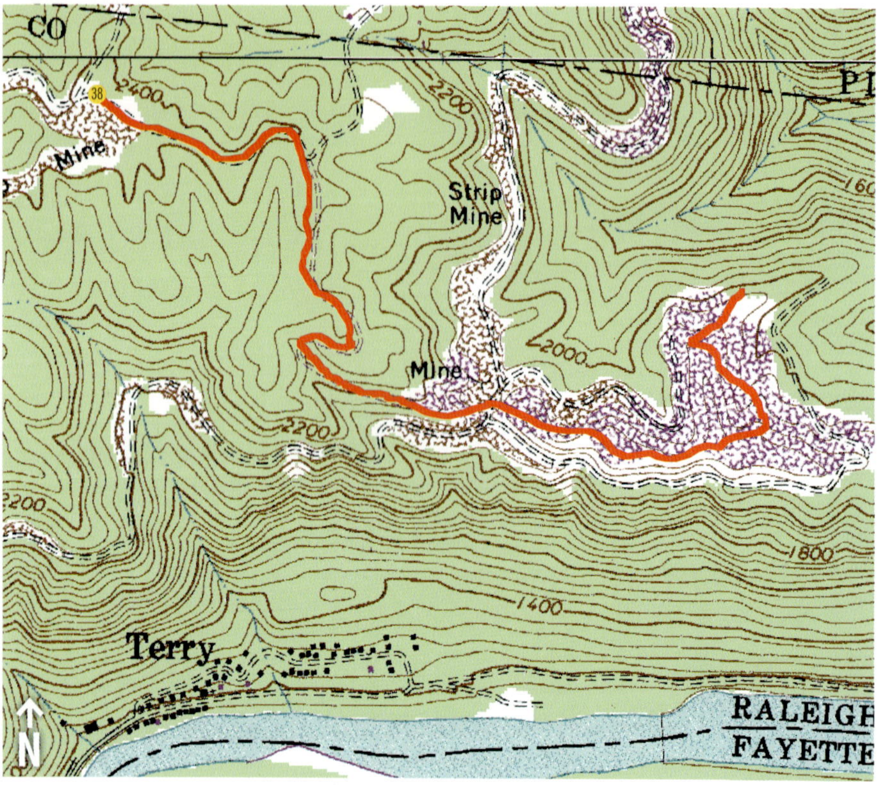

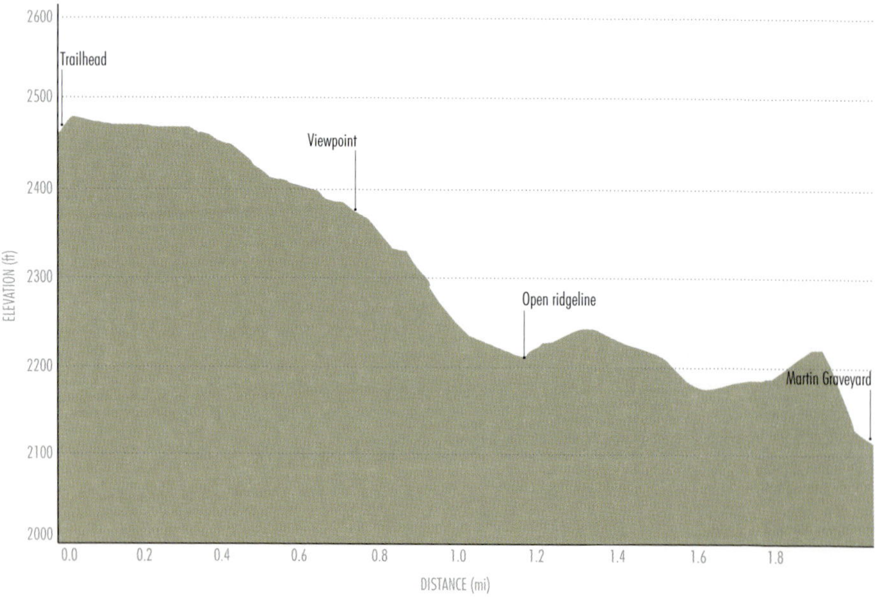

39 LITTLE LAUREL TRAIL

Little Laurel Trail is a wide and well-graded path leading from Grandview down into the gorge and to the New River. The trail ends at Glade Creek Road. Cross the road and visit the remains of Royal, an old coal town reclaimed by Mother Nature.

4 | 2 ft | 1125 ft | 2.5 mi

Location: North of Interstate 64, Grandview Road exit 129
Maps: USGS Prince quad 1:24,000
Trail Options: Link to Glade Creek Trail via gravel road.
Facilities: The Grandview facilities include an abundance of parking, toilets, picnic facilities, and an amphitheater for special events.
Highlights: A gently sloping trail leading to the New River. The surrounding terrain is steep and gives the visitor the feeling that he is walking in the treetops. At the end of the trail and across the gravel road, learn more about the old coal town of Royal, now but a memory.

Trail Milestones:

0.0 mi – Grandview (37°50.265 N, 081°04.201 W)
0.4 mi – View of New River/rock formations (37°50.476 N, 081°04.458 W)
0.6 mi – Power-line cut (37°50.730 N, 081°04.434 W)
1.4 mi – Long switchbacks (37°50.969 N, 081°04.512 W)
2.0 mi – River view/narrowing trail (37°51.030 N, 081°04.621 W)
2.2 mi – Second power-line cut (37°51.104 N, 081°04.427 W)
2.5 mi – Trail's end/town of Royal (37°51.184 N, 081°04.156 W)

Finding the Trailhead

Grandview trailhead: (37°50.265 N, 081°04.201 W)
Take exit 129 (Grandview Road) and travel 4.8 miles to the national-park entrance. Once in the Grandview Region of the park, follow signs to shelters No. 3 and 4. The trail begins at the end of the parking area for these two shelters.

Glade Creek trailhead: (37°51.184 N, 081°04.156 W)
From US Route 19 take the Glen Jean exit. The exit leads immediately to a stop sign. Turn right here and travel on WV Route 16/61 for 2.8 miles. Turn left onto WV 61 and travel 4.4 miles to a Y intersection. Turn left onto WV Route 41 and travel 4.0 miles. Turn right onto the gravel Glade Creek Road (just before crossing the New River) and follow it 0.2 miles to the trailhead on the right.

Trail Description

Note: Hike descdribed from Grandview trailhead. The trailhead is located at the end of the paved parking area for Grandview shelters Nos. 3 and 4. The trail begins as a wide gravel road that the NPS uses as a service road. Reach some NPS maintenance buildings not long after starting, and keep right along the main trail. At 0.4 miles the trail makes a sharp bend to the right, with minor views of the New River far below and some very interesting rock formations to the right and uphill. Continue descending and cross through a power-line cut. At 1.0 miles the trail steepens for approximately 100 meters. Throughout the hike, the trail crosses seasonal streams.

At 1.4 miles the track begins a series of long switchbacks, the first of which has a large moss-covered bank. At 2.0 miles you are rewarded with up-close "peek-a-boo" views of the river and the sound of the rapids roaring below. Just beyond this turn, a landslide has greatly narrowed the trail — proceed with caution! Continue along the trail and at 2.2 miles pass beneath a second power-line cut to soon arrive at the trail's terminus at Glade Creek Road. Cross the road and read about the history of Royal.

LITTLE LAUREL TRAIL

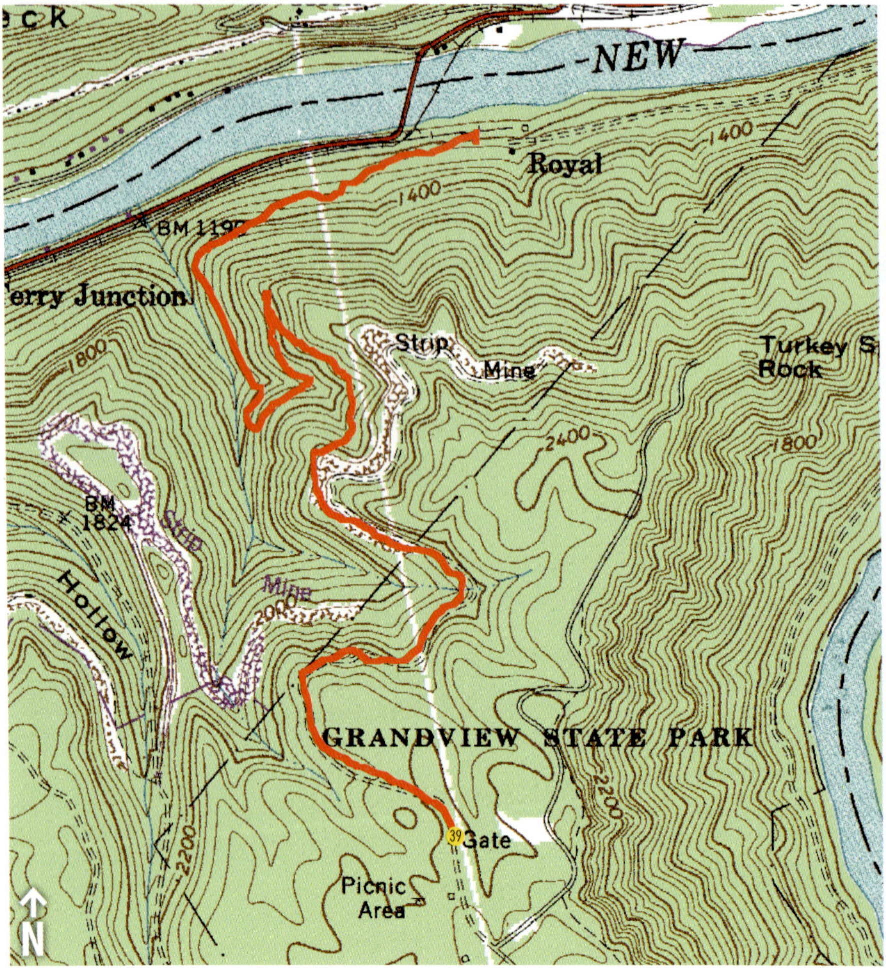

Trail Combinations/Options

At the end of Little Laurel Trail, turn right onto the gravel Glade Creek Road and follow it 5.4 miles to the trailhead for Glade Creek Trail (Trail 43) on the right.

Additional Notes

The Town of Royal: James Kay and James Laing founded Royal in 1891, and it soon became the center of activity for the Royal Coal and Coke Company. In its heyday, the town of Royal numbered 75 homes, a school, a church, and a theater. The mines near Royal produced coal for 37 consecutive years before eventually closing down in 1940.

LITTLE LAUREL TRAIL

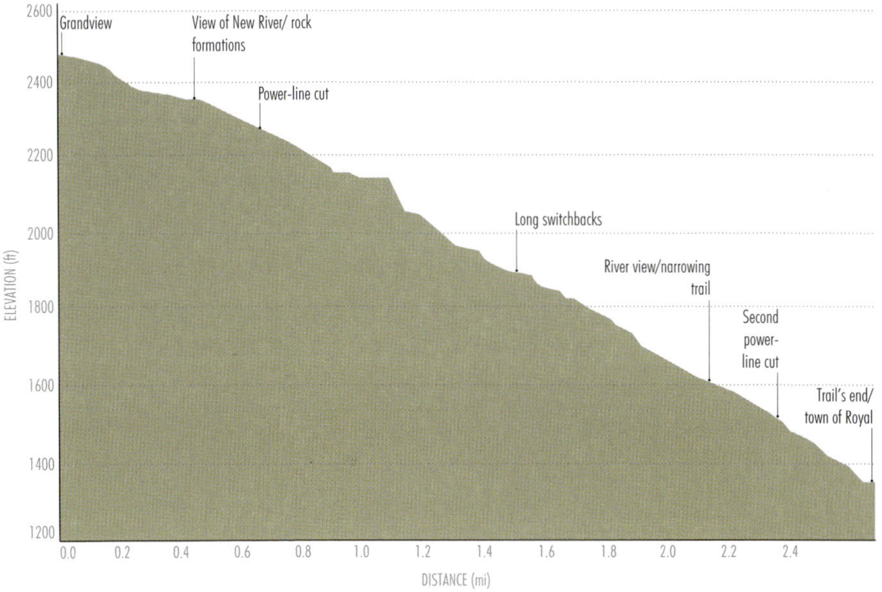

Glade Creek as seen from the northern trailhead.

10 GLADE CREEK REGION

Overview and Highlights

This region is an outdoor playground for hikers, bikers, kayakers, and fishermen. Its paths are less frequented than many of the more popular and easily accessible trails around Fayetteville, WV, but that is not for lack of beauty or adventure. Glade Creek, known for its outstanding trout fishing and runnable rapids, is the centerpiece of the region, with Glade Creek Falls a highlight for visitors. Kates Falls, a 25-foot wonder just off the Glade Creek Trail, is also a must-see. For hikers interested in getting away from it all, Kates Plateau and Polls Plateau trails are about as "out there" as you can get in the New River Gorge National River.

How to Get There

The Glade Creek Region, situated southeast of the Grandview Region of the New River Gorge, is mostly contained within and above a narrow valley formed by Glade Creek. Two trailheads access this portion of the park, described below:

Northern trailhead (Prince/New River Gorge): From US Route 19 take the Glen Jean exit. The exit leads immediately to a stop sign. Turn right here and travel on WV Route 16/61 for 2.8 miles. Turn left onto WV 61 and travel 4.4 miles to a Y intersection. Turn left onto WV Route 41 and travel 4.0 miles. Turn right on the gravel Glade Creek Road (just before crossing the New River). Follow this road 5.6 miles to find the trailhead on the right.

Southern trailhead (Interstate 64/Beaver): Take exit 129 off Interstate 64 toward Shady Spring. Drive south along WV Route 9 (Grandview Road) for 0.5 miles, following signs for Little Beaver State Park. Turn left on County Route 22, Scott Branch Road. Continue to the trailhead. *Note: As of January 2013, access to this trailhead was closed due to construction on the road and bridge. Please check with NPS rangers regarding access to the southern trailhead for Glade Creek Trail (Trail 43).*

Rules and Regulations

Please see "Rules and Regulations for the New River Gorge National River" (page 22) for rules and regulations governing the area.

History and Culture

The towns of Hamlet, located within the Glade Creek Region, played significant roles in the logging of the New River Gorge's old-growth forests. From the 1880s through the 1930s, loggers completely timbered the majority of the forests in and around the New River Gorge. The narrow gauge railway, where today's Glade Creek Trail runs, was built to assist in the removal of downed logs, as were many of the region's rail lines.

You can reach the ruins of Hamlet from the northern trailhead for the Glade Creek Region. Among the many foundations visible at the intersection of Glade Creek and the New River, it is easy to imagine the scope of the town that once stood in this location. While here, also check out the pillars of a former railroad bridge across the New River. The steel from this structure was removed and reprocessed for use during World War II.

GLADE CREEK REGION HIKES

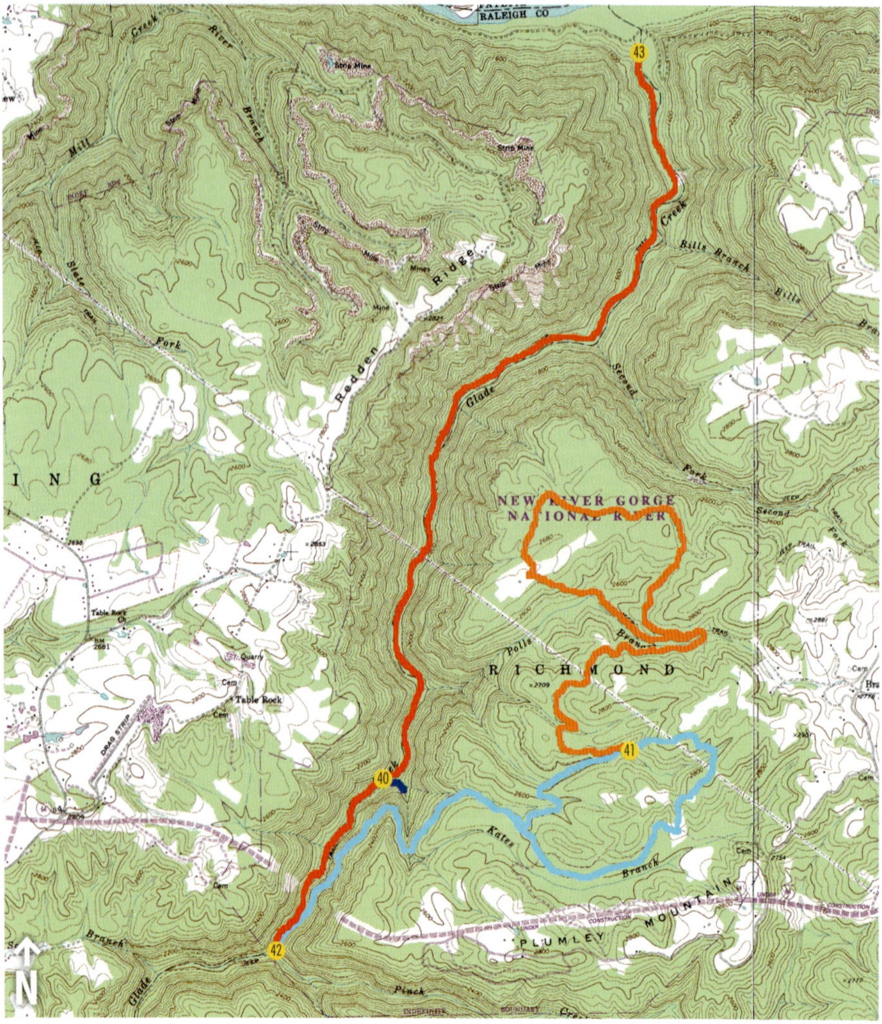

Map Key

Trail 40 – Kates Falls Trail – dark blue

Trail 41 – Polls Plateau Trail – orange

Trail 42 – Kates Plateau Trail – light blue

Trail 43 – Glade Creek Trail – red

Polls Branch Creek tumbling from the plateau above.

40 KATES FALLS TRAIL

This short trail, accessed from Glade Creek Trail, climbs steadily among moss-covered rocks to a beautiful two-part 25-foot waterfall.

3 | 80 ft | 0 ft | 0.11 mi

Location: North of Interstate 64, east of Beckley, WV
Maps: USGS Prince quad 1:24,000
USGS Meadow Creek quad 1:24,000
Trail Options: Accessed via the Glade Creek Trail.
Facilities: No facilities.
Highlights: Two-part 25-foot waterfall, cascades, and an abundance of spring wildflowers.

Trail Milestones:

0.05 mi – Trail alongside Kates Branch creek
(37°46.544 N, 081°01.915 W)
0.11 mi – Trail ends at falls
(37°46.511 N, 081°01.880 W)

Finding the Trailhead

(37°46.549 N, 081°01.967 W)
Access the trailhead via the Glade Creek Trail (Trail 43). From the northern Glade Creek trailhead (off Glade Creek Road, near Prince) travel 4.6 miles south/upstream to the intersection and trailhead. From the southern Glade Creek trailhead (accessed from Beaver, WV) travel north/downstream along the Glade Creek Trail 1.09 miles to the intersection and trailhead. See Finding the Trailhead for Glade Creek Trail (page 154) for detailed directions to both trailheads.

Trail Description

From the trailhead move though a small clearing as the trail bends left. Moving through rhododendrons, approach Kates Branch creek at 0.05 miles and bear right, paralleling the stream. Enjoy the bountiful wildflowers that grow here in the spring and the moss-covered boulders that frame the cascading stream as you climb higher toward the falls. Watch your step amongst the stones, as mist from the falls soaks everything nearby. At 0.11 miles arrive at the end of the trail near the base of the falls. Enjoy the views from here or scramble up amongst the rocks to get closer to the stream and waterfall.

Kates Falls.

Trail Combinations/Options

You can access this hike from the Glade Creek Trail (Trail 43). It is a nice place to stop and enjoy the coolness provided by the stream before continuing along Glade Creek.

41 POLLS PLATEAU TRAIL

The New River Gorge's most remote trail offers outstanding opportunities for wildlife viewing as well as the opportunity to check out an old homestead tucked into the woods.

4 | 475 ft | 424 ft | 4.81 mi

Location: North of Interstate 64, east of Beckley, WV
Maps: USGS Prince quad 1:24,000 USGS Meadow Creek quad 1:24,000
Trail Options: Approach the trailhead from Kates Plateau Trail or combine for a longer loop trail.
Facilities: No facilities available.
Highlights: Remote trail, an old homestead, and a forest thick with oak, hemlock, hickory, and rhododendron.

Trail Milestones:

0.7 mi – Turn right at fork (37°46.902 N, 081°01.061 W)
0.9 mi – Power-line cut (37°46.976 N, 081°00.886 W)
1.5 mi – Rhododendron grove (37°47.106 N, 081°00.456 W)
1.7 mi – Keep left at intersection (37°47.177 N, 081°00.282 W)
1.74 mi – Y intersection (37°47.170 N, 081°00.300 W)
2.5 mi – Keep left at intersection (37°47.515 N, 081°00.380 W)
3.3 mi – Sharp left turn (37°47.746 N, 081°01.092 W)
3.8 mi – Old homestead (37°47.449 N, 081°01.183 W)
4.7 mi – Rhododendrons and stream (37°47.322 N, 081°00.825 W)

Finding the Trailhead

(37°46.697 N, 081°00.668 W)
Take exit 129 off Intersate 64 toward Shady Spring. Drive 0.5 miles south along WV Route 9 (Grandview Road), following signs for Little Beaver State Park. Turn left on County Route 22, Scott Branch Road. Continue to the Kates Plateau Trail trailhead, your starting point. (To reach the Polls Plateau Trailhead, you must hike the Kates Plateau Trail to its Y intersection [1.8 miles] then take the left-hand branch for an additional 0.91 miles, creating a 2.71-mile approach. For further details, see trail description for Kates Plateau Trail [Trail 42].) *Note: As of January 2013, access to the Kates Plateau Trail trailhead was closed due to construction on the road and bridge. Please check with NPS Rangers regarding access.*

Trail Description

Note: This trail is marked intermittently with a white blaze, in addition to detailed signage at the trail intersection of Polls Plateau and Kates Plateau trails. From the trailhead and intersection with Kates Plateau Trail, cross a small, rocky stream and at 0.4 miles ascend through a hemlock grove while veering left. Cross another stream at 0.5 miles and turn left along the stream until at 0.7 miles you reach a trail intersection — stay right and continue 0.2 more miles to a power-line cut.

Continue hiking along the well-established trail, entering a thick stand of rhododendron. Cross a stream at 1.7 miles and arrive at a trail intersection. Stay straight/left here rather than taking the sharp-right alternative. This intersection is a bit tricky, but it will be obvious that you took the correct trail when after 0.04 miles you reach the Y intersection for the loop portion of Polls Plateau Trail, as designated by an NPS signpost. Here, take the right branch and begin a steady climb out of the rhododendron and into a forest filled with oak and hickory trees.

At 2.5 miles walk through a sunken portion of the trail, emerging onto a site often used for backcountry camping, and a trail intersection. Stay left here and continue hiking just below a ridgeline. At 3.3 miles the trail takes a sharp left, leaving the well-graded former road and setting off along single-track. After 0.2 miles the trail

POLLS PLATEAU TRAIL

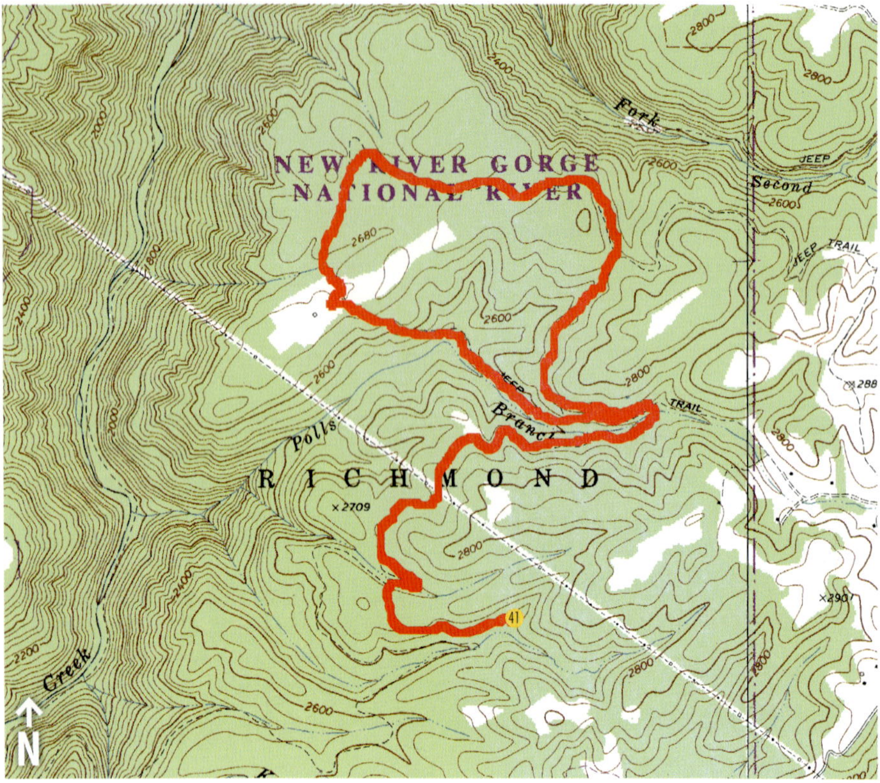

enters a stand of hemlocks, and at 3.7 miles crosses a stream via rock hopping. Just beyond, you'll first encounter the remnants of an old homestead. An old truck chassis, an ancient cooking stove with a porcelain front, and the remnants of outbuildings mark a family home from the early 1900s. The trail turns sharply left here in the middle of a field and continues straight for 100 meters before turning right at an old fence line and descending into the woods. Keep a sharp eye for this right turn and for the old glass bottles that litter the forest. Continue along the trail and at 4.7 miles come to an area thick with rhododendrons and a stream, following the path up to the Y intersection at 4.81 miles. This completes the Polls Plateau loop; now refer to the Polls Plateau Return to reach the original trailhead.

Trail Combinations/Options

You must use the Kates Plateau Trail to reach the trailhead for Polls Plateau Trail. Refer to the "Finding the Trailhead" section on the preceding page for directions. To combine this trail with Kates Plateau Trail, follow the trail description for Kates Plateau Trail to the intersection with Polls Plateau, turn right and complete the Polls Plateau Trail and Return, then turn right again and complete the Kates Plateau loop. From that point, follow the description for the Kates Plateau Return to its trailhead. This creates a 13.48-mile backcountry loop.

POLLS PLATEAU RETURN

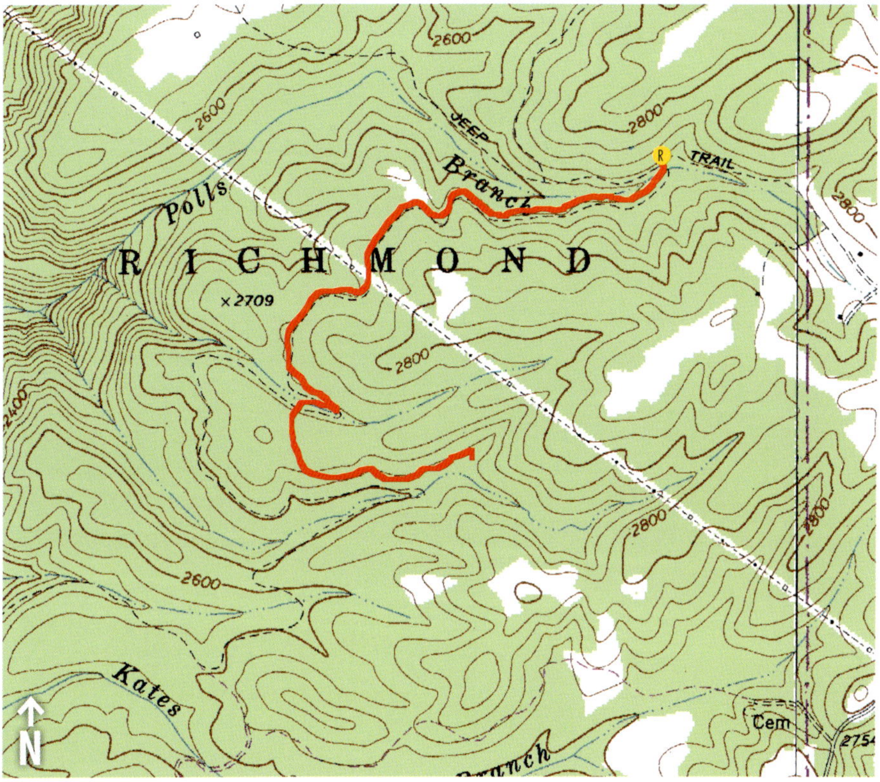

1 | 88 ft 144 ft | 1.74 mi

Trail Milestones:

0.0 mi – Y intersection
(37°47.170 N, 081°00.300 W)
0.04 mi – Keep right at intersection
(37°47.177 N, 081°00.282 W)
0.24 mi – Rhododendron grove
(37°47.106 N, 081°00.456 W)
0.84 mi – Power-line cut
(37°46.976 N, 081°00.886 W)
1.04 mi – Turn left at fork
(37°46.902 N, 081°01.061 W)

Trail Description

Following the same trail that leads to the Y intersection, use the following directions to assist in the return: From the Y intersection continue 0.4 miles before encountering another intersection. Keep right and enter a thick rhododendron grove. At 0.84 miles break out into the open along a power-line cut before returning to the forest. At 1.04 miles keep left at a trail intersection and continue 0.70 miles to the intersection with Kates Plateau Trail.

Additional Notes

In past guides and NPS material, the return mileages for the Kates Plateau and Polls Plateau trails were not included in total trail distance. The "Returns" for both trails correct this and give accurate mileage to complete each trail, with no surprises!

POLLS PLATEAU TRAIL

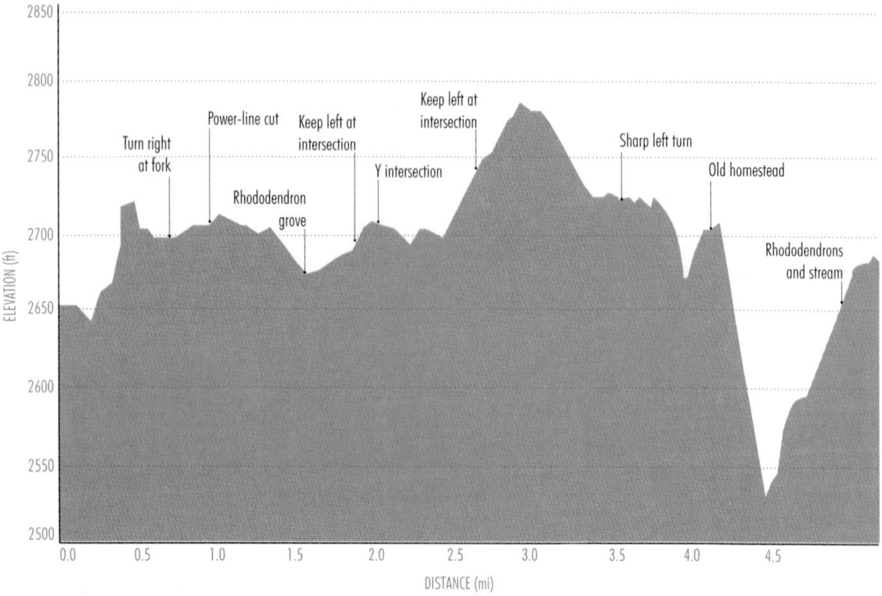

POLLS PLATEAU RETURN

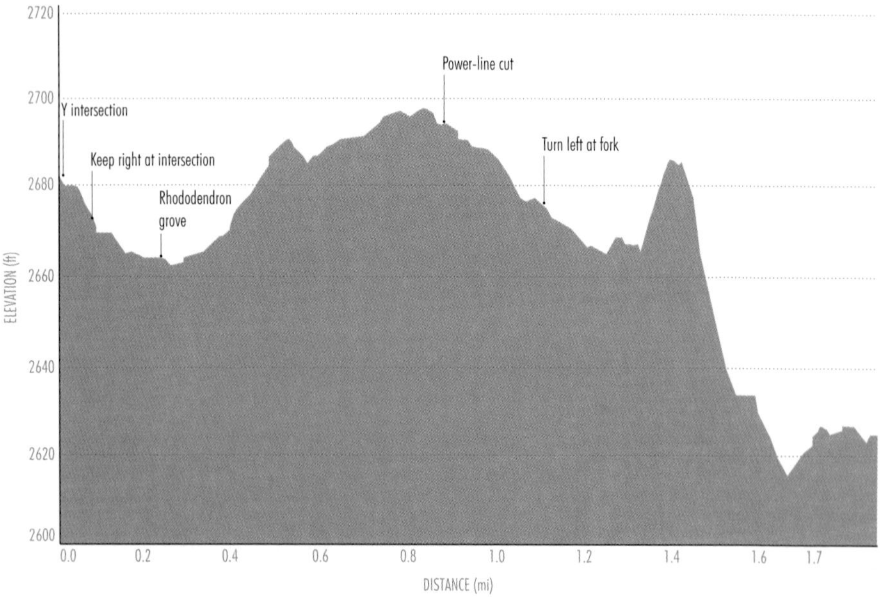

42 KATES PLATEAU TRAIL

A relatively remote trail that rises from Glade Creek to a plateau featuring wonderful opportunities to view wildlife, including beaver, deer, and turkey, giving a true backcountry feel to a day in the forest.

4 | 1040 ft | 429 ft | 5.02 mi

Location: North of Interstate 64, east of Beckley, WV
Maps: USGS Prince quad 1:24,000
USGS Meadow Creek quad 1:24,000
Trail Options: This trail shares a trailhead with the southern terminus of Glade Creek Trail. It is also used to reach Polls Plateau Trail.
Facilities: Gravel parking for ten vehicles, garbage receptacles.
Highlights: Highlights include Kates Branch creek, beaver activity, an old homestead, and access to Polls Plateau Trail.

Trail Milestones:

0.3 mi – Interstate 64
(37°46.083 N, 081°02.357 W)
1.0 mi – Trail marker
(37°46.436 N, 081°01.929 W)
1.2 mi – Kates Branch creek
(37°46.266 N, 081°01.872 W)
1.91 mi – Y intersection
(37°46.392 N, 081°01.282 W)
2.4 mi – Beaver pond
(37°46.154 N, 081°00.890 W)
3.1 mi – Homestead
(37°46.344 N, 081°00.412 W)
3.5 mi – Power-line cut
(37°46.603 N, 081°00.211 W)
4.1 mi – Polls Plateau Trail
(37°46.697 N, 081°00.668 W)

Finding the Trailhead

(37°45.882 N, 081°02.570 W)
Take exit 129 off Intersate 64 toward Shady Spring. Drive 0.5 miles south along WV Route 9 (Grandview Road), following signs for Little Beaver State Park. Turn left on County Route 22, Scott Branch Road. Continue to the trailhead. *Note: As of January 2013, access to this trailhead was closed due to construction on the road and bridge. Please check with NPS rangers regarding access.*

Trail Description

Note: The trail is marked intermittently with white blazes. From the trailhead, begin a steady ascent that continues for the initial 2.09 miles. While continuous, this climb is gradual, with myriad opportunities to rest and enjoy the surrounding scenery. At 0.3 miles cross under Interstate 64, suspended high above, and continue through a portion of trail at 0.4 miles that has narrowed due to a landslide. This area is stable, but watch your step. At 0.5 miles intersect an unused trail and continue straight (signs mark the path). Cross a seasonal stream at 0.6 miles, and come across a fallen concrete trail marker at 1.0 miles.

Soon after, you'll be able to hear Kates Branch creek tumbling down the mountainside and will begin to see the stream at 1.1 miles. At 1.2 miles carefully cross the stream in a tricky spot and, once across, take a moment to enjoy this rhododendron-shaded creek. Hike 0.71 miles to a Y intersection that marks the beginning of the loop portion of this trail. Take the right branch; the trail levels off after a short time and enters a thick grove of Eastern hemlocks. At 2.4 miles keep a close watch to your right for a pond, created by beavers within the rhododendron encircling the area. It's worth leaving the trail for a closer look. Upon returning, continue 0.6 miles to an old stand of hemlocks that tower above the trail. This entire area is covered with ground pine, and is beautiful in the spring and fall.

Just beyond, encounter the remnants of an old homestead, featuring an old barbed-wire fence to the right of the trail, with rusted metal tubs and mason jars scattered about. Please enjoy looking at these relics, but leave them in place. The trail now turns sharply left and climbs steeply for 0.2 miles through the hemlock forest, arriving

KATES PLATEAU TRAIL

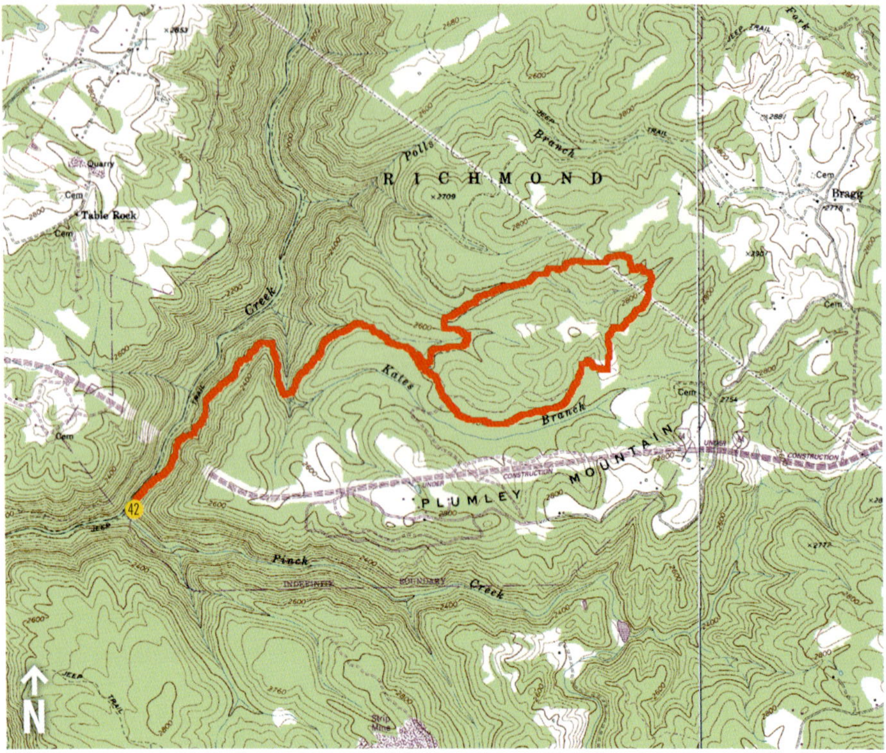

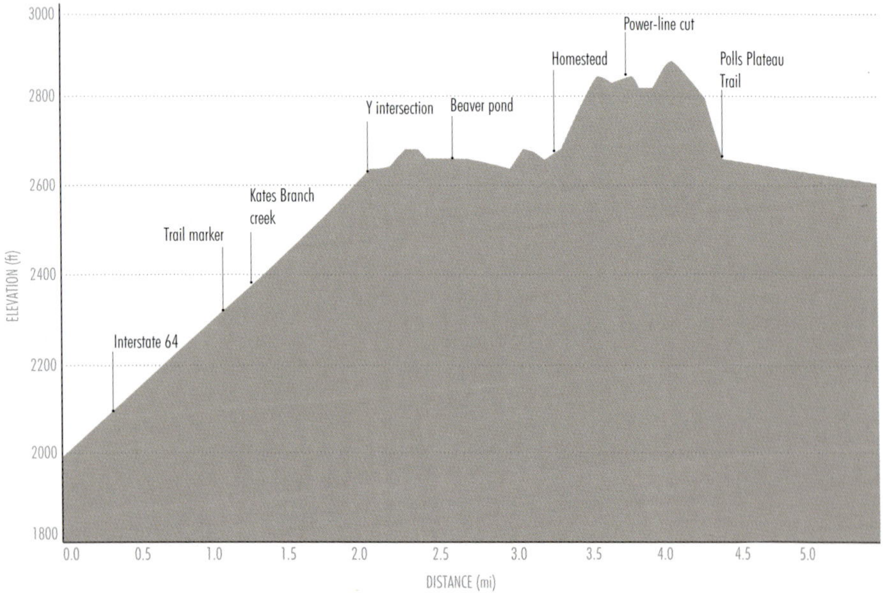

Beaver pond along Kates Plateau Trail.

at a ridgeline and then turning right. Not long after, the trail bursts into a power-line cut and turns sharply left on the far side. At 3.6 miles cross a stream and begin to see yellow "Private Property" signs posted beyond. Cross the power-line cut again at 3.8 miles, being watchful for deer and turkey. At 3.9 miles descend steeply and arrive at the intersection with the Polls Plateau Trail trailhead on the right. (If including Polls Plateau Trail in your hike, refer to Trail 41 for additional information.)

Stay straight at this intersection, crossing an open area sometimes used for camping, and cross a pretty stream. Continue 0.5 miles to an interesting area where the trail takes on a sunken feel as it tucks between two large berms. Emerge from the berms, descend slightly, and cross an open area with a multitude of small streams. Listen carefully, as many of these streams flow partially underground — you can hear them gurgling beneath your feet. After an additional 0.3 miles arrive at the Y intersection that marked the loop's beginning at 1.91 miles. To return to the trailhead, follow the description for Kates Plateau Return.

Trail intersection.

Trail Combinations/Options

The Kates Plateau Trail is an approach trail for those interested in hiking the Polls Plateau Trail (Trail 41), or can be combined with the Polls Plateau Trail and the associated trail returns for each trail. *Note: The "Returns" for both the Kates Plateau and Polls Plateau trails are essential for reaching each trail's original trailhead.* These are listed in order to provide accurate mileage for interested hikers. In other publications and NPS documents, this additional mileage is not listed, making for a much longer day than anticipated. Combining these trails creates a loop total mileage of 13.48 miles. It is also possible to combine this trail with Glade Creek Trail (Trail 43), as both trails share the same trailhead.

KATES PLATEAU RETURN TRAIL

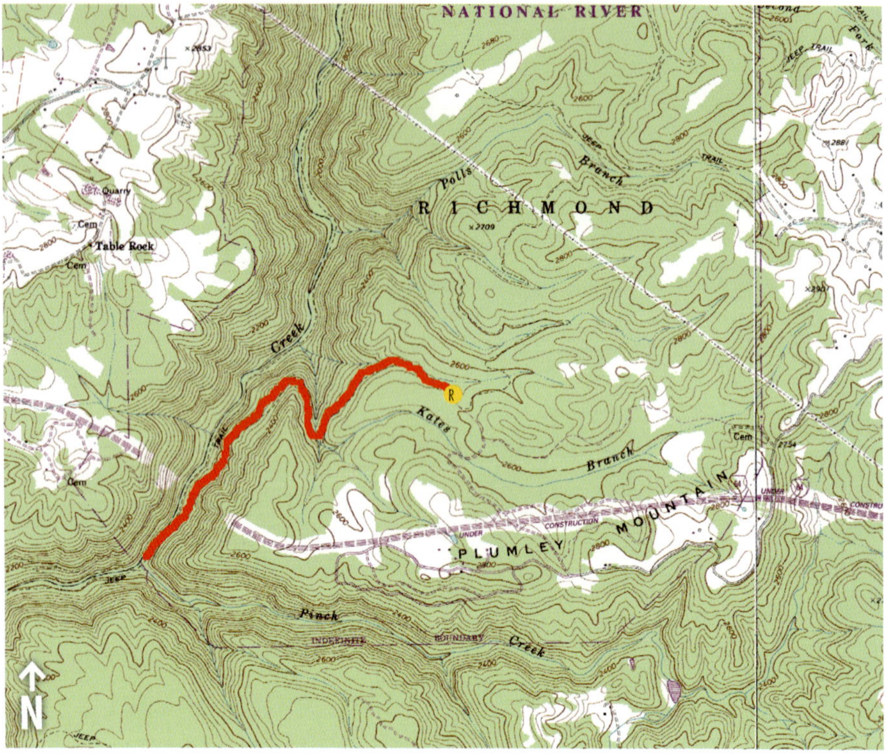

2 | 2 ft | 595 ft | 1.91 mi

Trail Milestones:

0.0 mi – Y intersection
(37°46.392 N, 081°01.282 W)
0.71 mi – Kates Branch creek
(37°46.266 N, 081°01.872 W)
0.91 mi – Trail marker
(37°46.436 N, 081°01.929 W)
1.61 mi – Interstate 64
(37°46.083 N, 081°02.357 W)
1.91 mi – Kates Plateau trailhead
(37°45.882 N, 081°02.570 W)

Trail Description

From the Y intersection of the Kates Plateau Trail begin a gradual descent to the trailhead. At 0.71 miles carefully cross Kates Branch creek and climb out of the creek bank, continuing along the well-delineated trail. At 0.91 miles pass a concrete trail marker lying on the ground; in winter, you can catch great views down the Glade Creek gorge here. Cross under Interstate 64 at 1.61 miles and arrive at the trailhead shortly thereafter.

Additional Notes

In past guides and NPS material, the return mileages for the Kates Plateau and Polls Plateau trails were not included in total trail distance. The Kates and Polls Plateau "Returns" correct this and give accurate mileage to complete each trail, with no surprises!

Small cascade along Kates Branch Creek.

KATES PLATEAU RETURN TRAIL

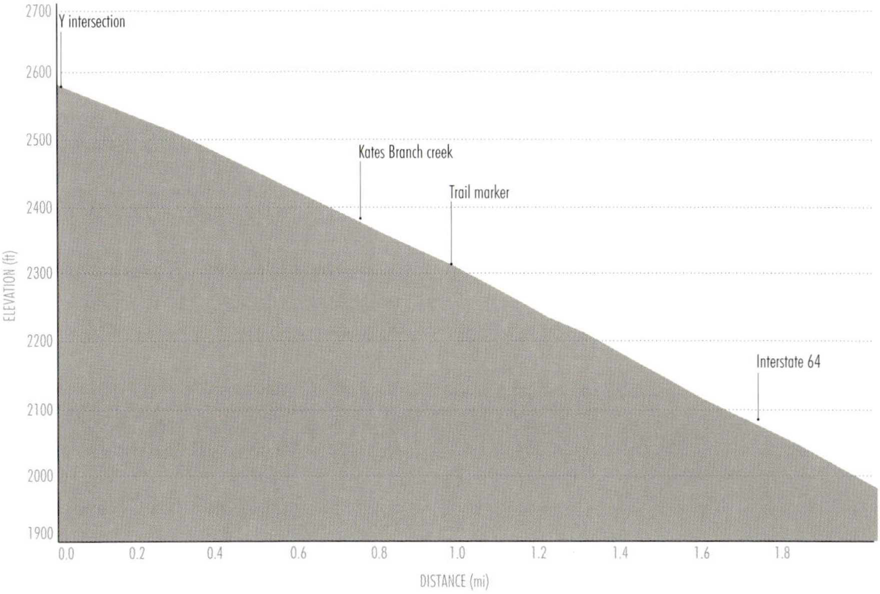

43 GLADE CREEK TRAIL

This beautiful creek-side trail, once home to a narrow gauge rail line, now lets hikers, bikers, kayakers, and fishermen access an abundant array of falls, pools, and islands tucked beneath rhododendron and hemlock groves. Towering ridgelines block the sun for lengthy parts of the day.

2 | 755 ft | 62 ft | 5.69 mi

Location: North of Interstate 64, east of Beckley, WV
Maps: USGS Prince quad 1:24,000 USGS Meadow Creek quad 1:24,000
Trail Options: Connect with Kates Falls Trail or link with Kates Plateau and Polls Plateau trails at the southern trailhead.
Facilities: Northern (Prince/Hamlet) trailhead: picnic facilities, ample gravel parking, toilets, boat ramp, primitive campground. Southern (Beaver) trailhead: limited gravel parking, trash bins.
Highlights: The town of Hamlet, Glade Creek Falls, numerous pools, rapids, and cascades, outstanding trout fishing.

Trail Milestones:

0.8 mi – Glade Creek Falls
(37°48.970 N, 081°00.486 W)
1.2 mi – Island
(37°48.732 N, 081°00.614 W)
3.0 mi – Bridge
(37°47.739 N, 081°01.711 W)
4.0 mi – Polls Branch stream
(37°46.956 N, 081°01.789 W)
4.3 mi – Falls/rapids
(37°46.775 N, 081°01.870 W)
4.6 mi – Kates Falls Trail
(37°46.549 N, 081°01.967 W)
5.3 mi – Landslide
(37°46.159 N, 081°02.344 W)
5.4 mi – Interstate 64
(37°46.083 N, 081°02.357 W)

Finding the Trailhead

Northern trailhead (Prince/Hamlet): (37°49.608 N, 081°00.619 W)
From US Route 19 take the Glen Jean exit. The exit leads immediately to a stop sign. Turn right here and travel on WV Route 16/61 for 2.8 miles. Turn left onto WV 61 and travel 4.4 miles to a Y intersection. Turn left onto WV Route 41 and travel 4.0 miles. Turn right onto the gravel Glade Creek Road (just before crossing the New River); follow this road 5.6 miles to the trailhead on the right.

Southern trailhead (Beaver): (37°45.882 N, 081°02.570 W)
Take exit 129 off Intersate 64 toward Shady Spring. Drive south along WV Route 9 (Grandview Road) for 0.5 miles, following signs for Little Beaver State Park. Turn left on County Route 22, Scott Branch Road. Continue to the trailhead. *Note: As of January 2013, access to this trailhead was closed due to construction on the road and bridge. Please check with NPS rangers regarding access.*

Trail Description

Note: Hike described from northern trailhead. At the northern trailhead, first take a moment to explore the former town of Hamlet. This town boomed along with the timber industry in the early 1900s, but is now nearly forgotten. Cross the bridge to the eastern side of Glade Creek and wander around the ruins. Follow unmarked trails toward the New River to see the concrete pillars that used to support a steel railroad bridge, dismantled in the 1940s and repurposed for the World War II war effort. This location is also the proposed future home of the Panther Branch Connector Trail, which will run across the bridge and continue three miles upstream along the New River.

Now head upstream and along the western side of Glade Creek, crossing a small stream at 0.3 miles before coming upon Glade Creek Falls at 0.8 miles. Although only 10 feet tall, these falls are a pretty sight, as they span the width of the stream. At this point it becomes necessary to climb up and over a set of stone steps. At 1.2 miles pass a stony island in the stream, and at 1.9 miles ascend over a small rise. Cross another small stream at 2.1 miles and take a moment to enjoy the small waterfall up and right of the trail.

Glade Creek Falls.

At 3.0 miles cross Glade Creek using a large wood-and-steel bridge. From this point continue upstream on the eastern side of Glade Creek. At 3.3 miles cross another small stream to the left, and at 4.0 miles cross over Polls Branch, a stream leading from Polls Plateau at the valley rim. Watch closely throughout this area for old crossties and rail beams once used to transport coal. Glade Creek narrows in this vicinity and creates interesting falls and rapids.

At 4.5 miles cross over Kates Branch creek and then intersect with Kates Falls Trail, on the left, after an additional 0.1 miles. Take a break here to climb to the falls then continue another 0.7 miles. Be careful in this area — a landslide has greatly narrowed the trail — but in the meantime don't overlook the forceful rapids to the right. At this point, listen also for the thunder as tractor-trailers roll across the bridge that serves Interstate 64 high above. Cross beneath the bridge and arrive at the southern trailhead, shared with Kates Plateau Trail, at 5.7 miles.

Glade Creek Trail.

GLADE CREEK TRAIL

Trail Combinations/Options

You can easily combine the Glade Creek Trail with the Kates Falls Trail (Trail 40) during your hike. Kates Falls Trail is a short, 0.11-mile trail located 4.6 miles from the northern trailhead or 1.09 miles from the southern trailhead. See Kates Falls Trail for more details.

Combine Glade Creek Trail with Kates Plateau Trail (Trail 42) and Polls Plateau Trail (Trail 41) for a true backcountry experience. Kates Plateau Trail connects to Glade Creek Trail at the southern trailhead and leads to a high mountain plateau. A combination of Glade Creek Trail (from the northern trailhead) plus Kates Plateau Trail/Return, and the retracing of Glade Creek Trail back to the northern trailhead, creates an 18.31-mile loop; adding in the Polls Plateau Trail/Return results in an even longer, 24.86-mile loop. You'll find multiple backcountry campsites throughout this region. Please see "Rules and Regulations for the New River Gorge National River" (page 22) and consult with NPS rangers for detailed information regarding backcountry camping.

Bridge at the 3.0-mile mark.

GLADE CREEK TRAIL

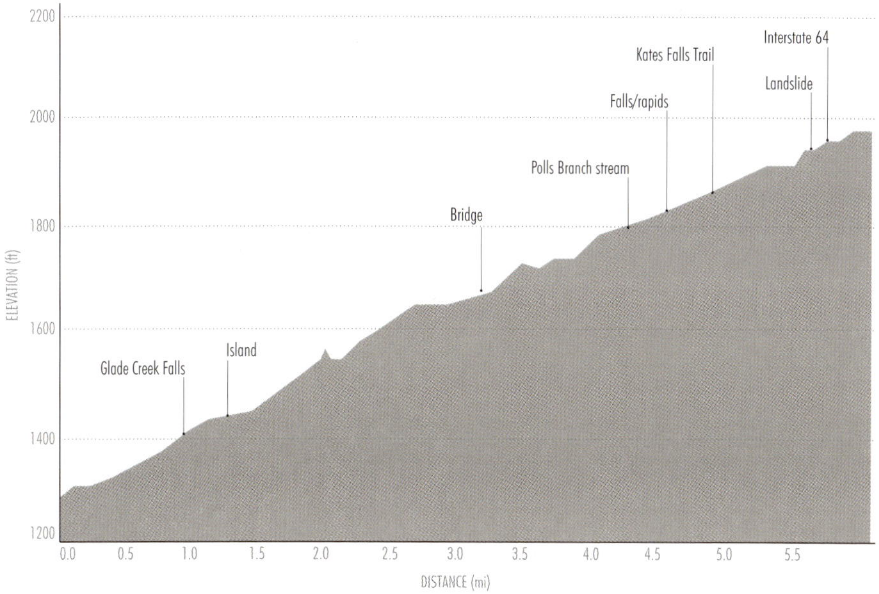

One of the many beautiful cascades
along Big Branch Creek.

11 BROOKS & SANDSTONE REGION

Overview and Highlights

The Brooks and Sandstone Region is not to be missed on a visit to the New River Gorge National River. The character of the river in this area is much different than in any other portion of the park. Here, the wide and relatively shallow river plays host to Brooks Falls and Sandstone Falls, allowing close-up views of each. Additionally, the Big Branch and Gwinn Ridge trails offer hikers the opportunity to explore areas less frequented by other visitors. The bald eagle nest at the northern end of Brooks Island is a draw for all visitors, but especially birdwatchers.

The Sandstone Visitor Center serves this portion of the New River and sits just off Interstate 64, exit 139. This center, built in 2003, is a model of green design, incorporating multiple facets of the LEED green-building system. It was built on the site of an old school, is warmed by geothermal heat, insulated with newspaper and cellulose, and uses storm-water runoff to water the native plants that surround the structure. I highly recommend a stop here prior to visiting the trails to learn more about the natural treasures of the New River Gorge National River.

How to Get There

The Brooks and Sandstone Region is located on the southern end of the park. The best access to the trails is via Interstate 64, exit 139. If visiting from Pipestem Resort or Bluestone state parks, you can also reach this region by traveling north along WV 20.

Rules and Regulations

Please see "Rules and Regulations for the New River Gorge National River" (page 22) for rules and regulations governing the area.

History and Culture

Hinton, perched above the New River, and the largest town in the Brooks and Sandstone Region, was founded in 1897. The entire downtown area is listed on the National Register of Historic Places and hosts many museums, shops, and eateries.

Parking area at Sandstone Falls.

BROOKS & SANDSTONE REGION HIKES

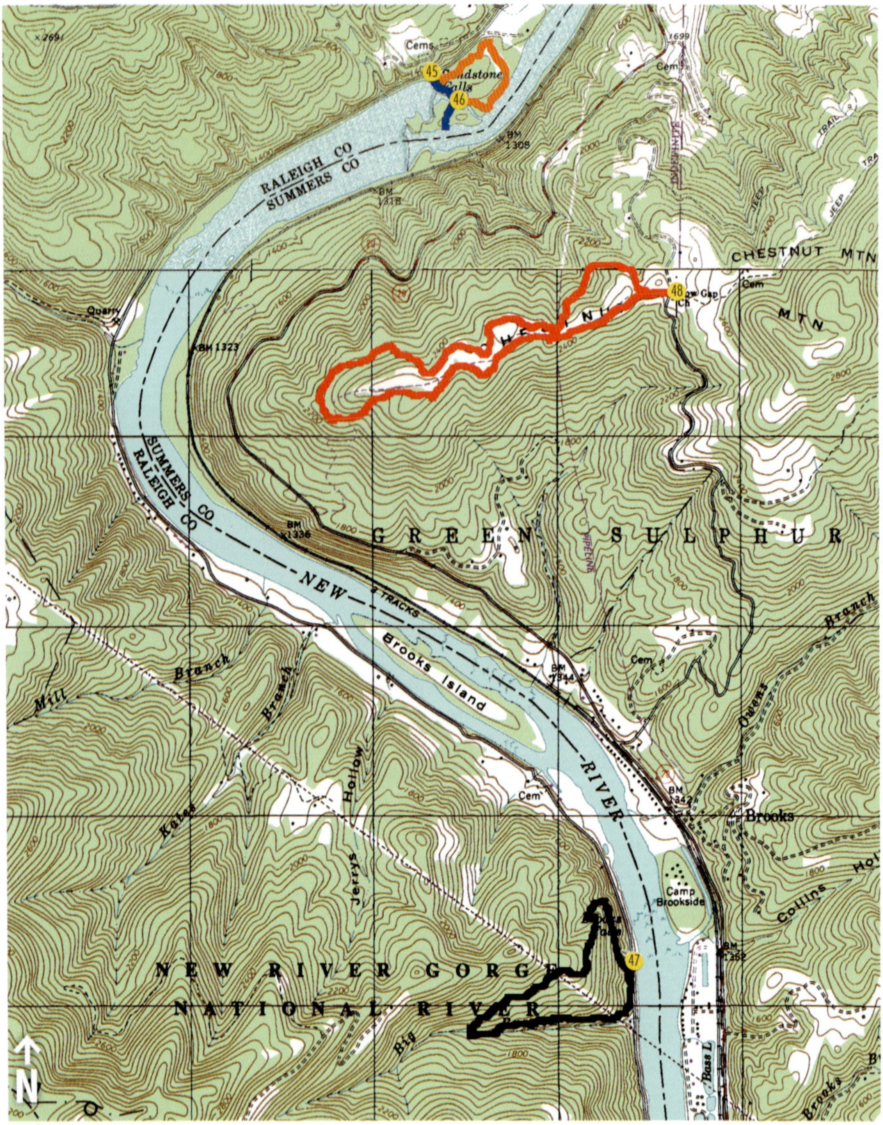

Map Key

Trail 45 – Sandstone Falls Boardwalk – blue

Trail 46 – Island Loop Trail – orange

Trail 47 – Big Branch Trail – black

Trail 48 – Gwinn Ridge Trail – red

44 SANDSTONE FALLS OVERLOOK TRAIL

A brief hike to an overlook with commanding views of the entirety of Sandstone Falls as well as farmland on the opposite side of the New River.

1 | 6 ft 139 ft | 0.07 mi

Location: South of Interstate 64, east of the New River in the Brooks and Sandstone Region of the New River Gorge National River
Maps: USGS Meadow Creek quad 1:24,000
Facilities: Parking for eight vehicles, toilets, and picnic area.
Highlights: Easily accessible, with nice views of Sandstone Falls.

Trail Milestones:

0.07 mi – Overlook (37°45.148 N, 080°54.236 W)

Finding the Trailhead

(37°45.172 N, 080°54.246 W)
To reach Sandstone Falls Overlook, take exit 139 from Interstate 64. Follow WV 20 south toward Hinton for 3.0 miles. Trailhead is on the right, just past a curve on WV 20.

Trail Description

A short and easy trail leads from the parking area just off the road. You can see the overlook from parking area. Trail is wide and consists of small gravel.

Additional Notes

Bald eagles! After visiting the Sandstone Falls Overlook Trail, continue south along WV 20 another 1.5 miles until you reach Brooks Overlook. This small overlook affords views of Brooks Island. Over the last few years, bald eagles have nested in a large white sycamore tree on the northern edge of the island. If you come at the right time and with good binoculars, you will be treated with views of our national bird in its natural habitat.

Serene view from Brooks Overlook.

45 SANDSTONE FALLS BOARDWALK

A wooden boardwalk leading to the beautiful Sandstone Falls, the largest waterfall on the New River.

1 | 6 ft 20 ft | 0.24 mi

Location: South of Interstate 64, west bank of New River, north of Hinton, WV
Maps: USGS Meadow Creek quad 1:24,000
Trail Options: Combine with the Island Loop Trail for a comprehensive look at the riverside ecosystem.
Facilities: Large gravel parking area, beautiful picnic tables along the water, toilets, multiple benches along boardwalk.
Highlights: This boardwalk allows access to multiple viewpoints of the majestic Sandstone Falls — almost 1,500 feet wide, with heights ranging from 10–25 feet. In addition, this hike allows visitors to experience the riverside flat-rock ecosystem, rarely found in West Virginia. You'll see multiple pools and smaller falls on the journey to the main viewpoints, while multiple smaller paths lead from the well-maintained and easily accessible boardwalk. If you venture from established trails, please use caution around the water's edge.

Trail Milestones:

0.05 mi – Intersection with Island Loop trailhead
(37°45.528 N, 080°54.286 W)
0.1 mi – Intersection with second Island Loop trailhead
(37°45.493 N, 080°54.227 W)
0.2 mi – Trail's end at viewpoint
(37°45.410 N, 080°54.272 W)

Finding the Trailhead

(37°45.550 N, 080°54.310 W)
To reach the Sandstone Falls parking area, take exit 139 off Interstate 64 and continue south along State Route 20 to the town of Hinton (14.1 miles). Pass through Hinton and turn right, staying on State Route 20 and crossing a low bridge over the New River. At the end of the bridge, turn right on State Route 26/River Road and continue 8.2 miles. The trailhead is located in the middle of the parking lot.

Trail Description

The boardwalk begins at the midpoint of the Sandstone Falls parking area. At this trailhead you'll find numerous information boards discussing the falls and the area's ecosystem. Pass the first trailhead for Island Loop Trail (Trail 46) to the left at 0.05 miles. Continue along the boardwalk, passing sparkling pools and trickling falls to the right. At 0.15 miles pass the second trailhead to Island Loop Trail and reach a large bridge crossing a flat, stone-bottom channel of the New River. Linger here and you will be rewarded with sightings of smallmouth bass and other fish of the New. A short walk takes you to the main viewpoint of Sandstone Falls. Trails lead from the main boardwalk to smaller cascades, streams, large boulders, and pools of the New River. Some of these lead to closer views of the main falls. Please use caution along these areas, as drownings have unfortunately occurred in seemingly shallow and slow-moving areas of the New. Return to the trailhead using the boardwalk, or turn right after the large bridge and enjoy a closer view of the island ecosystem via the Island Loop Trail.

Trail Combinations/Options

Include the Island Loop Trail (Trail 46) on the trip out or back and see more of the island. This combination creates a nearly 1.0-mile round-trip hike.

46 ISLAND LOOP TRAIL

A short trail that loops around an island below Sandstone Falls.

1 | 34 ft 25 ft | 0.62 mi

Location: South of Interstate 64, west bank of New River, north of Hinton, WV
Maps: USGS Meadow Creek quad 1:24,000
Trail Options: Combine with Sandstone Falls Boardwalk for a comprehensive round-trip hike of almost one mile.
Facilities: Large gravel parking area, beautiful picnic tables along the water, toilets.
Highlights: An interesting walk around an island that takes in views of woodlands and up-close views of the New River.

Trail Milestones:

0.2 mi – Trail intersection (37°45.653 N, 080°54.105 W)
0.4 mi – Water's edge (37°45.465 N, 080°54.113 W)
0.62 mi –Second trailhead (37°45.493 N, 080°54.227 W)

Finding the Trailhead

(37°45.528 N, 080°54.286 W)
To reach the Sandstone Falls parking area, take exit 139 off Interstate 64 and continue south along State Route 20 to the town of Hinton (14.1 miles). Pass through Hinton and turn right, staying on State Route 20 and crossing a low bridge over the New River. At the end of the bridge, turn right on State Route 26/River Road and continue 8.2 miles to the Sandstone Falls Boardwalk parking area.

The nearer trailhead is located 0.05 miles along the Sandstone Falls Boardwalk. Alternatively, hike the trail in reverse from the farther trailhead, 0.15 miles along the boardwalk.

Trail Description

Note: Hike described from the nearer trailhead, 0.05 miles along the Sandstone Falls Boardwalk. Island Loop Trail is a short path that runs through a young forest at the river's edge. At 0.2 miles, keep right, staying on the main trail as it intersects an unnamed path that leads to the parking lot (to left). Continue along easy but uneven and sometimes rocky terrain until at 0.5 miles you reach the slowly flowing New River. At this point, you can hear the falls off to the south. At 0.62 miles intersect the Sandstone Falls Boardwalk (Trail 45) and continue to the amazing viewpoints below the falls.

Trail Combinations/Options

You can easily combine the Island Loop Trail with the Sandstone Falls Boardwalk (Trail 45) to create a slightly longer loop.

Sandstone Falls, the largest waterfall along the New River.

ISLAND LOOP TRAIL

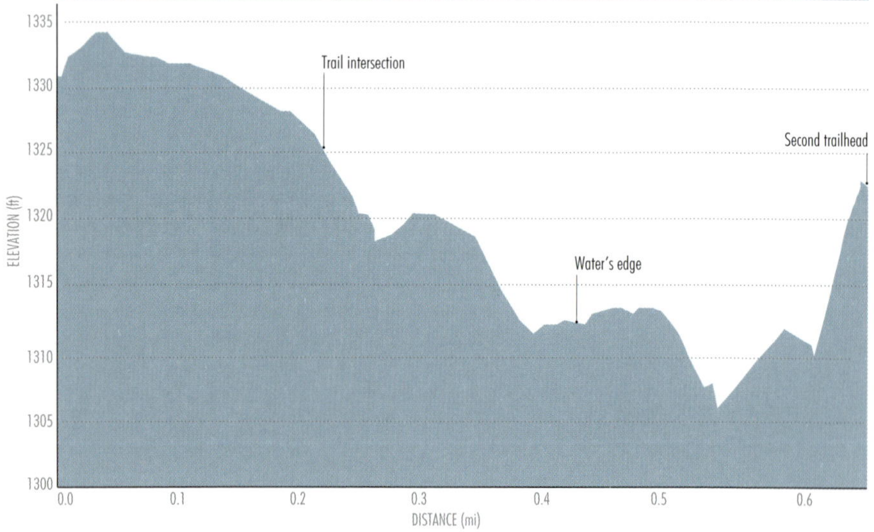

47 BIG BRANCH TRAIL

A strenuous trail that runs along a beautiful mountain stream, with a surprise bit of history hidden nearby.

4 | 571 ft | 571 ft | 1.97 mi

Location: South of Interstate 64, near Hinton, WV
Maps: USGS Hinton quad 1:24,000
Facilities: The Brooks Falls parking lot offers parking for approximately 15 vehicles, with multiple picnic tables, grills, and a porta-potty. This parking area is right beside the New River and offers outstanding places for a picnic.
Highlights: This hike offers close-up views of a mountain stream, with numerous waterfalls along the way. Near the top of the incline, you'll see remnants of a 1930s homestead. Keep your eyes peeled for a tree growing through an old washbasin. Seasonal wildflowers are an additional highlight.

Trail Milestones:

0.6 mi – Wooden bridge over Big Branch Creek
(37°42.857 N, 080°53.967 W)
0.7 mi – 30-foot waterfall
(37°42.837 N, 080°54.085 W)
0.8 mi – 1930s homestead
(37°42.822 N, 080°54.178 W)

Finding the Trailhead

(37°43.022 N, 080°53.592 W)
From Interstate 64, take exit 139. Travel 14.1 miles down WV 20 south and enter Hinton, WV. Cross the bridge at the end of town and turn right on WV 26. The trailhead is located across the road from the southern end of the Brooks Falls parking lot.

Trail Description

Starting at the southern end of the Brooks Falls parking lot, cross WV 26 and move into the forest. This trail, once a wagon road to the farm and gristmill above, is now a rough and rocky path. The first 0.2 miles follow alongside the road, crossing numerous seasonal drainages until bearing right, crossing, and then paralleling Big Branch Creek. At 0.4 miles cross the stream just below a small four-foot waterfall that flows over moss-covered boulders and fallen logs. At 0.6 miles re-cross the stream. You'll see a moss-covered and partially rotten bridge at this point, which can be bypassed by using well-placed stones within the streambed. Just beyond, at 0.7 miles, reach a thirty-foot waterfall that, while always a treat, becomes gorgeous after a spring rain. Above and to the left of the trail you might note the remains of an old homestead; the first indication is a moss-covered rock wall that parallels Big Branch Creek. If you venture just beyond the wall you can see portions of a foundation, and if you're lucky you'll spot the "washbasin tree." As you walk among the ruins, envision this area as the farm it was in the early 1900s, with a vegetable garden planted beside the house and farm animals grazing on the hillside above. Please do not disturb any artifacts in this area. At 1.0 miles reach the high

The washbasin tree.

point of this hike and begin winding down to the New River along a wide path. Throughout the year you can hear the roar of Brooks Falls, and in the late fall and winter you can catch glimpses of the river along the descent. At 1.6 miles the path turns sharply right near a stream. Do not cross the stream, but parallel it down, around a spur, and back to the starting point for this trail.

BIG BRANCH TRAIL

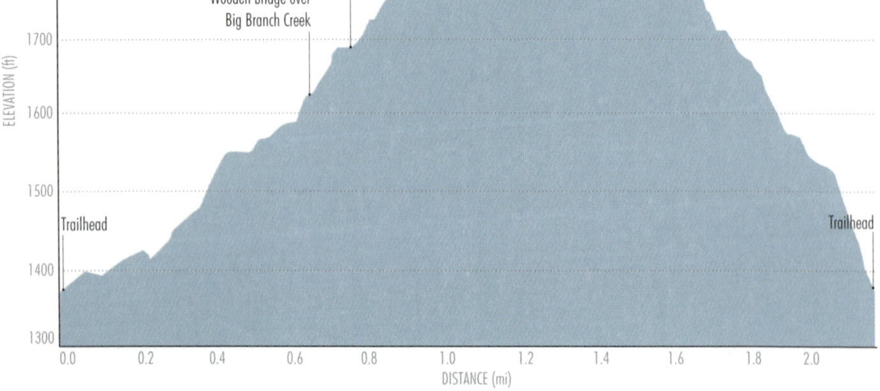

48 GWINN RIDGE TRAIL

A moderate hike that begins in a hill meadow and continues into a rocky, older forest.

3 643 ft 522 ft 3.16 mi

Location: South of Interstate 64 in the Brooks and Sandstone Region of the New River Gorge National River

Maps: USGS Meadow Creek and Hinton quad 1:24,000

Trail Options: By using a bypass trail, it is possible to shorten this hike to 1.0 miles or 2.9 miles.

Facilities: Gravel parking for six vehicles, picnic table, and grill.

Highlights: A lesser-traveled trail that meanders high above the New River, offering great opportunities to see wildlife, wildflowers, and an older forest.

Trail Milestones:

0.4 mi – Power-line cut (37°44.811 N, 080°53.870 W)

1.7 mi – Boulder field (37°44.735 N, 080°54.600 W)

1.8 mi – Begin ascent (37°44.781 N, 080°54.473 W)

2.5 mi – Power-line cut (37°44.811 N, 080°53.870 W)

Finding the Trailhead

(37°44.934 N, 080°53.445 W)

Exit 139 from Interstate 64. Follow WV 20 south toward Hinton for 5.8 miles. Turn left onto Brooks Mountain Road, a well-maintained gravel road. At 1.5 miles reach an intersection and keep left toward "Three Rivers Avian Center." Continue along road for 1.0 miles and arrive at a gravel parking lot on left.

Trail Description

From the trailhead, begin along a flat, gentle path in an old hill meadow that is slowly being reclaimed by young saplings. At 0.4 miles cross a power-line cut and see views north toward Interstate 64. Reenter the forest by walking around a large downed tree. At the time of publication, this trail was marked periodically with blue ribbon, though the trail is well defined throughout. At 1.0 miles the trail intersects an old logging road. A brown trail sign marks the correct direction (right). After 0.1 miles, the trail begins to descend to the south side of the ridgeline (left). Reach the bottom of this well-graded decline at 1.4 miles and follow a series of three wooden markers as the trail winds through the forest. At this point the trail begins to return toward the trailhead. At 1.7 miles move through an area of moss-covered boulders that looks like an alluvial fan, to the right of the trail. The track begins a slow ascent at 1.8 miles and levels out shortly thereafter on the ridgeline. Continue along a relatively flat portion for the next 0.6 miles until intersecting the power-line cut and downed tree once again. Continue straight across the cut and descend into forest, winding around the northern side of the ridge until finally ascending back to the trailhead.

A leaf-covered Gwinn Ridge Trail during an Indian summer day.

GWINN RIDGE TRAIL

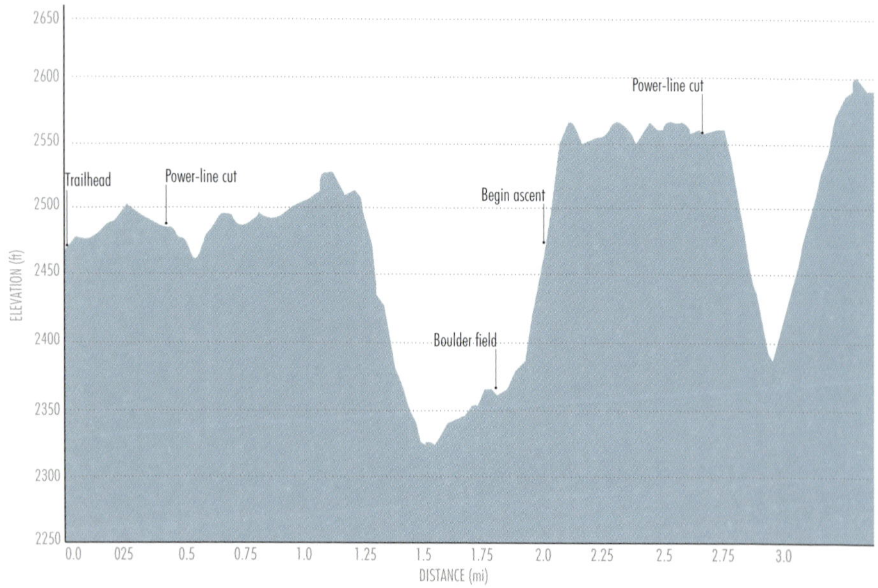

GWINN RIDGE TRAIL

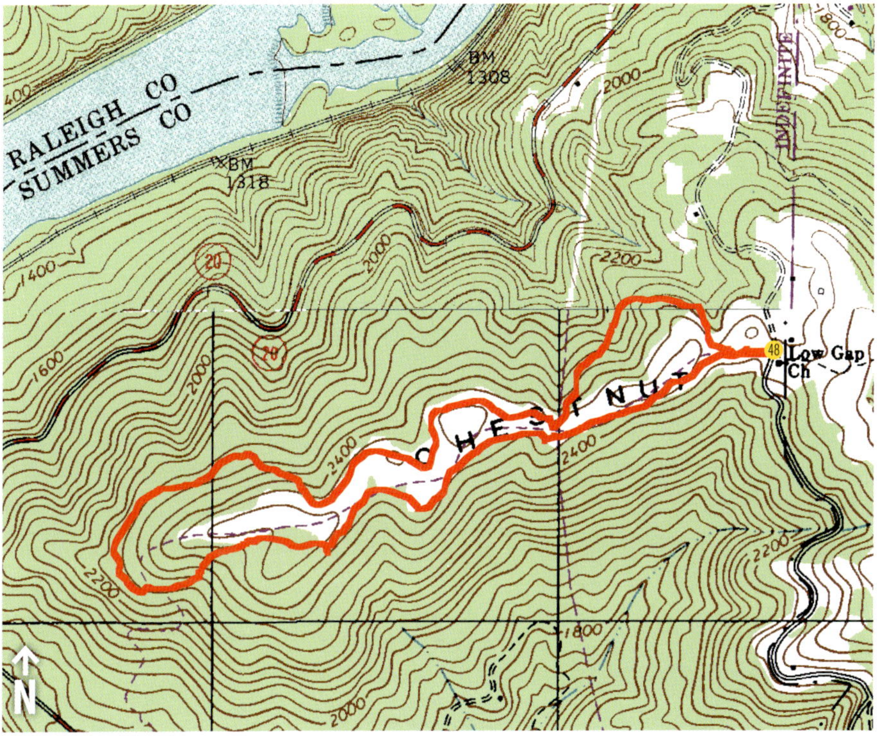

Trail Combinations/Options

Two options shorten this hike. The first allows you to bypass the last 0.6 miles of trail: At 2.5 miles, upon re-entering the power-line cut, turn right along a short connector trail and regain the original trail. Turn left and follow this trail 0.4 miles along flat terrain to return to the trailhead. This option bypasses the descent and ascent required for the normal trail, and shortens the hike to 2.9 miles total. The second option is to turn right at the power-line cut (0.4 miles) and connect to the end of the trail just below, again turning right for the final 0.6 miles. This option results in a 1.0-mile total hiking distance.

Looking toward Gwinn Ridge.

Part 2:

Hiking in Nearby West Virginia State Parks

An autumn morning along Glade Creek, Babcock State Park.

Summersville Lake from Long Point overlook.

12 SUMMERSVILLE LAKE WILDLIFE MANAGEMENT AREA

Overview and Highlights

Summersville Lake Wildlife Management Area is managed by the US Army Corps of Engineers (Huntington District) and the West Virginia Division of Natural Resources (WVDNR).

In addition to hiking and mountain biking trails, Summersville offers a wide range of outdoor options including climbing, boating, swimming, and scuba diving. In fact, Summersville Lake boasts the clearest and cleanest waters east of the Mississippi and has been described in diving magazines as the "Little Bahamas of the East."

How to Get There

You can easily access the Summersville Lake Wildlife Management Area trails from US Route 19. Long Point Trail, Salmon Run Trail, and Salmon Run Spur Trail are located off "Summersville Lake Airport Road," while Battle Run Trail is located near the Battle Run Campground just off WV Route 129.

Rules and Regulations

Rules and regulations here are different from other state parks listed in this section of the guide, due to the difference in management responsibilities by the US Army Corps of Engineers and the WVDNR. The following rules and regulations are by no means comprehensive, and all users are responsible for identifying and following all posted regulations:

- A cliff-jumping ban is strictly enforced at Summersville Lake. This ban includes jumping from heights above six feet and deep-water soloing. The fine, if caught, is said to be $5,000.
- Hunting and fishing are allowed during appropriate seasons. Trail users should be aware of the hunting seasons, generally September through March (see wvdnr.gov/Hunting/Regs1213/Season_dates.pdf for specific dates). It is also recommended that hikers and mountain bikers wear blaze-orange clothing and remain aware of their environment during these times. (The following link, again from the WVDNR, provides more hunting information: wvdnr.gov/Hunting/hunting_regs.shtm)
- The Battle Run Campground has its own regulations. Please ask campground employees for information.

History and Culture

The Summersville Dam was built between 1960 and 1966 in order to assist with flood control for the area, and President Lyndon B. Johnson dedicated it upon its completion. This structure is the second largest rock-filled dam in the eastern United States, while the massive lake covers over 2,700 acres and has a shoreline that runs for 60 miles.

Naming of the Summersville Dam provided a quandary for the US Army Corps of Engineers. Traditionally, every dam the corps built was named for the town closest to the construction; in the case of Summersville Dam, the closest town was a burg named Gad. Breaking tradition, and at the request of locals, the US Army Corps of Engineers decided that Summersville Dam was more appropriate than Gad Dam.

Summersville Lake Wildlife Management Area now provides recreation opportunities for thousands of visitors every year, from hikers, climbers, and rafters, to hunters, boaters, and fishermen.A number of historically significant buildings remain at this site, and each is worth a visit. Stop by the visitor center for more information.

SUMMERSVILLE LAKE WILDLIFE MANAGEMENT AREA HIKES

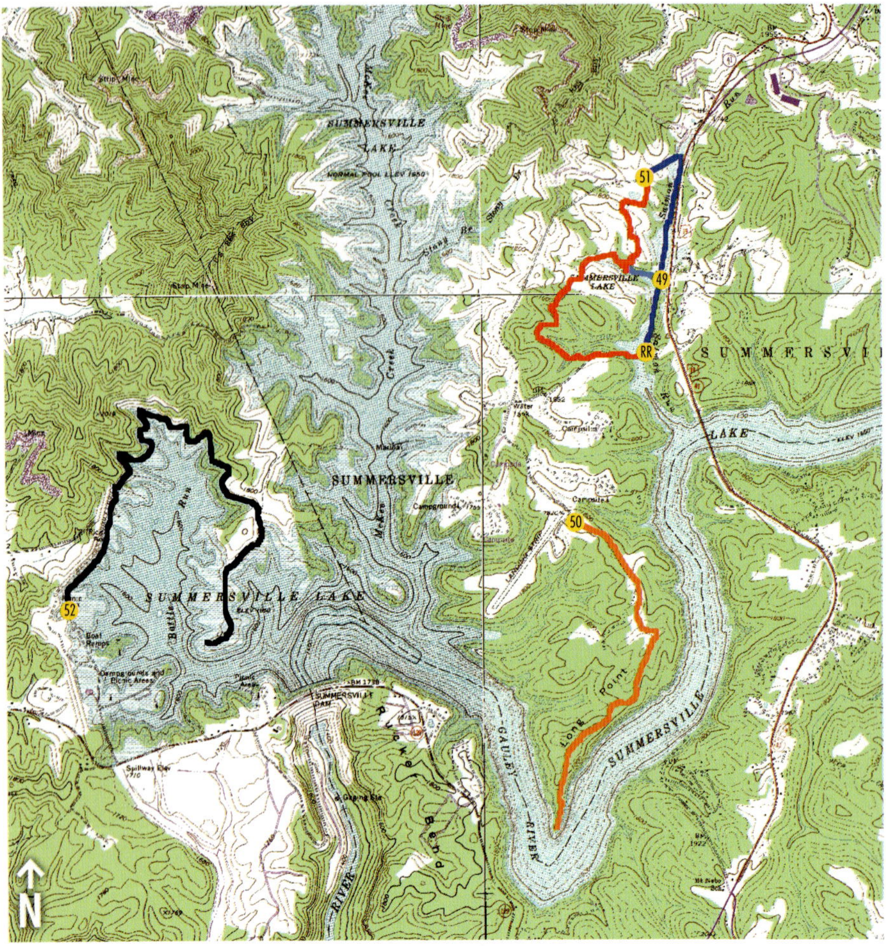

Map Key

Trail 49 – Salmon Run Spur Trail – light blue

Trail 50 – Long Point Trail – orange

Trail 51 – Salmon Run Trail – red

Trail 51 Road Return – dark blue

Trail 52 – Battle Run Trail – black

49 SALMON RUN SPUR TRAIL

This short spur trail allows easy access to and parking for the Salmon Run Trail, allowing you to create shorter loop hikes.

1 31 ft 4 ft 0.19 mi

Location: Just south of Summersville, WV; easily accessed from US Route 19
Maps: USGS Mount Nebo quad 1:24,000, USGS Summersville quad 1:24,000
Trail Options: Connects with Salmon Run Trail.
Facilities: Gravel parking for 15–20 vehicles, picnic area.
Highlights: A short trail that crosses Salmon Run and links to the longer Salmon Run Trail, allowing for shorter loop hikes when using road returns.

Trail Milestones:

0.19 mi – Intersection with Salmon Run Trail (38°15.109 N, 080°51.698 W)

Finding the Trailhead

(38°15.060 N, 080°51.520 W)
From Fayetteville, travel 21.6 miles north on US Route 19. Turn left on "Summersville Lake Airport Road" (see Additional Notes) and then immediately turn left again onto a paved road. Follow this straight road for 0.6 miles and park at a gravel lot on the left across from the footbridge (Hypes Bridge).

Trail Description

There is no sign at this trailhead. Cross the paved road to Hypes Bridge, a wooden footbridge crossing Salmon Run, and then continue along a wide and well-used trail into the forest. Intersect with Salmon Run Trail at 0.19 miles.

Trail Combinations/Options

The Salmon Run Spur Trail connects with the Salmon Run Trail (Trail 51) after 0.19 miles. The right fork of the Salmon Run Trail leads to the upper trailhead after 0.8 miles; there, you can return via the trail or road. The road-return distance from this point is also 0.8 miles and creates a 1.6-mile loop. The left fork of the Salmon Run Trail leads through the forest for 1.36 miles to the lower trailhead, near the lake. Return by backtracking along the same trail or along the paved road for 0.4 miles. Returning via the road creates a 1.95-mile loop.

Additional Notes

The Salmon Run Trail and Salmon Run Spur Trail were developed in cooperation with Glade Creek Boy Scout Troop 220. This area is extremely popular with locals throughout the year both for its easy access and gentle grades.

"Summersville Lake Airport Road" is the descriptor used on the WV Department of Transportation signs leading from US Route 19. Other less common names for this road include Long Point Access Road and CO Route 19/32.

50 LONG POINT TRAIL

A moderate trail through mature forest leading to an outstanding view of Summersville Lake from atop a tall rock cliff.

3 | 202 ft | 371 ft | 1.96 mi

Location: Just south of Summersville, WV; easily accessed from US Route 19
Maps: USGS Mount Nebo quad 1:24,000, USGS Summersville quad 1:24,000
Facilities: Roadside parking for four vehicles.
Highlights: This moderate trail leads through forest, with opportunities to see turkey and deer before heading through a rhododendron grove and ending at a tall cliff with a scenic view of Summersville Lake.

Trail Milestones:

0.7 mi – Sharp right turn
(38°13.585 N, 080°51.546 W)
0.8 mi – Stay right
(38°13.500 N, 080°51.602 W)
1.96 mi – Viewpoint/trail's end
(38°12.767 N, 080°52.096 W)

Additional Notes

"Summersville Lake Airport Road" is the descriptor used on the WV Department of Transportation signs leading from US Route 19. Other less common names for this road include Long Point Access Road and CO Route 19/32.

While the trail markers along this trail are helpful, the posted mileage is often incorrect.

Finding the Trailhead

(38°14.054 N, 080°51.988 W)
From Fayetteville, travel 21.6 miles north on US Route 19. Turn left on "Summersville Lake Airport Road" (see Additional Notes) and travel 2.4 miles. This road will pass the Mountain Lake Campground and Summersville Airport (on right). The trailhead is marked with a sign, as the road turns right. Stay straight and park along the roadside. Do not block the gate.

Trail Description

After parking (and not blocking the gate!), continue around the red-and-white gate down a gravel road, passing RV parking for Mountain Lake Campground on your left. This portion of trail is relatively flat and wide, following an old access road. At 0.1 miles pass a blue gate with a trail sign on the left, and after another 0.1 miles pass a second blue gate. At 0.4 miles rise gradually through the forest, and at 0.7 miles pass through an open field. Plastic hiking signs mark the way, with a sharp right turn at the end of the field. Reenter the mostly deciduous forest and at 0.8 miles the trail splits — stay to the right here. As of January 2013, a tree partially blocked the path to the right.

At 1.1 miles begin to see Summersville Lake off to the left through the trees. Descend slightly to the right and through a group of boulders and Eastern hemlocks before regaining the ridgeline. At 1.7 miles encounter a thick grove of rhododendron trees that gradually gives way to a mix of rhododendron and Virginia pines as you near the cliff edge. Fifteen meters before the trail's end, watch for a foot-wide crevice to the right that drops deeply and is often missed (careful here!). Continue to the cliff edge for fantastic views of the lake below. Again, please take care in this area, especially during rain as the rocks can get slippery and there are no guardrails along the cliff line.

Long Point Trail amongst hardwoods.

LONG POINT TRAIL

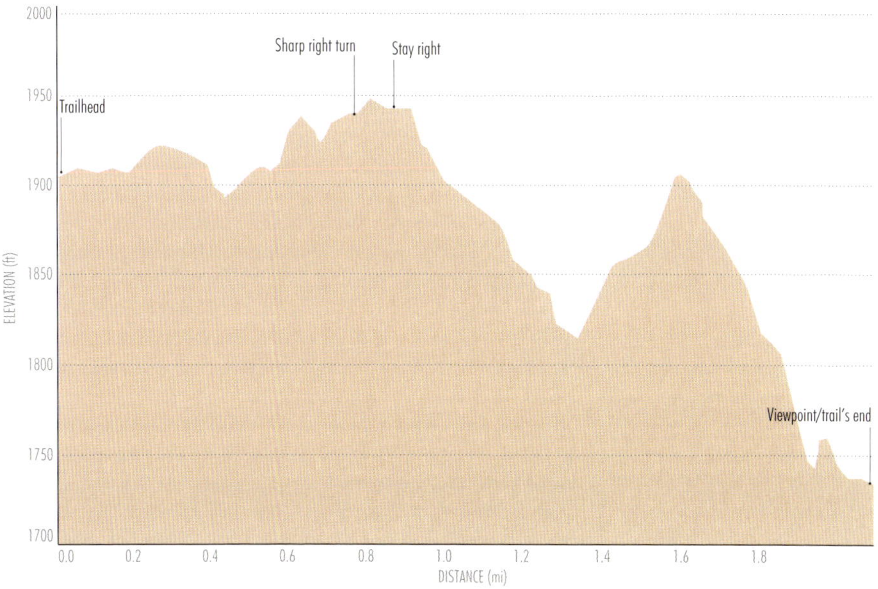

51 SALMON RUN TRAIL

A popular and well-maintained trail that ventures through fields and forests, to end at Summersville Lake.

3 | 307 ft 385 ft | 2.15 mi

Location: Just south of Summersville, WV; easily accessed from US Route 19
Maps: USGS Mount Nebo quad 1:24,000, USGS Summersville quad 1:24,000
Trail Options: Connect with Salmon Run Spur Trail to create shorter loops, or use the road return for a longer (3.38-mile) loop.
Facilities: Upper trailhead: gravel parking for three vehicles. Lower trailhead: ample paved parking, picnic facilities, toilets, benches, boat launch.
Highlights: A well-maintained trail through fields and forest that passes an old cemetery and old homesteads, to end at Summersville Lake.

Trail Milestones:

1.0 mi – Upper trailhead (38°15.474 N, 080°51.615 W)
0.8 mi – Intersection with Salmon Run Spur Trail (38°15.109 N, 080°51.698 W)
0.9 mi – Rock wall/bridge (38°15.162 N, 080°51.698 W)
1.1 mi – Old farm (38°15.104 N, 080°51.941 W)
1.2 mi – Stream/intersection (38°15.030 N, 080°52.015 W)
1.9 mi – Paved road (38°14.742 N, 080°51.892 W)
2.16 mi – Lower trailhead (38°14.742 N, 080°51.612 W)

Finding the Trailhead

Upper trailhead: (38°15.474 N, 080°51.615 W)
From Fayetteville, travel 21.6 miles north on US Route 19. Turn left on "Summersville Lake Airport Road" (see Additional Notes) and travel 0.23 miles. You'll see a small gravel turnoff on the left, with a trailhead sign just over the bank marking the upper trailhead.

Lower trailhead: (38°14.742 N, 080°51.612 W)
To reach the lower trailhead, turn left onto "Summersville Lake Airport Road" and immediately turn left onto the paved road. Drive 1.0 miles to large paved parking area with a boat launch; the trailhead is near the water on the right side of the lot.

Trail Description

Note: Description begins at upper trailhead. From the roadside, drop down into a field slowly being reclaimed by the surrounding forest and pass the trailhead sign. After 50 meters cross a stream and encounter a hill meadow. Stay left of the field and look carefully for an old cemetery hidden in the woods off to the right. At 0.3 miles reach another larger field, this time skirting to the right side before turning sharply left at the end of the open area and reentering the forest. Look for deer in this area in the evenings, as they come to feed on meadow grass.

Slowly descend, and at 0.8 miles intersect the Salmon Run Spur Trail and turn sharply right. Stay right and parallel a small stream before crossing it via a wooden bridge at 0.9 miles; watch for a moss-covered rock wall to the left. Ascend for the next 0.3 miles and look for evidence of an old farm on the right-hand side. At 1.2 miles easily cross an intermittent stream — the path branches both right and left just beyond this stream. Stay right to travel up and over a small rise, or skirt left to avoid this area; the two paths eventually reconnect on the opposite side of the high ground. (The trail to the right, while ascending slightly, is better maintained.) Continue along the trail, crossing an intermittent stream at 1.3 miles and another at 1.8 miles. Continue another 0.1 miles to reach a paved road. Turn left along this abandoned road and continue past the lake to the lower trailhead, at 2.16 miles.

The rock wall, with wooden bridge in the distance.

SALMON RUN TRAIL

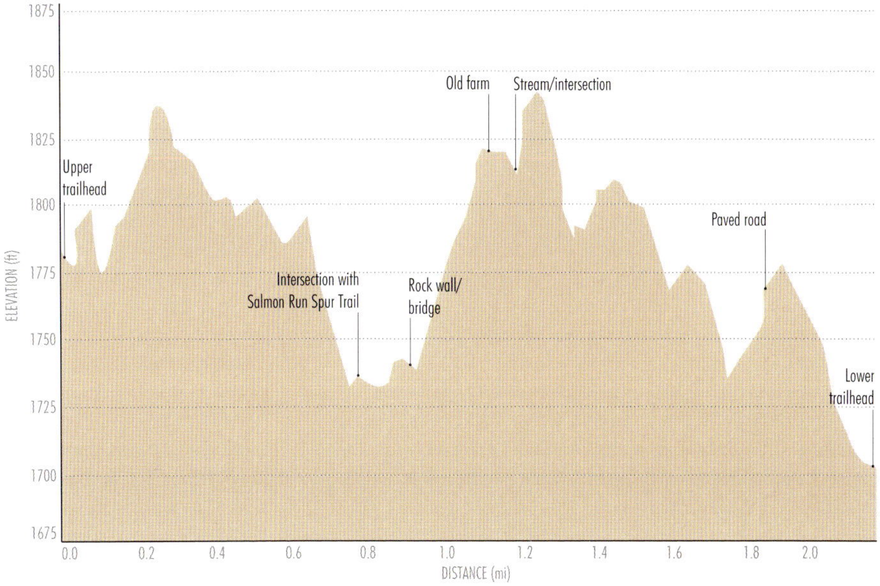

SALMON RUN TRAIL AND ROAD RETURN

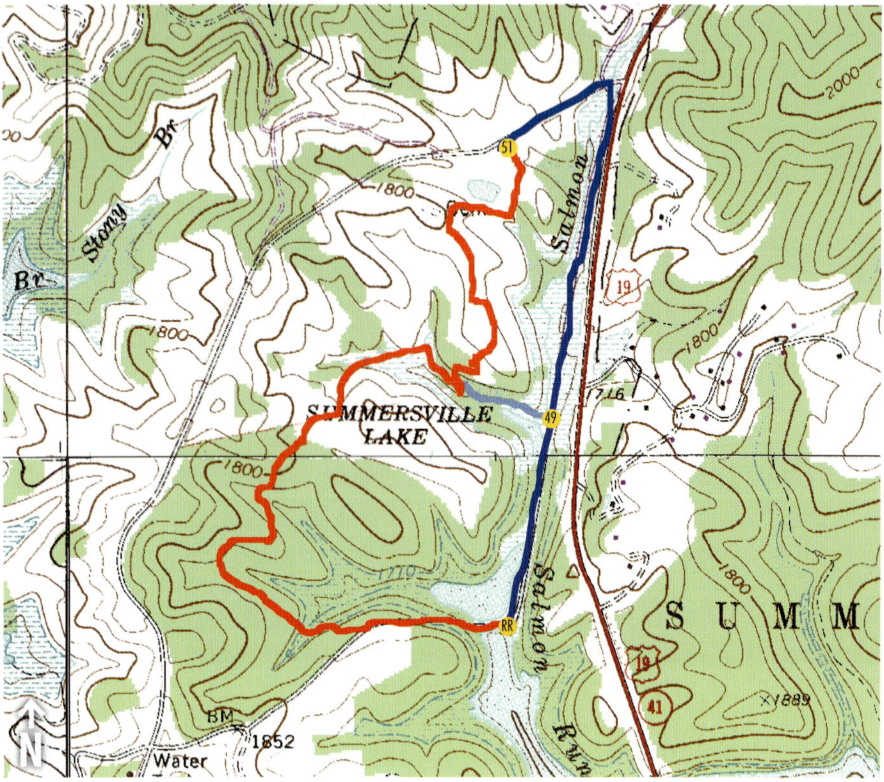

Trail Combinations/Options

Combining the Salmon Run Road Return, described on the facing page, with the Salmon Run Trail creates an enjoyable 3.38-mile loop. For a shorter loop, use the Salmon Run Spur Trail (Trail 49).

From the upper trailhead, the Salmon Run Trail connects with the Salmon Run Spur Trail after 0.8 miles. Rather than continuing along the Salmon Run Trail, turn left onto the spur and reach the road after 0.19 miles. Turn left and follow the paved road 0.6 miles before turning left again at the intersection with "Summersville Lake Airport Road." Travel 0.23 miles to the trailhead for a total loop of 1.82 miles.

From the lower trailhead, the Salmon Run Trail connects with the Salmon Run Spur Trail at 1.36 miles. Stay right at the intersection and travel 0.19 miles to the road. Turn right and travel 0.4 miles along the paved road to the lower-trailhead parking. This option results in a 1.95-mile loop.

Additional Notes

The Salmon Run Trail and Salmon Run Spur Trail were developed in cooperation with Glade Creek Boy Scout Troop 220. This area is extremely popular with locals throughout the year both for its easy access and gentle grades.

"Summersville Lake Airport Road" is the descriptor used on the WV Department of Transportation signs leading from US Route 19. Other less common names for this road include Long Point Access Road and CO Route 19/32.

SALMON RUN ROAD RETURN

2

121 ft 21 ft

1.23 mi

Trail Milestones:

0.0 mi – Lower trailhead (38°14.742 N, 080°51.612 W)

0.4 mi – Hypes Bridge/Salmon Run Spur trailhead (38°15.060 N, 080°51.520 W)

1.0 mi – Intersection with "Summersville Lake Airport Road" (38°15.578 N, 080°51.409 W)

1.23 mi – Upper trailhead (38°15.474 N, 080°51.615 W)

Trail Description

The Salmon Run Road Return creates an enjoyable loop that lets you return to the upper trailhead via the road paralleling the beautiful stream of Salmon Run. From the lower trailhead and the end of the Salmon Run Trail turn left, crossing the parking area, and continue along the paved road. At 0.4 miles pass the Hypes Bridge (Salmon Run Spur trailhead) on the left and continue on, keeping the stream to your left. At 1.0 miles come to the intersection with "Summersville Lake Airport Road" and turn left. Travel along this busier road 0.23 miles to the upper trailhead.

SALMON RUN ROAD RETURN

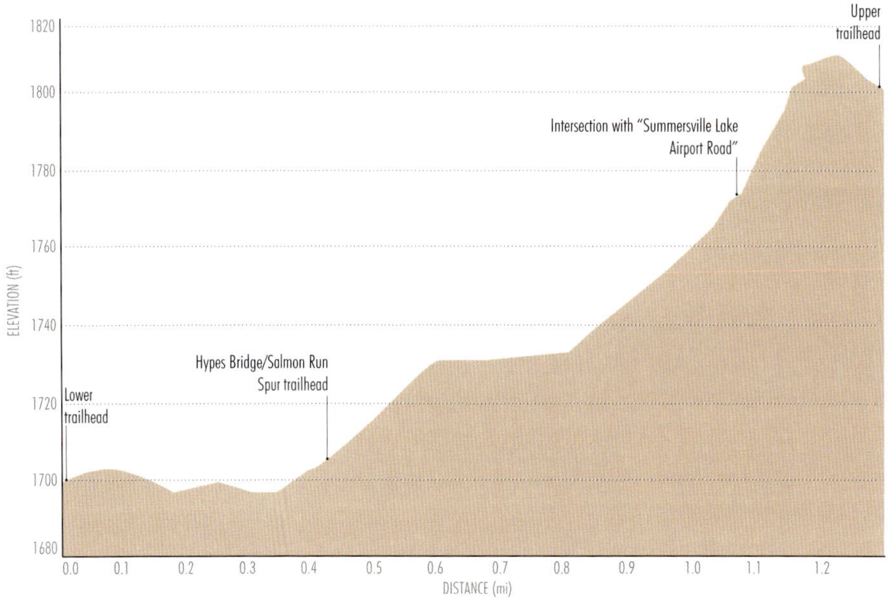

52 BATTLE RUN TRAIL

A nice hike along the water and through the forest near the Battle Run Campground, with multiple excellent spots for a picnic.

3 | 418 ft 418 ft | 3.18 mi

Location: Southwest of Summersville, WV; west of US Route 19
Maps: USGS Mount Nebo quad 1:24,000, USGS Summersville quad 1:24,000
Facilities: Paved parking, camping (114 sites), toilets/showers/laundry, picnic facilities, beach, boat docks, vending machines.
Highlights: A nice stroll along the water followed by a long hike along a wide trail through the forest. Multiple pretty spots to picnic along the water.

Trail Milestones:

0.3 mi – Picnic spot (38°13.917 N, 080°54.576 W)
0.8 mi – Turn left into forest (38°14.209 N, 080°54.479 W)
1.6 mi – Small stream (38°14.524 N, 080°54.359 W)
2.3 mi – Small stream and younger forest (38°14.276 N, 080°53.877 W)
2.6 mi – Small stream (38°14.148 N, 080°53.767 W)
2.7 mi – Trail splits (38°14.107 N, 080°53.715 W)
3.18 mi – Trail's end (38°13.553 N, 080°54.003 W)

Finding the Trailhead

(38°13.710 N, 080°54.750 W)
To access the trailhead from Fayetteville, WV, drive 17 miles north along US Route 19 to WV Route 129. Turn left and travel 3.7 miles to the entrance for Battle Run Campground. Keep straight 1.1 miles along the main campground road until it ends in a parking lot. There is no trailhead sign, but the trail is visible beyond an orange gate.

Trail Description

Starting at the end of the parking lot, hike along the edge of the water, soon entering an area between a rock dike on the left and the water's edge on the right. At 0.15 miles, if the water is low enough, you can spot two sunken boats on the bottom of the lake. This is a favorite spot for divers. Continue along the water until ascending slightly and entering a copse of trees along a finger that protrudes into the water — a beautiful picnic spot.

Return to the trail, veering away from the water and entering the forest. Here, you'll see a small plastic trail marker. The trail turns sharply left not long after entering the forest. This turn is easily missed — if you arrive in an open field, you've gone too far. Continue along a wide path through a forest dominated by mature deciduous trees. At 1.6 miles cross a small stream, and after another 0.7 miles cross a second stream and enter an area of younger forest with a dense population of American holly (*Llex opaca*). At 2.6 miles cross a third stream and move into an open area where the trail splits. Turning right, choose the middle trail that heads to the left of the ridgeline. The trail gradually leads into open fields and ends with views of the dam and lake.

Additional Notes

- No pets are allowed in and around Battle Run Campground.
- As of 2013, the trail is poorly maintained beyond 0.8 miles, with numerous downed trees.

BATTLE RUN TRAIL

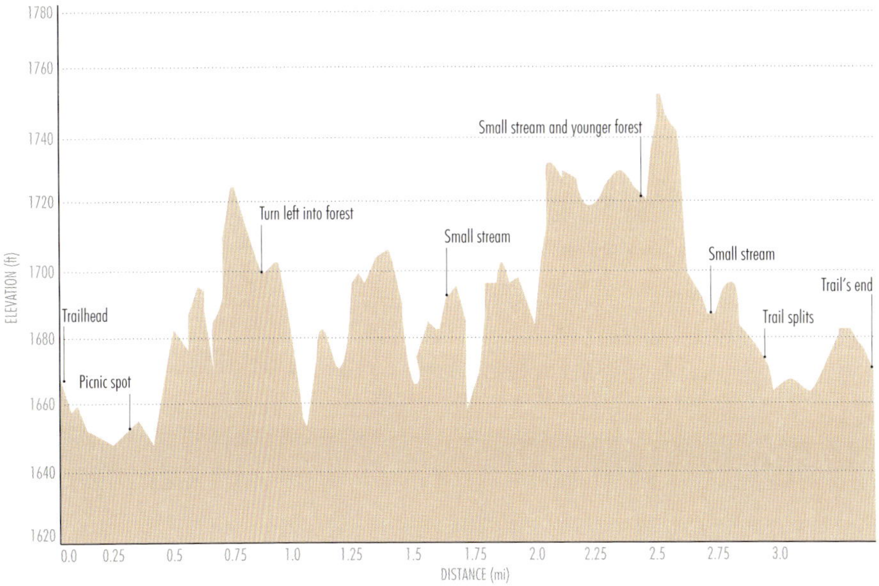

The mighty Gauley River during rafting season.

13 CARNIFEX FERRY BATTLEFIELD STATE PARK

Overview and Highlights

Carnifex Ferry Battlefield State Park is the best-preserved Civil War battlefield in the area, and is an official Civil War Discovery Trail location. The battle for Carnifex Ferry is reenacted every other year (odd years) on September 10.

How to Get There

Carnifex Ferry Battlefield State Park is located just outside Summersville, WV. From Fayetteville, WV, head north on US Route 19 for 17 miles to WV Route 129. Take a left and travel five miles until reaching Carnifex Ferry Battlefield State Park.

Rules and Regulations

Please see "Rules and Regulations for West Virginia State Parks" (page 24) for rules and regulations governing Carnifex Ferry Battlefield State Park and all other state parks in the region. In addition to the rules listed in that section, the following additional regulations apply:

- No alcoholic beverages permitted within park boundaries.
- Removal of any artifact is prohibited.

History and Culture

The battle for Carnifex Ferry occurred late in the day on September 10, 1861, when Federal forces, commanded by Brigadier General William S. Rosecrans, moved through thick forest from the northeast and encountered the defensive positions of the Confederate Army. The engagement continued until approaching darkness caused the Union forces to suspend their attack. Early on September 11, 1861, and under cover of night, Confederate forces under the command of Brigadier General John B. Floyd retreated across the Gauley River, thus ending the battle. Although suffering a greater number of killed and wounded in the engagement, the Union won the battle for Carnifex Ferry. This success helped secure the Kanawha Valley and prevent access to the Ohio River by the Confederates.

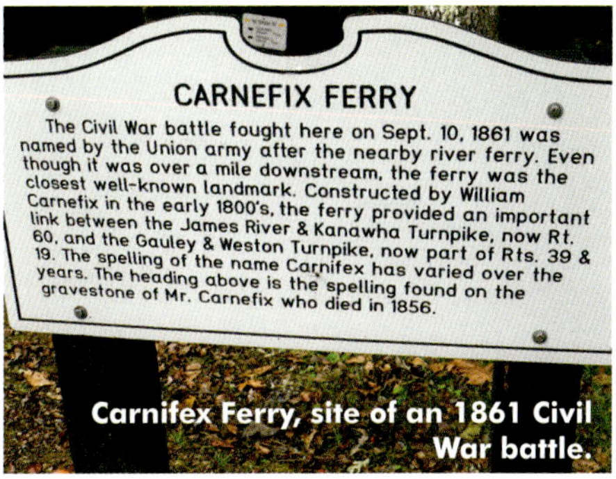

Carnifex Ferry, site of an 1861 Civil War battle.

CARNIFEX FERRY BATTLEFIELD STATE PARK HIKES

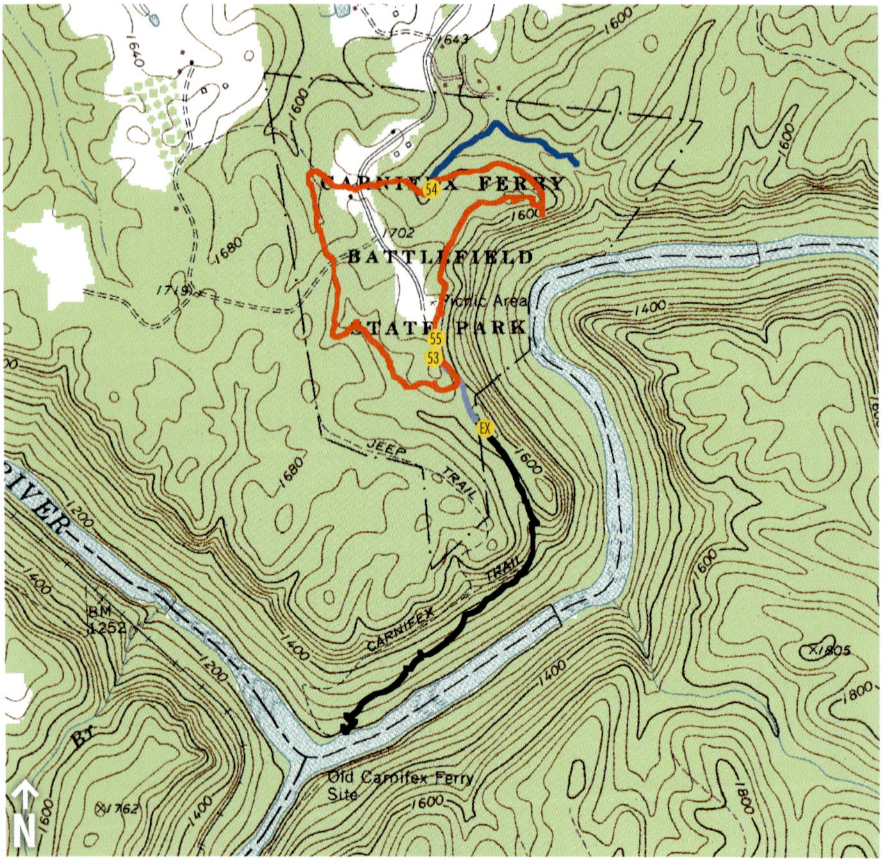

A kayaker enjoying a reprieve after Pillow Rock Rapids, Gauley River.

Map Key

Trail 53 – Old Carnifex Ferry Road Trail – light blue

Trail 53 Extension – black

Trail 54 – Pierson Hollow Trail – dark blue

Trail 55 – Patterson Trail – red

53 OLD CARNIFEX FERRY ROAD TRAIL

A short hike that traces the Confederate line of retreat during the night of September 10, 1861. Tack on a trip along an unmaintained trail into the Gauley River National Recreation Area for a longer hike of 1.17 miles.

3 | 20 ft 49 ft | 0.18 mi | 17 ft 445 ft (extension) | 1.17 mi (with extension)

Location: Close to Summersville, WV, just west of US Route 19

Maps: USGS Summersville Dam quad 1:24,000

Trail Options: Combine with the Patterson Trail for an additional 0.16 miles of hiking. Continue to river for 1.17 miles total distance.

Facilities: Carnifex Ferry State Park has a full complement of facilities, including picnic tables, grills, restrooms, vending machines, shelters, and ample paved parking.

Highlights: Follow in the path of Civil War soldiers along this wagon trail to the Carnifex Ferry fording site over the Gauley River.

Trail Milestones:

0.1 mi – Intersection with Patterson Trail (38°12.289 N, 080°56.281 W)

0.18 mi – End of official trail/ state-park boundary (38°12.220 N, 080°56.243 W)

Unmaintained Trail Milestones:

0.3 mi – Stream crossing (38°12.003 N, 080°56.109 W)

0.6 mi – Echo Boulder (38°11.819 N, 080°56.313 W)

0.9 mi – Intersection with larger trail/road (38°11.682 N, 080°56.545 W)

0.99 mi – Gauley River/end of trail (38°11.658 N, 080°56.545 W)

Finding the Trailhead

(38°12.337 N, 080°56.334 W)

From Fayetteville, WV, head north on US Route 19 for 17 miles to WV Route 129. Take a left and travel five miles until reaching Carnifex Ferry Battlefield State Park. Turn left into the park and drive approximately 1.3 miles until the road ends in a paved parking lot. Walk toward Shelter No. 3. The trailhead is located just beyond.

Trail Description

Red Diamond Blaze

From the trailhead proceed into the tree line. This trail shares its route with the Patterson Trail for the first 0.1 miles. At this point, the Patterson Trail breaks sharply right. Continue instead through a mix of rhododendron and deciduous trees, descending gradually toward the ferry. While this is an easy trail to navigate by daylight, consider the thoughts of the Confederate soldiers as they silently retreated through darkness from the larger Union Army surrounding their positions. At 0.18 miles reach the state-park boundary and the end of the official trail.

The trail continues another 0.99 miles into the Gauley River National Recreation Area, to the former site of the ferry. Though not maintained, this trail is open to the public. Continue descending along thick rhododendrons, crossing a rocky stream at 0.3 miles. At this point, listen for the roar of the river below and then continue another 0.3 miles to reach "Echo Boulder" to the right of the trail. This bus-sized boulder reflects the sound of the Gauley River for a "surround sound" experience. Continue down the trail and begin to catch glimpses of the river to your left. At 0.9 miles reach an intersection with a larger trail/dirt road. Stay left here, and shortly thereafter reach the river. During Gauley rafting season (September/October) you can watch rafters and kayakers negotiate obstacles; otherwise, enjoy the views and catch some rays on one of the many boulders along the river. Return to the trailhead via the same trail.

Echo Boulder.

Trail Combinations/Options

This trail runs contiguously with portions of the Patterson Trail (Trail 55). Combine with the Patterson Trail for a 2.16-mile hike.

Historical Notes

The Old Carnifex Ferry Road Trail was the path taken by Brigadier General John B. Floyd and his Confederate troops during their retreat of September 10, 1861. Under cover of darkness, this force slipped away from the Union Army, utilizing a rope bridge constructed the day prior. After crossing the Gauley River, the rebel forces destroyed the bridge and continued south along Sunday Road.

Caution

Live artillery projectiles are still present on the battlefield. If found, do not handle them. Please notify park staff immediately.

Take care if continuing to the Gauley River. The current is swift, and drownings do occur.

OLD CARNIFEX FERRY ROAD TRAIL

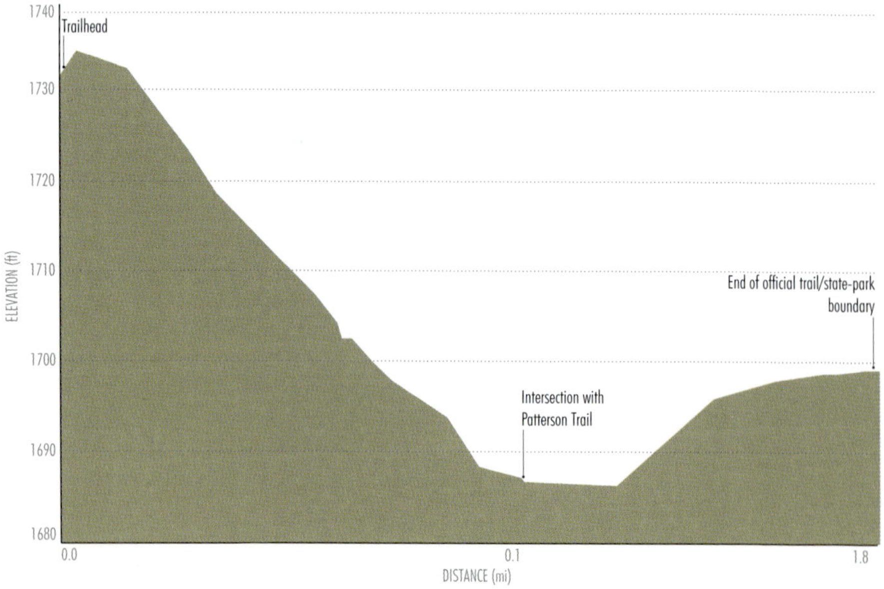

OLD CARNIFEX FERRY ROAD TRAIL AND EXTENSION

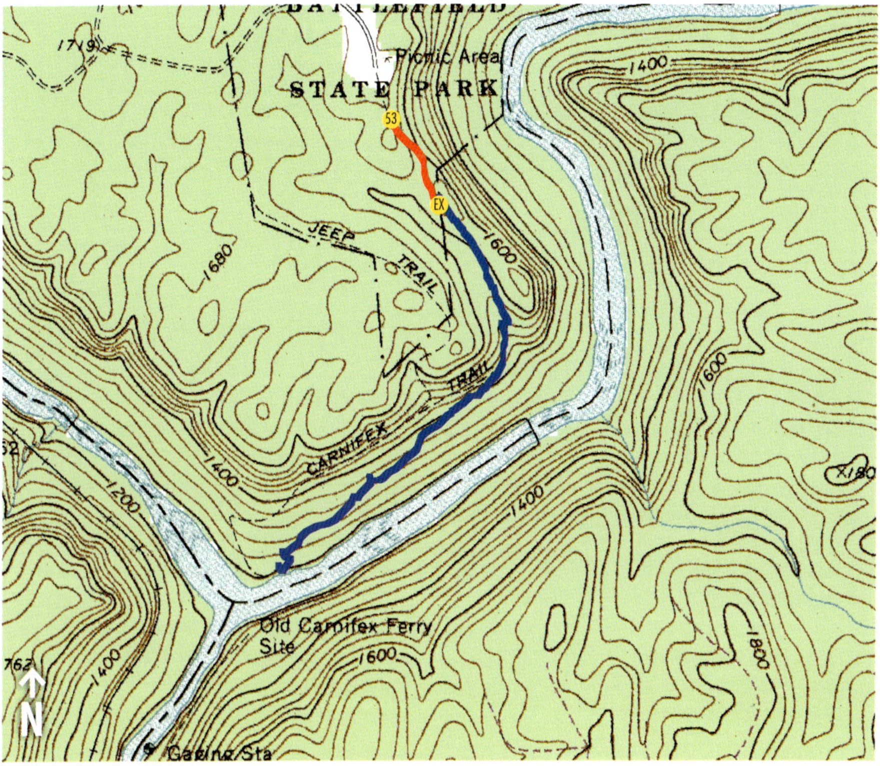

OLD CARNIFEX FERRY ROAD TRAIL EXTENSION

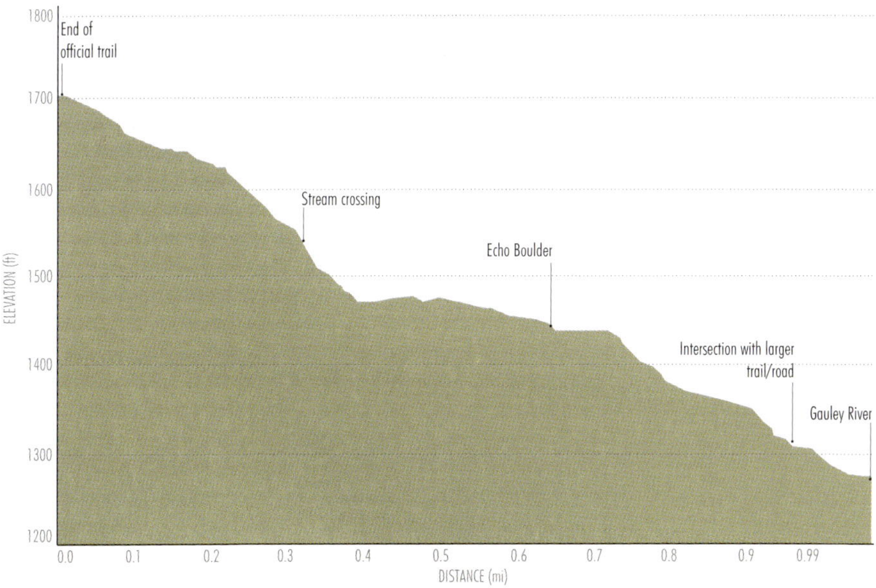

54 PIERSON HOLLOW TRAIL

A short branch trail accessible from Patterson Trail that journeys deeper into the forest. This area is known for a "friendly fire" incident that occurred between different units of the Union Army during the battle for Carnifex Ferry.

2 — 2 ft / 80 ft — 0.42 mi

Location: Close to Summersville, WV, just west of US Route 19
Maps: USGS Summersville Dam quad 1:24,000
Trail Options: A great add-on hike to combine with Patterson Trail.
Facilities: No facilities on the trail, but the state park has picnic tables, grills, restrooms, vending machines, shelters, and ample paved parking.
Highlights: A short branch trail that sustained severe damage during the June 2012 derecho windstorm and was the location of an unfortunate episode during the Civil War battle that occurred here.

Trail Milestones:

0.2 mi – Stream crossing (38°12.749 N, 080°56.199 W)
0.4 mi – Trail's end (38°12.682 N, 080°56.002 W)

Caution

Live artillery projectiles are still present on battlefield. If found, do not handle. Please notify park staff immediately.

Finding the Trailhead

(38°12.634 N, 080°56.349 W)

From Fayetteville, WV, head north on US Route 19 for 17 miles to WV Route 129. Take a left and travel five miles to Carnifex Ferry Battlefield State Park. For just this hike, turn left into the park to the Patterson House, and park beside it. If adding Pierson Hollow Trail as part of the longer Patterson Trail, continue to the main parking lot where the park road dead-ends.

The trailhead is located off Patterson Trail and can be accessed either from the Patterson House (closest) or as part of the main Patterson Trail. From the house, cross the main park drive, descend across the field, and enter the woods. The trailhead is 0.2 miles from the house. If approaching from the main Patterson Trail trailhead, follow the Patterson Trail, reaching Pierson Hollow Trail after 0.9 miles.

Trail Description

Blue Diamond Blaze

From the trailhead, parallel the stream and venture deeper into the woods. At 0.2 miles cross the stream along a wooden bridge, and over the next 0.2 miles witness the devastation wrought by the June 2012 windstorm. The trail ends at a sign. Return by the same path.

Trail Combinations/Options

This trail is a perfect addition to the longer Patterson Trail (Trail 55), adding 0.84 miles.

Historical Notes

During the Battle for Carnifex Ferry, Union troops attempted to push their assault against Confederate forces entrenched on the Patterson Farm. Units of the 13th, 23rd, and 28th Ohio occupied the area of Pierson Hollow, and in the fading daylight and fog of battle, portions of the 28th Ohio fired on their fellow soldiers, killing two and wounding 30 more. General Rosecrans ordered the advance stopped, and Union forces prepared for a renewed assault on the morning of September 11, 1861.

Rock formations along Pierson Hollow Trail.

PIERSON HOLLOW TRAIL

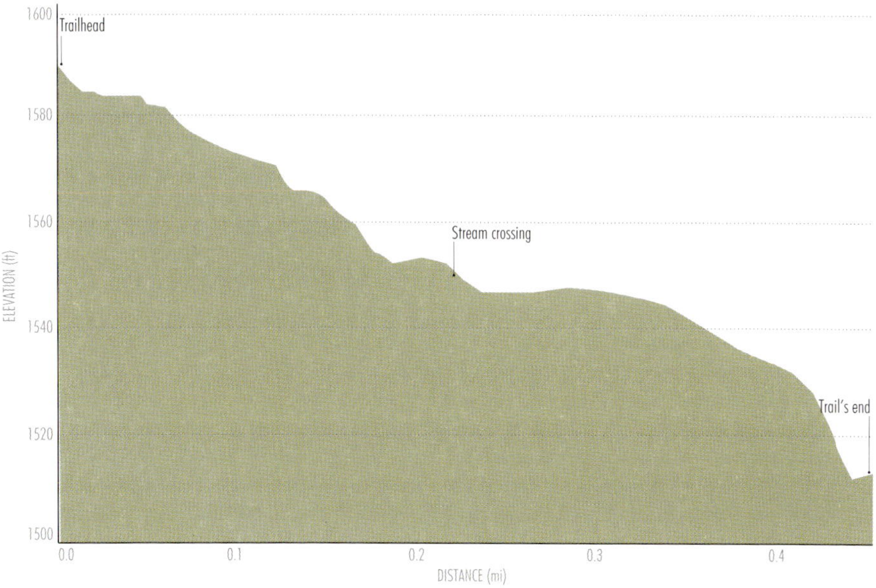

55 PATTERSON TRAIL

This trail loops around the entire park, offering visitors scenic views of the Gauley River and an in-depth tour of the battlefield.

3 | 344 ft | 384 ft | 2 mi

Location: Close to Summersville, WV, just west of US Route 19

Maps: USGS Summersville Dam quad 1:24,000

Trail Options: Combine with the Pierson Hollow Trail and Old Carnifex Ferry Road Trail to gain a comprehensive understanding of the battle.

Facilities: Carnifex Ferry State Park has a full complement of facilities, including picnic tables, grills, restrooms, vending machines, shelters, and ample paved parking.

Highlights: Spectacular views of the Gauley River Canyon paired with historical markers explaining the Battle of Carnifex Ferry.

Trail Milestones:

0.3 mi – Access trail (38°12.608 N, 080°56.233 W)

0.4 mi – Viewpoint No. 2 (38°12.618 N, 080°56.148 W)

0.5 mi – Viewpoint No. 3 (38°12.601 N, 080°56.084 W)

0.9 mi – Intersection with Pierson Hollow Trail (38°12.633 N, 080°56.350 W)

1.1 mi – Patterson House (38°12.640 N, 080°56.497 W)

1.4 mi – Gravel road (38°12.502 N, 080°56.574 W)

1.1 mi – Intersection with Old Carnifex Ferry Road Trail (38°12.289 N, 080°56.281 W)

Finding the Trailhead

(38°12.363 N, 080°56.343 W)

From Fayetteville, WV, head north on US Route 19 for 17 miles to WV Route 129. Take a left and travel five miles until reaching Carnifex Ferry Battlefield State Park. Turn left into the park and drive approximately 1.3 miles until the road ends in a paved parking lot. Walk toward Shelter No. 3. The trailhead is just left of the shelter.

Trail Description

Yellow Diamond Blaze

While you can access this trail from multiple points within the park, this description begins at the designated trailhead beside Shelter No. 3. Named after Henry Patterson, the unlucky landowner whose family farm became a battleground on September 10, 1861, this trail encompasses the majority of the state park. Beginning at the shelter, walk along the wood line and almost immediately arrive at a newly built overlook that provides an outstanding view of the Gauley River. During rafting season on the Gauley (September/October), you can hear the roar of the rapids and the screams of rafters from this lofty perch. Enter the forest and at 0.1 miles encounter a spur trail to the right; this trail is not maintained and leads to private property. As you continue along the trail notice the large number of downed trees to either side — this damage is from a major windstorm, called a *derecho*, which hit the area in June 2012.

At 0.3 miles a spur trail (on the left) leads to the softball field, and at 0.4 miles you'll encounter a second overlook. From here you can see Pillow Rock Rapids. A third and final overlook is located at 0.5 miles — descend 55 steps to "Copperhead Overlook." Return to the trail and continue hiking through the forest, reaching the intersection with Pierson Hollow Trail at 0.9 miles. Turn sharply left and ascend, crossing a field, to arrive at the Patterson House. The trail continues to the right of the house and reenters the forest. At 1.3 miles cross a wooden bridge over a seasonal stream, and after a further 0.1 miles cross a gravel road (WV Route 23). At 1.6 miles encounter a spur trail that leads to the main parking lot. Stay right and descend slightly, crossing and then paralleling a small stream. The trail then becomes enveloped by a rhododendron grove until emerging at the intersection with Old Carnifex Ferry Road Trail. Turn left and continue 0.1 miles to the trailhead, back at Shelter No. 3.

Trail Combinations/Options

You can shorten the hike by utilizing the spur trail at 0.3 miles (total length: 0.4 miles) or the spur trail at 1.6 miles (total length: 1.9 miles). You can also combine Patterson Trail with Pierson Hollow Trail (Trail 54; adding 0.84 miles round-trip) or Old Carnifex Ferry Road Trail (Trail 53; adding 0.16 miles round-trip).

Patterson House.

Historical Notes

The Patterson Farm and House for which this trail is named became a battlefield between Union and Confederate forces on September 10, 1861. Built in the 1850s, the property was acquired by West Virginia in 1935. It now serves as a museum, open seasonally.

Caution

Live artillery projectiles are still present on battlefield. If found, do not handle. Please notify park staff immediately.

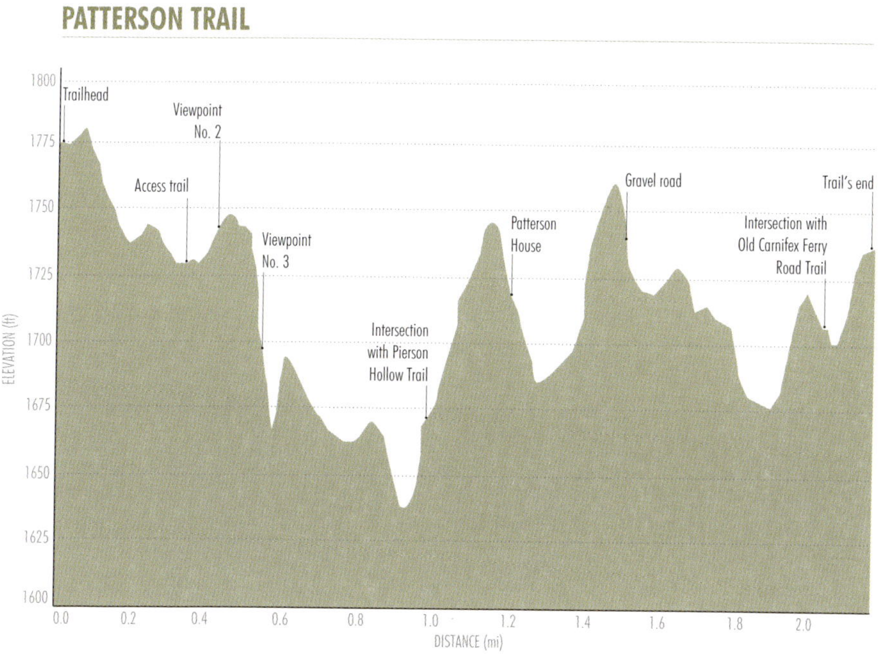

14 HAWK'S NEST STATE PARK

Overview and Highlights

Hawk's Nest State Park, established in 1935, is a 276-acre area bordering the New River. The park takes its name from the number of osprey (fish-hawks) that nest in the cliffs. The park's main facilities perch high above the river along US Route 60, also known as the Midland Trail, a designated National Scenic Byway. The state park offers a host of facilities that include a lodge, aerial tram, museum, swimming pool, game courts, a golf course, and access to the jet boats that operate in summer.

How to Get There

To reach the main lodge at Hawk's Nest, drive 8.1 miles from the intersection of US Route 60 (Midland Trail) and US Route 19. US Route 60 is located 5.2 miles north of the New River Gorge Bridge near Fayetteville, WV. See individual trails for directions to the various trailheads.

Rules and Regulations

Please see "Rules and Regulations for West Virginia State Parks" (page 24) for rules and regulations governing Hawk's Nest State Park and all other state parks in the region.

General Trail Information

Note that Hawk's Nest State Park lies at the juncture of three separate USGS map sheets. These sheets are listed for every hike and cover all of the acreage within the state park. Also, in addition to the seven trails listed in this chapter, I should mention two trails I didn't describe:

Lover's Leap Trail: At the time of publication, this trail is closed. It does, however, have an interesting story: Legend has it that two Native American lovers, one a Shawnee and the other a Cherokee, leapt to their deaths from these rocks after they were refused permission to be together.

Hawk's Nest Connector Trail: This trail, not yet completed, will connect the Hawk's Nest Rail Trail to Fayette Station Road between the visitor center (at the New River Gorge Bridge) and the New River.

History and Culture

While the legend of star-crossed Native American lovers is the stuff of local lore, this area also played host to one of the worst industrial disasters in the United States. In the 1930s, a hydroelectric project began with the construction of the Hawk's Nest Dam and water-diversion tunnel. The purpose of this construction was to generate power for a plant downstream. The dearth of jobs during this era lured workers to West Virginia from throughout the country, but especially African Americans from the Deep South. Of the more than three thousand men who entered these mines, most worked only two to three months. The cause of their short tenure was the silica dust generated by the mining operation, leading to silicosis among the workers. Estimated fatalities due to this tragedy range from 109 admitted deaths (at the time of the incident), to 476 deaths (from a 1936 congressional investigation), to 764 (in another government investigation in 1986).

View of the New River from the Hawk's Nest Overlook Trail.

In reality, we will never know the true number of deaths caused by this environmental disaster. For more information, the book *The Hawks Nest Tunnel: An Unabridged History,* by Patricia Spangler, is an outstanding resource. A cemetery for the workers who died here was rededicated in September 2012. It is located on Whippoorwill Road, 20.8 miles north of Fayetteville, WV, on US Route 19. Turn left on this road and then immediately right, following it to its end.

Aerial Tram Operating Days and Hours of Operation

Operating Days:
May through Memorial Day: Saturdays and Sundays only
Memorial Day through Labor Day: Daily except Wednesdays
September: Saturdays and Sundays only
October: Daily except Wednesdays
November through April: CLOSED

Tram Hours:
Weekdays: 11 a.m. - 4:45 p.m.
Weekends: 11 a.m. - 6:45 p.m. (June, July, August)

Ticket Costs:
Adult: $4
Child: $2.50
Senior: $3
(Prices subject to change)

HAWK'S NEST STATE PARK HIKES

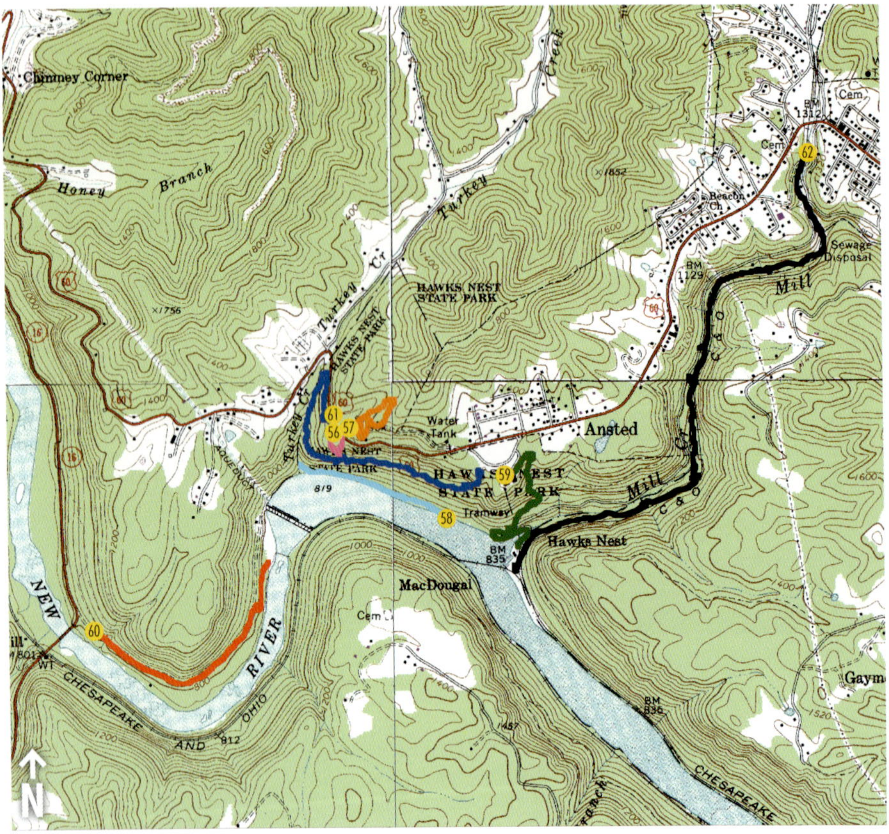

Mallards enjoying a swim on Hawk's Nest Reservoir.

Map Key

Trail 56 – Hawk's Nest Overlook Trail – pink
Trail 57 – Loop Trail – orange
Trail 58 – Fisherman's Access Trail – light blue
Trail 59 – G.S.Y.P. Trail – dark green
Trail 60 – Cotton Hill to Hawk's Nest Dam Trail – red
Trail 61 – Cliffside Trail – dark blue
Trail 62 – Hawk's Nest Rail Trail – black

56 HAWK'S NEST OVERLOOK TRAIL

This short paved loop trail, originally built by the Civilian Conservation Corps in the 1930s, leads to stunning views of the New River Gorge and the expanse of the Hawk's Nest Dam.

1 | 22 ft 27 ft | 0.17 mi

Location: Near Ansted, WV. Located on US Route 60 (Midland Trail); west of US Route 19

Maps: USGS Ansted quad 1:24,000
USGS Beckwith quad 1:24,000
USGS Fayetteville quad 1:24,000

Trail Options: No combinations or options available, though the Loop Trail (Trail 57) and Cliffside Trail (Trail 61) trailheads are nearby.

Facilities: Paved parking, picnic tables and shelters, modern toilets, gift shop.

Highlights: Incredible lookout above a bend in the New River that offers stunning views of the gorge and the Hawk's Nest Dam.

Trail Milestones:

0.1 mi – Overlook
(38°07.317 N, 081°07.667 W)

Finding the Trailhead

(38°07.368 N, 081°07.677 W)
The trailhead is located in a parking area just off US Route 60 (Midland Trail) — locally, this area is often referred to as "Lower Park." From the main portion and lodge of Hawk's Nest State Park, drive 0.4 miles west along US Route 60. The trailhead is located in the middle of this parking lot.

Trail Description

This paved and well-maintained trail leads to an overlook above the New River Gorge; a stone-and-beam rail protects visitors along the length of the trail. At 0.1 miles find a wheelchair-accessible viewpoint followed by a set of 34 stairs that lead to a lower viewpoint. For twenty-five cents, children and adults alike can use a telescope to identify wildlife around the gorge or get a closer view of the Hawk's Nest Dam, completed in 1936. Other interesting sites visible from here include the Hawk's Nest Railway bridge and rail system on the opposite side of the gorge where trains lumber along daily, carrying loads of coal.

Trail Combinations/Options

No combinations or options available, though you'll find the Loop Trail (Trail 57) and Cliffside Trail (Trail 61) trailheads nearby.

Additional Notes

This portion of the state park closes nightly at 10 p.m.

57 LOOP TRAIL

A short trail that ventures uphill into the forest before looping back along a ridge and descending stone stairs to the trailhead.

2 | 133 ft | 150 ft | 0.46 mi

Location: Near Ansted, WV. Located on US Route 60 (Midland Trail); west of US Route 19
Maps: USGS Ansted quad 1:24,000
USGS Beckwith quad 1:24,000
USGS Fayetteville quad 1:24,000
Trail Options: No trail options or combos available, but there's easy access to the Cliffside Trail (Trail 61) and Hawk's Nest Overlook Trail (Trail 56).
Facilities: Paved parking, picnic tables and shelters, modern toilets, gift shop.
Highlights: A short trail that leads into a typical West Virginia forest.

Trail Milestones:

0.4 mi – Stone stairs
(38°07.365 N, 081°07.586 W)

Finding the Trailhead

(38°07.391 N, 081°07.623 W)
The trailhead is located at the parking area just off US Route 60 (Midland Trail) — locally, this area is often referred to as "Lower Park." From the main portion and lodge of Hawk's Nest State Park, drive 0.4 miles west along US Route 60 and park your car. Cross US Route 60 and walk toward the gift shop on the right; the trailhead is located just above, along a paved walkway.

Trail Description

From the trailhead (by the gift shop) begin walking along a broken paved walkway. This section is relatively straight and leads directly up a small gully formed by a stream, with picnic tables situated periodically throughout. Follow this path approximately 0.15 miles and bear right to ascend to the ridgeline. At the top of the ridge you'll see a stone-and-beam park building to the left. At 0.4 miles begin descending stone stairs back to the trailhead. This excursion makes for a great short hike and picnic.

Trail Combinations/Options

Across US Route 60, find easy access to the start points for the Cliffside Trail (Trail 61) and the Hawk's Nest Overlook Trail (Trail 56).

Moss-covered stairs of the Loop Trail.

58 FISHERMAN'S ACCESS TRAIL

An easy hike along Hawk's Nest Reservoir that leads to Turkey Falls and close-up views of Hawk's Nest Dam.

2 | 22 ft 16 ft | 0.48 mi

Location: Near Ansted, WV. Located on US Route 60 (Midland Trail); west of US Route 19
Maps: USGS Ansted quad 1:24,000
USGS Beckwith quad 1:24,000
USGS Fayetteville quad 1:24,000
Trail Options: Access this trail from the G.S.Y.P. Trail or the Hawk's Nest Rail Trail.
Facilities: Toilets and picnic tables available at the aerial tram station.
Highlights: Turkey Falls, Hawk's Nest Reservoir and Dam.

Trail Milestones:

0.49 mi – Turkey Falls
(38°07.290 N, 081°07.800 W)

Finding the Trailhead

From the G.S.Y.P. Trail (Trail 59): (38°07.151 N, 081°07.299 W)
Turn right at the G.S.Y.P. Trail's 0.6-mile mark. Stay straight at the intersection rather than turning sharply left, and pass a parking area and boat launch to arrive at the trailhead, as designated by a gate.

From the aerial tram or Hawk's Nest Rail Trail (Trail 62):
Pass under the tram cables and follow a path across a vehicle bridge over Mill Creek. Continue along the path to an intersection (G.S.Y.P. Trail will be above and right) and stay straight, passing a parking area and boat launch before arriving at the trailhead.

Trail Description

From the trailhead walk along the wide and grassy trail, with the reservoir to the left. Views abound along the water, from river level to the cliffs above. Pass multiple cleared areas that are popular with fisherman and watch for ducks and geese nesting along the banks. To your right the ground rises steeply toward the upper portion of Hawk's Nest State Park. Continue along this gentle trail 0.49 miles until reaching a bridge over Turkey Creek. To your right you'll see the fabulous falls, which fill with runoff after spring rains to make for a great scene. This is the end of the official trail, though the path continues a short ways beyond the falls and allows closer views of the Hawk's Nest Dam complex. The unofficial trail ends at a chain-link fence.

Trail Combinations/Options

You can reach the Fisherman's Access Trail from the G.S.Y.P. Trail (Trail 59), the tram, or the Hawk's Nest Rail Trail (Trail 62). If using the tram, check with Hawk's Nest staff, as the operating hours vary depending on the day and season.

59 G.S.Y.P. TRAIL

Descend along switchbacks to the bottom of the gorge, crossing below the cascades of Mill Creek before arriving at the Hawk's Nest Aerial Tram.

3 48 ft 384 ft 0.75 mi

Location: Near Ansted, WV. Located on US Route 60 (Midland Trail); west of US Route 19
Maps: USGS Ansted quad 1:24,000
USGS Beckwith quad 1:24,000
USGS Fayetteville quad 1:24,000
Trail Options: Connect with the Fisherman's Access Trail at 0.6 miles or the lower trailhead of the Hawk's Nest Rail Trail at the tram.
Facilities: Toilets, snack bar, picnic facilities, and tram at trail's end.
Highlights: Views of the gorge and reservoir, Mill Creek, aerial tram.

Trail Milestones:

0.4 mi – Bench
(38°07.169 N, 081°07.033 W)
0.5 mi – Gravel road
(38°07.120 N, 081°07.074 W)
0.6 mi – Sharp left turn
(38°07.106 N, 081°07.151 W)
0.75 mi – Mill Creek
(38°07.077 N, 081°07.060 W)

Additional Notes

So what does G.S.Y.P. stand for anyway? It stands for the Governor's Summer Youth Program, a state program that gives participants, usually ages 14–21, practical work experience during the summer months. Members of the program assisted in the construction of this trail in the late 1980s or early 90s.

Finding the Trailhead

(38°07.256 N, 081°07.096 W)
The trailhead is located beside the tennis courts by the main lodge at Hawk's Nest. To reach the lodge, drive 8.1 miles along US Route 60 (Midland Trail) from the intersection of this road and US Route 19.

Trail Description

From the lodge entrance walk toward the tennis courts and follow the paved path. Just beyond the courts, a sign points to the right — follow it across the basketball courts, and then the trail moves into the wood line. At 0.1 miles turn right down steps made of railroad crossties alongside a tiny stream to the left. Continue descending past a large downed tree at 0.2 miles. Notice the rock overhang to the right, and at 0.4 miles reach a flat portion of trail with a wooden bench near a couple of large boulders. Take a break here or continue along the path as it begins to widen. At 0.5 miles the trail intersects and combines with a gravel road; bear right and continue descending. *Note: This is an actively used road.* At 0.6 miles the trail turns sharply left and parallels the mouth of Mill Creek. Walk to the bridge and cross downstream from a sample of Mill Creek's many cascades. The trail ends at the lower aerial tram station. Return by the same route or ride the tram back to the lodge. For additional information on tram operating hours and ticket costs, see page 195 in the introductory portion of this chapter.

Trail Combinations/Options

Connect with the Fisherman's Access Trail (Trail 58) by staying straight at 0.6 miles, passing the parking area and boat dock. This combination creates a 1.1-mile trek (one-way). It is also possible to link to the Hawk's Nest Rail Trail (Trail 62) by passing the tram and accessing the lower trailhead; this yields a total hike of 3.12 miles (one-way).

The mouth of Mill Creek.

G.S.Y.P. TRAIL

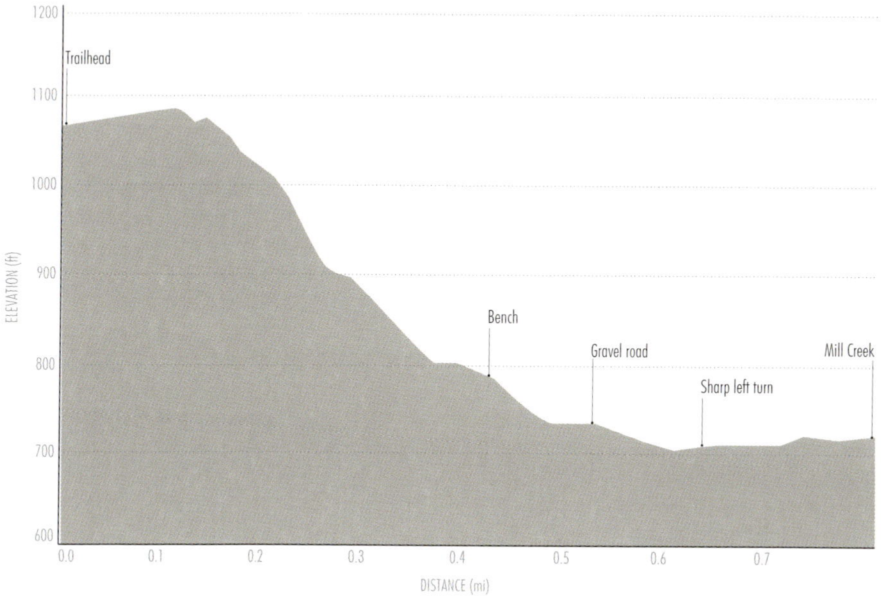

60 COTTON HILL TO HAWK'S NEST DAM TRAIL

An easy walk along an access road that culminates with a close-up view of the Hawk's Nest Dam and the enormous boulders that litter the riverbed below.

2 | 24 ft | 271 ft | 0.86 mi

Location: Near Ansted, WV. Located on US Route 60 (Midland Trail); west of US Route 19
Maps: USGS Ansted quad 1:24,000
USGS Beckwith quad 1:24,000
USGS Fayetteville quad 1:24,000
Facilities: Gravel parking for approximately 20 vehicles.
Highlights: Close-up views of Hawk's Nest Dam, enormous boulders.

Trail Milestones:

0.06 mi – Trail No. 1
(38°06.822 N, 081°08.463 W)
0.61 mi – Trail No. 2
(38°06.879 N, 081°07.980 W)
0.67 mi – Trail leaves access road
(38°06.919 N, 081°07.920 W)
0.86 mi – Trail's end at boulder field
(38°07.024 N, 081°07.927 W)

Finding the Trailhead

(38°06.865 N, 081°08.548 W)
From Fayetteville (US Route 19) take a left at the intersection with WV Route 16 and travel seven miles until you cross a bridge over the New River; turn right immediately after the bridge at "Cotton Hill Public Fishing Access Area."

Access from US Route 19 is also available if traveling from Summersville. Take the US Route 60 exit (Midland Trail) and follow signs west toward Charleston. Drive 10.78 miles — past Hawk's Nest State Park (at 8.1 miles) — and turn left onto WV Route 16 at Chimney Corner. Drive 1.9 miles along WV Route 16 and turn left into the Cotton Hill parking area, just prior to crossing the New River. The trailhead is located by the tall chain-link fence that prevents vehicular access to the trail.

Trail Description

At the trailhead, pass to the right of the chain-link fence. Please note the warnings signs related to water release from the dam and pay close attention to any sirens. Almost immediately, pass a sign for Trail No. 1 to the right. Bypass this side trail and continue straight along the gravel road; at 100 meters a small cascading stream intersects the trail. With the New River to your right, the trail begins a slow ascent through a deciduous forest, with a stand of hickory trees that deposit their nuts on the track. Numerous unmarked trails created by local fishermen lead off from the larger path here.

At 0.61 miles pass Trail No. 2, leading off to the right. Again, pass this trail and stay straight along the gravel trail until at 0.67 miles the trail branches off to the right. Follow the sign toward "Hawk's Nest Dam." The trail now becomes single-track and begins to descend toward the river; this trail is rocky in spots, and at 0.86 miles opens up onto flat rock with numerous boulders distributed throughout. You can now see the Hawk's Nest Dam. Take time to explore the boulders. Some are the size of small houses, with unique patterns carved into their sides from years of water erosion. Heads up: While the New River here looks much less menacing than at the rapids upstream, it's still dangerous. Return by the same track to the parking lot.

Hawk's Nest Dam, as seen from below.

COTTON HILL TO HAWK'S NEST DAM TRAIL

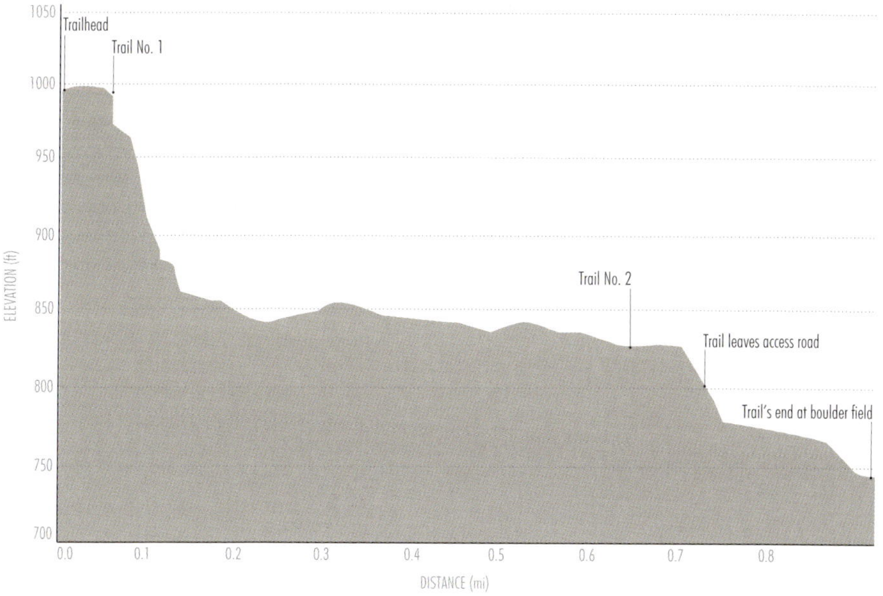

COTTON HILL TO HAWK'S NEST DAM TRAIL

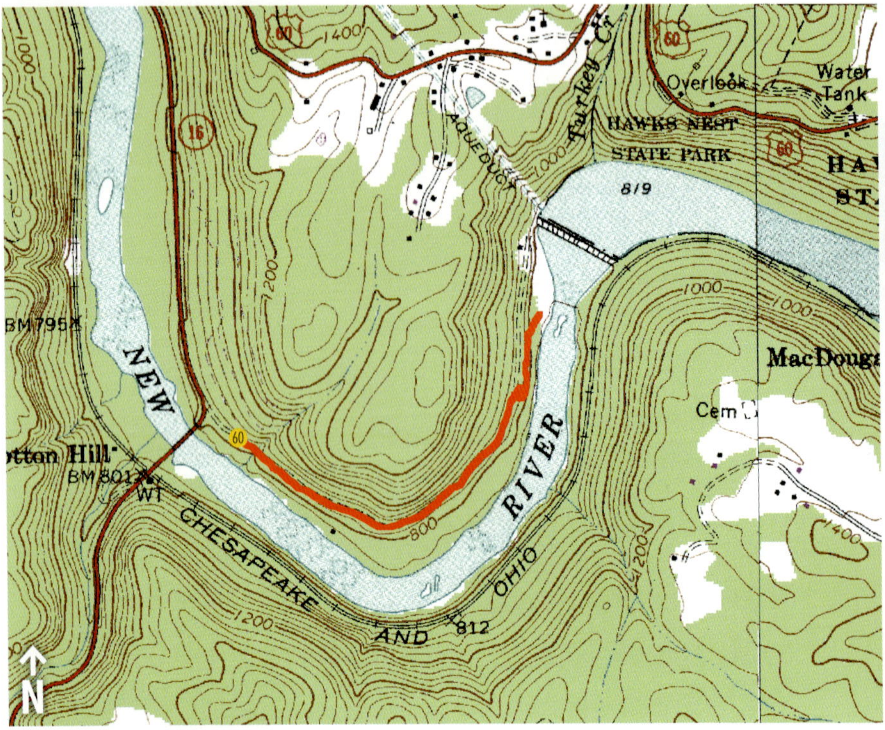

Cotton Hill.

Additional Notes

This area is popular with climbers, and a climber access trail at the parking area climbs a steep hill to a cliff line dubbed "Cotton Hill." At the end of the Cotton Hill to Hawk's Nest Dam Trail, you may also see climbers on the numerous boulders below the dam. See Mike Williams' *New River Gorge Rock Climbs* for more information regarding climbing and bouldering in this area.

Caution

This trail is located downstream from the Hawk's Nest Dam. While hiking on the access road is relatively safe, once you turn onto the single-track trail and venture down to the boulder field and near the New River, be very cautious. As the signs in the area declare: "Warning: DAM UPSTREAM, Water may rise rapidly at any time WITHOUT WARNING. Siren will warn of definite water rise. Avoid placing yourself where quick exit from the river is difficult. Personal awareness at all times is required due to the noise from trains, water, and other environmental factors. Sirens may not always be heard. You are at risk to remain near the water after the water starts to rise or you hear a siren." Got that? Siren = imminent water release = get away from the river and up to higher ground!

High above the Hawk's Nest Dam.

61 CLIFFSIDE TRAIL

A challenging trail that begins along Turkey Creek before turning into the New River Gorge and following the base of a rock wall, with views of the river far below.

3 | 346 ft | 331 ft | 1.28 mi

Location: Near Ansted, WV. Located on US Route 60 (Midland Trail); west of US Route 19
Maps: USGS Ansted quad 1:24,000
USGS Beckwith quad 1:24,000
USGS Fayetteville quad 1:24,000
Trail Options: No combinations or options available, though the Hawk's Nest Overlook Trail (Trail 56) and the Loop Trail (Trail 57) are nearby.
Facilities: Paved parking, picnic tables and shelters, modern toilets, gift shop.
Highlights: Turkey Creek cascades and waterfall, rock wall and overhangs, views of the New River.

Trail Milestones:

0.15 mi – Turkey Creek
(38°07.528 N, 081°07.722 W)
0.4 mi – Waterfall
(38°07.392 N, 081°07.783 W)
0.6 mi – Rock overhang
(38°07.300 N, 081°07.683 W)
1.11 mi – Stairs
(38°07.231 N, 081°07.245 W)
1.28 mi – Trail's end
(38°07.267 N, 081°07.183 W)

Finding the Trailhead

(38°07.398 N, 081°07.694 W)
The trailhead is located in a parking area just off US Route 60 (Midland Trail) — locally, this area is often referred to as "Lower Park." From the main portion and lodge of Hawk's Nest State Park, drive 0.4 miles west along US Route 60. The trailhead is located on the western side of the parking lot.

Trail Description

From the trailhead, descend immediately into the forest. This trail is single-track throughout and can be slippery at times along steep embankments. Negotiate a series of switchbacks through an evergreen grove and encounter a rocky outcropping at 0.1 miles. Continue down the trail, veering left along Turkey Creek. Through the trees notice a series of pretty cascades flowing over exposed sandstone.

Continue to 0.4 miles and enjoy the 20-foot waterfall to the right. Round a bend in the trail and cross a feeder stream using rocks. Careful here — the wet stones are slippery. The trail now turns away from Turkey Creek and begins to parallel a rock wall high above the New River, with views of the gorge through the trees.

At 0.6 miles encounter an enormous rock overhang, a perfect hideaway if you're caught in a midsummer thunderstorm. Notice the different tree types around you: Above the cliff evergreens dominate, while below the cliff deciduous trees reign supreme. At 1.1 miles come to the foot of a set of stairs (24 total steps) and continue on the trail above. A small branch trail at the stairs' base leads to the top of a cliff — please take care if approaching this area. From atop the stairs, follow the trail an additional 0.18 miles to the trail's end near the lodge. Watch for deer in this area as you return to the lodge or back to Lower Park.

Trail Combinations/Options

No combos or options available, though the Hawk's Nest Overlook Trail (Trail 56) and the Loop Trail (Trail 57) trailheads are nearby.

Additional Notes

The trail as described leads from Lower Park to the main lodge at Hawk's Nest. It is possible to return to the Lower Park parking by way of US Route 60. This road is busy, but it does have a large shoulder that accommodates foot traffic. Hike 0.4 miles to Lower Park to complete the loop.

Falls along Turkey Creek.

CLIFFSIDE TRAIL

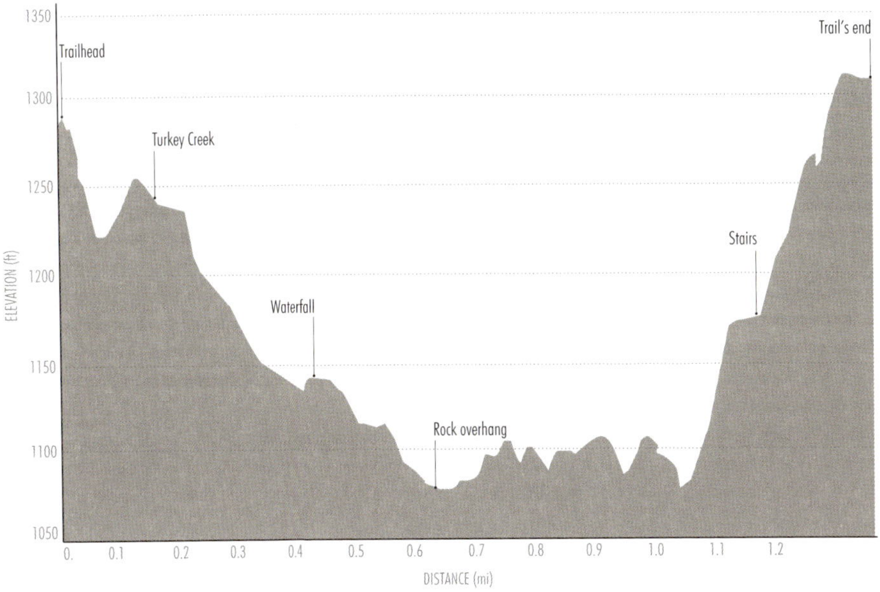

62 HAWK'S NEST RAIL TRAIL

One of the area gems, this well-maintained trail parallels Mill Creek, with its beautiful cascades and waterfalls. This trail also provides a healthy dose of history related to the former railroad that once occupied the trail bed as well as the mines the railroad served.

3 | 43 ft 371 ft | 2.37 mi

Location: Near Ansted, WV. Located on US Route 60 (Midland Trail); west of US Route 19
Maps: USGS Ansted quad 1:24,000
USGS Beckwith quad 1:24,000
USGS Fayetteville quad 1:24,000
Trail Options: Connect with the Fisherman's Access Trail (Trail 58) or G.S.Y.P. Trail (Trail 59).
Facilities: Large gravel parking, toilets, picnic facilities.
Highlights: Mill Creek cascades and waterfalls, mining and railroad history.

Trail Milestones:

0.3 mi – Trestle
(38°08.086 N, 081°06.068 W)
0.9 mi – Stream to left
(38°08.086 N, 081°06.068 W)
1.1 mi – Mill Creek Falls
(38°08.086 N, 081°06.068 W)
1.3 mi – Water tower
(38°08.086 N, 081°06.068 W)
1.5 mi – Mill Creek Colliery Company mine
(38°08.086 N, 081°06.068 W)
1.8 mi – Fox Branch Falls
(38°08.086 N, 081°06.068 W)
2.37 mi – Trail's end
(38°08.086 N, 081°06.068 W)

Finding the Trailhead

(38°08.086 N, 081°06.068 W)
Take US Route 19 5.2 miles north from the New River Gorge Bridge to the intersection with US Route 60 (Midland Trail). From this intersection drive 6.3 miles west along US Route 60 to the town of Ansted, WV. Signs point to the trailhead, but the easiest route is to turn right on Ansted Bank Road just after passing through the main portion of town (the turn comes directly after the Rite Aid), and then almost immediately turn left on Hawk's Nest Road. This road goes under US Route 60 and leads to the trailhead parking at 0.3 miles.

Trail Description

Beginning at the trailhead near Ansted, the trail descends along a wide and well-maintained trail alongside the gravel Hawk's Nest Road, soon crossing the road and continuing to a trestle bridge over Mill Creek at 0.3 miles. Just above the bridge, Westlake Creek falls into Mill Creek (on the left). Look closely and you'll see the foundation of Lykens Mill, built by Joseph Skaggs in 1830. In this area you'll pass numerous benches along the trail before continuing steadily downward to the 0.9-mile mark. At this point note a small, pretty stream that feeds into Mill Creek on the left.

At 1.1 miles encounter a highlight of the trail, Mill Creek Falls. This waterfall, the tallest on Mill Creek at 20 feet, is a favorite of visitors, including the kayakers who run the stream when water levels are high. Information boards here recount the geologic story of the area both in terms of rock formation and the region's modern history of mining.

After another 0.2 miles encounter a water tower left of the trail. A tree growing through and around the structure testifies to its age. This tower supplied water to the steam engines that once plied this route between Ansted and Hawk's Nest. At 1.4 miles the view opens up on the right due to a number of downed trees, victims of the June 2012 *derecho* windstorm that ravaged the area. Just beyond, at 1.5 miles, a small spur trail leads down and to the right of the trail. This leads to a Mill Creek Colliery Company mine that dates back to 1921. After exploring this area, return to the trail and continue 0.3 miles to reach

Train trestle at Hawk's Nest.

Fox Branch Falls on the left. A bench here provides a perfect place to take a break and enjoy this wonderful waterfall. Cross the trestle bridge and continue along the trail to its terminus at 2.37 miles. Turn right toward the aerial tram to connect to the G.S.Y.P. Trail, or use the tram to return to the lodge at Hawk's Nest State Park. For additional information on tram operating hours and ticket costs, see page 195 in the introductory portion of this chapter.

Trail Combinations/Options

G.S.Y.P. Trail (Trail 59): At the trail's end, you can link into the G.S.Y.P. Trail. Continue past the tram station to the bridge that crosses Mill Creek. Follow the gravel road (part of the G.S.Y.P. Trail) to the trail sign (approximately 0.2 miles) and move left into the forest, following trail signs. This trail is for hiking or trail running only.
Fisherman's Access Trail (Trail 58): After connecting with the G.S.Y.P. Trail for 0.15 miles, cross Mill Creek and follow the gravel road until it turns sharply right. Rather than turning right and staying on the G.S.Y.P. Trail, keep straight and walk past the parking area and boat launch to reach the trailhead for Fisherman's Access Trail, at the gate.
Hawk's Nest Connector Trail: This trail, not yet completed, will connect the Hawk's Nest Rail Trail with Fayette Station Road. This trail is designed to be an intermediate-level trail for mountain biking or hiking, offering views of the New River.

HAWK'S NEST RAIL TRAIL

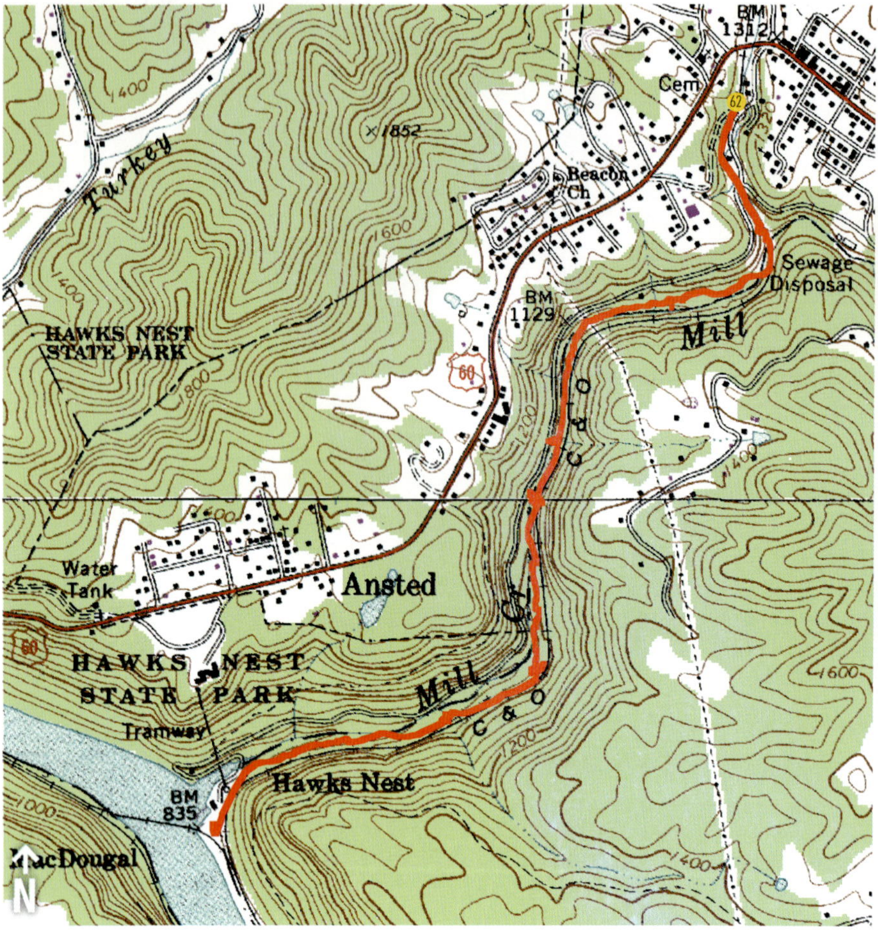

Additional Notes

Hawk's Nest Rail Trail: A debt of gratitude goes out to the many people who made this trail a reality. The town of Ansted, local volunteers, and local contractors worked together to provide this wonderful resource in 2004. As you travel down this trail, remember the volunteers who made this trail possible for all to enjoy!

Town of Ansted: Ansted, incorporated in 1891, is named for the British geologist Dr. David Ansted, who mapped coal deposits in this region in the 1850s. In addition to coal and railroad history, this area was home to both Union and Confederate troops during the Civil War, and hosts three individual sites of relevant historical importance: Tyree Tavern, a favorite haunt that served as headquarters for units of both sides; Westlake Cemetery, the burial place of Thomas "Stonewall" Jackson's mother; and Contentment, the home of Confederate Colonel George Imboden, which now serves as a museum.

HAWK'S NEST RAIL TRAIL

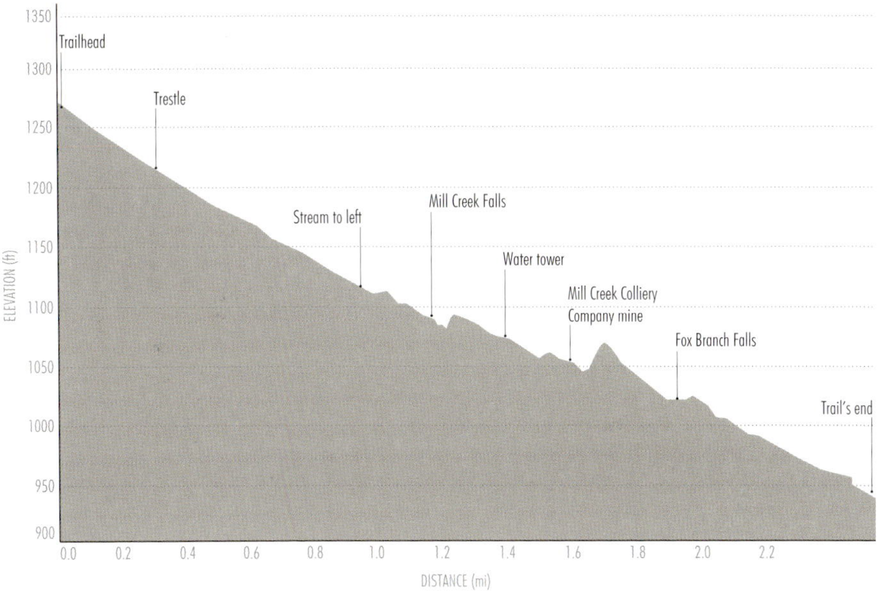

Glade Creek Grist Mill.

15 BABCOCK STATE PARK

Overview and Highlights

Babcock State Park, completed in July 1937 through the efforts of the Civilian Conservation Corp (CCC), is a 4,127-acre state park that borders the New River Gorge National River. Known for the Glade Creek Grist Mill and home to superb trout fishing, Babcock State Park also offers a wide variety of trails, from flat and easy, to rugged and strenuous.

Here, you'll find an abundance of lodging options, from camping to cabins. Some of the cabins are constructed of chestnut logs from trees that died during the chestnut blight of the early twentieth century. It is estimated that the American chestnut once accounted for one out of every four trees in the Appalachian Mountains, and the logs in these cabins serve as a stark reminder of what the forest of the New River Gorge region once looked like.

How to Get There

From Fayetteville, WV, and all points south, follow US Route 19 north to the US Route 60 (Midland Trail) intersection. Drive east for 9.5 miles on US Route 60 until reaching its intersection with WV Route 41. Take WV Route 41 south 1.6 miles to reach the upper access into the park, or continue another 2.0 miles to the main entrance. From the east and Interstate 64, take the Sam Black Church exit (exit 156) and follow US Route 60 west 25.2 miles to WV Route 41 south.

Rules and Regulations

Please see "Rules and Regulations for West Virginia State Parks" (page 24) for rules and regulations governing Babcock State Park and all other state parks in the region.

General Trail Information

Ten trails within Babcock State Park are open to hikers, mountain bikers, trail runners, and cross-country skiers. You'll also find equestrian trails — however, only the concessionaire uses these trails, and no private horseback riding is allowed without permission from the park superintendent. For this reason, these trails are not included in this guide. Consult with Babcock State Park staff for additional information.

History and Culture

Glade Creek Grist Mill: Assembled in 1976 at the site of Cooper's Mill, the Glade Creek Grist Mill is one of the most-photographed spots in West Virginia. It was built using portions of three historic mills from around the state: The structure dates back to 1890 and is from Pocahontas County, WV; the waterwheel came from the Spring Run Grist Mill in Petersburg, WV (a fire destroyed the majority of this mill, but spared the wheel); and other portions of the mill came from the Onego Grist Mill in Seneca Rocks, WV.

BABCOCK STATE PARK HIKES

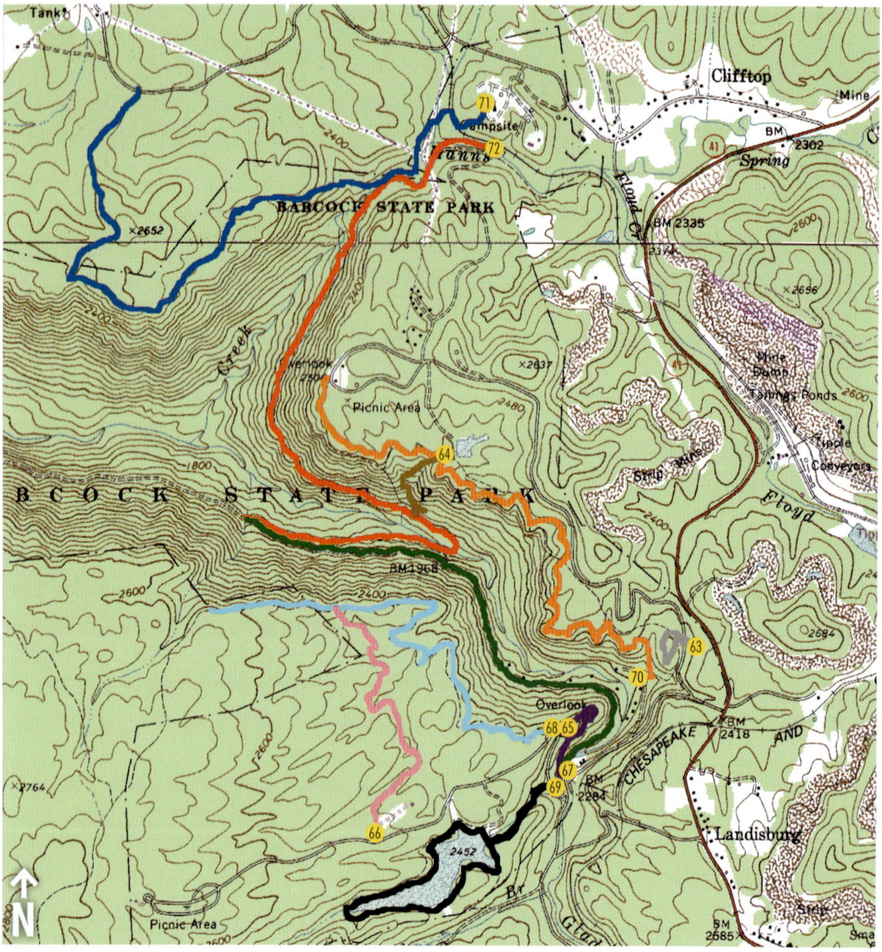

View from the stone shelter along the Island in the Sky Trail (Trail 65).

Map Key

Trail 63 – Mountain Heath Trail – gray
Trail 64 – Rocky Trail – brown
Trail 65 – Island in the Sky Trail – purple
Trail 66 – Triple Creek Trail – pink
Trail 67 – Old Sewell Road Trail – dark green
Trail 68 – Wilderness Trail – light blue
Trail 70 – Skyline Trail – orange
Trail 71 – Manns Creek Trail – dark blue
Trail 72 – Narrow Gauge Trail – red

63 MOUNTAIN HEATH TRAIL

A short educational trail that introduces young people to the various plants and trees of the forest.

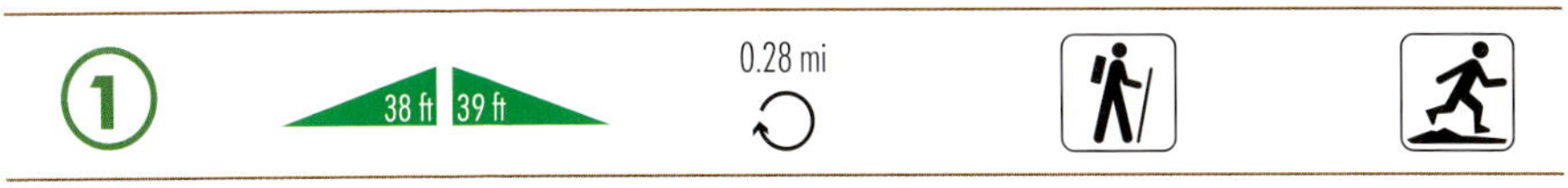

Location: Accessed from WV Route 41, east side of New River Gorge
Maps: USGS Thurmond quad 1:24,000, USGS Danese quad 1:24,000
Facilities: Small gravel turnoff across from trailhead for three vehicles.
Highlights: Educational opportunity, view from Point 15.

Trail Milestones:

0.2 mi – Cliff's edge/viewpoint (37°59.030 N, 080°56.496 W)

Finding the Trailhead

(37°59.064 N, 080°56.425 W)
Turn into the main park entrance from WV Route 41. At the Y intersection take the right-hand branch and travel 300 meters. The trailhead is on the left, with a small parking turnoff on the right.

Trail Description

No Blaze
From the trailhead enter the woods and move right, following the trail markers from No. 1 through No. 29. (Brochures available at the visitor center guide you through the local flora.) The trail ascends to the right for a little more than 0.1 miles before leveling off. At 0.2 miles (Point 15) you can see glimpses of the valley through the trees; there is also a short cliff line here, so take care. Turn sharply left from this point and begin a steady descent toward Point 29. Turn right and return to the trailhead at 0.28 miles.

Winter in Babcock State Park.

64 ROCKY TRAIL

This short yet rugged trail connects Skyline Trail (Trail 70) with the Narrow Gauge Trail (Trail 72).

4 | 0 ft 378 ft | 0.31 mi

Location: Accessed from WV Route 41, east side of New River Gorge
Maps: USGS Thurmond quad 1:24,000, USGS Danese quad 1:24,000
Trail Options: Connects Skyline and Narrow Gauge trails.
Facilities: No facilities available.
Highlights: Stone staircase built in the 1930s.

Finding the Trailhead

Upper trailhead: (37°59.505 N, 080°57.180 W)
The upper trailhead is located along Skyline Trail at its 1.5-mile point as described in this guide.

Lower trailhead: (37°59.372 N, 080°57.255 W)
The lower trailhead is sited along the Narrow Gauge Trail at its 1.7-mile point as described in this guide.

Trail Description

White Diamond Blaze
Note: Hike described from upper trailhead. Descend from the intersection with Skyline Trail, paralleling a small stream amongst a grove of rhododendrons. Cross this stream at 0.2 miles and continue downward. The Civilian Conservation Corp (CCC) built this trail in the 1930s, and great portions of the original stairs survive today. Continue steeply downward until just before reaching the flat and wide Narrow Gauge Trail. At this point, the trail loses definition and requires attention to navigate the final 10 meters without falling.

Trail Milestones:

0.0 mi – Upper trailhead at Skyline Trail (37°59.505 N, 080°57.180 W)
0.2 mi – Cross stream (37°59.412 N, 080°57.278 W)
0.31 mi – Lower trailhead at Narrow Gauge Trail (37°59.372 N, 080°57.255 W)

Trail Combinations/Options

Use this trail to combine portions of the Skyline Trail (Trail 70) and Narrow Gauge Trail (Trail 72). See the Narrow Gauge Trail description for loop options.

65 ISLAND IN THE SKY TRAIL

A short hike that features beautiful vistas and allows the visitor an up-close view of the park's rock formations.

2 | 51 ft 185 ft | 0.42 mi

Location: Accessed from WV Route 41, east side of New River Gorge

Maps: USGS Thurmond quad 1:24,000, USGS Danese quad 1:24,000

Trail Options: Wilderness Trail (Trail 68) trailhead nearby.

Facilities: Paved parking for multiple vehicles.

Highlights: Beautiful vista over the park and up-close views of cliffs.

Trail Milestones:

0.01 mi – Intersection (37°58.909 N, 080°56.728 W)

0.1 mi – Overlook and stone shelter (37°58.909 N, 080°56.717 W)

0.4 mi – Glade Creek Grist Mill main trailhead (37°58.756 N, 080°56.816 W)

Trail Combinations/Options

Two options return you to the starting trailhead: Either retrace the exact path you came by or use the paved road that leads to Boley Lake. (If using the paved road to ascend or descend after completing the hike, you'll pass the trailhead for the Lake View Trail [Trail 69].) The upper trailhead also allows access to the Wilderness Trail (Trail 68), which is located in the same curve.

Finding the Trailhead

Upper trailhead: (37°58.866 N, 080°56.807 W)
Reach the upper trailhead from the visitor center by crossing the bridge at the Glade Creek Grist Mill and continuing toward Boley Lake. At the second sharp turn, find a small paved parking lot to the right; the upper trailhead is located here.

Main trailhead: (37°58.756 N, 080°56.816 W)
The main trailhead is located beside the gristmill and is accessed from the parking lot either at the visitor's center or the mill itself.

Trail Description

White Diamond Blaze

Note: Hike described from the upper trailhead, as it's less difficult in this direction. This trail is marked throughout with a white diamond blaze. Almost immediately, thick rhododendron encroaches on the trail until you reach an intersection at 150 meters. Keep right to a stone-and-beam shelter with beautiful views of a large portion of the park. This shelter and the surrounding area are located atop a cliff, so please watch your step.

After taking in the vista, retrace your steps to the intersection, take a right, and begin to descend to the cliff bottom. Duck beneath boulders and use wooden ladders to make your way to the cliff base. From this point the trail becomes more moderate in nature and meanders gradually along the cliff and then through deciduous forest to the Glade Creek Grist Mill.

If starting from the gristmill (main trailhead), the hike moves upward at a slight incline and requires maneuvering up the ladders to the cliff top and relatively level trail above.

66 TRIPLE CREEK TRAIL

A winding trail that crosses three streams and connects to the Wilderness Trail.

3 | 174 ft | 127 ft | 0.93 mi

Location: Accessed from WV Route 41, east side of New River Gorge
Maps: USGS Thurmond quad 1:24,000, USGS Danese quad 1:24,000
Trail Options: Connect with the Wilderness Trail (Trail 68).
Facilities: Paved parking, toilet facilities, and swimming pool near trailhead.
Highlights: Mature forest, with multiple stream crossings.

Trail Milestones:

0.3 miles – Stream No. 1
(37°58.818 N, 080°57.277 W)
0.51 mi – Stream No. 2
(37°58.915 N, 080°57.391 W)
0.8 miles – Stream No. 3
(37°59.083 N, 080°57.402 W)

Finding the Trailhead

(37°58.632 N, 080°57.377 W)

Reach the trailhead from the visitor center by crossing the bridge at the Glade Creek Grist Mill and continuing past Boley Lake to the swimming-pool parking area on the right. The trailhead is at the entrance to this parking area.

Trail Description

Orange Diamond Blaze

Move into forest from the trailhead just off the paved entrance to the swimming pool. The trail here is single-track and winds through the forest. This trail is well marked with orange diamond blazes, markers that are sorely needed due to the tortuous nature of the trail. At 0.27 miles encounter a large cluster of trees downed in summer 2012 during a massive windstorm, called a *derecho,* that struck southern West Virginia and caused major damage. Just beyond, at 0.3 miles, cross the first stream using a wooden bridge. The trail widens here and is better defined before coming around a sharp bend and crossing over the second creek, sometimes dry, at 0.51 miles.

For the next 0.29 miles the trail loops through the woods until crossing the final Triple Creek Trail stream at 0.80 miles. Ascend steeply for the final 0.13 miles and intersect the Wilderness Trail (Trail 68).

Trail Combinations/Options

The most-frequented option is to link up with the Wilderness Trail (Trail 68). Most often, hikers or trail runners combine these trails by beginning on the Wilderness Trail, connecting to the Triple Creek Trail, and then hiking or running the latter in reverse of the description above. A road connector 0.68 miles in length is then used to return to the Wilderness Trail's trailhead. See the Wilderness Trail description for more info.

Following Triple Creek Trail over a stream crossing.

TRIPLE CREEK TRAIL

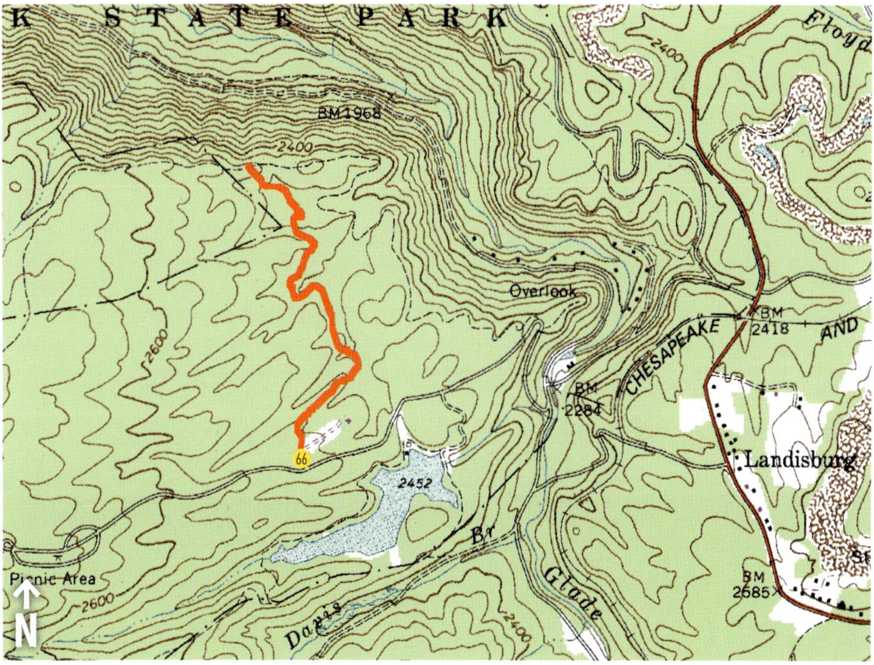

67 OLD SEWELL ROAD TRAIL

Old Sewell Road Trail, historically part of the Manns Creek Railway, is a well-developed road/trail that leads from the Glade Creek Grist Mill to the intersection with the Narrow Gauge Trail.

2 | 2 ft 314 ft | 1.59 mi

Location: Accessed from WV Route 41, east side of New River Gorge
Maps: USGS Thurmond quad 1:24,000, USGS Danese quad 1:24,000
Trail Options: Connect with the Narrow Gauge Trail (Trail 72).
Facilities: Ample paved parking, a gift shop, and toilet facilities are located near the trailhead at the visitor's center.
Highlights: Glade Creek Grist Mill, waterfalls, and cascades.

Trail Milestones:

0.6 mi – Paved road ends (37°59.019 N, 080°56.995W)
0.8 mi – Stream to left (37°59.148 N, 080°57.052W)

Finding the Trailhead

(37°58.772 N, 080°56.811W)
Reach the trailhead from the visitor center by crossing the bridge at the Glade Creek Grist Mill and turning right. The trail begins as a paved road leading toward cabins 8–13.

Trail Description

No Blaze
From the Glade Creek Grist Mill, built in 1976 as a re-creation of the original Cooper's Mill that once stood in the same location, move downhill along the paved road. Traffic along this road is minimal, but please be aware of cars. Remember to look over your right shoulder as you hike down the trail, lest you miss some of the area's most beautiful falls and cascades. At 0.2 miles pass under a rock outcropping on the left. Historical photos show trains pulling empty cars underneath this roof with barely an inch of room to spare. Continue a steady descent, with cabins tucked between massive boulders to the right between the trail and Glade Creek. At 0.6 miles the paved road ends at Cabin No. 13, and then moves around a gate blocking vehicular traffic at 0.7 miles. The trail remains wide but now consists of small gravel and dirt.

At 0.8 miles pass a pretty stream falling precipitously down the mountain to the left. It is possible, at 1.0 miles, to catch glimpses of the swinging bridge along the Narrow Gauge Trail below and right. Reach the trail's end at 1.59 miles. Here, the trail dead-ends due to a landslide that destroyed a large section of this former rail bed; meanwhile, Narrow Gauge Trail intersects and leads sharply right. The remainder of Old Sewell Road Trail is officially closed to visitors.

Trail Combinations/Options

Connect with the Narrow Gauge Trail (Trail 72) at the end of the trail, just before a significant landslide that has closed the remainder of the trail. See the Narrow Gauge Trail description for options.

Looking upstream to the Glade Creek Grist Mill.

OLD SEWELL ROAD TRAIL

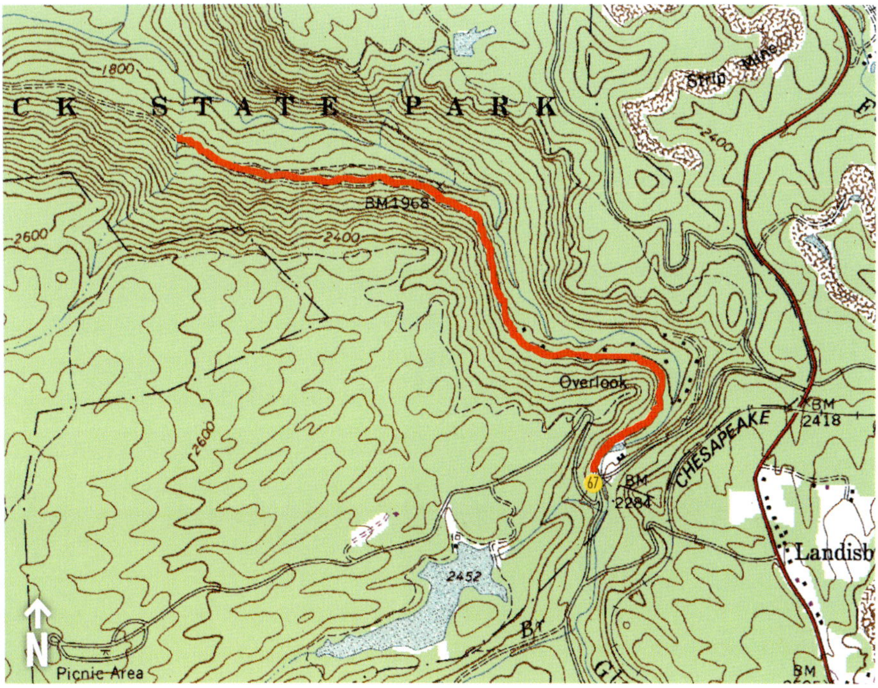

68 WILDERNESS TRAIL

This trail leads into a pretty forest and is popular with local trail runners.

3 | 362 ft | 111 ft | 1.60 mi

Location: Accessed from WV Route 41, east side of New River Gorge
Maps: USGS Thurmond quad 1:24,000, USGS Danese quad 1:24,000
Trail Options: Combine with Triple Creek Trail (Trail 66).
Facilities: Paved parking for multiple vehicles.
Highlights: Views into a valley.

Finding the Trailhead

(37°58.879 N, 080°56.835 W)
Reach the trailhead from the visitor center by crossing the bridge at the Glade Creek Grist Mill and continuing toward Boley Lake. At the second sharp turn find a small paved parking lot to the right; the trailhead is located opposite this parking area along the road.

Trail Description

Yellow Diamond Blaze
Ascend slightly from the trailhead and enter the forest. The trail winds through the trees until dropping in elevation to a stone bridge that crosses a seasonal stream at 0.64 miles. Climb steeply up the other side of the stream and venture downhill again at 0.8 miles to cross a smaller stream. From here the trail moves through nondescript forest until reaching the intersection with Triple Creek Trail at 1.3 miles. (You have three options at this junction: reverse back to the trailhead; continue 0.3 miles to the end of the trail; or turn left and begin hiking the Triple Creek Trail [Trail 66].) Staying on the Wilderness Trail, continue 0.3 miles, catching glimpses of the valley below and to the right. There are remnants of a stone fence in this area. The trail ends at a sign stating "Trail's end — Please return along same trail."

Trail Milestones:

0.64 mi – Stone bridge over stream (37°59.042 N, 080°57.224 W)
1.3 mi – Intersection with Triple Creek Trail (37°59.149 N, 080°57.500 W)

Wilderness Trail.

Trail Combinations/Options

Combine with the Triple Creek Trail (Trail 66) and a short section of park road to create a 3.51-mile loop. To close the loop, backtrack along the final 0.3 miles of Wilderness Trail and turn right onto Triple Creek Trail. At the end of Triple Creek Trail (parking lot), hike to the road (100 meters) and turn left. This paved road descends gradually for 0.68 miles to the original Wilderness Trail trailhead.

WILDERNESS TRAIL

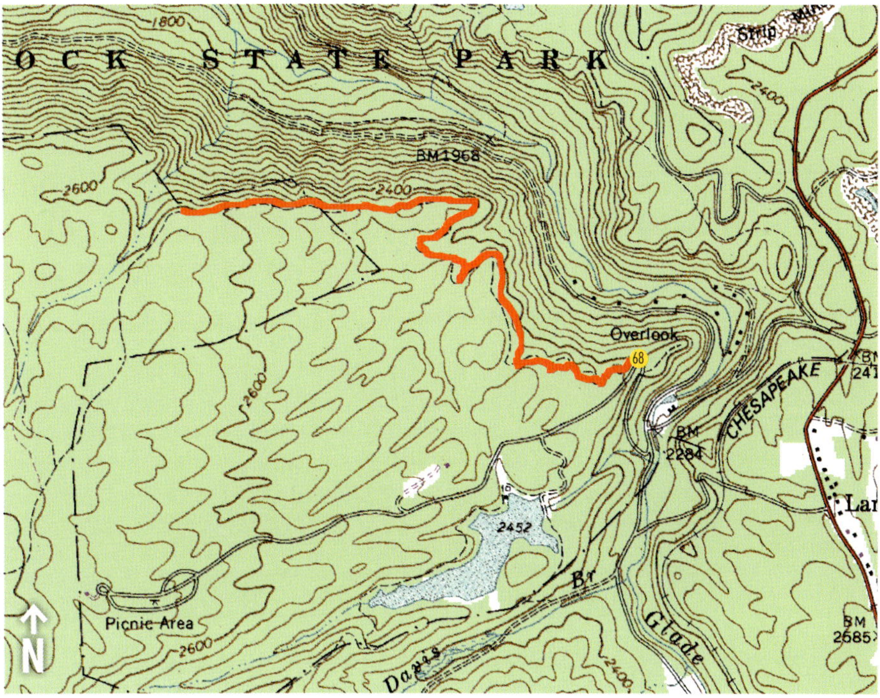

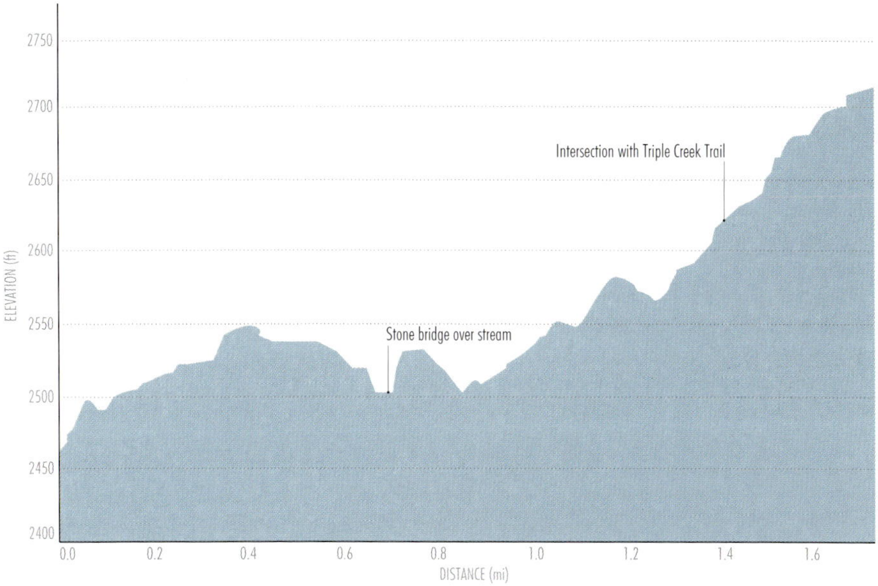

69 LAKE VIEW TRAIL

A nice hike along the shores of Boley Lake. Offers amazing colors in the autumn.

2 | 316 ft 298 ft | 1.76 mi

Location: Accessed from WV Route 41, east side of New River Gorge
Maps: USGS Thurmond quad 1:24,000, USGS Danese quad 1:24,000
Facilities: None at trailhead; parking available at Glade Creek Grist Mill and at 1.4 miles (toilets, picnic tables).
Highlights: Boley Lake, stream, autumn colors.

Trail Milestones:

0.3 mi – Intersect with lake (37°58.909 N, 080°57.026 W)
0.6 mi – Field with views (37°58.458 N, 080°57.169 W)
0.9 mi – Bridge (37°58.445 N, 080°57.461 W)
1.4 mi – Parking area (37°58.640 N, 080°57.113 W)

Finding the Trailhead

(37°58.735 N, 080°56.842 W)
The trailhead is located along Boley Lake Road. From the visitor's center and gristmill, walk toward the lake. The trailhead is on the left, just after the first curve.

Alternatively, drive to Boley Lake and begin the trail from the parking area. This option bypasses the 0.3-mile approach to the lake from the trailhead described above.

Trail Description

Orange Diamond Blaze
From the trailhead ascend through thick rhododendron until reaching a small stream. Cross a wooden bridge and climb up a steeper bank. Continue along the stream until reaching Boley Lake at 0.3 miles. From this point, the trail moves in both directions — turn left along the lake edge, following trail signs. In an additional 0.3 miles the trail moves out of the forest and into a small field. This area offers great views of a large portion of the lake. Move off the trail here to the water's edge to get a better look at the tall grass and lily pads that hug the banks. Watch for small frogs.

The trail reenters the forest and meanders along just above shoreline until reaching a bridge at 0.9 miles. Continue through mature woods until reaching the lake parking at 1.4 miles. This paved lot has spaces for 20 vehicles, toilets, picnic facilities, a dock, and boat rentals. Stay close to the lake and return to the trail on the far side. At 1.5 miles reach the lakeside intersection near the trailhead and turn left, returning 0.3 miles to the trail's end.

LAKE VIEW TRAIL

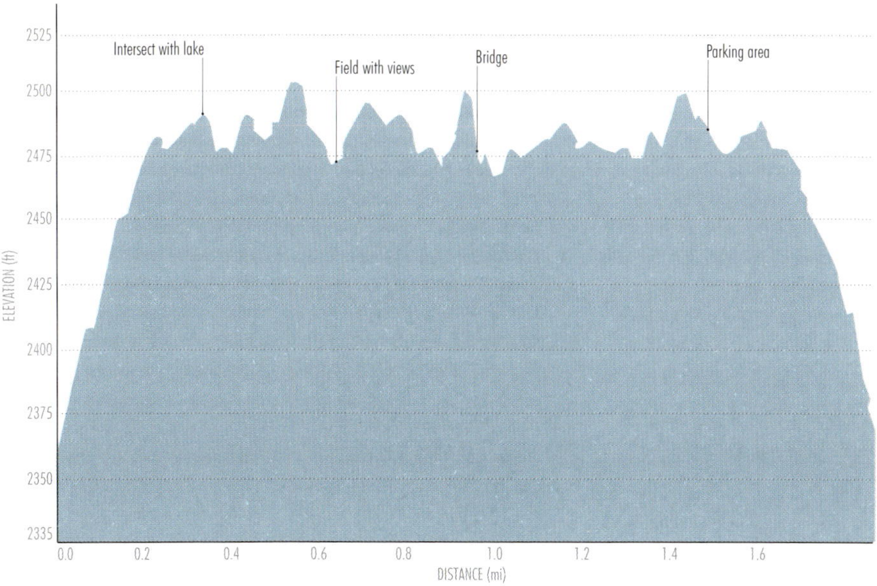

70 SKYLINE TRAIL

Skyline Trail, one of the most popular trails in the park, offers viewpoints throughout its length, including one considered to be among the best in the region.

3 | 485 ft | 234 ft | 2.07 mi

Location: Accessed from WV Route 41, east side of New River Gorge
Maps: USGS Thurmond quad 1:24,000, USGS Danese quad 1:24,000
Trail Options: Connects the Rocky Trail (Trail 64) to the Narrow Gauge Trail (Trail 72).
Facilities: Toilet and picnic facilities at Manns Creek Overlook.
Highlights: Distant views of West Virginia's mountains.

Trail Milestones:

0.2 mi – Attain cliff top (37°59.061 N, 080°56.608 W)
0.8 mi – Viewpoint (37°59.250 N, 080°56.817 W)
1.5 mi – Intersection with Rocky Trail (37°59.505 N, 080°57.180 W)

Finding the Trailhead

Lower trailhead: (37°58.995 N, 080°56.558 W)
Access this trailhead by following WV Route 41 south to the main park entrance. Enter the park and turn left at the Y intersection. Take the next possible right (toward cabins 1–5); the trailhead is located in the tree line across from Cabin No. 5.

Upper trailhead: (37°59.690 N, 080°57.523 W)
The upper trailhead (Manns Creek Overlook) is located near the picnic area. To get here, follow WV Route 41 south to the main park entrance. Enter the park and turn right at the Y intersection. Continue along this road until you reach the Manns Creek Overlook. The road becomes one-way in this area — loop to the right, passing cabins No. 14 and 15 to the left. The picnic area is located to the right, with the trailhead just adjacent.

Trail Description

Yellow Diamond Blaze
Note: Hike described from lower trailhead. Starting at the lower trailhead across from Cabin No. 5, hike uphill beside a stream (to the right) and amidst a thicket of rhododendrons. Turn right and continue to ascend. At 0.2 miles notice a rock cleft to the right, and shortly thereafter cross it via a wooden bridge. After this steep ascent, the trail begins to level out atop the cliff line. Take special care at this point, as the trail closely parallels the cliff edge.

At 0.4 miles intersect a small branch trail (10 meters long) that leads to an outstanding viewpoint. Continue along the main trail. Multiple branch trails in this area lead to overlooks, but the main trail remains well defined. Throughout the first 0.6 miles of the hike, the forest consists mainly of rhododendrons, but at this point it begins to transition to hardwoods. At 0.8 miles come upon one of the highlights of this trail and the park where the forest gives way to a small opening with benches: This overlook, on a clear day, offers views along the Manns Creek Gorge and beyond. Considered one of the region's best viewpoints, this spot alone is worth the drive to Babcock State Park. Reenter the forest on the far side of this clearing, and at 1.2 miles the trail narrows and hugs the cliff edge. Continue to another viewpoint

SKYLINE TRAIL

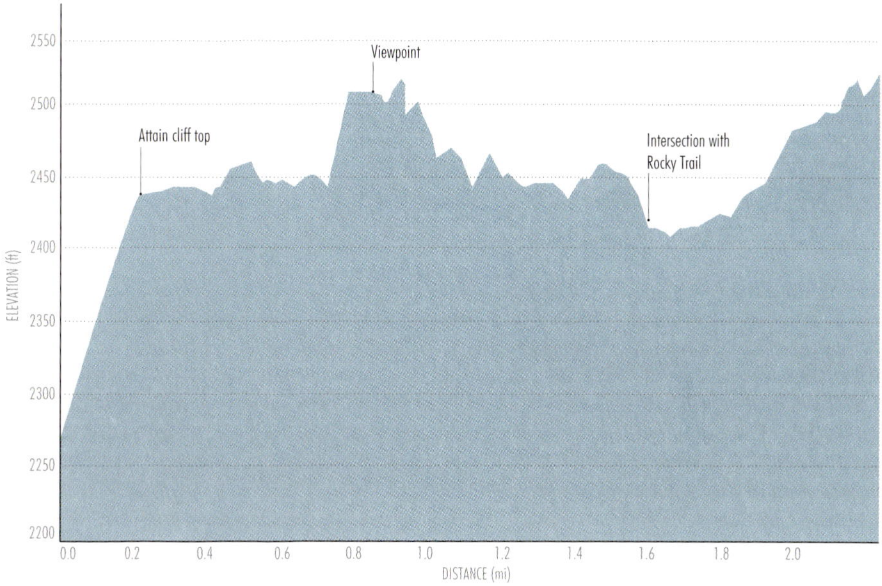

after 0.1 miles, and at 1.5 miles intersect Rocky Trail and a streambed. Rocky Trail parallels this stream and moves downhill. Continue straight over the stream and move upward out of this depression. At 1.7 miles the trail weaves through a small boulder field. After another 0.2 miles you'll begin to see picnic facilities to the right before moving through boulders and reaching the upper trailhead (Mann's Creek Overlook) at 2.07 miles.

Trail Combinations/Options

Use Rocky Trail (Trail 64) to connect with Narrow Gauge Trail (Trail 72) — a nice loop using these trails, along with Old Sewell Road Trail (Trail 67) and a short portion of paved road, creates a 4.62-mile excursion. Starting at the trailhead near Cabin No. 5, travel 1.5 miles to the intersection with Rocky Trail. Descend Rocky Trail to Narrow Gauge Trail and turn left. Follow Narrow Gauge Trail 0.82 miles to its terminus and intersection with Old Sewell Road Trail, turning left and following this latter to the Glade Creek Grist Mill. From the mill turn left and follow the paved park road to the intersection with the access road to cabins 1–6, and then arrive back at the trailhead.

Additional Notes

Be especially cautious throughout this trail, as it parallels a tall cliff line for the majority of its length.

71 MANNS CREEK TRAIL

Waterfalls, boulders, and distant views are just a few of the highlights of the pleasant Manns Creek Trail.

3 | 528 ft | 519 ft | 2.28 mi

Location: Accessed from WV Route 41, east side of New River Gorge
Maps: USGS Thurmond quad 1:24,000, USGS Danese quad 1:24,000
Trail Options: No connections available, though you can return by using the Camp Carver Road (CR 11/3) and turning right onto the Old Clifftop Road (CR 11).
Facilities: Campground, toilets, showers, and ample parking.
Highlights: Manns Creek, viewpoint.

Trail Milestones:

0.4 mi – Stone building (38°00.193 N, 080°57.258 W)
1.2 mi – Boulders (37°59.883 N, 080°57.992 W)
1.4 mi – Overlook (37°59.856 N, 080°58.149 W)
1.6 mi – Sharp right turn (37°59.919 N, 080°58.309 W)
2.28 mi – Camp Washington Carver (38°00.362 N, 080°58.102 W)

Trail Combinations/Options

No combination to other trails is available. However, rather than returning to the trailhead via the same route, you can take the Camp Carver Road (CR 11/3) and turn right onto the Old Clifftop Road (CR 11) to return to the campground.

Finding the Trailhead

(38°00.315 N, 080°57.051 W)
From US Route 60, take WV Route 41 south 1.6 miles until intersecting with Clifftop Loop Road (CR 11/4). Turn right here and follow the road through the town of Clifftop to the park's campground entrance; the trailhead is located beside Campsite No. 26, at the rear of the campground.

Trail Description

Orange Diamond Blaze
From the trailhead at campsite No. 26 meander through the woods for 150 meters, passing boulders to the right, before reaching an opening where the trail veers sharply right along an old railroad bed. Proceed 50 meters before the trail turns sharply left and reenters a rhododendron forest. At 0.2 miles cross a stream over a wooden bridge and continue along a hillside covered thickly with low-hanging rhododendron. At 0.4 miles pass a stone building to the left and begin to parallel Manns Creek to the left not long after.

Begin to ascend, and cross a rocky, cascading stream using a wooden bridge. At this point the trail steepens and moves away from Manns Creek. At 1.2 miles cross a stream that flows, for a time, within the trail before dropping off to the left. Weave through boulders as the rhododendrons begin to give way to mountain laurel. Take some time to explore these boulders, or just have a rest on a log bench under one of the massive overhangs.

Continue 0.2 miles to an overlook on the left that offers a fantastic view toward the New River. Continue along the now relatively flat path until at 1.6 miles the trail turns sharply right at a sign that reads "Do Not Enter: This trail is not a state park trail." Move through mature forest for the next 0.69 miles before skirting a field to the left and arriving at Camp Washington Carver.

Looking down-valley from the overlook at 1.4 miles.

MANNS CREEK TRAIL

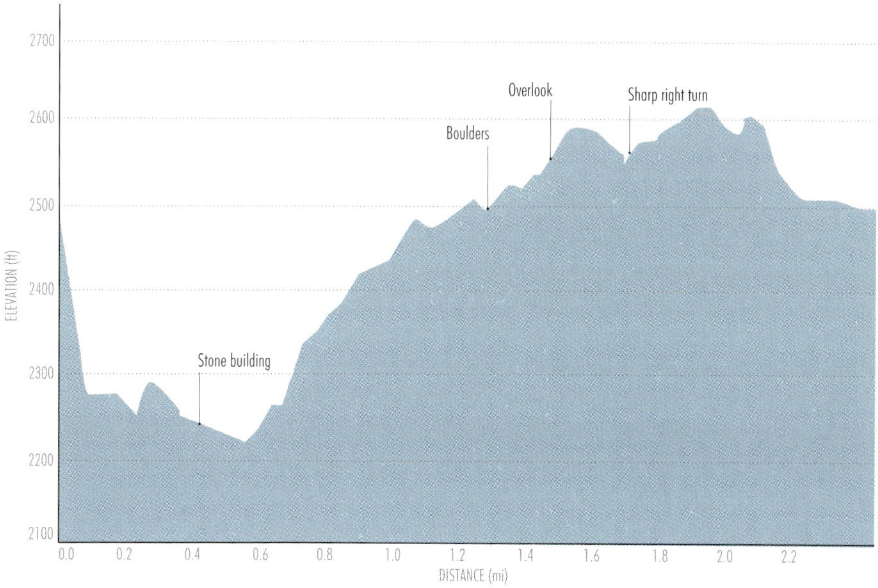

72 NARROW GAUGE TRAIL

This fun trail follows the rail bed for the Manns Creek Railway, and moves along Manns and Glade creeks before arriving at a park highlight, the swinging bridge over Glade Creek.

2 | 44 ft 412 ft | 2.52 mi

Location: Accessed from WV Route 41, east side of New River Gorge
Maps: USGS Thurmond quad 1:24,000, USGS Danese quad 1:24,000
Trail Options: This trail connects with Rocky Trail (Trail 64) and Old Sewell Road Trail (Trail 67).
Facilities: No facilities at the trailhead, but parking and toilet facilities are readily accessible in the campground above.
Highlights: Manns and Glade creeks, swinging bridge.

Trail Milestones:

0.2 mi – Trail splits left
(38°00.202 N, 080°57.208 W)
1.52 mi – First barricade
(38°59.406 N, 080°57.394 W)
1.65 mi – Second barricade
(38°59.337 N, 080°57.286 W)
1.9 mi – Swinging bridge
(38°59.286 N, 080°57.142 W)

Finding the Trailhead

(38°00.221 N, 080°57.030 W)
The trailhead is located in the northern portion of the park. From US Route 60, travel 1.6 miles south along WV Route 41. Turn right on Clifftop Loop Road (CR 11/4) until reaching the park campground. The trailhead is located on the right side of the park road that leads to the northern cabin area. Signs located throughout the park guide you there.

Trail Description

Yellow Diamond Blaze
Leaving the park road at the trailhead on the right, follow the trail (also an access road) alongside Manns Creek for 0.2 miles. At this point the trail moves to the left and narrows slightly — this area is heavily populated with rhododendrons. At 0.5 miles Manns Creek begins to fall away from the trail and the roar of the cascades lessens. In the next 0.1 miles remember to look to the right and over your shoulder to appreciate the falls along the stream below.

Now the trail begins to emerge from the thick rhododendrons, often found along streambeds, and to move into a more mature deciduous forest. The trail continues to descend gradually as rock walls begin to materialize to your left. At 1.3 miles Manns Creek is but a memory, and you can now catch glimpses of Glade Creek far below.

At 1.52 miles reach the first barricade that impedes progress along the trail, a washed-out portion of the original rail line. Move down and right, cross the stream, and ascend the opposite side back to the trail. Just 0.13 miles farther along encounter the second barricade and detour again to the right and below, crossing the stream over a wooden bridge. You'll find a small waterfall above with a cave behind it, but don't let that distract you from the hidden railroad gem below: the axle to a narrow gauge railcar that lies in the streambed below the bridge. Take some time here to explore these two sights before ascending steeply to regain the trail.

Slightly past this second barricade, come upon the sign for Rocky Trail, leading steeply to the left. Continue straight until reaching the highlight of your hike, the swinging bridge over Glade Creek, a 20-foot span that rocks slightly up and down between the pillars

Glade Creek.

with human passage. This bridge utilizes the concrete pillars that once supported what was known as the Tank Trestle or Horseshoe Trestle of the Manns Creek Railway. Careful crossing this bridge, as it is extremely slippery when wet. Continue another 0.62 miles to the trail's end and intersection with the Old Sewell Road Trail.

Trail Combinations/Options

The Narrow Gauge Trail connects with Rocky Trail (Trail 64) and the Old Sewell Road Trail (Trail 67). Utilizing a car shuttle, a great one-way hike is to combine the Narrow Gauge Trail and Old Sewell Road Trail. At the Narrow Gauge Trail's terminus and intersection with Old Sewell Road Trail, turn left and steadily climb along the trail and road until you reach the Glade Creek Grist Mill. Return by car. This one-way jaunt is 4.11 miles.

To create a loop with the Narrow Gauge Trail, complete the above one-way trail and turn left at the gristmill. Pass the visitor center on the left and climb along the park road until you reach the first road leading left. Turn on this road (which leads to cabins 1–6). At Cabin No. 5 watch for the trailhead to Skyline Trail (Trail 70). Take Skyline Trail 1.5 miles until it intersects with Rocky Trail. Turn left on Rocky Trail, descending to Narrow Gauge Trail. At this intersection, turn right and return via the remaining portion of the Narrow Gauge Trail (1.7 miles). This combination results in a 7.92-mile loop.

NARROW GAUGE TRAIL

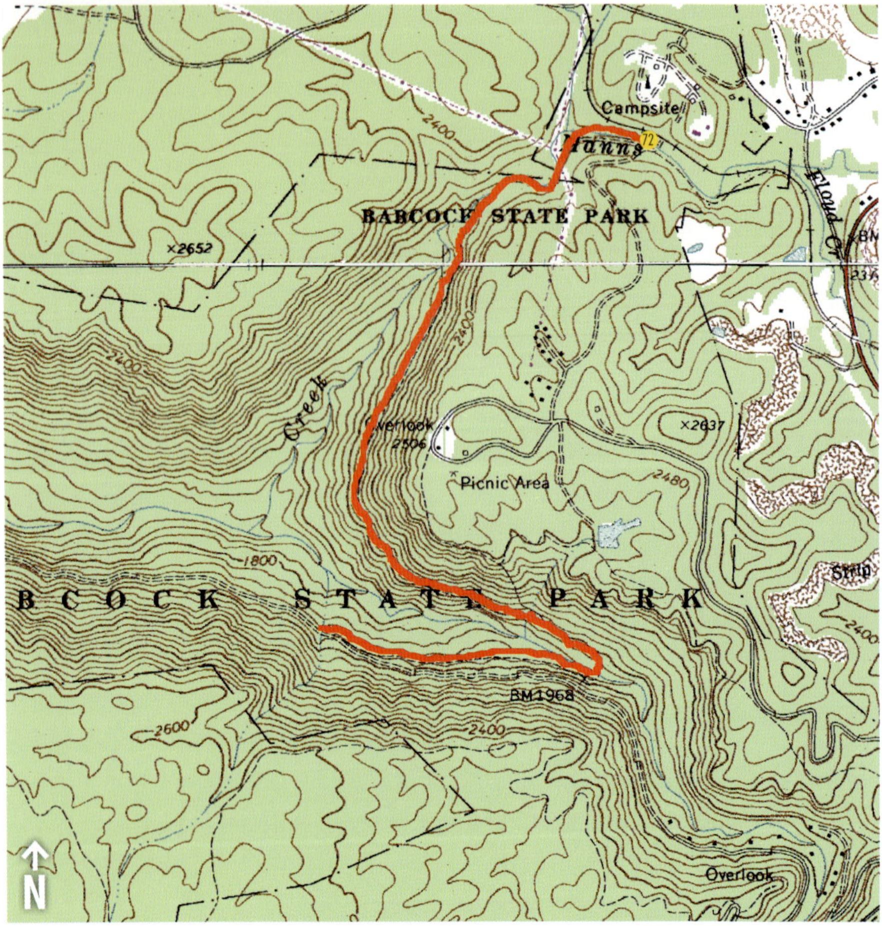

Additional Notes

From 1873 until 1956, the Manns Creek Railway operated along the path of the Narrow Gauge Trail and Old Sewell Road Trail, carrying coal from the mines at Clifftop and lumber from Landisburg. This small railroad, only 40 miles in length, moved coal and timber from these two towns to the main Chesapeake and Ohio (C&O) lines in the New River Gorge. A sharp eye will find remnants of this past throughout the hike.

Mountain-Bike Note

Two locations on this trail require mountain bikers to dismount and carry their bicycles: one at 1.5 miles and the second at 1.6 miles. It is also advisable to walk your bicycle across the swinging bridge.

NARROW GAUGE TRAIL

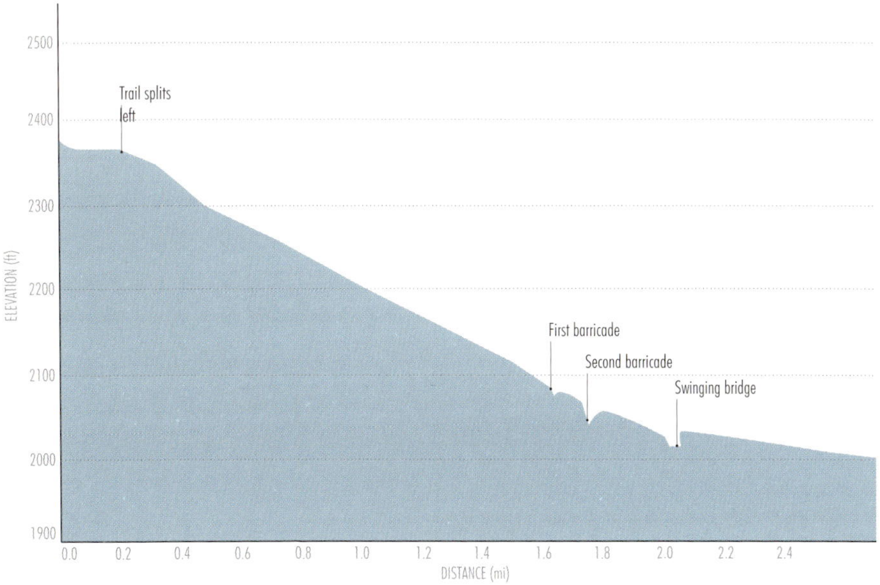

A fisherman along Little Beaver Lake.

16 LITTLE BEAVER STATE PARK

Overview and Highlights

Little Beaver State Park, a 562-acre state park due south of Fayetteville and near the Grandview Region of the New River Gorge National River, is home to an 18-acre lake built from 1938–1942. This park offers a host of recreational activities, including hiking, biking, fishing, camping, and boating. It also includes a newly built campground with 46 sites, completed in 2011.

The area around the lake is particularly beautiful in the fall, with the changing of the leaves. Additionally, the many trails that border area streams offer brilliant displays of color from blooming rhododendron in late spring.

How to Get There

From Interstate 64, take exit 129A toward Shady Spring. Turn onto Grandview Road (CR 9) south and travel 1.8 miles to the entrance for Little Beaver State Park on the left.

Rules and Regulations

Please see "Rules and Regulations for West Virginia State Parks" (page 24) for rules and regulations governing Little Beaver State Park and all other state parks in the region.

Additional regulations, posted at the campground office, apply to Little Beaver's campsites. For additional information, please consult with campsite employees.

General Trail Information

You'll find eighteen trails within the boundaries of Little Beaver State Park that are open to hikers, trail runners, and mountain bikers. All are well marked with diamond trail blazes of various colors. Many trails share the same color, but are located in different areas and should not cause confusion.

History and Culture

The dam at Little Beaver State Park was built between 1938 and 1942 as part of a Works Progress Administration (WPA) and Civilian Conservation Corps (CCC) project. Mrs. Carrie Morgan Wright of Cincinnati, Ohio, and Mr. George H. Smith of Chillicothe, Ohio, donated 50 acres of land for the project. Made of locally quarried sandstone, the dam was added to the National Register of Historic Places in 1998.

LITTLE BEAVER STATE PARK HIKES

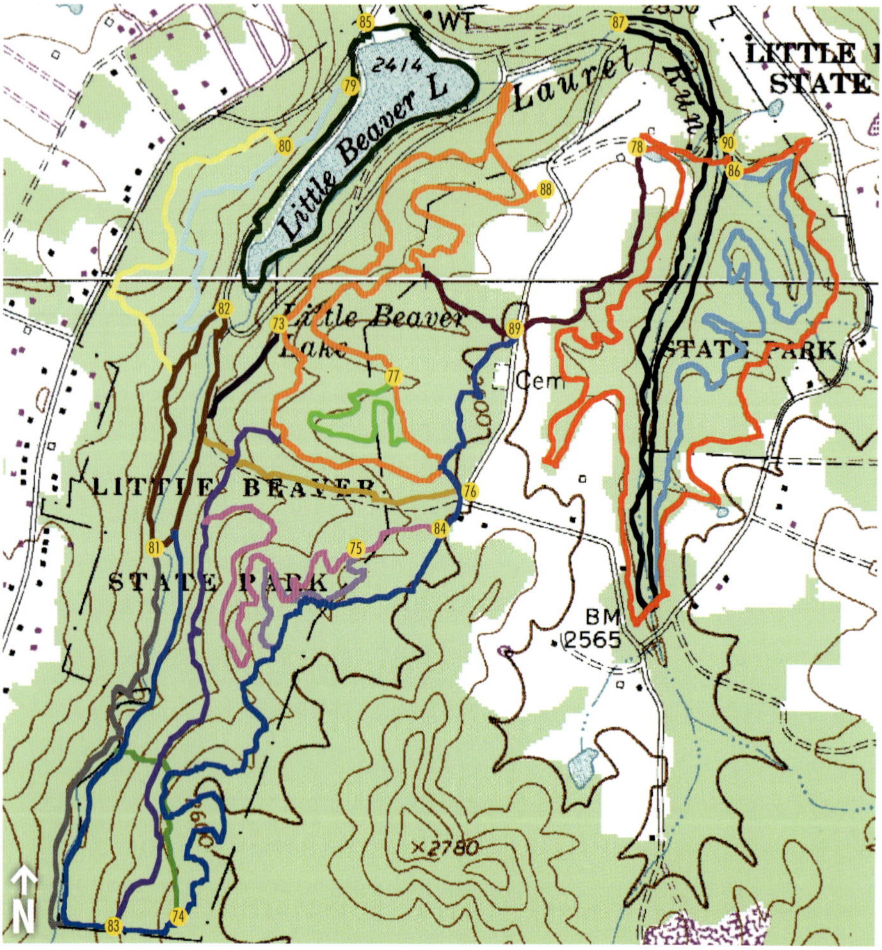

Map Key

Trail 73 – Hemlock Trail – dark purple
Trail 74 – Drop Off Trail – green
Trail 75 – Turkey Spur Trail – lavender
Trail 76 – Creek Bed Trail – tan
Trail 77 – Easy Street Trail – light green
Trail 78 – Deer Trail – brick red
Trail 79 – Billy Goat's Gruff Trail – aqua
Trail 80 – Topper's Ridge Trail – yellow
Trail 81 – Black Bear Run Trail – gray
Trail 82 – Beaver Creek Trail – brown
Trail 83 – Stone Trough Trail – purple
Trail 84 – Crooked Rock Trail – pink
Trail 85 – Lake Front Trail – dark green
Trail 86 – Weaver Way Trail – light blue
Trail 87 – Railroad Grade Trail – black
Trail 88 – Nature Ridge Trail – orange
Trail 89 – Rhododendron Run Trail – dark blue
Trail 90 – Laurel Creek Trail – red

73 HEMLOCK TRAIL

The Hemlock Trail is a short access trail linking the Nature Ridge Trail to Beaver Creek Trail through a forest of hemlocks, Virginia pine, rhododendron, and mountain laurel.

2 | 3 ft | 80 ft | 0.16 mi

Location: South of Interstate 64, exit 129A
Maps: USGS Prince quad 1:24,000, USGS Shady Spring quad 1:24,000
Trail Options: Connector trail from Nature Ridge Trail (Trail 88) to Beaver Creek Trail (Trail 82).
Facilities: Little Beaver State Park offers a full range of picnic, recreation, camping, and toilet facilities.
Highlights: Wonderful greenery year-round.

Trail Milestones:

1.0 mi – Intersection with Nature Ridge Trail/upper trailhead (37°44.944 N, 081°04.983 W)
0.16 mi – Intersection with Beaver Creek Trail/lower trailhead (37°44.839 N, 081°05.089 W)

Finding the Trailhead

From Interstate 64, take exit 129A toward Shady Spring. Turn onto Grandview Road (CR 9) south and travel 1.8 miles to the entrance for Little Beaver State Park on the left.

Upper trailhead: (37°44.944 N, 081°04.983 W)
Access the trail from its upper trailhead, 1.4 miles along the Nature Ridge Trail (Trail 88) — please see the Nature Ridge Trail description for details to reach that trailhead.

Lower trailhead: (37°44.839 N, 081°05.089 W)
The trail's lower trailhead is located 0.15 miles along Beaver Creek Trail (Trail 82). This intersection/trailhead is not marked and may be difficult to find. See the Beaver Creek Trail write-up for more.

Trail Description

Yellow Diamond Blaze

Note: Hike described from upper trailhead. From the upper-trailhead intersection, 1.4 miles along Nature Ridge Trail, turn left and descend amongst the trail's namesake, Eastern hemlock. The name neglects the other sources of greenery along this short trail, which include rhododendrons, Virginia pine, and mountain laurel. The combination of these three types of trees plus a shrub creates a beautiful environment throughout this short jaunt. Arrive at the Beaver Creek Trail after hiking 0.16 miles. At the time of publication, this lower-trailhead intersection did not have a trail sign along Beaver Creek Trail — it is, however, located at the 0.15-mile mark of that trail and just before its intersection with Creek Bed Trail.

Trail Combinations/Options

This trail is often used to connect Nature Ridge Trail (Trail 88) to trails along the southwestern portion of the park.

74 DROP OFF TRAIL

A short alternate trail that connects different portions of the Rhododendron Run Trail and includes a steep descent of 140 feet.

3 | 16 ft | 157 ft | 0.37 mi

Location: South of Interstate 64, exit 129A
Maps: USGS Prince quad 1:24,000, USGS Shady Spring quad 1:24,000
Trail Options: Connect to three separate portions of Rhododendron Run Trail.
Facilities: Little Beaver State Park offers a full range of picnic, recreation, camping, and toilet facilities.
Highlights: Access to Rhododendron Run Trail, steep descent.

Trail Milestones:

1.0 mi – Southern trailhead (37°44.242 N, 081°05.140 W)
0.2 mi – Connects with Rhododendron Run Trail (37°44.366 N, 081°05.151 W)
0.3 mi – Intersection with Stone Trough Trail (37°44.434 N, 081°05.186 W)
0.37 mi – Final intersection with Rhododendron Run Trail near creek (37°44.440 N, 081°05.225 W)

Finding the Trailhead

From Interstate 64, take exit 129A toward Shady Spring. Turn onto Grandview Road (CR 9) south and travel 1.8 miles to the entrance for Little Beaver State Park on the left.

This trail intersects the Rhododendron Run Trail (Trail 89) in three different locations; please see its description for information regarding the trailhead and how to reach these intersections.

1: (37°44.242 N, 081°05.140 W) The main (southern) trailhead is located at the 1.6-mile mark of the Rhododendron Run Trail.

2: (37°44.366 N, 081°05.151 W) The intersection and combination of the two trails occurs at the Rhododendron Run Trail's 1.1-mile mark.

3: (37°44.440 N, 081°05.225 W) The lower trailhead is located at Rhododendron Run Trail's 2.0-mile mark.

Trail Description

Blue Diamond Blaze

From the southernmost trailhead, at the 1.6-mile mark of the Rhododendron Run Trail, move right onto the trail. Continue through mixed forest until intersecting the Rhododendron Run Trail again and traveling along the same path for 100 meters. In the winter, you'll be able to see the Stone Trough Trail (Trail 83) downhill and left. After another 100 meters, the trail veers left and downhill, away from Rhododendron Run Trail. At 0.3 miles the trail intersects the Stone Trough Trail. Move across this trail and descend steeply to the trail's end and final intersection with the Rhododendron Run Trail.

Trail Combinations/Options

This trail connects with the Rhododendron Run Trail (Trail 89) in three separate spots. It is not as frequently traveled as other trails but is useful for mountain bikers looking for a steep descent or a tough climb. The trail also connects with the Stone Trough Trail (Trail 83), allowing the hiker to continue north along the midline of the ridge and eventually reach the Nature Ridge Trail (Trail 88).

75 TURKEY SPUR TRAIL

A short trail that runs along a ridge spur, with multiple connections between Crooked Rock and Rhododendron Run trails.

3 | 52 ft 35 ft | 0.41 mi

Location: South of Interstate 64, exit 129A
Maps: USGS Prince quad 1:24,000, USGS Shady Spring quad 1:24,000
Trail Options: Connect Crooked Rock Trail (Trail 84) with Rhododendron Run Trail (Trail 89).
Facilities: Little Beaver State Park offers a full range of picnic, recreation, camping, and toilet facilities.
Highlights: Mixed hardwood forest.

Finding the Trailhead

The trailheads are located along the Crooked Rock Trail (Trail 84) and the Rhododendron Run Trail (Trail 89).

First trailhead: (37°44.675 N, 081°04.863 W)
The first trailhead is 0.2 miles along the Crooked Rock Trail; please see its trail description for directions.

Second trailhead: (37°44.569 N, 081°04.986 W)
The second trailhead is at an intersection 0.8 miles along Rhododendron Run Trail; please see its trail description for additional details.

Trail Description

White Diamond Blaze
Turkey Spur Trail is a great alternative that allows the hiker a little variation while traveling along the Crooked Rock or Rhododendron Run trails. Along the course of this short path, you can ping-pong yourself between these two trails and vary your route ever so slightly for a different experience. From the start, both main trails lie within sight, the first being Rhododendron Run Trail on the left after 180 meters and connecting for a short time at 0.13 miles. Soon after this connection, cross a short bridge, and in 100 meters move right and intersect Crooked Rock Trail. The trails merge for a short distance and then Turkey Spur splits left at 0.3 miles, moving uphill to the trail's end and final intersection with Rhododendron Run Trail at 0.41 miles.

Trail Milestones:

1.0 mi – Intersection with Crooked Rock Trail/first trailhead (37°44.675 N, 081°04.863 W)
0.13 mi – Intersection with Rhododendron Run Trail (37°44.620 N, 081°04.913 W)
0.19 mi – Intersection with Crooked Rock Trail (37°44.624 N, 081°04.955 W)
0.41 mi – Intersection with Rhododendron Run Trail/second trailhead (37°44.569 N, 081°04.986 W)

Trail Combinations/Options

Turkey Spur Trail allows multiple opportunities to vary your route along the Crooked Rock Trail (Trail 84) and Rhododendron Run Trail (Trail 89). Hikers, trail runners, and mountain bikers familiar with the park often use this trail to customize their experience.

76 CREEK BED TRAIL

A great connector trail that allows quick access to Beaver Creek Trail from the Rhododendron Run and Crooked Rock trails.

3 | 1 ft | 168 ft | 0.43 mi

Location: South of Interstate 64, exit 129A
Maps: USGS Prince quad 1:24,000, USGS Shady Spring quad 1:24,000
Trail Options: Connect the upper portion of Rhododendron Run Trail (Trail 89) to Beaver Creek Trail (Trail 82).
Facilities: Little Beaver State Park offers a full range of picnic, recreation, camping, and toilet facilities.
Highlights: Little Beaver Creek.

Trail Milestones:

0.0 mi – Intersection with Rhododendron Run Trail/upper trailhead (37°44.748 N, 081°04.693 W)
0.1 mi – Trail come close to Nature Ridge Trail (37°44.740 N, 081°04.793 W)
0.4 mi – Intersection with Stone Trough Trail (37°44.806 N, 081°05.075 W)
0.43 mi – Intersection with Beaver Creek Trail/lower trailhead (37°44.818 N, 081°05.099 W)

Finding the Trailhead

Upper trailhead: (37°44.748 N, 081°04.693 W)
To access the upper trailhead, via the Rhododendron Run Trail (Trail 89), continue straight along the main park road, passing the visitor center on the right and continuing uphill to the camping-registration office. Stay left at the office and continue along a gravel road toward an open field. From the registration office, travel 0.1 miles and stay right (field on the left and forest on the right). The parking area for the Creek Bed and Rhododendron Run trails is on the left, just before the cemetery; the latter's trailhead (37°44.932 N, 081°04.621 W) lies across the road, to the road's right. Creek Bed's upper trailhead is located 0.3 miles along Rhododendron Run Trail.

Lower trailhead: (37°44.818 N, 081°05.099 W)
The lower trailhead is accessed from Beaver Creek Trail (Trail 82); hike 0.15 miles along it as described to get there.

Trail Description

Blue Diamond Blaze
Note: Hike described from upper trailhead. From Rhododendron Run Trail (upper trailhead), begin to steadily descend along a wide but rocky path. At 0.1 miles the trail runs near the Nature Ridge Trail (Trail 88). In late fall and early winter, be careful throughout the trail, as newly fallen leaves cover the majority of the stones, making it somewhat treacherous to navigate the path. Young Virginia pine and hemlock surround the trail and are tucked beneath the larger, more mature oaks looming above.

At 0.4 miles intersect Stone Trough Trail (Trail 83) and continue just 0.03 miles farther to reach the lower trailhead and intersection with Beaver Creek Trail (Trail 82). Move across the trail and duck beneath rhododendrons to access Little Beaver Creek for a nice view of the stream.

Trail Combinations/Options

Creek Bed Trail is a short east-west connector that allows access from trails along the central ridgeline of the park and campsite area to the park's lower portion near Little Beaver Creek and Little Beaver Lake. The higher, eastern trails include: Rhododendron Run Trail (Trail 89), Crooked Rock Trail (Trail 84), and Nature Ridge Trail (Trail 88). The lower, western trails include Beaver Creek Trail (Trail 82) and Stone Trough Trail (Tral 83).

CREEK BED TRAIL

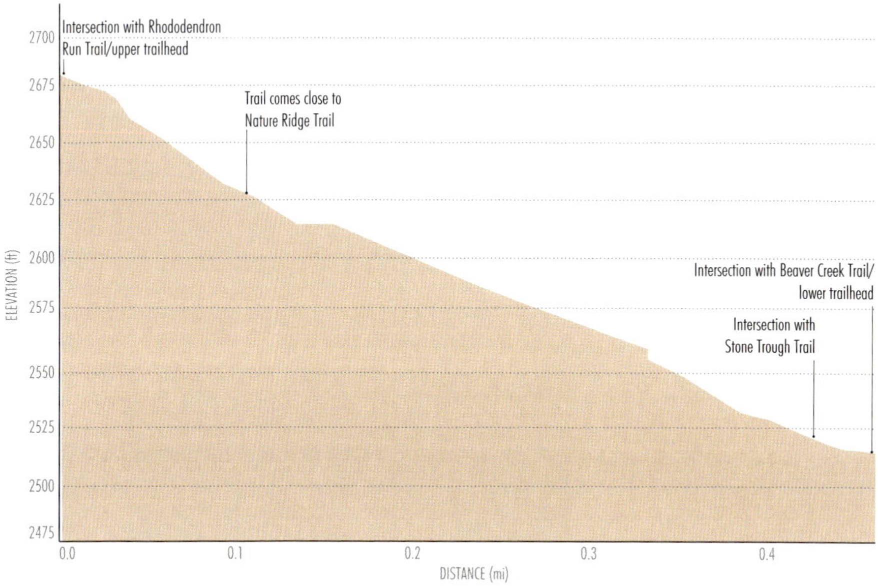

77 EASY STREET TRAIL

Easy goes it along this short loop detour off the Nature Ridge Trail.

1 | 39 ft 45 ft | 0.43 mi

Location: South of Interstate 64, exit 129A
Maps: USGS Prince quad 1:24,000, USGS Shady Spring quad 1:24,000
Trail Options: A short loop trail off Nature Ridge Trail (Trail 88).
Facilities: Little Beaver State Park offers a full range of picnic, recreation, camping, and toilet facilities.
Highlights: Young Virginia pine and hemlock grove.

Trail Milestones:

0.0 mi – First trailhead, at 0.7-mile mark of Nature Ridge Trail (37°44.883 N, 081°04.805 W)
0.43 mi – Second trailhead, at 0.8-mile mark of Nature Ridge Trail (37°44.810 N, 081°04.776 W)

Finding the Trailhead

From Interstate 64, take exit 129A toward Shady Spring. Turn onto Grandview Road (CR 9) south and travel 1.8 miles to the entrance for Little Beaver State Park on the left.

First trailhead: (37°44.883 N, 081°04.805 W)
Second trailhead: (37°44.810 N, 081°04.776 W)
To reach the Nature Ridge trailhead, follow the main park road past the visitor center and uphill to the campground office. The trailhead is just off the road to the southwest. Hike 0.7 miles along Nature Ridge Trail (Trail 88) to the first trailhead.

Trail Description

White Diamond Blaze
This trail is the least challenging outing within the park. From 0.7 miles along the Nature Ridge Trail, move into a small grove of rhododendrons, which bloom from late May to June. Break out of this grove and enter a forest of young Virginia pine and Easter hemlocks that line the trail to either side. Wind through this young forest, not far from the Nature Ridge Trail. The trail ends after 0.43 miles back at the Nature Ridge Trail, just 0.1 miles farther along from where you originally departed.

Trail Combinations/Options

Take this short side trail from Nature Ridge Trail (Trail 88) to arrive 0.1 miles farther down the same trail.

EASY STREET TRAIL

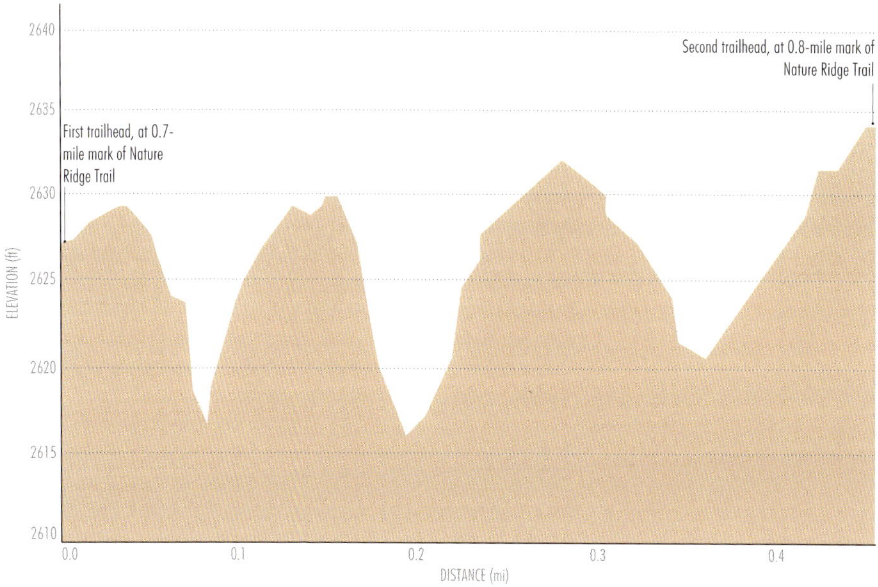

78 DEER TRAIL

A meandering trail through field and forest that connects two of the longer trails in the park, the Laurel Creek Trail and the Nature Ridge Trail.

2 | 71 ft | 97 ft | 0.56 mi

Location: South of Interstate 64, exit 129A
Maps: USGS Prince quad 1:24,000, USGS Shady Spring quad 1:24,000
Trail Options: Connects Laurel Creek Trail (Trail 90) and the Nature Ridge Trail (Trail 88).
Facilities: Little Beaver State Park offers a full range of picnic, recreation, camping, and toilet facilities.
Highlights: Wildlife, pond, fields, and forest.

Trail Milestones:

0.0 mi – Intersection with Laurel Creek Trail/eastern trailhead (37°45.154 N, 081°04.430 W)
0.2 mi – Hemlock grove (37°45.007 N, 081°04.420 W)
0.38 mi – Road/cemetery/Rhododendron Run trailhead (37°44.939 N, 081°04.619 W)
0.56 mi – Intersection with Nature Ridge Trail/western trailhead (37°45.007 N, 081°04.756 W)

Finding the Trailhead

From Interstate 64, take exit 129A toward Shady Spring. Turn onto Grandview Road (CR 9) south and travel 1.8 miles to the entrance for Little Beaver State Park on the left.

Eastern trailhead: (37°45.154 N, 081°04.430 W)
The eastern trailhead is located at the 2.4-mile mark of Laurel Creek Trail (Trail 90). Please see this trail's description for information regarding the trailhead and how to reach this intersection.

Western trailhead: (37°45.007 N, 081°04.756 W)
The western trailhead is located at an intersection with Nature Ridge Trail (Trail 88) at 0.4 miles. Please see this trail's description for additional details.

Trail Description

Blue Diamond Blaze

Note: Hike described from eastern trailhead, at intersection with Laurel Creek Trail. With a small pond nearby, move past the trailhead sign and immediately hike into a beautiful forest of large Virginia pines. The trail here is well defined as you weave amongst the evergreens and walk upon their needles. The forest quickly transitions to a mix of hardwoods, with a field above and to the right.

At 0.2 miles enter a small hemlock grove. Continue along the trail until reaching a field, and move right and uphill. Atop the incline, at 0.38 miles, arrive at a gravel road with a cemetery and the Rhododendron Run trailhead to the left along the road. Walk directly across the road and re-enter the wood line. Descend 0.18 miles until reaching the western trailhead and intersection with Nature Ridge Trail.

Trail Combinations/Options

Deer Trail is a popular connector between Laurel Creek Trail (Trail 90) and Nature Ridge Trail (Trail 88). It is the easiest connection between the eastern grouping of trails and the larger western group of trails within the park. The trail also passes close to the upper trailhead for Rhododendron Run Trail (Trail 89).

The gravel road at 0.38 miles.

DEER TRAIL

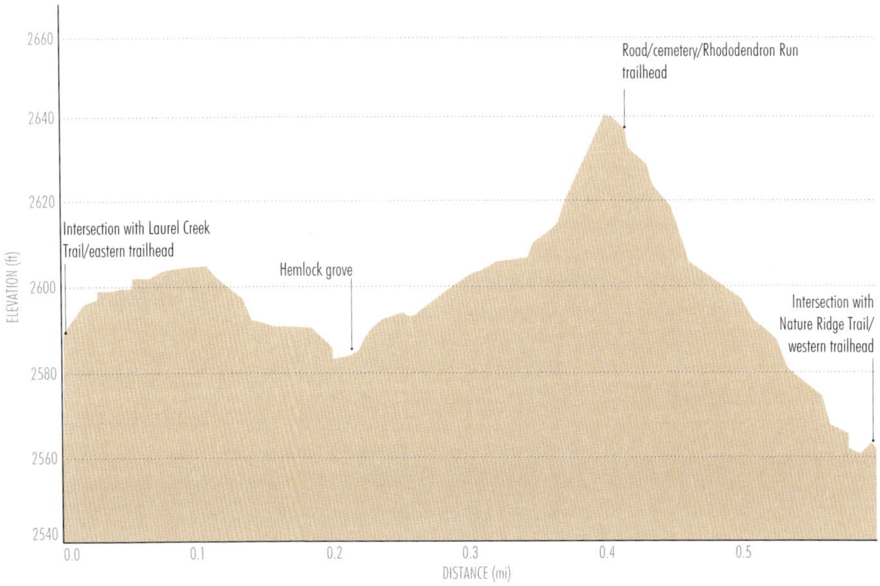

79 BILLY GOAT'S GRUFF TRAIL

This short trail features an abundance of moss-covered boulders and ferns galore, and is well worth the detour from the lake.

2 | 126 ft | 127 ft | 0.6 mi

Location: South of Interstate 64, exit 129A

Maps: USGS Prince quad 1:24,000, USGS Shady Spring quad 1:24,000

Trail Options: Connect with Topper's Ridge Trail (Trail 80) or Beaver Creek Trail (Trail 82).

Facilities: Little Beaver State Park offers a full range of picnic, recreation, camping, and toilet facilities.

Highlights: Beautiful moss-covered boulders and a forest thick with ferns.

Trail Milestones:

0.1 mi - Intersection with Topper's Ridge trailhead (37°45.170 N, 081°04.934 W)

0.2 mi – Boulder field (37°45.127 N, 081°05.020 W)

0.4 mi – Converge with Topper's Ridge Trail (37°45.035 N, 081°05.119 W)

0.6 mi – Trail's end at Beaver Creek Trail (37°44.963 N, 081°05.084 W)

Finding the Trailhead

From Interstate 64, take exit 129A toward Shady Spring. Turn onto Grandview Road (CR 9) south and travel 1.8 miles to the entrance for Little Beaver State Park on the left.

Lake Front Trail access: (37°45.225 N, 081°04.872 W)
Beaver Creek Trail access (37°44.963 N, 081°05.084 W)
This trail has two trailheads: The most commonly used option is 0.1 miles along the Lake Front Trail (Trail 85), while a second trailhead is accessible from the Beaver Creek Trail (Trail 82) at its 0.7-mile mark. See respective trail descriptions for additional details.

Trail Description

Red Diamond Blaze

Departing from the intersection with the Lake Front Trail, begin climbing into the forest. At 0.1 miles intersect the trailhead for Topper's Ridge Trail (Trail 80) to the right. Continue deeper into the woods and at 0.2 miles arrive at a boulder field covered in vivid green moss. From this point, ferns and moss dominate the forest floor. At 0.3 miles come upon a rock wall to the right, and at 0.4 miles move close to Topper's Ridge Trail — the two trails parallel briefly before diverging. Keeping left and descending from the highpoint of the trail, move through thick rhododendrons and arrive at the trail's end and intersection with Beaver Creek Trail (Trail 82). Turn left here to reach a park road or turn right to hike Beaver Creek Trail (reversing that hike as it's described).

Trail Combinations/Options

An easy loop possibility is available by linking up with the Topper's Ridge Trail (Trail 80). Follow Billy Goat's Gruff Trail to its end, turn right on Beaver Creek Trail (Trail 82), and turn right at the farther trailhead for Topper's Ridge Trail. Hike Topper's Ridge Trail in reverse to the intersection at the beginning of the Billy Goat's Gruff Trail.

Numerous combinations are also available from the trail's end and intersection with Beaver Creek Trail. As mentioned in the chapter introduction, the possibilities for combinations are endless and allow exploration for all ability levels and desired lengths.

Lake view from the trailhead.

BILLY GOAT'S GRUFF TRAIL

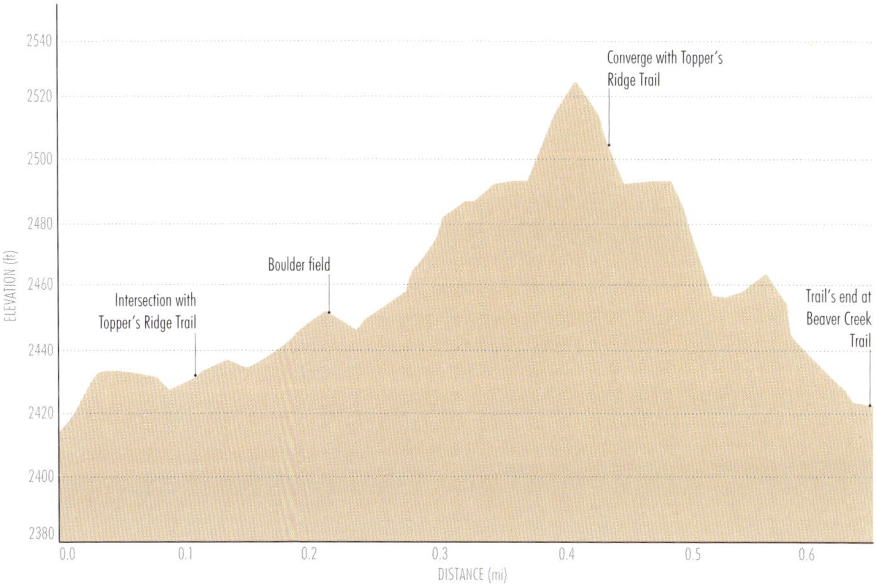

80 TOPPER'S RIDGE TRAIL

A short trail on the western edge of Little Beaver State Park that rises above the lake and runs through an evergreen forest before descending to Beaver Creek Trail.

3 | 124 ft | 126 ft | 0.6 mi

Location: South of Interstate 64, exit 129A
Maps: USGS Prince quad 1:24,000, USGS Shady Spring quad 1:24,000
Trail Options: Connect to Billy Goat's Gruff Trail (Trail 79) and Beaver Creek Trail (Trail 82).
Facilities: Little Beaver State Park offers a full range of picnic, recreation, camping, and toilet facilities.
Highlights: Evergreen forest, moss-covered boulders.

Trail Milestones:

0.3 mi – Billy Goat's Gruff Trail nearby (37°45.053 N, 081°05.141 W)
0.5 mi – Begin descending (37°44.961 N, 081°05.198 W)

Finding the Trailhead

From Interstate 64, take exit 129A toward Shady Spring. Turn onto Grandview Road (CR 9) south and travel 1.8 miles to the entrance for Little Beaver State Park on the left.

Main trailhead: (37°45.154 N, 081°04.970 W)
This trail has two trailheads: The main, most commonly used trailhead is accessed by hiking 0.1 miles from the start of the Lake Front Trail (Trail 85), and then turning right onto Billy Goat's Gruff Trail (Trail 79) for 0.1 miles to reach the trailhead. A second, less-used trailhead is accessible from the Beaver Creek Trail (Trail 82) at its 0.6-mile mark. See respective trail descriptions for additional details.

Trail Description

Yellow Diamond Blaze
From the intersection at Billy Goat Gruff's Trail, turn right onto the trail and begin moving uphill to reach a ridgeline and move into an evergreen forest. Continue along this rocky ridge, and at 0.3 miles the trail moves close to the Billy Goat's Gruff Trail to the left. (A short black-diamond connector trail runs between the trails in this location, for use by mountain bikers.) Keep right and begin to see a paved road (CR 307) to the distant right. Keep straight and at 0.5 miles bear sharply left and begin to descend.

At 0.6 miles arrive at the trail's end and intersection with Beaver Creek Trail. Turn left to reach the park road and Beaver Creek Trail parking area, or right to move south along Beaver Creek Trail and encounter intersections with multiple trails in that direction (Black Bear Run Trail [Trail 81] and Rhododendron Run Trail [Trail 89]).

Trail Combinations/Options

While numerous options are available, a nice 1.4-mile combination that takes in the trails on the extreme western edge of the park links up Lake Front Trail (Trail 85), Billy Goat's Gruff Trail (Trail 79), and Topper's Ridge Trail. Start from the Lake Front trailhead at the main parking area; travel to the intersection with Billy Goat's Gruff Trail and turn right onto it. Hike this trail to its terminus then turn right on Beaver Creek Trail until it intersects Topper's Ridge Trail. Turn right here and hike Topper's Ridge Trail to its end (main trailhead), where it connects with Billy Goat's Gruff Trail and Lake Front Trail. Turn left here to return to the parking area, or turn right to complete the Lake Front Trail loop around the lake for a longer loop of 2.33 miles.

A rocky stretch of Topper's Ridge Trail.

TOPPER'S RIDGE TRAIL

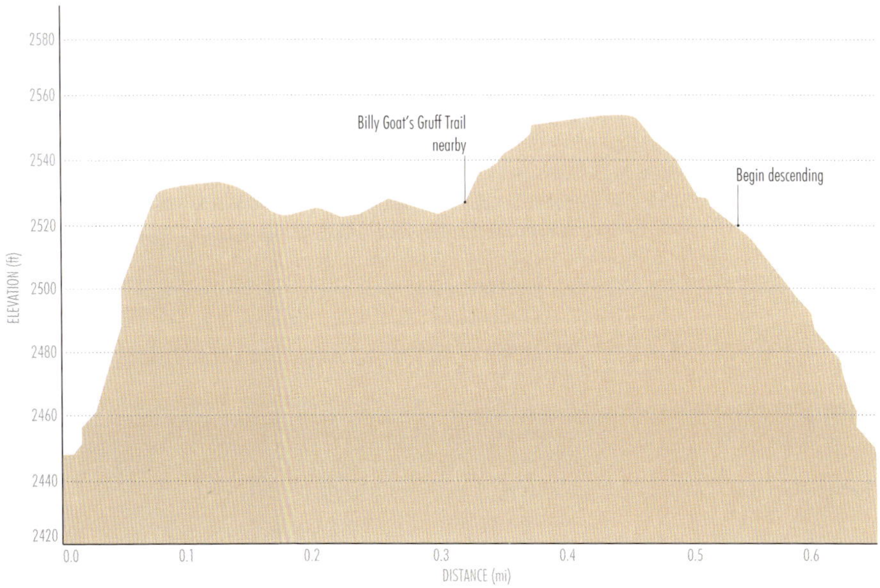

81 BLACK BEAR RUN TRAIL

A favorite trail for many who visit, the Black Bear Run Trail parallels Little Beaver Creek through rhododendrons that completely encapsulate the path and stream. A hike that's not to be missed!

1 | 52 ft | 20 ft | 0.65 mi

Location: South of Interstate 64, exit 129A
Maps: USGS Prince quad 1:24,000, USGS Shady Spring quad 1:24,000
Trail Options: Connects Beaver Creek Trail (Trail 82) to Rhododendron Run Trail (Trail 89).
Facilities: Little Beaver State Park offers a full range of picnic, recreation, camping, and toilet facilities.
Highlights: Rhododendron "tunnel" and blooms, deep pools of water.

Trail Milestones:

1.0 mi – Intersection with Beaver Creek Trail/main trailhead (37°44.688 N, 081°05.167 W)
0.4 mi – Move out of rhododendrons (37°44.410 N, 081°05.289 W)
0.62 mi – Cross Little Beaver Creek (37°44.239 N, 081°05.328 W)
0.65 mi – Intersection with Rhododendron Run Trail/secondary trailhead (37°44.243 N, 081°05.308 W)

Finding the Trailhead

Main trailhead: (37°44.688 N, 081°05.167 W)
The main trailhead is located 0.4 miles along Beaver Creek Trail (Trail 82). Please see the Beaver Creek Trail for information regarding its trailhead and how to reach this intersection.

Secondary trailhead: (37°44.243 N, 081°05.308 W)
A secondary and less-used trailhead is located 1.8 miles along Rhododendron Run Trail (Trail 89). Please see this trail's description for additional details.

Trail Description

Red Diamond Blaze

Note: Hike described from main trailhead, at Beaver Creek Trail intersection. The trailhead is located 0.4 miles along the Beaver Creek Trail, just after it crosses Little Beaver Creek — turn left here onto Black Bear Run Trail. The trail parallels and runs just to the right of the creek. Immediately move into thick rhododendrons that form a "tunnel" over the trail. This area is particularly beautiful in late spring when the trees are blooming or with a wet snow that clings to the branches, turning the forest white.

The creek along the trail alternates between babbling flows and deep-green pools that entice the visitor to "dip a toe" during the hot summer months. Watch closely within the clear waters for a glimpse of the trout that live here.

At 0.4 miles the trail opens up into taller hardwoods. This area is not well marked, though the trail is well defined. Continue along the stream and at 0.62 miles cross Little Beaver Creek via well-placed rocks to arrive at the intersection with Rhododendron Run Trail. Turn left here and hike back toward Beaver Creek Trail and that trail's parking area.

Along the trail.

Trail Combinations/Options

This trail is easily combined with the Beaver Creek Trail (Trail 82) and a portion of Rhododendron Run Trail (Trail 89) to create a long but mellow loop that parallels the stream in a figure 8 pattern. Starting at the Beaver Creek trailhead, hike 0.4 miles and intersect the Black Bear Run Trail. Turn left and continue along Black Bear Run Trail until it ends and intersects with Rhododendron Run Trail; turn left here and travel 0.54 miles to the trail's end and intersection with Beaver Creek Trail. Turn left, cross the stream, and stay right along the Beaver Creek Trail to its end after 0.37 miles. This trail loop is very easy and covers 1.96 total miles.

The rhododendron "tunnel."

BLACK BEAR RUN TRAIL

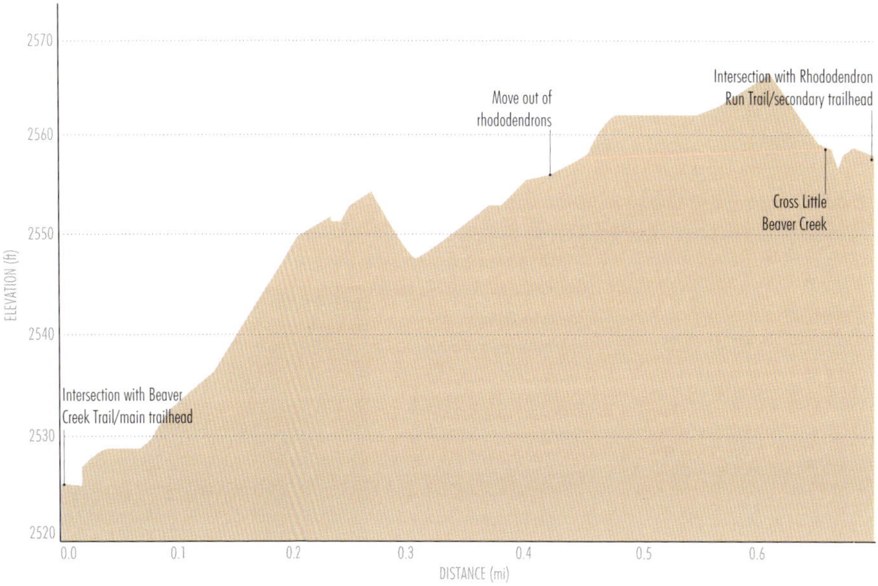

82 BEAVER CREEK TRAIL

An easy hike along both sides of Little Beaver Creek that intersects with multiple trails, and with a fun, but potentially tricky, stream crossing!

1 | 50 ft | 50 ft | 0.77 mi

Location: South of Interstate 64, exit 129A

Maps: USGS Prince quad 1:24,000, USGS Shady Spring quad 1:24,000

Trail Options: Connect with Creek Bed Trail (Trail 76), Rhododendron Run Trail (Trail 89), Black Bear Run Trail (Trail 81), Topper's Ridge Trail (Trail 80), and Billy Goat's Gruff Trail (Trail 79).

Facilities: Little Beaver State Park offers a full range of picnic, recreation, camping, and toilet facilities.

Highlights: Little Beaver Creek, multiple trail intersections, tricky stream crossing.

Trail Milestones:

0.15 mi – Intersection with Hemlock and Creek Bed trails (37°44.818 N, 081°05.099 W)

0.3 mi – Intersection with Rhododendron Run Trail/stream (37°44.698 N, 081°05.144 W)

0.4 mi – Intersection with Black Bear Run Trail (37°44.688 N, 081°05.167 W)

0.6 mi – Intersection with Topper's Ridge Trail (37°44.894 N, 081°05.084 W)

0.7 mi – Intersection with Billy Goat's Gruff Trail (37°44.963 N, 081°05.143 W)

Finding the Trailhead

(37°44.936 N, 081°05.071 W)

From Interstate 64, take exit 129A toward Shady Spring. Turn onto Grandview Road (CR 9) south and travel 1.8 miles to the entrance for Little Beaver State Park on the left.

To reach the trailhead, continue along the main park road past the visitor center. Take the first right after the visitor center and pass a large parking area to the left. Continue high above the lake (on your right) for 0.5 miles until reaching a parking area on the left with space for approximately six vehicles, just prior to a bridge. The trailhead is located on the far end of this lot.

Trail Description

White Diamond Blaze

From the trailhead, move into a rhododendron grove with Little Beaver Creek to the right. At 0.15 miles intersect first with Hemlock Trail (unmarked) and almost immediately with Creek Bed Trail as it descends to the trail from the left. Continue straight until coming to a wider area and intersection with Rhododendron Run Trail. Keep right here and immediately cross the stream using well-placed steps along the rocks that line the creek. In higher water this may prove to be a little tricky. Take care here, and if the water is too high, use one of the many other options available to continue hiking in the park.

After emerging from the streambed, intersect Black Bear Run Trail on the left. Keep right here and begin to parallel Little Beaver Creek (stream is on the right). Pass Topper's Ridge Trail and Billy Goat's Gruff Trail (both on the left) and arrive at the park road at 0.77 miles. Turn right, cross a vehicle bridge, and arrive back at the trailhead parking.

Tricky stream crossing.

BEAVER CREEK TRAIL

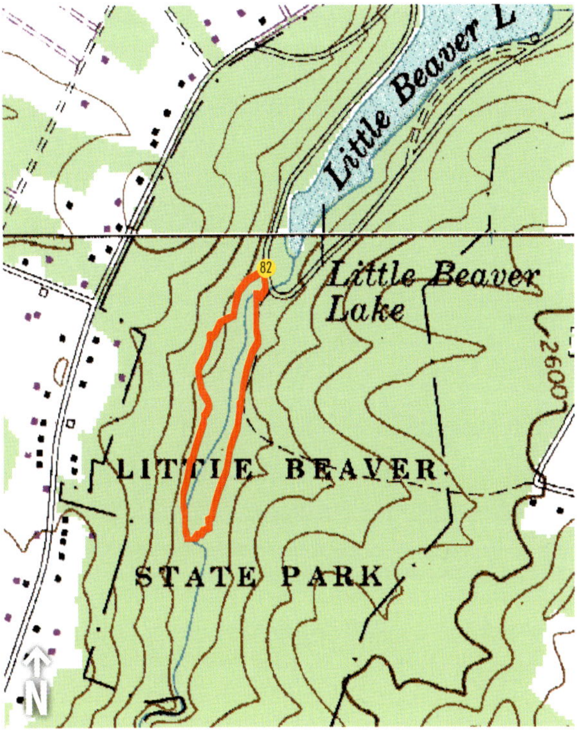

Trail Combinations/Options

Connect with Hemlock Trail (Trail 73), Creek Bed Trail (Trail 76), Rhododendron Run Trail (Trail 89), Black Bear Run Trail (Trail 81), Topper's Ridge Trail (Trail 80), and Billy Goat's Gruff Trail (Trail 79) for a number of possible combinations and links to other portions of the park.

One fun combination hikers often use is to connect Beaver Creek Trail with Rhododendron Run Trail and eventually return via Creek Bed Trail. Hiking or running the trail in this direction allows for a warm-up before tackling the incline along Rhododendron Run Trail. Returning along Creek Bed Trail, though rocky, brings you back to your starting point for a nice loop totaling 3.07 miles.

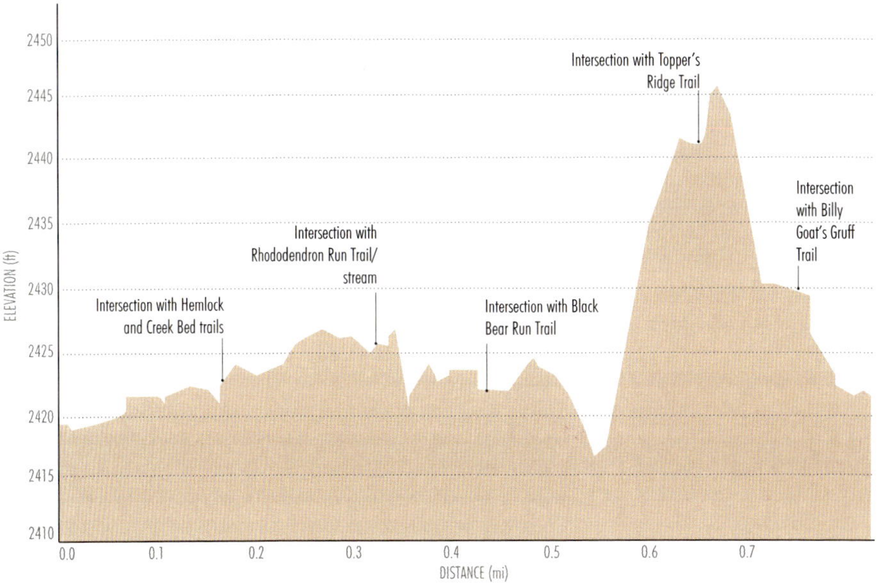

83 STONE TROUGH TRAIL

Stone Trough Trail journeys from the southernmost point of Little Beaver State Park through a beautiful evergreen forest to Nature Ridge Trail.

3 | 134 ft | 137 ft | 0.91 mi

Location: South of Interstate 64, exit 129A
Maps: USGS Prince quad 1:24,000, USGS Shady Spring quad 1:24,000
Trail Options: Connects with Rhododendron Run Trail (Trail 89), Drop Off Trail (Trail 74), Crooked Rock Trail (Trail 84), and Creek Bed Trail (Trail 76); ends at Nature Ridge Trail (Trail 88).
Facilities: Little Beaver State Park offers a full range of picnic, recreation, camping, and toilet facilities.
Highlights: Beautiful year-round through an evergreen forest.

Finding the Trailhead

From Interstate 64, take exit 129A toward Shady Spring. Turn onto Grandview Road (CR 9) south and travel 1.8 miles to the entrance for Little Beaver State Park on the left.

Southern trailhead: (37°44.241 N, 081°05.234 W)
The southern trailhead is located at the 1.7-mile mark along Rhododendron Run Trail (Trail 89); please see the Rhododendron Run Trail for information regarding the trailhead and information to reach this intersection.

Northern trailhead: (37°44.812 N, 081°04.981 W)
The northern trailhead is located at an intersection with Nature Ridge Trail (Trail 88) at 1.2 miles; please see this trail's description for additional details.

Trail Milestones:

0.0 mi – Intersection with Rhododendron Run Trail/southern trailhead (37°44.241 N, 081°05.234 W)
0.2 mi – Intersection with Drop Off Trail (37°44.434 N, 081°05.088 W)
0.4 mi – Thick stand of hemlocks (37°44.520 N, 081°05.096 W)
0.7 mi – Intersection with Crooked Rock Trail (37°44.740 N, 081°05.186 W)
0.8 mi – Intersection with Creek Bed Trail (37°44.806 N, 081°05.075 W)
0.91 mi – Intersection with Nature Ridge Trail/northern trailhead (37°44.812 N, 081°04.981 W)

Trail Description

White Diamond Blaze

Note: Hike described from southern trailhead. The trailhead is accessed 1.7 miles along Rhododendron Run Trail (Trail 89), midway down a steep section of path. Begin the Stone Trough Trail by travelling uphill and through a small pine thicket. The trail is well defined here, and after 200 meters begins to bear left. At 0.1 miles you can see the Drop Off Trail (Trail 74) through the trees to the right. Stay left of a cluster of rhododendrons here.

At 0.2 miles intersect the Drop Off Trail as it descends across the path — keep right at this intersection. At 0.4 miles bear left and descend slightly through a thick stand of Eastern hemlock. Encounter a black-diamond connector trail in 0.1 miles that leads left to the lower portion of the Rhododendron Run Trail. Stay right and move through a rocky bit of trail before entering an area of five-to-six-foot Virginia pines. At 0.7 miles intersect Crooked Rock Trail (Trail 84). The evergreen forest becomes thick with trees in this area but opens up again at 0.8 miles and the intersection with the Creek Bed Trail (Trail 76). Cross straight through this opening and move steeply upwards to the trail's end at 0.91 miles, intersecting Nature Ridge Trail (Trail 88).

STONE TROUGH TRAIL

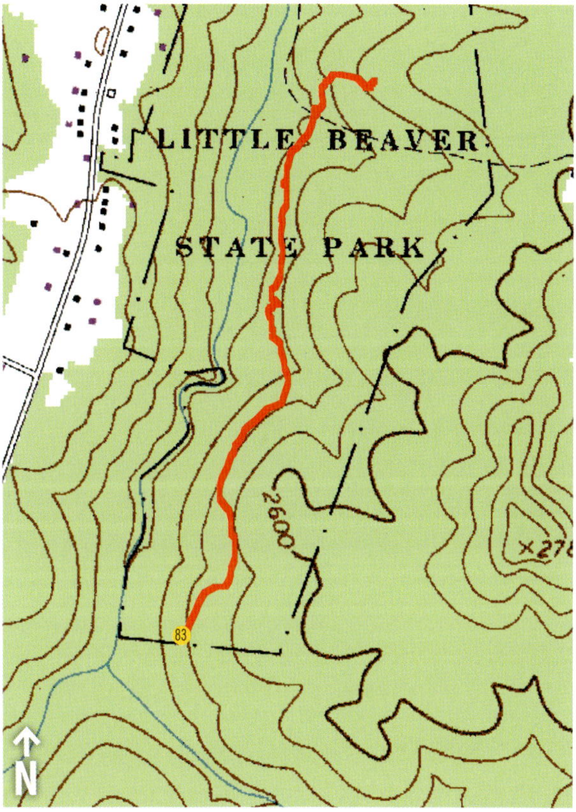

Trail Combinations/Options

Stone Trough Trail is an outstanding trail that allows links to multiple trails. It is great for campers, as it allows a quick return toward Nature Ridge Trail (Trail 88) and the campsite above. This option is especially useful for families with children who might wish to return to the campsite along a shorter route.

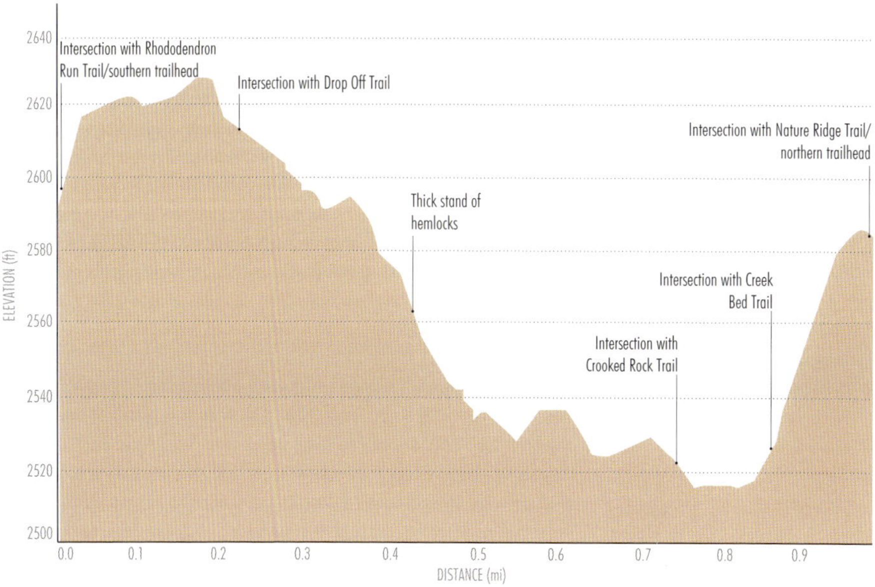

84 CROOKED ROCK TRAIL

This trail is an excellent shortcut for the hiker, trail runner, or mountain biker, bypassing the longer southern loop of the Rhododendron Run Trail and allowing access to the lower, western portion of the park.

3 | 123 ft | 265 ft | 0.98 mi

Location: South of Interstate 64, exit 129A
Maps: USGS Prince quad 1:24,000, USGS Shady Spring quad 1:24,000
Trail Options: Connects Rhododendron Run Trail (Trail 89) with Stone Trough Trail (Trail 83).
Facilities: Little Beaver State Park offers a full range of picnic, recreation, camping, and toilet facilities.
Highlights: Excellent shortcut, forest, and boulders.

Trail Milestones:

0.0 mi – Intersection with Rhododendron Run Trail/upper trailhead (37°44.707 N, 081°04.729 W)
0.1 mi – Curved bridge (37°44.701 N, 081°04.825 W)
0.2 mi – Intersection with Turkey Spur trailhead (37°44.675 N, 081°04.863 W)
0.4 mi – Second intersection with Turkey Spur Trail (37°44.624 N, 081°04.955 W)
0.6 mi – Boulder on left (37°44.559 N, 081°05.027 W)
0.98 mi – Intersection with Stone Trough Trail/lower trailhead (37°44.740 N, 081°05.186 W)

Finding the Trailhead

From Interstate 64, take exit 129A toward Shady Spring. Turn onto Grandview Road (CR 9) south and travel 1.8 miles to the entrance for Little Beaver State Park on the left.

Upper trailhead: (37°44.707 N, 081°04.729 W)
The upper trailhead is located at the 0.4-mile mark along Rhododendron Run Trail (Trail 89) near the border of Beaver Creek Farm (private property); please see the Rhododendron Run Trail for information regarding the trailhead and information to reach this intersection.

Lower trailhead: (37°44.740 N, 081°05.186 W)
A lower trailhead is located at an intersection with Stone Trough Trail (Trail 83) at its 0.7-mile mark; please see this trail's description for additional details.

Trail Description

Red Diamond Blaze
Beginning at the intersection with the Rhododendron Run Trail, travel downhill and reach a curved wooden bridge at 0.1 miles. Ascend slightly and after a short distance intersect the Turkey Spur trailhead at 0.2 miles. Move downward though a mixed forest until intersecting Turkey Spur Trail a second time and paralleling it almost 50 meters before splitting and moving right. The trail swings south for 0.2 miles until reaching a large boulder on the left. At 0.63 miles the trail bends 180 degrees and travels north just over 0.3 miles until dropping to and intersecting the Stone Trough Trail at 0.98 miles.

Trail Combinations/Options

The Crooked Rock Trail connects Rhododendron Run Trail (Trail 89) to the Stone Trough Trail (Trail 83), with two intersections to the Turkey Spur Trail (Trail 75) along its course. While the intersections with Turkey Spur add variation, hikers often use the connection between the Rhododendron Run and Crooked Rock trails as an interesting link from the higher trails along the ridgeline to the lower trails near Little Beaver Creek and Lake.

CROOKED ROCK TRAIL

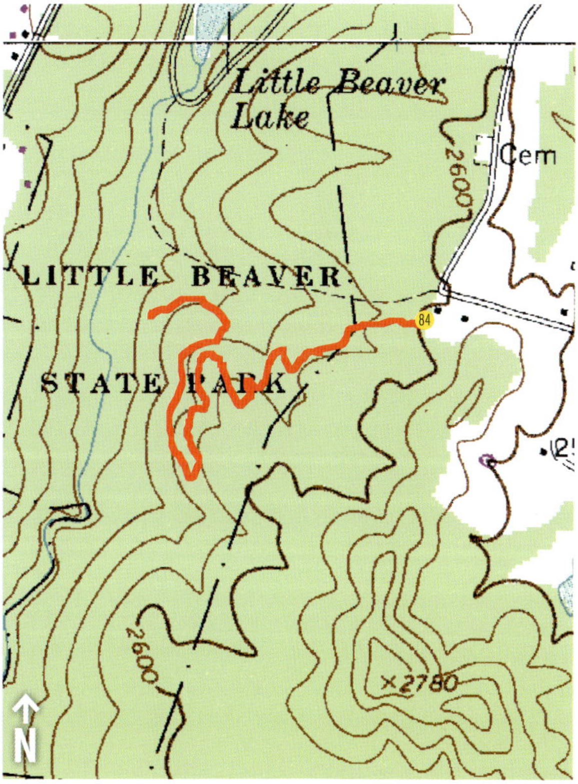

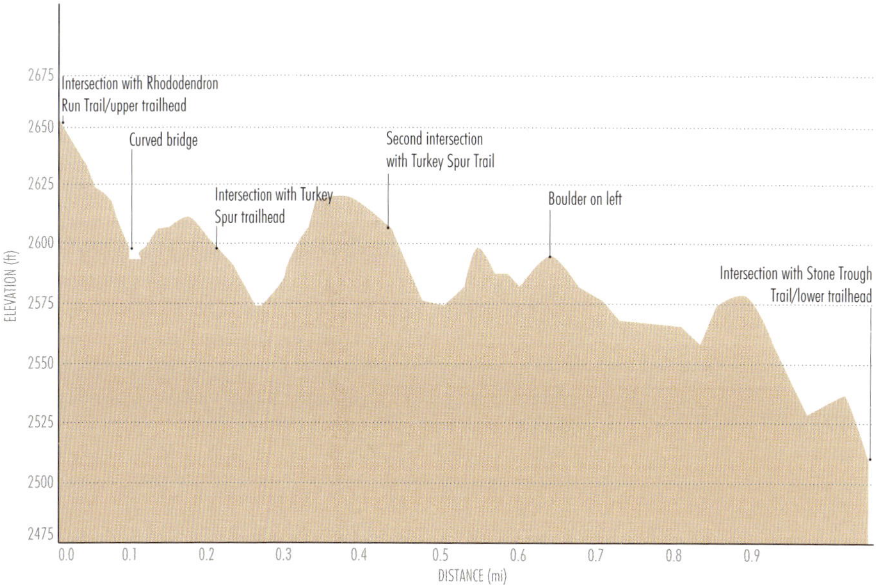

85 LAKE FRONT TRAIL

This trail loops an 18-acre lake and is particularly pretty on early fall mornings, as a mist rises off the waters.

1 | 61 ft 74 ft | 1.13 mi

Location: South of Interstate 64, exit 129A
Maps: USGS Prince quad 1:24,000, USGS Shady Spring quad 1:24,000
Trail Options: Connect to Billy Goat's Gruff Trail (Trail 79).
Facilities: Little Beaver State Park offers a full range of picnic, recreation, camping, and toilet facilities.
Highlights: Lake, wildlife (ducks and geese), fishing.

Trail Milestones:

0.1 mi – Intersection with Billy Goat's Gruff Trail (37°45.093 N, 081°04.996 W)
0.5 mi – Cross Little Beaver Creek (37°45.005 N, 081°05.010 W)
0.9 mi – Picnic area/playground (37°45.215 N, 081°04.697 W)

Finding the Trailhead

(37°45.294 N, 081°04.847 W)
From Interstate 64, take exit 129A toward Shady Spring. Turn onto Grandview Road (CR 9) south and travel 1.8 miles to the entrance for Little Beaver State Park on the left.

To reach the trailhead, take the first possible right upon entering the park. The trailhead is on the far side of this parking area near Little Beaver Creek where the water flows over the spillway at the dam.

Trail Description

White Diamond Blaze
Before starting off, make sure to take in the dam and spillway to your left. Cross a wooden bridge that spans Little Beaver Creek and climb up and around the side of the lake. At 0.1 miles intersect the Billy Goat's Gruff Trail on the right and tucked into the forest. Continue paralleling the lake along a partially paved walk — ducks and geese populate this area. Continue 0.2 miles and come upon a wooden overlook and fishing spot. Just beyond, the trail intersects a paved turnaround point; stay left here, along the road for a short time, and find the obvious dirt path of the trail on the far side.

At 0.5 miles cross the mouth of Little Beaver Creek on a longer wooden bridge. The water is clear and shallow here, and it's possible to see some of the bass, crappie, bluegill, channel catfish, and trout that populate this lake. Rhododendrons envelop the next 0.4 miles of trail as you continue to wind around and parallel the lake. At 0.9 miles break out into the open and pass a picnic shelter and playground to the right. Stay left and cross Laurel Run Creek just before it empties into the lake. Bear left toward the visitor center and boat-rental area (1.0 miles), moving onto a concrete area between the visitor center and the lake. On the far side, climb a set of stairs and descend back to the parking area and trail's end.

Trail Combinations/Options

Connect with the Billy Goat's Gruff Trail (Trail 79) at 0.1 miles and access Topper's Ridge Trail (Trail 80) or Beaver Creek Trail (Trail 82) to create a longer adventure.

Morning fog lifting off Little Beaver Lake.

LAKE FRONT TRAIL

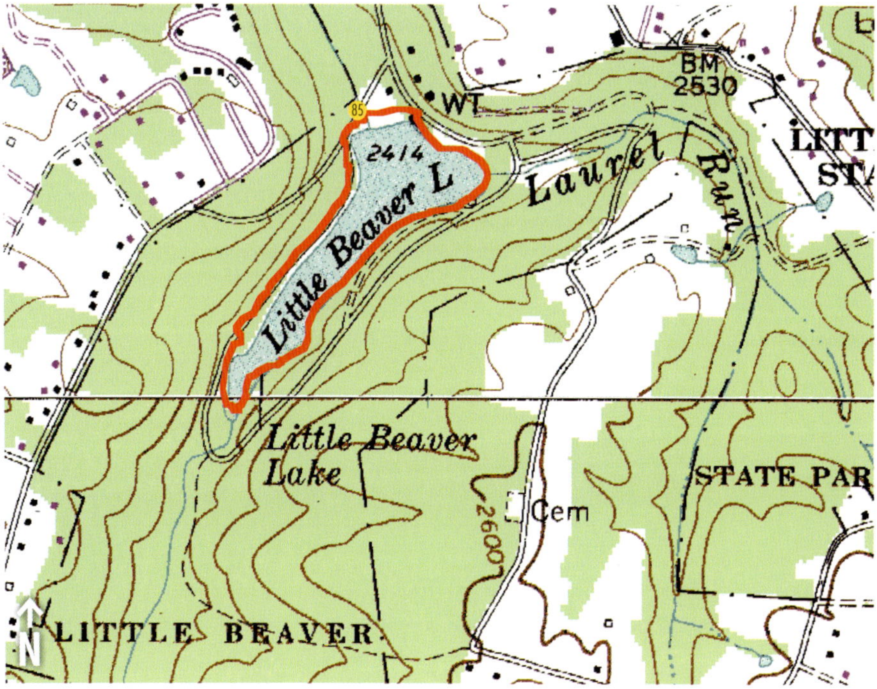

86 WEAVER WAY TRAIL

A challenging trail through thick rhododendron and mature hemlocks, with opportunities to see wildlife.

4 | 194 ft 163 ft | 1.43 mi

Location: South of Interstate 64, exit 129A
Maps: USGS Prince quad 1:24,000, USGS Shady Spring quad 1:24,000
Trail Options: Connects to Railroad Grade Trail (Trail 87) and Laurel Creek Trail (Trail 90).
Facilities: Little Beaver State Park offers a full range of picnic, recreation, camping, and toilet facilities.
Highlights: Rhododendrons, hemlocks, and an old stone fence.

Trail Milestones:

0.0 mi – Intersection with Railroad Grade Trail/Laurel Creek Trail/lower trailhead (37°45.147 N, 081°04.295 W)
0.35 mi – Bridge (37°44.972 N, 081°04.176 W)
1.2 mi – Hemlocks/stone fence (37°44.804 N, 081°04.375 W)
1.43 mi – Intersection with Railroad Grade Trail/Laurel Creek Trail/upper trailhead (37°44.619 N, 081°04.409 W)

Finding the Trailhead

From Interstate 64, take exit 129A toward Shady Spring. Turn onto Grandview Road (CR 9) south and travel 1.8 miles to the entrance for Little Beaver State Park on the left.

Lower trailhead: (37°45.147 N, 081°04.295 W)
Continue along the main park road approximately 0.4 miles until reaching a sharp curve; the Railroad Grade Trail's lower trailhead (37°45.314 N, 081°04.461 W) is located at this point. Hike 0.3 miles to Weaver Way's lower trailhead.

Upper trailhead: (37°44.619 N, 081°04.409 W)
Follow Railroad Grade Trail 0.9 miles to Weaver Way's upper trailhead.

Trail Description

Blue Diamond Blaze
The lower (main) trailhead for the Weaver Way Trail is located at a four-way intersection at the 0.3-mile mark of the Railroad Grade Trail. It is marked with a blue diamond blaze and is to the left-hand side of the Railroad Grade Trail, marked by a sign. Move into the forest here and quickly gain an understanding for the naming of the trail as you weave through the thick rhododendrons that surround the trail. At 0.35 miles come to a wooden bridge over a small stream.

Continue again through a thick grove of rhododendrons until moving into a stand of mature hemlocks at 1.2 miles. To the right and through the trees you can see the remains of an old stone fence, now covered in moss, about 20 meters off the trail. At 1.3 miles spot the Laurel Creek Trail to the left as it descends, and the Railroad Grade Trail to the right as the three trails move to their mutual intersection at 1.43 miles, marking the trail's end.

Trail Combinations/Options

The only options for this trail are as an alternative route for a portion of the Railroad Grade Trail (Trail 87), making for a more strenuous and longer loop that totals 2.73 miles, or to lengthen the Laurel Creek Trail (Trail 90) to render a 2.86-mile loop.

WEAVER WAY TRAIL

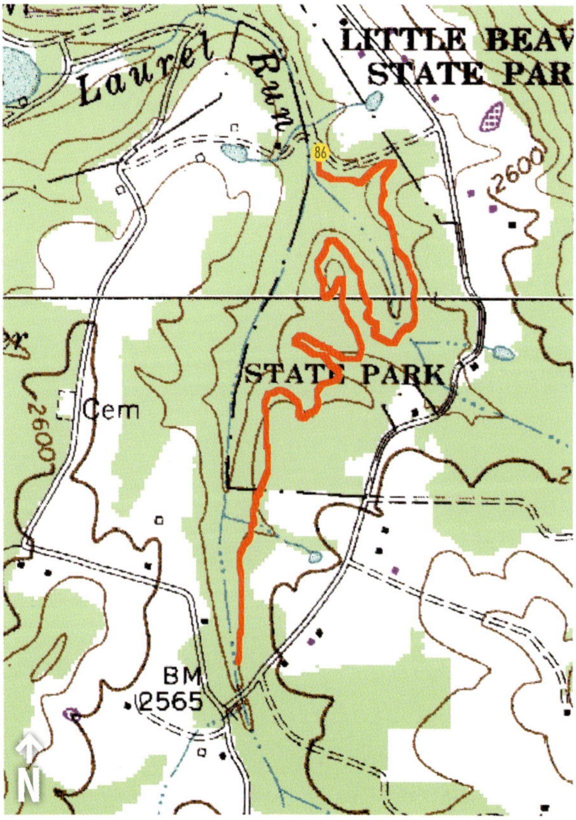

The stone fence, glimpsed through the trees.

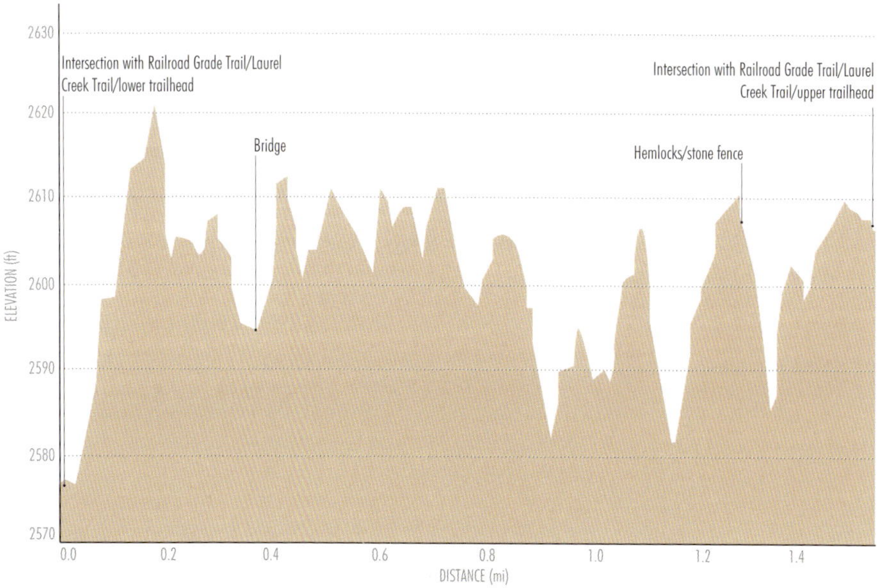

87 RAILROAD GRADE TRAIL

A gentle loop that follows Laurel Creek south until intersecting Laurel Creek and Weaver Way trails twice before returning to the road, just above the original trailhead.

2 | 184 ft | 86 ft | 1.9 mi

Location: South of Interstate 64, exit 129A
Maps: USGS Prince quad 1:24,000, USGS Shady Spring quad 1:24,000
Trail Options: Connects with Weaver Way Trail (Trail 86) and Laurel Creek Trail (Trail 90).
Facilities: Little Beaver State Park offers a full range of picnic, recreation, camping, and toilet facilities.
Highlights: Laurel Creek, rhododendrons, wildlife.

Trail Milestones:

0.0 mi – Lower trailhead (37°45.314 N, 081°04.461 W)
0.3 mi – Intersection with Weaver Way/Laurel Creek trails (37°45.147 N, 081°04.295 W)
0.9 mi – Second intersection with Weaver Way/Laurel Creek trails (37°44.619 N, 081°04.409 W)
1.6 mi – Final intersection with Laurel Creek Trail (37°45.145 N, 081°04.326 W)
1.9 mi – Upper trailhead (37°45.305 N, 081°04.462 W)

Finding the Trailhead

From Interstate 64, take exit 129A toward Shady Spring. Turn onto Grandview Road (CR 9) south and travel 1.8 miles to the entrance for Little Beaver State Park on the left.

Lower trailhead: (37°45.314 N, 081°04.461 W)
Upper trailhead: (37°45.305 N, 081°04.462 W)
Continue along the main park road approximately 0.4 miles until reaching a sharp curve. Here, you'll find the two trailheads just meters apart and on opposite sides of Laurel Creek. The best parking is located above these trailheads at the camping-registration building, 0.15 miles from the trailheads along the paved road.

Trail Description

Yellow Diamond Blaze
From the lower trailhead, on the left side of Laurel Creek, move into the forest, keeping the creek to your right. This trail is wide and rocky throughout. Continue along a gentle grade and at 0.3 miles arrive at a four-way intersection with two trails to the left and one trail to the right. The trail farthest left, Laurel Creek Trail, is marked with a red diamond blaze. The next trail to the left is the Weaver Way Trail, designated with a blue diamond blaze. The trail to the right is the return portion of the Laurel Creek Trail. Stay straight through this intersection along the obvious wider path.

The trail continues to parallel Laurel Creek, which provides the background "music" of a babbling stream to accompany your journey. Continue along this path and shortly cross a feeder stream over a rock bridge. Deer are plentiful in this area, and if you're lucky you might also see a turkey or two. Off to the left you can spot the remains of a stone wall at 0.7 miles; at 0.9 miles intersect the end of the Weaver Way Trail and a portion of the Laurel Creek Trail. Just ahead (east) of this intersection you'll see a paved road called Country Club Road; turn right at this intersection and cross a wooden bridge over Laurel Creek.

After crossing the bridge, almost immediately turn right and begin descending, again with Laurel Creek to your right. Weave through hemlocks and rhododendron until intersecting Laurel Creek Trail

RAILROAD GRADE TRAIL

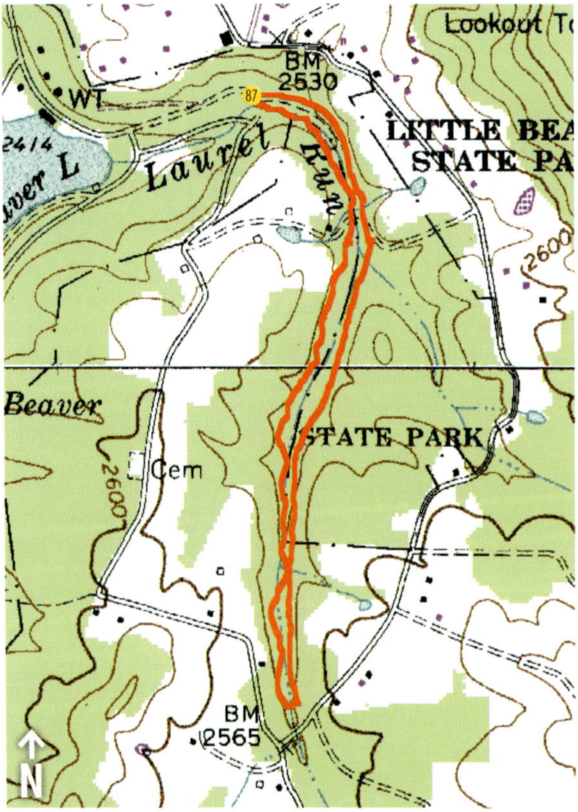

the final time at 1.6 miles. (Looking right, you'll spot the original four-way intersection just beyond the creek.) Continue straight, and at 1.9 miles reach the upper trailhead along the park road, just above the original trailhead.

Trail Combinations/Options

Connect with the Weaver Way Trail (Trail 86) or Laurel Creek Trail (Trail 90) at two different points. Connecting with the Weaver Way Trail at the 0.3-mile mark allows for a more difficult and longer (2.73-mile) loop that moves through thick rhododendron.

Connecting with the Laurel Creek Trail creates a longer (2.83-mile) and very scenic loop encompassing many of the park's highlights. At 0.3 miles move left along the Laurel Creek Trail and follow it as per its route description.

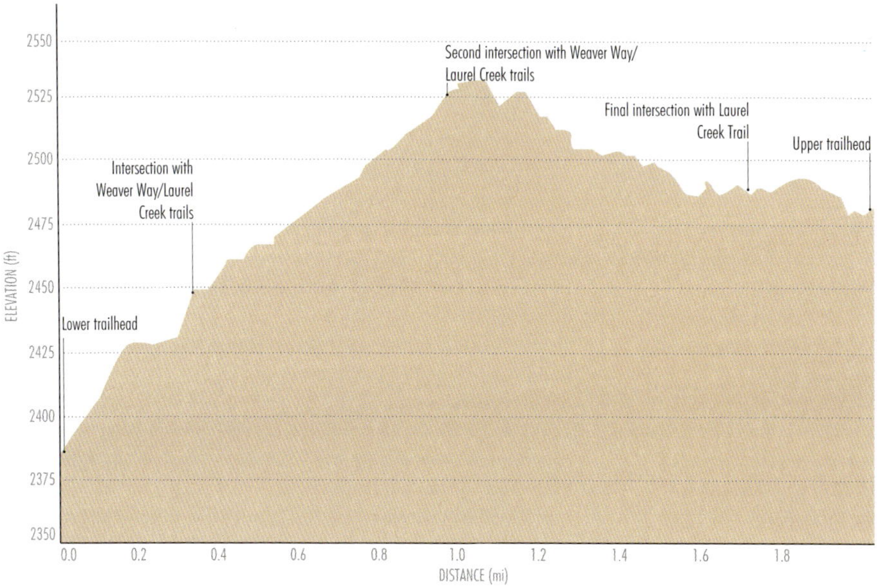

88 NATURE RIDGE TRAIL

This trail borders the majority of the campground, allowing visitors easy access to a host of trails and the lake below.

3 | 311 ft | 255 ft | 2.22 mi

Location: South of Interstate 64, exit 129A
Maps: USGS Prince quad 1:24,000, USGS Shady Spring quad 1:24,000
Trail Options: Connects with Deer Trail (Trail 78), Easy Street Trail (Trail 77), Rhododendron Run Trail (Trail 89), Stone Trough Trail (Trail 83), and Hemlock Trail (Trail 73).
Facilities: Little Beaver State Park offers a full range of picnic, recreation, camping, and toilet facilities.
Highlights: Boulders with small cave, mixed forest, wildlife, access to campground.

Trail Milestones:

0.4 mi – Intersection with Deer Trail (37°45.007 N, 081°04.756 W)
0.7 mi – Intersection No.1 with Easy Street Trail (37°44.883 N, 081°04.805 W)
0.8 mi – Intersection No. 2 with Easy Street Trail (37°44.810 N, 081°04.776 W)
0.9 mi – Intersection with Rhododendron Run Trail (37°44.780 N, 081°04.733 W)
1.2 mi – Intersection with Stone Trough Trail (37°44.812 N, 081°04.981 W)
1.4 mi – Intersection with Hemlock Trail (37°44.944 N, 081°04.983 W)
2.07 mi – Parking area (37°45.229 N, 081°04.628 W)

Finding the Trailhead

(37°45.106 N, 081°04.587 W)
From Interstate 64, take exit 129A toward Shady Spring. Turn onto Grandview Road (CR 9) south and travel 1.8 miles to the entrance for Little Beaver State Park on the left.

Continue straight along the main park road, passing the visitor center on the right and continuing uphill to the camping-registration office. The trailhead is located across the paved road from the office on the southwest side

Trail Description

Red Diamond Blaze
From the trailhead below the campground-registration office, enter the forest and immediately cross a wooden bridge. The trail moves left and skirts the campground, just inside the wood line. At 0.3 miles the trail veers right, away from the camping area, and crosses a wooden bridge. Stay in the forest and do not move onto the service road. At 0.4 miles intersect the Deer Trail. Pay close attention to the trail blaze, as this intersection can be tricky. Continue another 0.1 miles as the trail curves to the right before entering a meadow with a pine thicket beyond. Now move into a stand of rhododendron with hemlocks and Virginia pines looming overhead.

At 0.6 miles you can catch distant views in the fall and winter. Closer to the trail, to its right, you'll also note some interesting boulders that create a small cave-like structure. Cross a small stream over a rock bridge at 0.7 miles and reach the first intersection with Easy Street Trail. Continuing another 0.1 miles, reach the second Easy Street trailhead, to the right.

Continue straight, and at 0.9 miles intersect the Rhododendron Run Trail. At this point the trail turns sharply right. Continue 0.3 miles to the intersection with Stone Trough Trail and move into an area densely populated with rhododendrons that form a foliage tunnel over the trail. Within this grove, a large moss-covered boulder offers the perfect spot for a mid-hike break.

At 1.4 miles connect with the Hemlock Trail. Keeping right, continue 0.5 miles until reaching a wooden bridge. Cross and continue downhill to a parking lot for visitors and overflow campground park-

Trailhead for Nature Ridge Trail.

NATURE RIDGE TRAIL

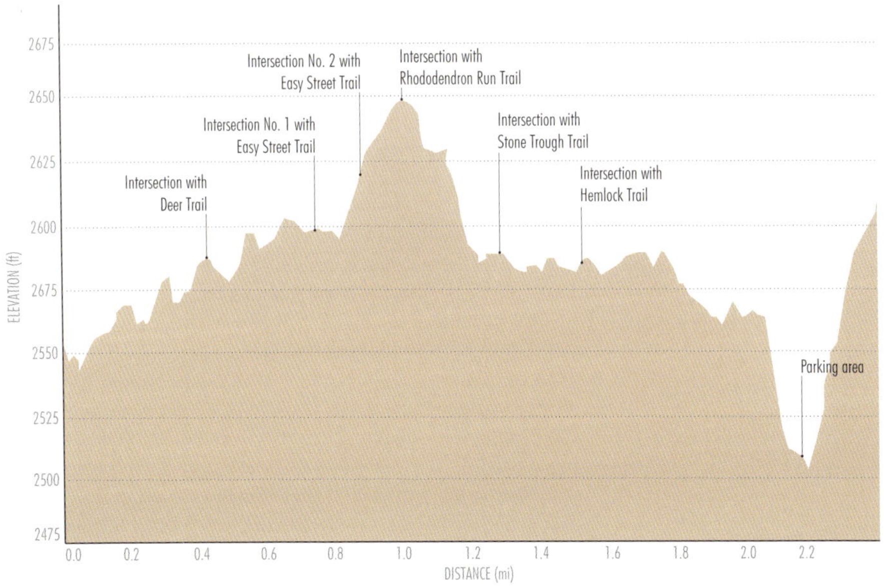

NATURE RIDGE TRAIL

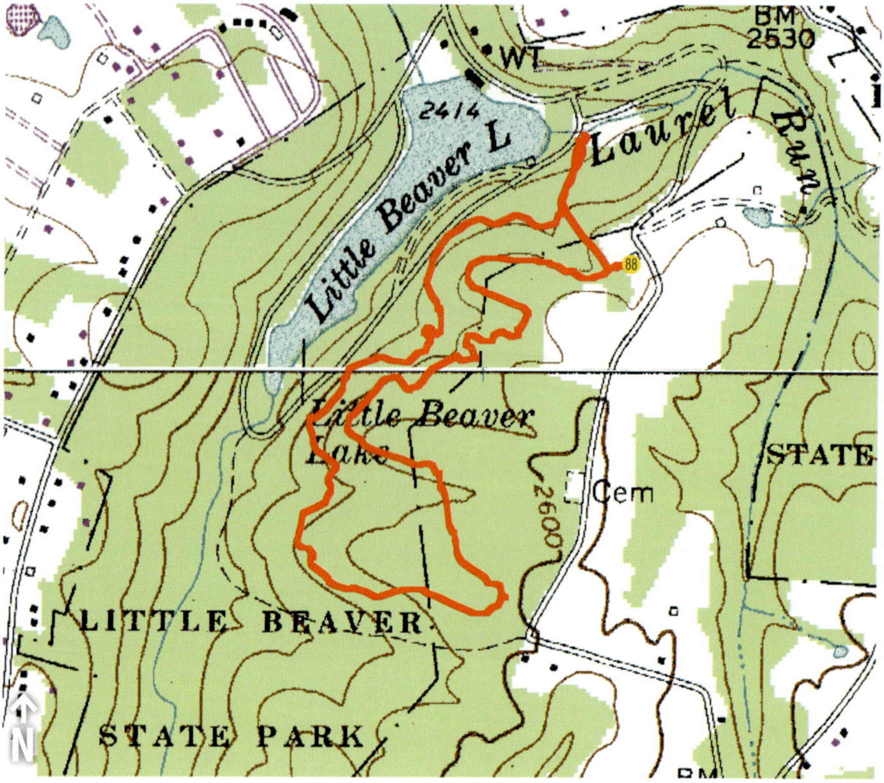

ing at 2.07 miles. At the parking area turn around and almost immediately turn steeply uphill and to the left to return to the original trailhead.

Trail Combinations/Options

The Nature Ridge Trail is frequently used by visitors staying at the campground, as it is the nearest and most easily accessed of all the park's trails. Some common connections include:

Nature Ridge Trail – Easy Street Trail: This combination adds 0.43 miles to the total mileage, resulting in a 2.55-mile loop.

Nature Ridge Trail – Hemlock Trail – Beaver Creek Trail: This combination allows access to the lower portion of the park and adds the beautiful area surrounding Little Beaver Creek for a spectacular 3.37-mile hike. To complete this linkage, hike the Nature Ridge Trail 1.4 miles to the Hemlock Trail (Trail 73). At the intersection turn left and hike 0.16 miles to the Beaver Creek Trail (Trail 82). Turn left along the Beaver Creek Trail and complete the 0.77-mile circuit, returning to the Hemlock Trail's lower trailhead (37°44.839 N, 081°05.089 W) and reversing the 0.16 miles back to the Nature Ridge Trail. Here, turn left and complete the Nature Ridge Trail, returning to its trailhead and the campground.

89 RHODODENDRON RUN TRAIL

Rhododendron Run Trail is the ultimate trail in Little Beaver State Park, connecting to no fewer than eight other trails and offering a multitude of challenges and options.

4 270 ft 464 ft 2.34 mi

Location: South of I-64, exit 129A
Maps: USGS Prince quad 1:24,000, USGS Shady Spring quad 1:24,000
Trail Options: Connects with Nature Ridge Trail (Trail 88), Creek Bed Trail (Trail 76), Crooked Rock Trail (Trail 84), Turkey Spur Trail (Trail 75), Drop Off Trail (Trail 74), Stone Trough Trail (Trail 83), Black Bear Run Trail (Trail 81), and Beaver Creek Trail (Trail 82).
Facilities: Little Beaver State Park offers a full range of picnic, recreation, camping, and toilet facilities.
Highlights: Scenic, connects to multiple trails, wildlife.

Trail Milestones:

0.2 mi – Intersection with Nature Ridge Trail (37°44.780 N, 081°04.733 W)
0.3 mi – Intersection with Creek Bed Trail (37°44.748 N, 081°04.693 W)
0.4 mi – Intersection with Crooked Rock Trail (37°44.707 N, 081°04.729 W)
0.6 mi – Intersection No. 1 with Turkey Spur Trail (37°44.620 N, 081°04.913 W)
0.8 mi – Intersection No. 2 with Turkey Spur Trail (37°44.569 N, 081°04.986 W)
1.1 mi – Intersection No. 1 with Drop Off Trail (37°44.366 N, 081°05.151 W)
1.6 mi – Intersection No. 2 with Drop Off Trail (37°44.440 N, 081°05.225 W)
1.7 mi – Intersection with Stone Trough Trail (37°44.241 N, 081°05.234 W)
1.8 mi – Intersection with Black Bear Run Trail (37°44.243 N, 081°05.308 W)

Finding the Trailhead

From Interstate 64, take exit 129A toward Shady Spring. Turn onto Grandview Road (CR 9) south and travel 1.8 miles to the entrance for Little Beaver State Park on the left.

Upper trailhead: (37°44.932 N, 081°04.621 W)
To access the upper trailhead, continue straight along the main park road, passing the visitor center on the right and continuing uphill to the camping-registration office. Stay left at the office and continue along a gravel road toward an open field. Travel 0.1 miles from the office and stay right when the road reaches the field (field on the left and forest on the right). The parking area for the Rhododendron Run Trail is located on the left side of the gravel road just before the cemetery, while the trailhead is located to the right of the road just before the cemetery. The distance from the main park entrance to the trailhead is 0.89 miles.

Lower trailhead: (37°44.698 N, 081°05.144 W)
To access the lower trailhead, follow the Beaver Creek Trail (Trail 82) 0.3 miles to its intersection with Rhododendron Run Trail.

Trail Description

Yellow Diamond Blaze
Note: Hike described from upper trailhead. From the trailhead, move into the woods and skirt right past the cemetery. Follow this single-track though the forest until intersecting the Nature Ridge Trail at 0.2 miles. Keep left, and after an additional 0.1 miles intersect the Creek Bed Trail and a dirt road. Follow the trail blaze and sign straight across this intersection.

At 0.4 miles come to the third trail intersection, this time with Crooked Rock Trail. On the left, you'll see Beaver Creek Farm, an area of private property and a park boundary. Ascend a short distance and veer right, away from the boundary, before descending and intersecting Turkey Spur Trail the first time — the two trails travel the same path for a short distance. Break left as these trails diverge, and at 0.8 miles intersect Turkey Spur Trail the second and final time.

RHODODENDRON RUN TRAIL

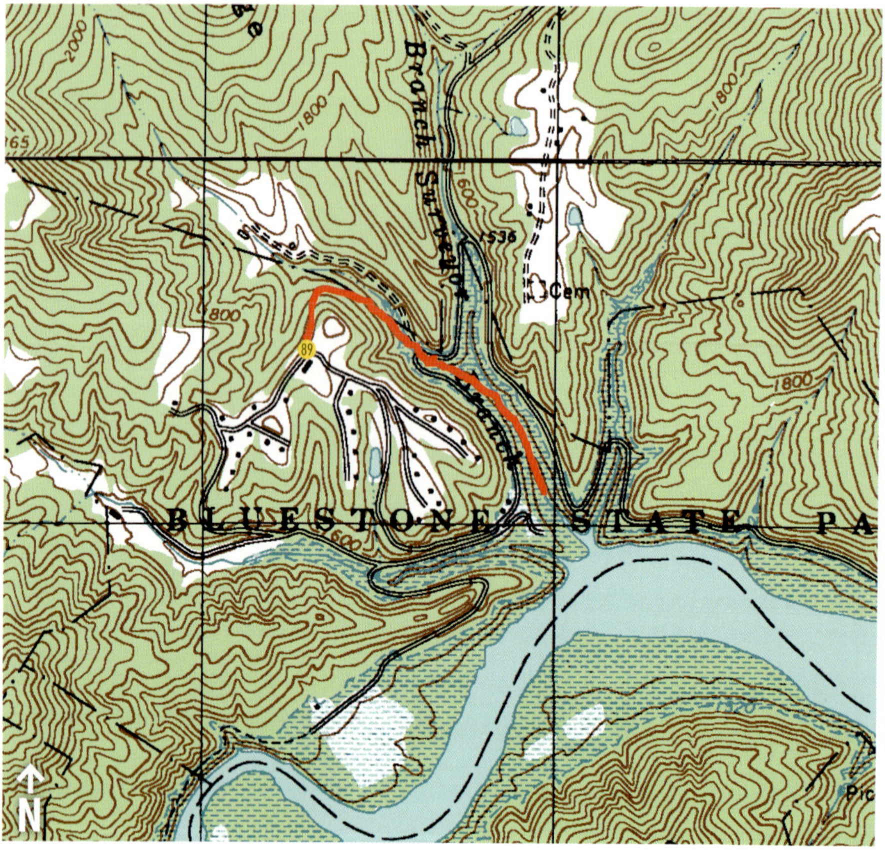

Descend steeply in this area through boulders and rhododendrons, coming to a particularly large boulder at 0.9 miles. Hike up and over this garage-sized bit of stone and continue along the trail. At 1.0 miles arrive at a boulder that provides a nice shelter, perfect for a midsummer rainstorm, then descend amongst additional boulders, arriving at the first intersection with the Drop Off Trail at 1.1 miles.

From this intersection, continue another half-mile to the second intersection with Drop Off Trail and views of a lake far off and to the left. Descend now steeply to the intersection with the Stone Trough Trail and at 1.8 miles arrive at the side of Little Beaver Creek and the intersection with Black Bear Run Trail. Turn right and follow the creek downstream. Through the last 0.54 miles of trail, relax on this relatively flat section and take time to explore the blue-green pools beside you. Late May through early June is a wonderful time to explore this bit of the hike, as the rhododendrons are full of blooms, and the forest floor and stream are littered with fallen petals.

Arrive at the trail's end at 2.34 miles, intersecting the Beaver Creek Trail 0.3 miles from its trailhead

Trail Combinations/Options

This trail intersects eight other trails within the state-park boundaries. Options are almost endless, and many are described within other hikes in this chapter.

A perfect place for a break during a thunderstorm.

RHODODENDRON RUN TRAIL

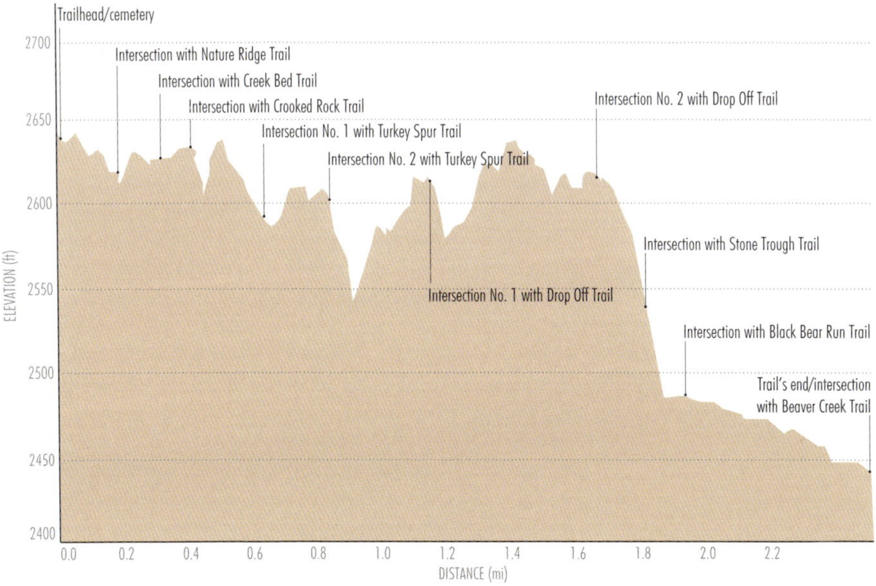

90 LAUREL CREEK TRAIL

One of the longest and most interesting trails in the park, the Laurel Creek Trail combines a scenic hike through forest with opportunities to view wildlife.

4 | 351 ft | 305 ft | 2.53 mi

Location: South of Interstate 64, exit 129A
Maps: USGS Prince quad 1:24,000, USGS Shady Spring quad 1:24,000
Trail Options: Connect with Railroad Grade Trail (Trail 87), Weaver Way Trail (Trail 86), and Deer Trail (Trail 78).
Facilities: Little Beaver State Park offers a full range of picnic, recreation, camping, and toilet facilities.
Highlights: Varied terrain, wildlife.

Trail Milestones:

0.0 mi – Intersection with Railroad Grade Trail/Weaver Way Trail/trailhead (37°45.147 N, 081°04.295 W)
0.27 mi – Series of three bridges (37°45.081 N, 081°04.162 W)
0.71 mi – Bridge (37°44.815 N, 081°04.268 W)
1.1 mi – Intersection with Railroad Grade and Weaver Way trails (37°44.619 N, 081°04.409 W)
2.3 mi – Pond (37°45.132 N, 081°04.366 W)
2.4 mi – Intersection with Deer Trail (37°45.154 N, 081°04.430 W)
2.53 mi – Intersection with Railroad Grade Trail/Weaver Way Trail/trailhead (37°45.147 N, 081°04.295 W)

Finding the Trailhead

(37°45.147 N, 081°04.295 W)
From Interstate 64, take exit 129A toward Shady Spring. Turn onto Grandview Road (CR 9) south and travel 1.8 miles to the entrance for Little Beaver State Park on the left.

Continue along the main park road approximately 0.4 miles until reaching a sharp curve where you'll find the trailhead for the Railroad Grade Trail (37°45.314 N, 081°04.461 W). Follow the Railroad Grade Trail 0.3 miles to the Laurel Creek trailhead.

Trail Description

Red Diamond Blaze
From the intersection with the Railroad Grade and Weaver Way trails, turn sharply left and begin on the trail marked with a red diamond blaze. Move uphill and at 0.1 miles enter an area of thinner forest with homes to the front and left of the trail. Move right and cross a small wooden bridge. At 0.27 miles cross the first of a series of three small wooden bridges spanning depressions and intermittent streams. At 0.4 miles cross the last bridge and climb a short, steep incline. You can hear local traffic along a nearby road; it soon comes very close at 0.71 miles before you cross a small wooden bridge and move away from the road. At 0.9 miles pass a marshy pond on your left and enter a large stand of hemlocks and Virginia pines before descending to meet the Railroad Grade and Weaver Way trails at 1.1 miles.

Cross Laurel Creek using the long wooden bridge and continue straight as the trail again moves close to the road and cattle farm beyond. Just before reaching the road, turn sharply right and parallel it until crossing a rocky, intermittent stream at 1.3 miles. A further 0.3 miles along, the trail begins to open into a younger forest with a meadow and Christmas-tree farm to the left. The trail turns sharply right here and at 1.9 miles enters multiple long, winding turns that are great fun for mountain bikers. Continue along and enter a patch of evergreens, with a steep hollow to the right of the trail. At 2.3 miles come upon a pond surrounded by a field — this area is popular with deer. After another 0.1 miles pass the trailhead for the Deer Trail on the left. Continue around the pond and descend along the now-rocky path to the Railroad Grade Trail. Pass this intersection, immediately cross Laurel Creek, and arrive back at the original trailhead at 2.53 miles.

Ice-covered pond along Laurel Creek Trail.

Trail Combinations/Options

The Laurel Creek Trail connects to the Railroad Grade Trail (Trail 87) and the Weaver Way Trail (Trail 86) at the trailhead and at the 1.1-mile mark. Many local trail runners use one of these two trails to vary their route through the forest. See the description for each hike to gain a better understanding of the route and difficulty level.

The Laurel Creek Trail also connects to the Deer Trail (Trail 78), which offers a wonderful opportunity to combine multiple options for a longer hike. By taking the Deer Trail, you can connect with the Rhododendron Run Trail (Trail 89) and create a loop that encompasses the south and east portions of the park. Follow the Deer Trail to its intersection with a gravel road and turn left along that road. Just before reaching the cemetery, turn right onto Rhododendron Run Trail and follow it its full 2.34 miles to its lower trailhead and intersection with Beaver Creek Trail (Trail 82). Connect with and follow Beaver Creek Trail until you reach its trailhead and parking (0.3 miles). Turn right onto the park road and follow it past a large parking area to the main park road (0.6 miles). Turn right and follow this road 0.17 miles back to the original Railroad Grade trailhead. At this point you can continue to the starting point for Laurel Creek Trail or call it a day at the parking lot. This loop is a strenuous but fun 6.29-mile outing that offers wonderful opportunities to see much varied terrain.

LAUREL CREEK TRAIL

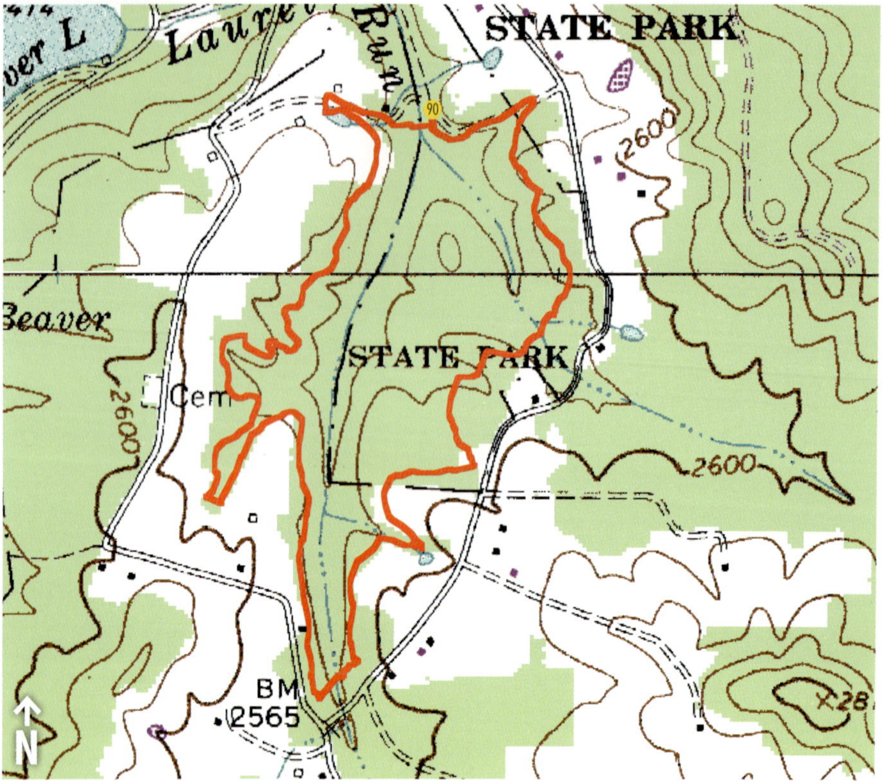

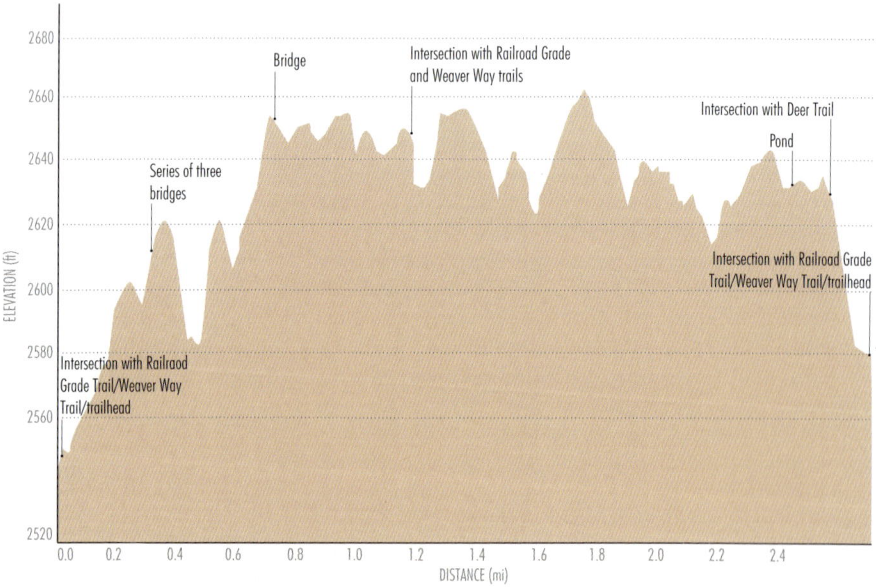

"Cave" near the camping area of Little Beaver State Park.

17 BLUESTONE STATE PARK & BLUESTONE NATIONAL SCENIC RIVER

Overview and Highlights

Bluestone State Park is a 2,154-acre park created in 1950. The park borders the western side of the Bluestone Lake and Dam. The area offers a variety of outdoor adventures, including hiking, camping, biking, hunting, fishing, and boating. The lake is very popular with fishermen, and the area entertains more than 1.3 million visitors each year.

How to Get There

From Interstate 64: Take exit 139 (Hinton/Sandstone) off Interstate 64 and travel 10.3 miles along WV Route 20 to Hinton. Follow WV Route 20 through the historic portion of Hinton and then an additional 4.9 miles to the entrance for Bluestone State Park. Turn right onto Bluestone Park Road (CR 20/2) and drive 2.15 miles to the visitor center/park headquarters.

From Interstate 77: Take exit 9 (Princeton) off Interstate 77. Travel 0.6 miles on US Route 460 west. Turn right onto WV Route 104, then immediately left along the same road (WV 104). Drive 1.0 miles and turn right onto WV Route 20. Travel on this road, passing the town of Athens and Pipestem Resort State Park, for 22.3 miles. Turn left at the Bluestone State Park entrance and drive 2.15 miles to the visitor center/park headquarters.

Rules and Regulations

Please see "Rules and Regulations for West Virginia State Parks" (page 24) for rules and regulations governing Bluestone State Park and all other state parks in the region. Additional regulations, posted at the visitor center, pertain to the campsites and cabins in Bluestone State Park. For additional information, please consult with park employees.

The National Park Service (NPS) is the administrative agency for the Bluestone Turnpike Trail (Trail 98), which lies in the Bluestone National Scenic River. Please consult "Rules and Regulations for the New River Gorge National River" (page 22) for rules and regulations governing the Bluestone National Scenic River. In addition to the rules listed in that section, the following rules also apply:

- No alcohol is permitted.
- Camping is not permitted at any location.

General Trail Information

You'll find eight trails within the boundaries of Bluestone State Park and Bluestone National Scenic River that are open to hikers and trail runners. Mountain biking and horseback riding are also permitted on the Bluestone Turnpike Trail (Trail 98). All of these trails are well marked with trail blazes of various colors.

The incredible Bluestone Lake.

History and Culture

President Franklin D. Roosevelt authorized the building of the Bluestone Dam and Lake in 1935, without congressional approval. However, preparation for and the building of the dam did not begin until the early 1940s due to a lawsuit that challenged the government's right to build the dam. Ultimately, the US Supreme Court heard the case and ruled in favor of the government. Construction was again delayed due to the onset of World War II but resumed in 1946. The dam was completed in 1949, while Bluestone State Park was created one year later.

A stream along the Bluestone Turnpike Trail.

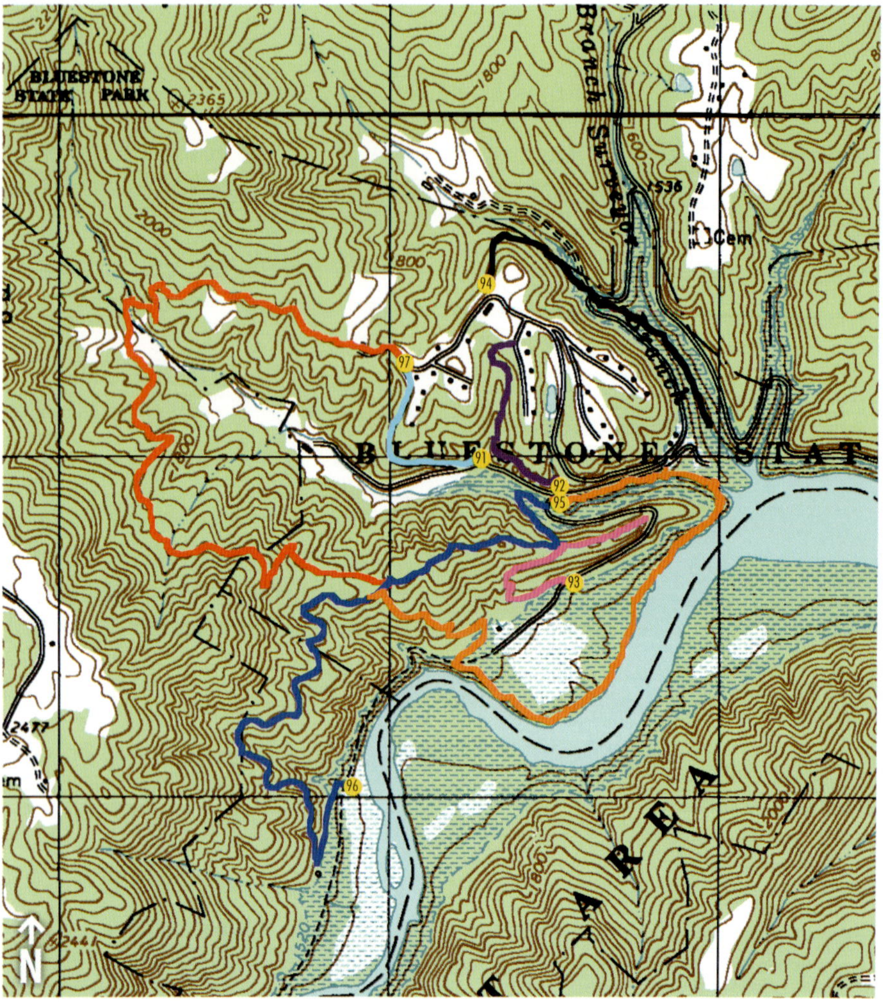

Map Key

Trail 91 – Giles, Fayette, Kanawha Turnpike Trail – light blue
Trail 92 – Cabin Trail – purple
Trail 93 – Overlook Trail – pink
Trail 94 – Rhododendron Trail – black
Trail 95 – Riverview Trail – orange
Trail 96 – Big Pine Trail – dark blue
Trail 97 – Boundary Trail – red

91 GILES, FAYETTE, KANAWHA TURNPIKE TRAIL

This trail is one of the few remaining and undisturbed portions of the Giles, Fayette, and Kanawha Turnpike, which in the 1860s was a major thoroughfare for the region. Walk along the path a young Booker T. Washington trod barefoot after the Civil War.

2 | 246 ft 0 ft | 0.36 mi

Location: South of Interstate 64 and Hinton, WV; east of Interstate 77
Maps: USGS Flat Top quad 1:24,000, USGS Hinton quad 1:24,000, USGS Pipestem quad 1:24,000
Trail Options: Connect with the Boundary Trail (Trail 97).
Facilities: No facilities along this trail.
Highlights: Historically significant trail.

Trail Milestones:

0.2 mi – Cabins on the right (37°36.991 N, 080°56.591 W)

Additional Notes

Booker T. Washington, civil rights leader of the late 1800s, renowned educator, and advisor to President Theodore Roosevelt, traveled along this trail with his mother and family after being freed at the end of the Civil War. Known for his Atlanta Address of 1895, Washington was a leader of the civil rights movement and spokesperson for African American citizens. He was the first leader of the Tuskegee Institute in Alabama and helped site West Virginia State University in the Kanawha Valley.

Finding the Trailhead

(37°36.953 N, 080°56.411 W)
From the park headquarters along Bluestone Park Road (CR 20/2), continue 0.27 miles to a deep bend in this road at an intersection and park at the small gravel lot. To reach the trailhead, you must walk down the road that leads west (and not the main Bluestone Park Road) for 0.2 miles to the trailhead on the right.

Trail Description

Orange Square Blaze
From the trailhead ascend gradually along the entire length of the trail through a mixed forest. This portion of the trail dates back to the early 1800s and witnessed pioneers moving west from Virginia through West Virginia, Ohio, and beyond. In the 1860s, armies from both sides in the Civil War used this trail to transport men and material, to secure valuable resources for their respective factions. Watch closely as you ascend for small details pointing to the trail's provenance, such as the worn cut of the bank above or the well-graded feature of the track below. At 0.2 miles begin to see cabins perched above and to the right. A little farther on, the trail comes to an end at 0.36 miles near Cabin No. 17.

This marks the end of the maintained official trail and the intersection with the Boundary Trail. While the Giles path does continue straight along its historic route into the forest above, it becomes rougher and more difficult to discern, and this distance is not included in the 0.36 miles as described.

Trail Combinations/Options

Connect with the Boundary Trail (Trail 97) and take a left, hiking it to its end for a 2.29-mile one-way journey. This combination necessitates a return via the same route.

It is also possible to hike the Boundary Trail to its intersection with the Big Pine Trail (Trail 96), turn left onto Big Pine, and return to the original gravel parking area at the bend in Bluestone Park Road. This route is a strenuous 2.9-mile round-trip.

92 CABIN TRAIL

This short trail leads from the junction of a park road, Big Pine Trail, and Riverview Trail to the cabins atop the ridge.

3 | 232 ft 28 ft | 0.43 mi

Location: South of Interstate 64 and Hinton, WV; east of Interstate 77

Maps: USGS Flat Top quad 1:24,000, USGS Hinton quad 1:24,000, USGS Pipestem quad 1:24,000

Trail Options: Connect with Riverview Trail (Trail 95) or Big Pine Trail (Trail 96).

Facilities: Limited parking at trailhead; picnic facilities, playground, and parking at trail's end.

Highlights: Access to cabins; deer and turkey feeding in area.

Trail Milestones:

0.1 mi – Power-line cut (37°36.937 N, 080°56.311 W)

Finding the Trailhead

(37°36.901 N, 080°56.244 W)

From the park headquarters along Bluestone Park Road (CR 20/2), continue 0.27 miles to a deep bend in this road at an intersection. The trailhead is to the right, with parking for a few vehicles in a gravel lot.

Trail Description

Yellow Triangle Blaze

From the trailhead at the intersection with Bluestone Park Road, climb steeply for a short time and veer left along the trail. The ascent almost immediately lessens in steepness, and at 0.1 miles the trail moves through an opening for a power-line cut. Continue around a spur of the ridge; as the trail begins to move deeper into the valley, it becomes enveloped by soft moss. At 0.2 miles the trail begins to parallel a seasonal stream. Continue along the trail as it ascends to the cabin area at trail's end. The trail tops out on a large, flat hilltop populated by cabins — the cabins nearest the trail's end are Nos. 11 and 12. At this point be sure to visit an enormous evergreen that dominates the area — a pitch pine (*Pinus rigida*). Return along the same route or use the cabin-access road to return to the trailhead.

Trail Combinations/Options

There are no combinations available to create loop hikes. It is possible to add the Cabin Trail to either the Big Pine Trail (Trail 96) or the Riverview Trail (Trail 95), as all three trails share a common trailhead.

93 OVERLOOK TRAIL

This trail leads to a ridgeline and scenic viewpoint looking out over Bluestone Lake.

3 | 224 ft | 50 ft | 0.47 mi

Location: South of Interstate 64 and Hinton, WV; east of Interstate 77
Maps: USGS Flat Top quad 1:24,000, USGS Hinton quad 1:24,000, USGS Pipestem quad 1:24,000
Trail Options: Connect with Big Pine Trail (Trail 96) and Riverview Trail (Trail 95).
Facilities: No facilities at trailhead; Meador Campground just 0.1 miles away.
Highlights: Scenic vista, rocky ridgeline.

Trail Milestones:

0.3 mi – Intersection with Big Pine Trail (37°36.815 N, 080°56.237 W)

Finding the Trailhead

(37°36.761 N, 080°56.231 W)

From the park headquarters along Bluestone Park Road (CR 20/2), continue 0.79 miles. This portion of the road drops down into a valley with a deep bend, and then climbs to a spur with a sharp right turn before finally descending to the trailhead on the right. There is no parking here, so continue to the Meador Campground; park here and return 0.1 miles uphill along the road.

Trail Description

Red Square Blaze

From the trailhead along the Bluestone Park Road, move uphill into a brushy forest. As you climb steadily along switchbacks, the forest becomes older in nature and the trees begin to tower over the trail. Using this series of well-graded switchbacks, the ascent softens at 0.21 miles. Continue to 0.3 miles and intersect the Big Pine Trail (Trail 96). Big Pine Trail makes a big bend at this point, with both branches lying off to your left. To stay on the Overlook Trail, turn right at this junction and continue along a rocky ridgeline. Weave amongst lichen- and moss-covered boulders along the narrow ridge until reaching the viewpoint at 0.47 miles. From here, you can look east along the Bluestone River to Bluestone Lake.

The trail ends at this point and requires backtracking to the trailhead or to the intersection with Big Pine Trail if including the latter as part of a larger loop (see Trail Combinations/Options). At the overlook, you'll see what looks to be a continuance of the trail descending steeply straight ahead, but this is NOT a trail. It leads to a cliff above the Bluestone Park Road and is extremely dangerous.

Trail Combinations/Options

A connection is available with Big Pine Trail (Trail 96). This connection allows for two loops, both of which return via Riverview Trail (Trail 95) to the parking area at Meador Campground.

Bluestone Lake at low water, from the scenic overlook.

Loop 1: At 0.3 miles intersect the Big Pine Trail. Take the branch of Big Pine that leads off the ridgeline (this will be obvious) and descend steeply to a stream where the trail turns sharply right. Continue to the trail's end and gravel parking area. Cross the road and find the trailhead for the Riverview Trail, and then follow Riverview 0.7 miles back to the Meador Campground. Visiting the viewpoint on Overlook Trail and completing this loop results in a pleasant and very scenic outing of 1.55 miles.

Loop 2: After visiting the scenic overlook, return along the Overlook Trail and connect to the other branch of Big Pine Trail — the one that leads west along the ridgeline — following it 0.4 miles to intersect the Riverview Trail's western terminus. Turn left onto Riverview Trail and descend 0.96 miles to reach Meador Campground. This route creates a loop of 2.00 miles.

Additional Notes

This trailhead is just 0.1 miles from the Meador Campground, home to 32 campsites (22 with electricity). This campground sits on the banks of the Bluestone River and is one of the prettiest in the area, with ample parking, toilets, and a bathhouse with hot water.

OVERLOOK TRAIL

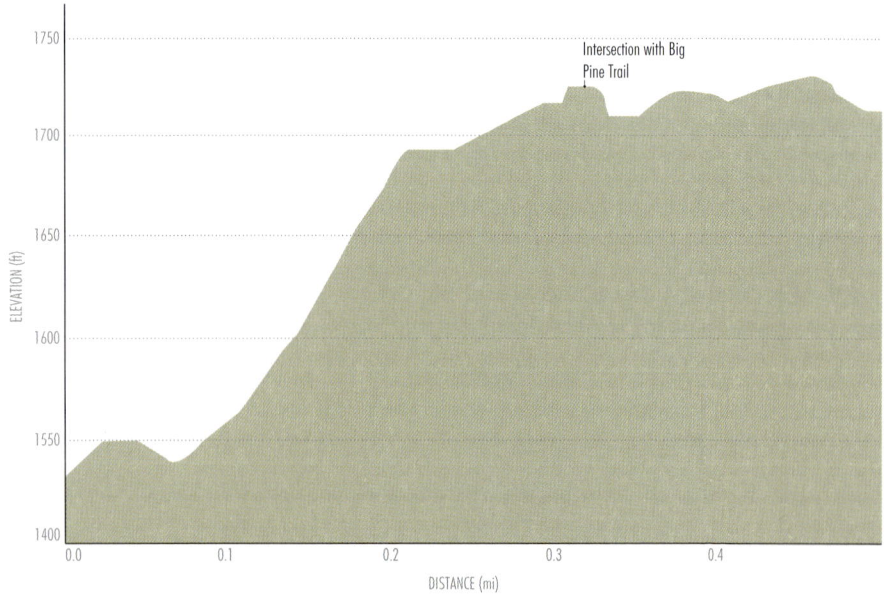

94 RHODODENDRON TRAIL

This trail descends to Surveyor's Creek amongst rhododendrons to the official trail's end, and then a waterfall just above the lake.

2 | 7 ft 300 ft | 0.67 mi

Location: South of Interstate 64 and Hinton, WV; east of Interstate 77
Maps: USGS Flat Top quad 1:24,000, USGS Hinton quad 1:24,000, USGS Pipestem quad 1:24,000
Trail Options: No combinations available, though park roads lead back to the trailhead.
Facilities: No facilities available at trailhead; toilets available at trail's end.
Highlights: Wildlife, stream, waterfall past official trail's end.

Trail Milestones:

0.29 mi – Cross Bluestone Park Road (37°37.227 N, 080°56.191 W)

Finding the Trailhead

(37°37.238 N, 080°56.391 W)
From the park headquarters along Bluestone Park Road (CR 20/2), turn right off this road and continue along a paved park road that ascends to the cabin area on the ridgeline. The trailhead is located 0.6 miles along this road, across from the activities center.

Trail Description

Red Triangle Blaze
Park at the activities center and cross the road to the trailhead. Immediately enter the woods and walk along single-track that's been narrowly cut into a steep mountainside. This trail can be difficult to hike in icy or wet weather. Please take care along the route.

Continue a gradual descent throughout the first 0.29 miles and watch for deer below. At this point descend steeply down a bank to the Bluestone Park Road (CR 20/2). Cross this busy road and pick up the trail on the far side. The trail flattens out in this section and parallels Surveyor's Creek. Over the next 300 meters you must cross the stream twice; this is easily done, as ample rocks permit a safe (and dry!) crossing.

The trail officially ends at 0.67 miles as it emerges into an open field near restrooms. If you wish, continue along the stream 0.2 miles to see a waterfall that's beautiful after a spring rain. When the area is not busy with boaters, deer often visit these fields to feed. Return by the same trail or use park roads to navigate back to the trailhead.

Trail Combinations/Options

No combinations available to other trails, though you can return to the trailhead via park roads.

95 RIVERVIEW TRAIL

If you have time for only one hike in Bluestone State Park, make it this one. Riverview Trail encompasses a beautiful stream, multiple waterfalls, close-up views of the lake, and a trip through a mixed deciduous and evergreen forest.

3 | 432 ft 187 ft | 1.66 mi

Location: South of Interstate 64 and Hinton, WV; east of Interstate 77
Maps: USGS Flat Top quad 1:24,000, USGS Hinton quad 1:24,000, USGS Pipestem quad 1:24,000
Trail Options: Combine with Big Pine Trail (Trail 96).
Facilities: Small parking area at trailhead, toilet facilities at Meador Campground at 0.7 miles.
Highlights: Waterfalls, stream, lake views, mixed forest.

Trail Milestones:

0.2 mi – Waterfall
(37°36.930 N, 080°56.022 W)
0.4 mi – Waterfall
(37°36.920 N, 080°55.920 W)
0.7 mi – Meador Campground
(37°36.730 N, 080°56.086 W)
1.3 mi – Bluestone Park Road
(37°36.633 N, 080°56.458 W)

Trail Combinations/Options

Combine Riverview Trail with the Big Pine Trail (Trail 96) to create a loop that returns to the Riverview trailhead. From the trail's end and intersection with Big Pine Trail, turn right along Big Pine Trail and follow it 0.61 miles. This creates a 2.27-mile loop.

Finding the Trailhead

(37°36.893 N, 080°56.255 W)
From the park headquarters along Bluestone Park Road (CR 20/2), continue 0.27 miles to a deep bend in this road at an intersection. The trailhead is to the left, below the road, with parking available for a few vehicles in a gravel lot.

Trail Description

Blue Square Blaze
From the lot, cross the Bluestone Park Road (CR20/2) to the trailhead. Immediately descend to reach a stream. Cross this stream at 100 meters and continue to parallel it. Enjoy the pretty cascades, and at 0.2 miles reach a six-foot waterfall that spills over flat rock. Take a moment to appreciate the falls, then continue hiking; at 0.4 miles reach a Y intersection. You will follow the right branch, but before continuing take the time to explore this area. To the left you'll see the top of a 20-foot waterfall — move below this waterfall for a beautiful view from downstream. Take care in this area, especially with small children. For the adventurous hiker, a small, tricky trail winds downstream and under an enormous rock roof to give you a closer look at the falls. Follow this path at your own risk!

Continuing along the right branch from the Y intersection, come upon a small spur trail that leads uphill. This accesses the Bluestone Park Road. Stay left here and look for views through the trees of Bluestone Lake. Descend gradually through the forest until reaching the lakeshore. The hike continues along relatively flat ground for the next 0.35 miles.

At 0.7 miles arrive at the Meador Campground and intersect a campground road. Stay left along this road for a short time and reconnect to the trail just left of Campsite No. 14. Visitors staying at this campground often end their hike here.

Continue to parallel the lake and cross two small streams at 0.9 miles. At 1.1 miles reenter a pine forest and cross a small rocky stream. At this point the trail begins to ascend, and at 1.3 miles crosses the Bluestone Park Road. Steeply ascend the opposite side of the road and begin to follow a series of switchbacks to the trail's end (western terminus) and intersection with Big Pine Trail at 1.66 miles.

RIVERVIEW TRAIL

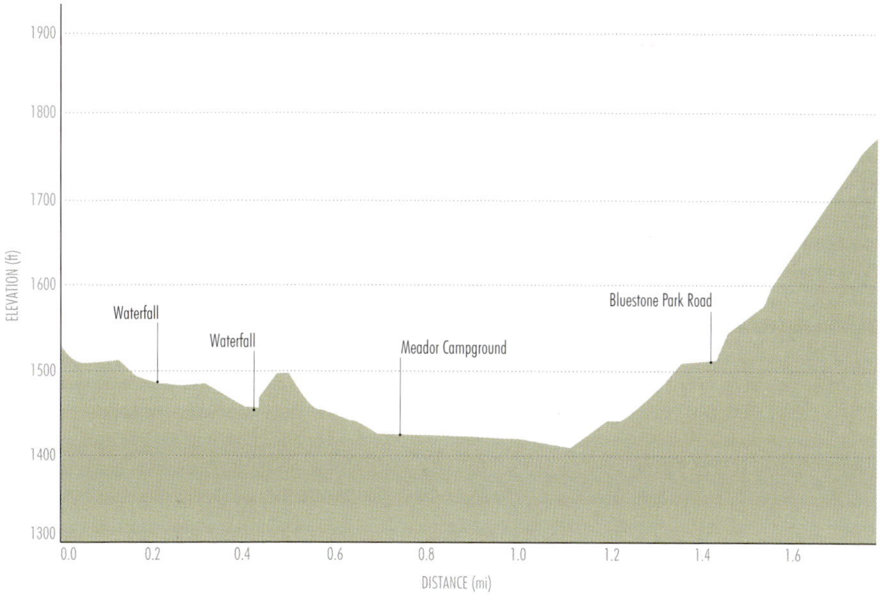

96 BIG PINE TRAIL

A moderate trail that connects the Old Mill Campground to other trails within the park, following a single-track path through a mature forest of hardwoods.

3 | 591 ft | 509 ft | 1.71 mi

Location: South of Interstate 64 and Hinton, WV; east of Interstate 77
Maps: USGS Flat Top quad 1:24,000, USGS Hinton quad 1:24,000, USGS Pipestem quad 1:24,000
Trail Options: Connects to Riverview Trail (Trail 95), Boundary Trail (97), and Overlook Trail (Trail 93).
Facilities: Parking, campsites, toilets, and bathhouse with cold showers at trailhead.
Highlights: Mature forest, views.

Trail Milestones:

0.2 mi – Old building (37°36.314 N, 080°56.739 W)
1.1 mi – Intersection with Riverview Trail (37°36.736 N, 080°56.625 W)
1.2 mi – Intersection with Boundary Trail (37°36.759 N, 080°56.593 W)
1.5 mi – Intersection with Overlook Trail (37°36.815 N, 080°56.237 W)

Finding the Trailhead

Old Mill Campground trailhead: (37°36.440 N, 080°56.678 W)
From the park headquarters located along Bluestone Park Road (CR 20/2), continue 1.34 miles to the Old Mill Campground. The trailhead is to the right as you drive to the campground entrance, beside a small stream. Park at the Old Mill Campground and hike back along the road to reach the trailhead.

Alternative trailhead: (37°36.880 N, 080°56.268 W)
From the park headquarters located along Bluestone Park Road (CR 20/2), continue 0.27 miles to a deep bend in this road at an intersection. The trailhead is to the right beside the gravel parking area and is marked by a sign.

Trail Description

Green Circle Blaze
Note: Hike described from the Old Mill Campground trailhead. To begin, walk back along the Bluestone Park Road 0.1 miles to the trailhead on the left, beside a small stream. Ascend the bank and move left and gently uphill. At 0.2 miles see an old concrete building half-hidden among the trees to the left while turning right into the first switchback. Continue along this moderately steep incline until leveling off at 0.5 miles and crossing a small stream. The trail remains at this mid-mountain level for the next 0.8 miles.

At 0.9 miles cross another stream, watching it fall quickly toward the Bluestone River, and at 1.1 miles reach the intersection with the Riverview Trail. To the left you can see the ridgeline and the Boundary Trail as it slowly descends and meets the trail at 1.2 miles. Stay straight at both of these intersections.

From the intersection with Boundary Trail begin to move uphill gradually until attaining the rocky ridgeline, catching nice views through the trees. This area is densely populated with squirrels, which play here year-round. Cross beneath a power line at 1.4 miles and intersect the Overlook Trail not long after. Turn left at this intersection and descend steeply to the trail's end, or alternatively, follow the Overlook Trail 0.17 miles to its scenic viewpoint, then return and

BIG PINE TRAIL

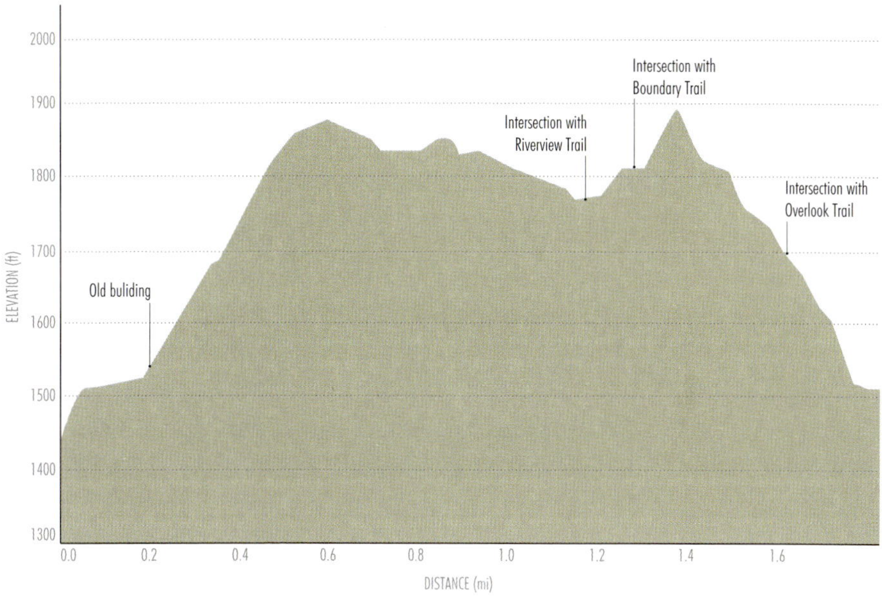

complete the Big Pine Trail. Take care on Big Pine's final descent, as it is narrow and the mountainside is extremely steep in this area.

Trail Combinations/Options

The Big Pine Trail connects with multiple trails within the park, but unfortunately does not lend itself to an easy loop when starting from the Old Mill Campground. Connecting with the Boundary Trail (Trail 97) creates a 3.03-mile one-way hike that requires a return along the same route or via park roads. You can also connect to the Riverview Trail (Trail 95) and descend to the Meador Campground and return by way of the Bluestone Park Road (CR 20/2) for 0.4 miles — this loop is 1.96 miles total.

Additional Notes

The Old Mill Campground is a 44-site rustic campground situated at the trailhead for Big Pine Trail and beside the Bluestone River as it empties into Bluestone Lake. This campground is also home to one of the two trailheads for the Bluestone Turnpike Trail (Trail 98). Facilities include toilets and a cold-water bathhouse.

97 BOUNDARY TRAIL

The most challenging trail within the state park, this path winds deeply into Gib Lilly Hollow before ascending to intersect the Big Pine Trail.

4 | 631 ft 504 ft | 1.93 mi

Location: South of Interstate 64 and Hinton, WV; east of Interstate 77
Maps: USGS Flat Top quad 1:24,000, USGS Hinton quad 1:24,000, USGS Pipestem quad 1:24,000
Trail Options: Connect with the Big Pine Trail (Trail 96) and the Giles, Fayette, Kanawha Turnpike Trail (Trail 91) to create a loop.
Facilities: No facilities along this trail.
Highlights: Older forest, stream, views through forested valley.

Trail Milestones:

0.71 mi – Stream
(37°37.206 N, 080°57.122 W)
0.8 mi – Spring and open area
(37°37.131 N, 080°57.124 W)
1.0 mi – Boulder field and stream
(37°37.020 N, 080°57.114 W)

Finding the Trailhead

(37°37.102 N, 080°56.554 W)
From the park headquarters along Bluestone Park Road (CR 20/2), turn right off this road and continue along a paved park road that ascends to the cabin area on the ridgeline. The trailhead is located 0.82 miles along this latter road and 50 meters northwest of Cabin No. 17.

Trail Description

White Diamond Blaze
From Cabin No. 17 walk northwest 50 meters to the trailhead, marked by a sign. The trail moves slightly uphill and to the right here. Follow the trail around and to the left, breaking away from the larger service road and now moving along single-track.

At 0.3 miles cross a small seasonal drainage, and at 0.5 miles begin to zigzag down switchbacks into the valley. At 0.71 miles reach a small stream; look to the right to see a small cascade, and just beyond, a barbed-wire fence marking the state-park boundary with private land. Ascend steeply up the opposite bank and bear left.

At 0.8 miles come upon a brushy, open area that can be somewhat muddy from a spring flowing from above. Move through this area, thick with briars, and reenter the forest. The trail now takes on a steeper nature, with a continuous ascent over the next 0.7 miles.

At 1.0 miles enter a boulder field and cross a stream. From this point, until the intersection with the Big Pine Trail, you can catch distant views of the surrounding area through the trees throughout late autumn and winter. At 1.5 miles begin to descend along switchbacks to the trail intersection with Big Pine Trail, along a ridgeline.

Trail Combinations/Options

At the trail's end turn left onto Big Pine Trail (Trail 96) and follow it 0.51 miles to its end. This area marks the junction of the Bluestone Park Road (CR 20/2) and a paved road leading off to the left. Follow this unnamed park road 0.2 miles to the Giles, Fayette, Kanawha Turnpike Trail (Trail 91); now hike this trail the full length of its maintained 0.36 miles to its end — the trailhead for the Boundary Trail is just beyond. This loop totals 3.08 miles.

The intersection of Boundary and Big Pine trails.

BOUNDARY TRAIL

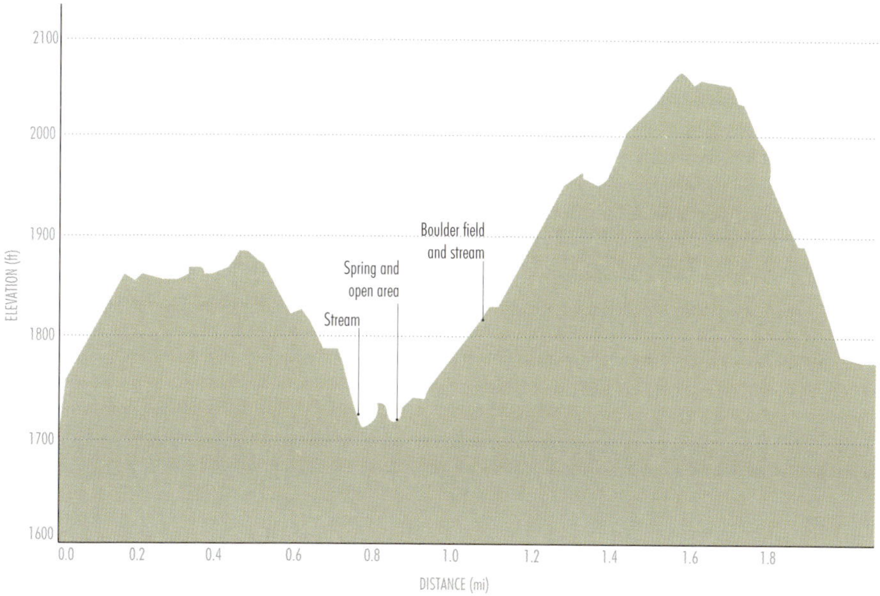

98 BLUESTONE TURNPIKE TRAIL

Follow this trail along the northwest bank of the scenic and wild Bluestone River, enjoying views of the waters and ridgeline while learning the history of this beautiful area.

2 | 646 ft | 592 ft | 7.44 mi

Location: South of Interstate 64 and Hinton, WV; east/northeast of Interstate 77

Maps: USGS Flat Top quad 1:24,000, USGS Hinton quad 1:24,000, USGS Pipestem quad 1:24,000

Trail Options: This trail connects Bluestone and Pipestem Resort state parks. In Pipestem, it connects to the Farley Loop Trail (Trail 113) and River Trail (Trail 114).

Facilities: Each state park has a full complement of facilities. The town of Lilly offers a large gravel parking area and picnic facilities (no toilets).

Highlights: Beautiful river, rapids, the town of Lilly, wildlife.

Trail Milestones:

1.3 mi – Cross stream (37°35.406 N, 080°57.625 W)

2.1 mi – Cross steel bridge/Lilly (37°35.020 N, 080°58.245 W)

2.3 mi – Cross stream (37°34.903 N, 080°58.450 W)

4.7 mi – First of several stream crossings (37°33.906 N, 080°59.873 W)

7.0 mi – Signboard for trail (37°32.573 N, 080°59.837 W)

River Levels Data Websites:

- waterdata.usgs.gov/usa/nwis/uv?03179000
- water.weather.gov/ahps2/hydrograph.php?wfo=rnk&gage=pipw2

Finding the Trailhead

Bluestone State Park trailhead: (37°36.138 N, 080°56.776 W)
See this chapter's intro (page 274) for driving directions to the park. From the park headquarters located along Bluestone Park Road (CR 20/2), continue 1.7 miles past the Old Mill Campground to a paved parking area for eight vehicles. The trailhead is designated with a sign, and blocked to vehicular traffic by a metal gate.

Lilly trailhead: (37°35.020 N, 080°58.245 W)
Take exit 125 off Interstate 64 toward Beaver. Follow US Route 19 south 4.1 miles and turn left onto WV Route 3. Follow WV Route 3 for 10 miles until arriving at the town of Nimitz. Turn right onto Ellison Ridge Road (WV Route 27) and drive 5.9 miles along paved double- and single-lane road. Turn left onto Bluestone River Road, a rough gravel road, to reach the parking area.

Pipestem Resort State Park trailhead: (37°32.734 N, 081°00.139 W)
Take exit 14 off Interstate 77 and travel along WV Route 20 north 11.2 miles to the park entrance. Follow the main park road 2.1 miles and turn left toward the Canyon Rim Visitor Center. Take the tram (see the Pipestem Resort State Park intro, page 292, for details) to the Mountain Creek Lodge. From the lodge, hike north along the River Trail 0.9 miles to the intersection of the Bluestone Turnpike Trail and the Farley Loop Trail.

At certain times of the year, you can also hike to the Mountain Creek Lodge via the River Trail, which begins at McKeever Lodge in Pipestem. Once on the main park road, drive 3.1 miles to the lodge and park in the large paved parking area. From the trailhead, hike 3.26 miles to the Bluestone River, cross the river at the fording site, and hike the remaining 1.8 miles to the trail intersection with the Bluestone Turnpike Trail.

Note: Before attempting to ford the Bluestone River, please consult with employees at the McKeever Lodge regarding current river levels and/or check with the US Army Corps of Engineers by calling (304) 466-0156 and listening to the recorded message regarding water levels at the "Bluestone River at Pipestem."

Looking upstream along the Bluestone River.

BLUESTONE TURNPIKE TRAIL

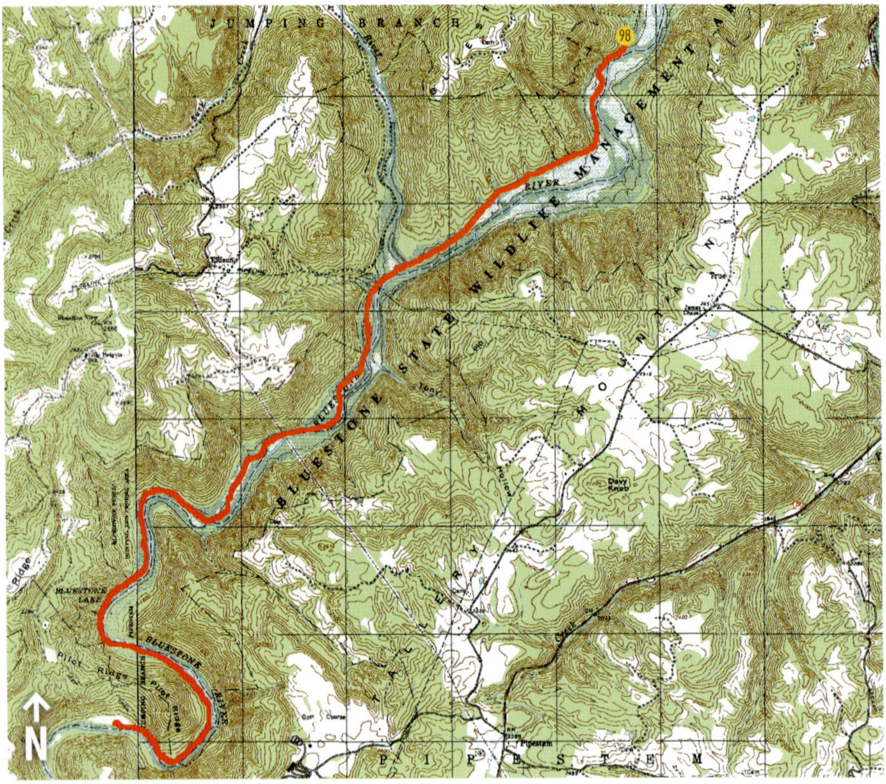

Trail Description

No Blaze

Note: Hike described from Bluestone State Park trailhead. From the trailhead at Bluestone State Park, move beyond the metal gate and continue along this wide and easy trail. The river, on your left, meanders gently along a rocky bottom as you head upstream. At 0.3 miles see a few of the many islands formed over the years as the river cut different channels. Continuing along the trail, watch for signs of the turkey and deer that frequent the area. At 1.3 miles cross a stream, and at 1.5 miles come across an area recently burned during a forest fire. Also at this location, a sign points out a spur trail to the grave of a soldier killed during World War II who was returned here for burial.

At 2.1 miles use a steel bridge to cross the Little Bluestone River and arrive at the former location of the town of Lilly, WV, one of the first pioneer settlements in the state and ancestral home to one of the largest families in the world. This town was uprooted by the government due to concerns that it would be flooded upon completion of the Bluestone Dam. While lying within the potential flood plain, the town's former site is still on dry ground (see Additional Notes on facing page for more information).

Cross another stream at 2.3 miles and then continue 0.8 miles, passing a small pond on the right that makes for a pretty picnic spot. The trail continues to hug the banks of the Bluestone River under a canopy of sycamore, oak, and maple trees. At 4.7 miles come across the first of several small streams that drain the mountains above and to the right. At 7.0 miles reach a signboard for the trail and the boundary of the national scenic river grounds. Continue past this signboard an additional 0.44 miles to reach the trail's end and intersection with the Farley Loop Trail and River Trail. From here, you can continue 0.9 miles to the Mountain Creek Lodge and Tram, or reverse your route back to the original Bluestone State Park trailhead.

Trail Combinations/Options

This trail connects Bluestone and Pipestem Resort state parks, and provides access to the trails within each. At the Pipestem trailhead, you can connect to the Farley Loop Trail (Trail 113) and the River Trail (Trail 114). If staying in the Mountain Creek Lodge, continue 0.9 miles along the River Trail to the lodge.

Additional Notes

Town of Lilly: Robert and Francis Lilly and Josiah Meador settled the town of Lilly, one of West Virginia's first settlements, in the early 1700s. Utilizing the natural resources within this valley, these families carved out a living and built a town that survived until the 1930s. The US government decided to build the Bluestone Dam to assist with flood control and determined that Lilly would be flooded by this project. The town's residents were forced to move, and the town was destroyed. Today, little evidence remains of this once-thriving town and early settlement deep within the Appalachian Mountains.

While their town may be gone, the Lilly family still thrives to this day. Each year in Flat Top, WV, they meet for a family reunion. Recognized by the *Guinness Book of World Records* as having the largest family reunion in the world, the Lilly family is also one of the largest clans on record.

Escape from the Shawnee, the Mary Draper Ingles Story: Mary Draper Ingles, born in 1732 and abducted in 1755 from Draper's Meadow by the Shawnee during the French and Indian War, provides one of the greatest survival stories in West Virginia history. She was taken with her two young sons to a village in Ohio, near present-day Chillicothe — the Shawnee took her sons and adopted them into their tribe, while Mary herself was sold to a French trader. Her determination not broken, Mary escaped along with an "old Dutch woman" and returned home, using in part what is now the Bluestone Turnpike Trail. Her epic journey of more than 500 miles is a testament to her will to survive. Upon Mary's escape, she reunited with her husband and lived until 1815 near Radford, Virginia.

BLUESTONE TURNPIKE TRAIL

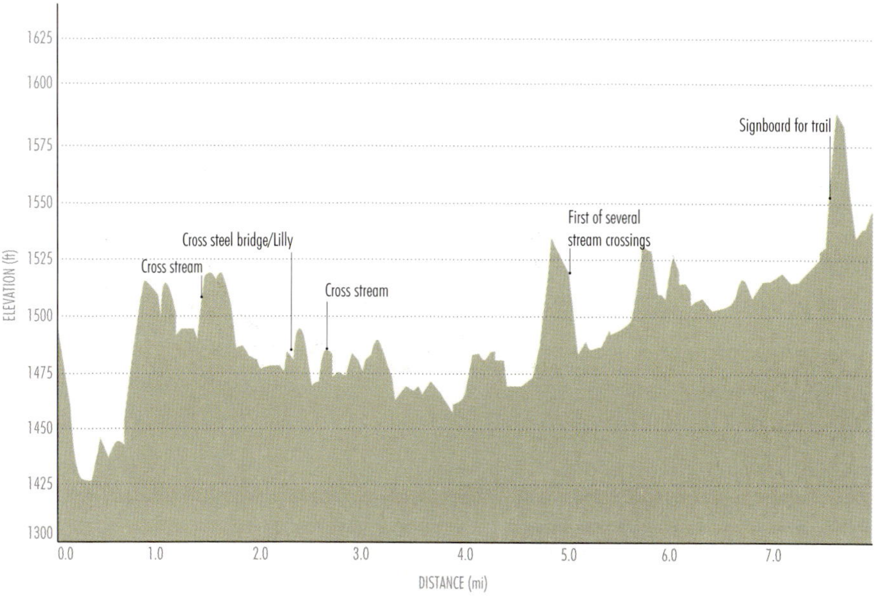

The Bluestone River Gorge from Heritage Point, Canyon Rim Trail.

18 PIPESTEM RESORT STATE PARK

Overview and Highlights

The 4,050-acre Pipestem Resort State Park was authorized during the John F. Kennedy administration and opened in 1967. The park is located within Mercer and Summers counties and borders portions of the Bluestone National Scenic River. It is one of West Virginia's most beautiful and luxurious state parks, and offers two lodges, 26 cottages, and a campground. There are also myriad recreational activities to enjoy, including 16 trails of varying degrees of difficulty.

How to Get There

From Interstate 64: Take exit 139 (Hinton/Sandstone) and travel 10.3 miles along WV Route 20 to Hinton. Follow WV Route 20 through the historic portion of Hinton and then an additional 12 miles to the Pipestem Resort State Park entrance. Turn right into the park and drive 3.1 miles to McKeever Lodge.

From Interstate 77: Take exit 9 (Princeton) and then travel 0.6 miles on US Route 460 west. Turn right onto WV Route 104, then immediately left along the same road (WV 104). Drive 1.0 miles and turn right onto WV Route 20, following it 13.4 miles and passing the town of Athens. Finally, turn left at the Pipestem Resort State Park entrance and travel 3.1 miles to McKeever Lodge.

Rules and Regulations

Please see "Rules and Regulations for West Virginia State Parks" (page 24) for rules and regulations governing Pipestem Resort State Park and all other state parks in the region.

Additional regulations pertain to the lodges, campsites, and cottages at Pipestem. These are available at the park headquarters, the campground, or McKeever Lodge. For additional information, please consult with park employees.

General Trail Information

There are sixteen trails within the boundaries of the Pipestem Resort State Park that are open to hikers and trail runners. Mountain biking, horseback riding, and cross-country skiing are permitted on some of these trails.

History and Culture

Pipestem Resort State Park is named for the local shrub narrowleaf meadowsweet (*Spiraea alba*), used by pioneers — and most likely even earlier by Native Americans — as the stem for pipes. Thus the name: Pipestem. In addition to the park, a nearby town and stream also bear the same moniker.

PIPESTEM RESORT STATE PARK LAKE HIKES

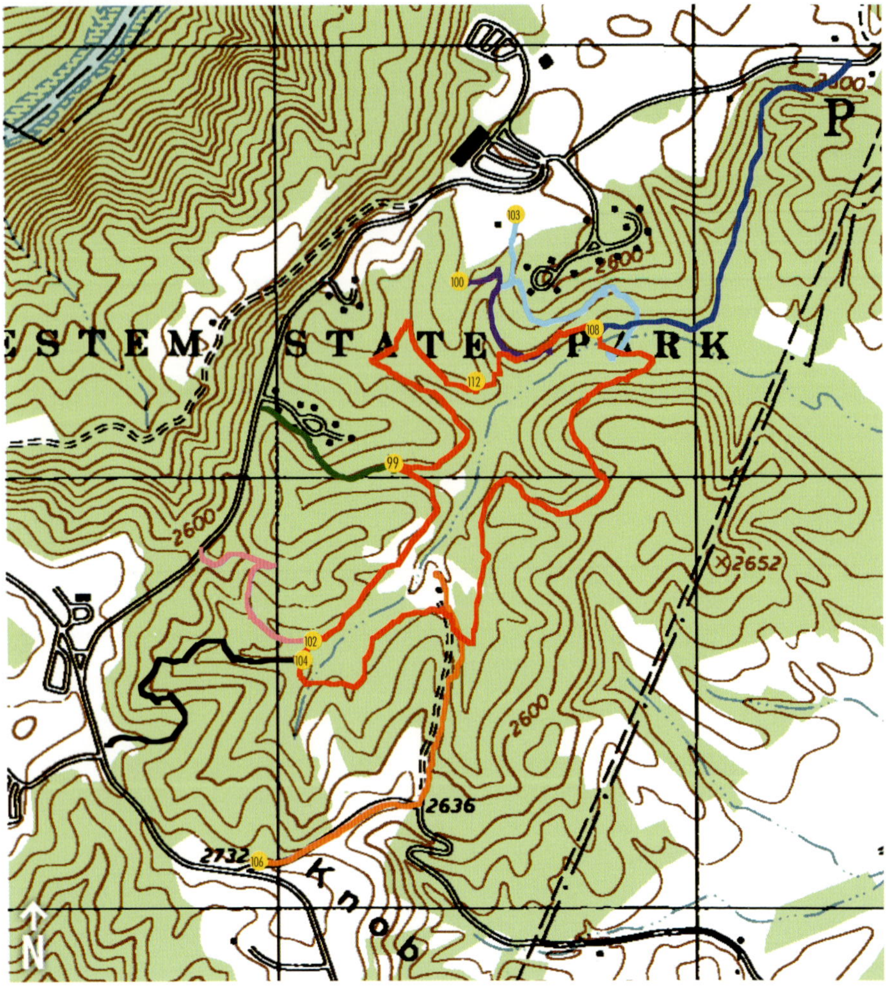

Map Key

Trail 99 – Cottage Trail – dark green

Trail 100 – Long Branch Trail – purple

Trail 102 – Turkey Spur Trail – pink

Trail 103 – Den Tree Trail – light blue

Trail 104 – South Side Trail – black

Trail 106 – Lake View Trail – orange

Trail 108 – Law Hollow Trail – dark blue

Trail 112 – Lake Shore Trail – red

PIPESTEM RESORT STATE PARK WEST SIDE HIKES

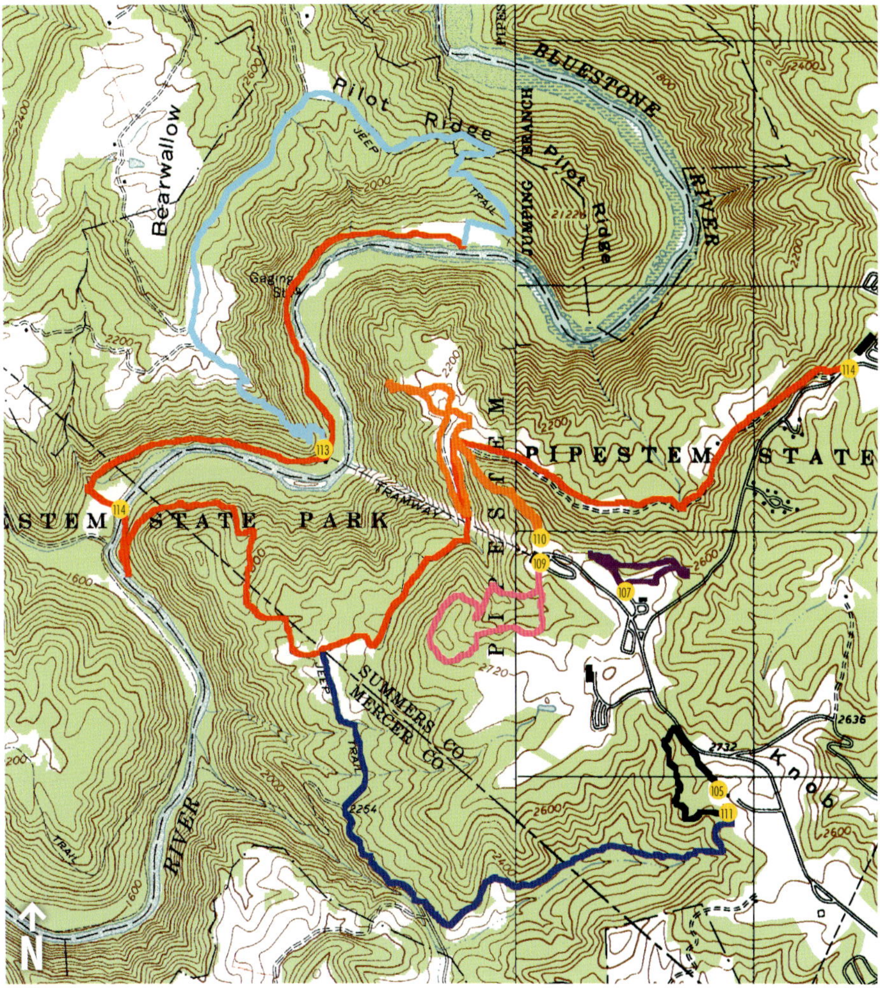

Map Key

Trail 105 – Dogwood Trail – black

Trail 107 – North Side Trail – purple

Trail 109 – Lick Hollow Trail – pink

Trail 110 – Canyon Rim Trail – orange

Trail 111 – County Line Trail – dark blue

Trail 113 – Farley Loop Trail – light blue

Trail 114 – River Trail 1 & 2 – red

99 COTTAGE TRAIL

A short trail that leads to Cottage Area A (cottages 1–9) and a beautiful viewpoint overlooking the Bluestone River Gorge.

2 | 143 ft | 1 ft | 0.27 mi

Location: East of Interstate 77, northeast of Princeton, WV, off WV Route 20
Maps: USGS Flat Top quad 1:24,000 USGS Pipestem quad 1:24,000
Trail Options: Connection with Lake Shore Trail (Trail 112).
Facilities: No facilities available.
Highlights: Forest, beautiful viewpoint.

Trail Milestones:

0.26 mi – Intersection with park road (37°32.184 N, 080°59.333 W)
0.27 mi – Viewpoint (37°32.202 N, 080°59.332 W)

Finding the Trailhead

Lake Shore Trail trailhead: (37°32.108 N, 080°59.098 W)
Access the lower trailhead via the Lake Shore Trail (Trail 112). From the Lake Shore trailhead, turn right and hike 0.5 miles counterclockwise around the lake to the intersection with and trailhead for the Cottage Trail.

To reach the intersection of Cottage Trail and the main park road, drive 2.7 miles from the park entrance. The trailhead is located beside the intersection used to access Cottage Area A, on the right.

Trail Description

White Square Blaze
Note: Hike described from Lake Shore Trail trailhead. From the intersection with the Lake Shore Trail, hike steadily uphill along this short and well-defined trail. After 0.1 miles begin to see cabins to the right through the trees. If staying in cottages 1–9, this trail provides an outstanding route to the Lake Shore Trail. Continue 0.16 miles and arrive at the park road. Carefully cross the road diagonally to the right and arrive at an outstanding viewpoint over Bluestone River Gorge.

Trail Combinations/Options

This trail connects to the Lake Shore Trail (Trail 112) and offers access to six other trails within Pipestem. See the Lake Shore Trail description for additional details on trail intersections.

Sunset at the Cottage Trail viewpoint.

100 LONG BRANCH TRAIL

A short paved trail that allows easy access to Long Branch Lake and ends at the fishing pier.

2 | 4 ft | 107 ft | 0.27 mi

Location: East of Interstate 77, northeast of Princeton, WV, off WV Route 20
Maps: USGS Flat Top quad 1:24,000, USGS Pipestem quad 1:24,000
Trail Options: Connects to the Lake Shore Trail (Trail 112), allowing access to numerous other trails.
Facilities: Benches at 50 meters and at 0.27 miles, boat rental.
Highlights: Access to lake.

Trail Milestones:

0.2 mi – Intersection with Lake Shore Trail
(37°32.245 N, 080°58.907 W)
0.27 mi – Boat rental
(37°32.255 N, 080°58.868 W)

Finding the Trailhead

(37°32.340 N, 080°59.005 W)
From the park entrance drive 3.1 miles to McKeever Lodge and the arboretum. Parking is available in the arboretum's gravel lot to the right, or across the street in the paved area below McKeever Lodge. The trailhead is located at the end of (and just below) the gravel lot at the arboretum. There is no trailhead marker, but the trail begins at a Y intersection with Long Branch Lake Road — take the paved path on the left.

The lower trailhead is located 0.08 miles left of the Lake Shore Trail trailhead near the boat-rental building along the lake.

Trail Description

Blue Square Blaze
From the arboretum lot, walk southeast toward the lake. The trailhead is located down a short decline and at the Y intersection with the Long Branch Lake Road. Gradually descend along this paved trail to reach a metal bench on the left at 50 meters. Continue until reaching the intersection with the Lake Shore Trail (Trail 112) at 0.2 miles — the Lake Shore Trail breaks off to the right on a dirt path at this point. Keep left along the paved trail until arriving at the boat-rental area and building along the lake. This is the end point for the Long Branch Trail.

Trail Combinations/Options

This trail connects to the Lake Shore Trail at the 2.4-mile mark as described in that hike. Continue along Lake Shore Trail past the dam to reach the Den Tree Trail (Trail 103) or the Law Hollow Trail (Trail 108), or turn right to reach the Lake Shore trailhead and/or other hikes farther south.

101 PIPESTEM KNOB TRAIL

A short but steep paved trail that leads to the Bolar Tower, offering unparalleled 360-degree views of West Virginia and Virginia.

2 | 169 ft | 0 ft | 0.32 mi

Location: East of Interstate 77, northeast of Princeton, WV, off WV Route 20
Maps: USGS Flat Top quad 1:24,000, USGS Pipestem quad 1:24,000
Facilities: Large paved parking area for 24 vehicles, water fountain, garbage.
Highlights: Spectacular views, mature forest.

Trail Milestones:

0.31 mi – Bolar Tower
(37°30.867 N, 080°58.360 W)

Finding the Trailhead

(37°30.957 N, 080°58.516 W)
From the main park entrance, drive 0.6 miles and turn right into a large paved parking area. A sign that reads "Lookout Tower – Pipestem Knob Trail" points the way.

Trail Description

Blue Square Blaze
The trailhead is on the east side of the lot. Move around a metal gate and begin hiking along a doublewide paved trail. This trail continues gradually upward, gaining 169 feet in elevation via a series of switchbacks. The forest here is almost exclusively composed of mature deciduous trees. At 0.3 miles move out of the forest and onto the bald top of Pipestem Knob at 3,000 feet. The trail takes you to the Bolar Tower, named after the park's sixth superintendent. Climb the 52 steps to the top for a 360-degree panoramic view of southern West Virginia and Virginia. Few viewpoints in the region can match sunrise or sunset seen from this spot.

Additional Notes

Steve Bolar, for whom the Bolar Tower is named, was the sixth superintendent of Pipestem Resort State Park, from 1996 to 2009. As a child, Steve always wanted to be a park ranger. He succeeded in and overshot that goal by making Pipestem a jewel of the West Virginia state-park system. This hike was a favorite of Steve's, and the tower was renamed for him after his passing in 2009.

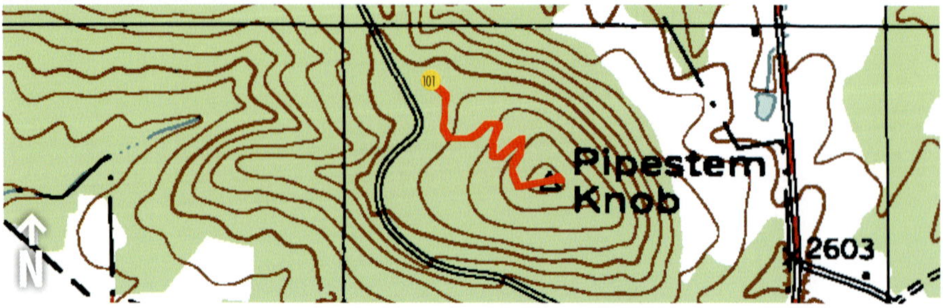

102 TURKEY SPUR TRAIL

This short spur trail leads from the Lake Shore Trail to the main park road between park headquarters and Cottage No. 1.

2 | 170 ft | 0 ft | 0.36 mi

Location: East of Interstate 77, northeast of Princeton, WV, off WV Route 20
Maps: USGS Flat Top quad 1:24,000, USGS Pipestem quad 1:24,000
Trail Options: Links into the Lake Shore Trail (Trail 112).
Facilities: No facilities available.
Highlights: Forest, beautiful hike.

Trail Milestones:

0.23 mi – Sharp left turn (37°31.987 N, 080°59.314 W)
0.36 mi – Intersection with park road/trail's end (37°32.008 N, 080°59.433 W)

Finding the Trailhead

Lower trailhead: (37°31.901 N, 080°59.225 W)
The lower trailhead is located at the 0.9-mile mark of the Lake Shore Trail. From the Lake Shore trailhead, turn right and travel this distance, going counterclockwise around the lake to an intersection that's well marked with a sign.

To reach the upper trailhead/intersection with the park road, drive 2.4 miles from the park entrance or 0.2 miles from park headquarters. A brown wooden sign on the right marks the upper trailhead.

Trail Description

Red Square Blaze

Note: Hike described from lower trailhead. From the trailhead and intersection with the Lake Shore Trail begin a slow and steady ascent. After 0.15 miles begin to hike through an area thick with a species of ground pine and continue uphill. At 0.23 miles the trail turns sharply left and ascends along a wider trail to the park road. Turn right here to reach Cottage Area A, or turn left to reach park HQ.

Trail Combinations/Options

This trail intersects the Lake Shore Trail (Trail 112) at 0.9 miles, allowing access to any of the other trails that also intersect the Lake Shore Trail.

A portion of the Turkey Spur Trail.

103 DEN TREE TRAIL

A short but fantastic trail that leads from the edge of the arboretum to the Long Branch Lake and Dam, with opportunities to see wildlife along the way.

3 — 44 ft 151 ft — 0.51 mi

Location: East of Interstate 77, northeast of Princeton, WV, off WV Route 20
Maps: USGS Flat Top quad 1:24,000, USGS Pipestem quad 1:24,000
Trail Options: Connects with the Lake Shore Trail (Trail 112) and Law Hollow Trail (Trail 108).
Facilities: Bench at 0.1 miles.
Highlights: Arboretum, pretty forest, lake, and dam.

Trail Milestones:

0.05 mi – Wooden bridge (37°32.381 N, 080°58.929 W)
0.5 mi – Intersection with Law Hollow Trail (37°32.291 N, 080°58.703 W)
0.51 mi – Intersection with Lake Shore Trail/dam (37°32.248 N, 080°58.750 W)

Finding the Trailhead

Main trailhead: (37°32.422 N, 080°58.921 W)
From the park entrance drive 3.1 miles to McKeever Lodge and the arboretum. Parking is available in the arboretum's gravel lot to the right, or across the street in the paved area below the lodge. The trailhead is located at the eastern edge of the arboretum and marked prominently with multiple signs.

Reach the lower trailhead (along Lake Shore Trail) by turning left at the Lake Shore trailhead and hiking 0.38 miles clockwise around the lake to the two trails' intersection below the dam, as marked by a trailhead sign.

Trail Description

Red Square Blaze
Note: Hike described from main trailhead. From the arboretum lot, take a few moments to enjoy the well-planned and -maintained area and learn about some of the trees that populate Appalachian forests. Move east to the rear portion of the tree garden and find the well-marked trailhead. Leave the open field and descend slightly, crossing a wooden bridge at 0.05 miles. Skirt the forest for a brief time before entering it at 0.1 miles — you'll see a metal bench along a road to the right. At 0.2 miles enter a power-line cut with views of the lake; continue angling left where the woods become more mature. Continue through this forest, which is thick with fallen leaves in autumn. At 0.5 miles intersect Law Hollow Trail and shortly thereafter cross a wooden bridge over Long Branch Creek to arrive at the lower trailhead and intersection with Lake Shore Trail below the dam.

Trail Combinations/Options

Connect with the Lake Shore Trail (Trail 112) to enjoy the lake or Law Hollow Trail (Trail 108) to return to the ridgeline and McKeever Lodge.

DEN TREE TRAIL

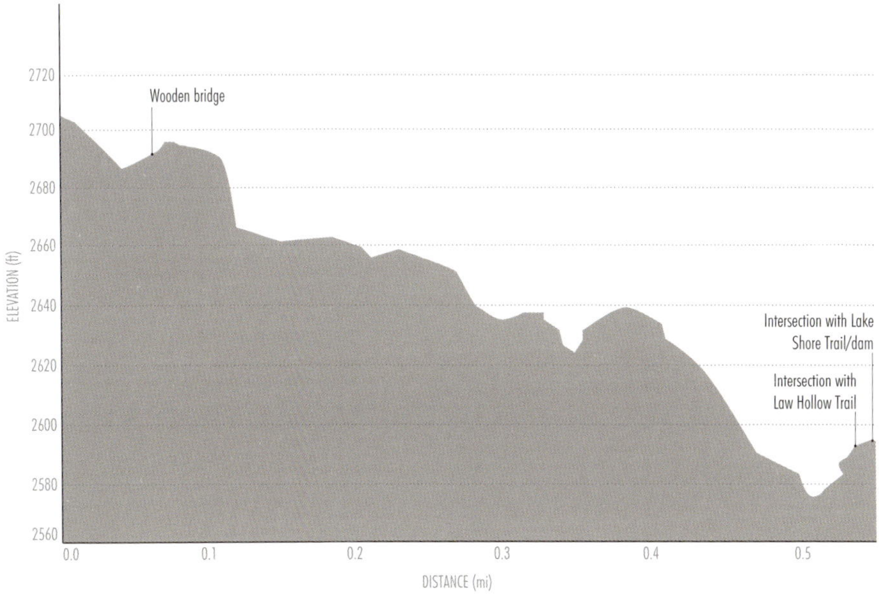

104 SOUTH SIDE TRAIL

This short trail leads from the Lake Shore Trail to the intersection of the main park road and Recreation Drive.

3 251 ft 15 ft 0.55 mi

Location: East of Interstate 77, northeast of Princeton, WV, off WV Route 20
Maps: USGS Flat Top quad 1:24,000, USGS Pipestem quad 1:24,000
Trail Options: Connects to Lake Shore Trail (Trail 112).
Facilities: No facilities available.
Highlights: Forest, wildlife.

Trail Milestones:

0.35 mi – Ground pine (37°31.822 N, 080°59.519 W) **0.55 mi –** Intersection with main park road (37°31.763 N, 80°59.589 W)

Finding the Trailhead

Lower trailhead: (37°31.875 N, 080°59.270 W)
Reach the lower trailhead, along Lake Shore Trail, by turning right at the Lake Shore trailhead and hiking 1.0 miles counterclockwise around Long Branch Lake to the trail intersection on the lake's southern end. The upper trailhead, near the intersection with Recreation Drive, is not marked and is extremely difficult to find — i.e., not recommended as a starting point.

Trail Description

Yellow Square Blaze
Note: Hike described from lower trailhead. Leave the trailhead along the Lake Shore Trail (Trail 112) and slowly ascend through the forest. The trail is single-track but well trod and obvious. At 0.35 miles enter an area covered with ground pine and small boulders randomly situated along the slope. The trail curls left here before moving right along a small spur. At 0.55 miles break out into a grassy area alongside the main park road. Deer frequent this area in the evenings.

Trail Combinations/Options

This trail intersects the Lake Shore Trail (Trail 112) at 1.0 miles, allowing access to any of the other trails that also intersect the Lake Shore Trail. There are no other combinations available for the South Side Trail.

Ground pine along the South Side Trail.

SOUTH SIDE TRAIL

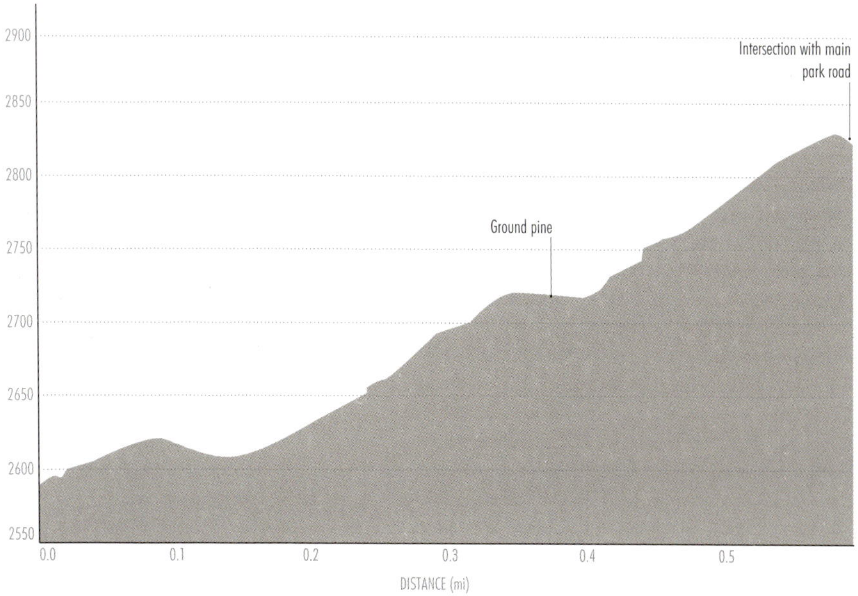

105 DOGWOOD TRAIL

A short loop trail with plenty of opportunity to see wildlife. This area is heavily populated by deer.

2 | 159 ft | 154 ft | 0.61 mi

Location: East of Interstate 77, northeast of Princeton, WV, off WV Route 20
Maps: USGS Flat Top quad 1:24,000, USGS Pipestem quad 1:24,000
Trail Options: Shares a trailhead with the County Line Trail (Trail 111).
Facilities: Nature Center, paved parking for 26 vehicles, picnic facilities.
Highlights: Pond, wildlife, re-creation of early 1900s cabin.

Trail Milestones:

0.0 mi – Trailhead/pond
(37°31.495 N, 080°59.392 W)
0.61 mi – Trail's end/field
(37°31.535 N, 080°59.410 W)

Finding the Trailhead

(37°31.495 N, 080°59.392 W)
From the park entrance drive 1.5 miles and turn left toward the Nature Center; park in the paved lot and walk toward the center. The trailhead is located downhill and to the left of the center, between the two settler-style buildings. A sign marks the beginning of the trail.

Trail Description

Blue Square Blaze
Take note of a small pond off to the right as you approach the trailhead. The Dogwood Trail shares a mutual trailhead with the County Line Trail (Trail 111) — these trails immediately split, and the Dogwood Trail moves right. Continue, and at 0.12 miles ascend a short but steep section of trail and immediately descend to the left. At 0.3 miles the trail turns sharply right. Follow the trail signs and climb toward the main park road. Prior to reaching the road, turn right and parallel the road just below it for 0.1 miles before returning to the woods. The trail ends at 0.61 miles, in the field northwest of the nature center.

Trail Combinations/Options

This trail shares a trailhead with County Line Trail (Trail 111). After completing the loop, it is easy to connect with and hike County Line Trail.

Additional Notes

The Nature Center at the trailhead is an outstanding stop for young and old alike. The naturalist on staff, Jim Phillips, goes to extraordinary lengths to help educate visitors about the flora and fauna of the region. Stop in, learn about the natural history of West Virginia, and count the number of different bird species that feed in the garden — then go and enjoy the Dogwood Trail!

The Nature Center is open from 12:30 p.m.–4:30 p.m. on Saturdays and 10:30 a.m.–2:30 p.m. on Sundays. For additional operating hours and activities at the center, please check with park staff.

Pond near the trailheads for Dogwood and County Line trails.

DOGWOOD TRAIL

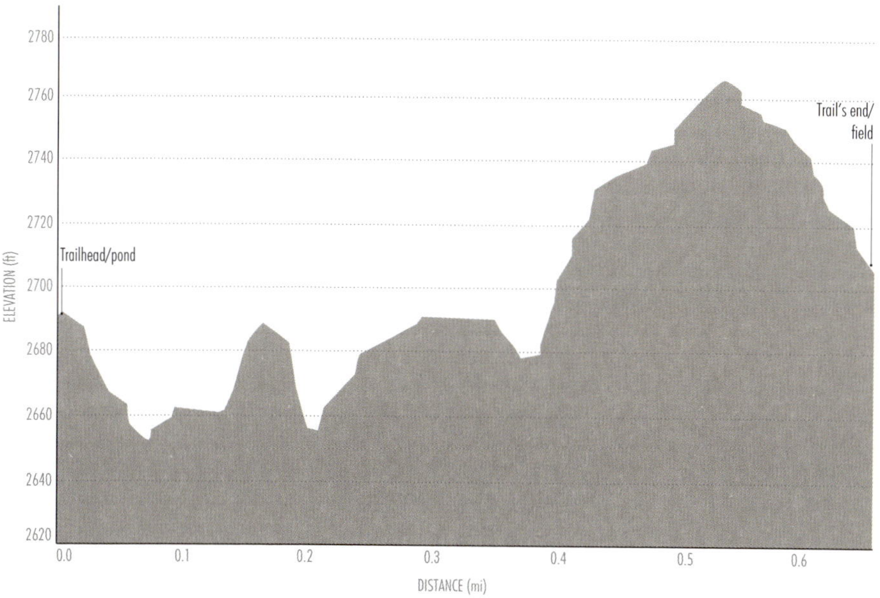

106 LAKE VIEW TRAIL

A nice hike that gradually descends through field and forest to Long Branch Lake.

Location: East of Interstate 77, northeast of Princeton, WV, off WV Route 20
Maps: USGS Flat Top quad 1:24,000, USGS Pipestem quad 1:24,000
Trail Options: Connection to Lake Shore Trail (Trail 112).
Facilities: Parking for eight vehicles.
Highlights: Long Branch Lake, wildlife.

Finding the Trailhead

(37°31.613 N, 080°59.341 W)
To reach the trailhead parking, drive 1.7 miles from the park entrance; the parking area is located to the right at a small turnoff overlooking a large field with distant views (parking coordinates: 37°31.587 N, 080°59.283 W). Walk 100 meters farther down the road (to the northwest) to reach the trailhead, tucked just inside the wood line.

Trail Description

White Square Blaze
As you walk toward the trailhead, watch to your right for deer grazing in the field below. Hunting is not allowed within Pipestem Resort State Park, and the deer are plentiful. At the trailhead move gently down along a very wide trail. This area is often rough, as this is a very popular section of trail for equestrians. At 0.2 miles encounter two large unmarked trails, the first to the left and the second to the right. The signage is good in this area and will keep you on the correct path. At 0.3 miles encounter a third unmarked trail to the left. Stay straight, again following the posted signs.

At 0.5 miles intersect the Lake Shore Trail. Keep straight here toward Long Branch Lake — the trail ends at the banks of the lake. Enjoy the view before returning to the trailhead or connecting to other trails in the area using the Lake Shore Trail.

Trail Milestones:

0.5 mi – Intersection with Lake Shore Trail
(37°31.927 N, 080°59.046 W)

Trail Combinations/Options

This trail intersects the Lake Shore Trail (Trail 112). To reach this intersection from the Lake Shore Trail, turn right at that trail's trailhead and hike counterclockwise 1.3 miles around the lake. The Lake Shore Trail offers access to six other trails within Pipestem. See the Lake Shore Trail description for additional details on other trail intersections.

107 NORTH SIDE TRAIL

This loop trail moves into the forest just below park headquarters and reenters a field on the opposite side.

Location: East of Interstate 77, northeast of Princeton, WV, off WV Route 20
Maps: USGS Flat Top quad 1:24,000, USGS Pipestem quad 1:24,000
Facilities: Picnic area with tables and grills, paved parking.
Highlights: Forest, wildlife.

Trail Milestones:

0.24 mi – Start of steep ascent (37°32.026 N, 080°59.671 W)
0.5 mi – Field (37°31.989 N, 080°59.591 W)

Finding the Trailhead

(37°31.976 N, 080°59.677 W)

From the park entrance follow the main park road for 2.2 miles. At this intersection, turn left and then immediately right into the park-headquarters lot. The trailhead is to the left of the HQ at the end of the paved parking area.

Trail Description

Red Square Blaze

From the trailhead, move past the picnic area and into an evergreen forest that quickly gives way to hardwoods. Continue along the ridgeline until at 0.1 miles the trail turns sharply right. Continue to move through the forest, and at 0.24 miles ascend steeply before leveling off. At 0.4 miles the trail reaches a Y intersection — keep left along the correct trail and see the park road to your front and left. The trail next turns sharply right and at 0.5 miles emerges from the forest into a field. Be quiet in this area, as deer often bed down on the fringes of the forest — you'll likely see them if you keep a watchful eye. Moving into the open field, move along the wood line with park HQ to your left until reaching the original trailhead.

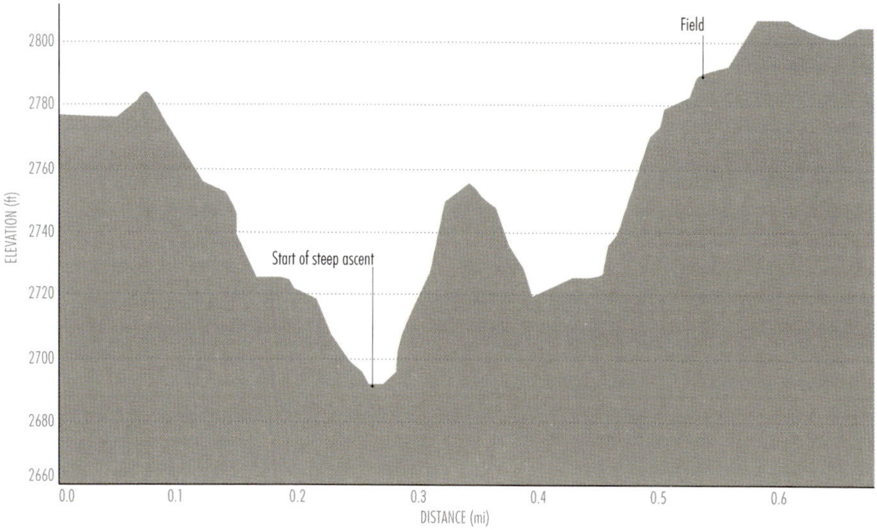

108 LAW HOLLOW TRAIL

A short trail that follows an old logging road and moves northeast toward the park driving range; also makes for a great alternate return to McKeever Lodge.

3 | 203 ft | 21 ft | 0.67 mi

Location: East of Interstate 77, northeast of Princeton, WV, off WV Route 20
Maps: USGS Flat Top quad 1:24,000, USGS Pipestem quad 1:24,000
Trail Options: Connects with Lake Shore Trail (Trail 112).
Facilities: No facilities available.
Highlights: Forest, dam, and lake.

Trail Milestones:

0.07 mi – Intersection with Den Tree Trail (37°32.291 N, 080°58.703 W)
0.67 mi – Private residence/trail's end (37°32.617 N, 080°58.377 W)

Finding the Trailhead

Main trailhead: (37°32.280 N, 080°58.786 W)
From the park entrance drive 3.1 miles to McKeever Lodge. Use the Long Branch Lake road or the Long Branch Trail (Trail 100) to reach the Lake Shore Trail (Trail 112). Once at the Lake Shore trailhead, turn left and hike 0.28 miles clockwise around the lake to the trailhead, located just below the dam.

For the upper trailhead, if using it to access additional hikes near the lake, walk 0.3 miles east from McKeever Lodge along Albert Hill Road (CR 18/2) to the trailhead on the right.

Trail Description

White Square Blaze
Note: Hike described from main trailhead. From the trailhead, located just below the dam and in an open field, begin your hike by moving into the forest. The trail gradually ascends throughout its 0.67-mile course. After 0.07 miles intersect the Den Tree Trail (Trail 103) as it moves perpendicularly west across the path. Keep straight, paralleling Law Branch Creek for a short period. At 0.1 miles the trail begins to move left away from the stream, and at 0.3 miles the slope begins to steepen somewhat. The trail is easily followed throughout and is very wide. Cross a seasonal stream that muddies the trail and continue upward until reaching the trail's end, with a private residence to your right. Turn left along Albert Hill Road (CR 18/2) and walk 0.3 miles back to McKeever Lodge.

Trail Combinations/Options

Connect to the Lake Shore Trail (Trail 112) from the driving range at the upper trailhead, or use as an alternate route to return to the lodge from Long Branch Lake.

109 LICK HOLLOW TRAIL

This loop trail descends into a beautiful hollow before ascending to a viewpoint over Bluestone River Gorge and returning again through the hollow near a golf course.

3 | 409 ft | 321 ft | 1.11 mi

Location: East of Interstate 77, northeast of Princeton, WV, off WV Route 20
Maps: USGS Flat Top quad 1:24,000, USGS Pipestem quad 1:24,000
Facilities: Canyon Rim Center is located at the trailhead and features a gift shop, tram station, toilet facilities, and vending machines.
Highlights: Rocky stream, views of gorge, forest.

Trail Milestones:

0.17 mi – Stream crossing
(37°31.962 N, 081°00.023 W)
0.4 mi – Viewpoint
(37°31.958 N, 081°00.150 W)
0.7 mi – Golf course on right
(37°31.828 N, 081°00.131 W)
0.9 mi – Wooden bridge
(37°31.875 N, 080°59.947 W)
1.0 mi – Stream
(37°31.934 N, 080°59.919 W)

Finding the Trailhead

(37°32.016 N, 080°59.926 W)
From the park entrance, follow the main park road 2.2 miles; turn left at this intersection and travel to the dead end. Parking is available at the Canyon Rim Center parking area. The trailhead is located left of this large building, beside a lower parking area, and is marked by a trailhead sign.

Trail Description

White Square Blaze
Move into the forest from the edge of the parking area along singletrack trail. Descend gradually to a fenced-off area — before reaching this point, the trail branches sharply right. Begin to parallel a small stream to the left, and at 0.17 miles cross the stream using rocks and a small wooden bridge. Begin a steep ascent of the hollow, passing by a group of large downed trees. The trail veers to the right and around the ridge, arriving at a viewpoint over Bluestone River Gorge at 0.4 miles.

After enjoying the view, continue just below the ridgeline on your left and circle until entering a small stand of Virginia pines at 0.6 miles. Move slightly uphill in this area to the ridge top and begin to see the golf course (Hole 4) to the front and right. Stay on the trail and to the left of the course over the next 0.2 miles.

At 0.9 miles use a wooden bridge to cross a stream and pass a Frisbee-golf "hole" on the course that's located throughout this area. Cross another small stream and ascend the final 0.1 miles to the parking lot near the original trailhead.

110 CANYON RIM TRAIL

One of the region's more difficult hikes, this trail moves sharply downward to a beautiful cliff at Heritage Point and then climbs steeply back to the original trailhead.

5 | 542 ft 542 ft | 1.91 mi

East of Interstate 77, northeast of Princeton, WV, off WV Route 20

Maps: USGS Flat Top quad 1:24,000, USGS Pipestem quad 1:24,000

Trail Options: Connect with the River Trail (Trail 114) to extend the hike.

Facilities: Canyon Rim Center, located at the trailhead, features a gift shop, tram station, toilet facilities, and vending machines.

Highlights: Beautiful views of the Bluestone River Gorge, wildlife.

Trail Milestones:

0.3 mi – Intersection No. 1 with River Trail
(37°32.294 N, 081°00.152 W)

0.75 mi – Heritage Point
(37°32.423 N, 081°00.354 W)

1.37 mi – Intersection No. 2 with River Trail
(37°32.144 N, 081°00.134 W)

1.57 mi – Right turn and steep ascent
(37°32.093 N, 080°59.927 W)

Finding the Trailhead

(37°32.093 N, 080°5 9.927 W)
From the park entrance, follow the main park road 2.2 miles; turn left at the intersection near park headquarters and travel to the dead end. Parking is available at the Canyon Rim Center lot — the trailhead is located to the right of this large building, beside the facility's service parking area, and is marked by a trailhead sign.

Trail Description

Blue Square Blaze
From the trailhead immediately enter the forest and hike along the ridgeline for the first 0.1 miles. At this point begin to descend steeply for the next 0.2 miles — the trail is easy to follow and moves to the left of the ridgeline. Take a moment to notice the lichen-covered boulders on the right side of the trail. At 0.3 miles intersect the River Trail the first time. Give your knees a break on this relatively flat stretch before continuing downhill on the far side of the intersection. At 0.4 miles enter a copse of pine trees and break out into an open area and power-line cut. Deer abound in this area: I once startled a large eight-point buck dozing in the sun here!

The descent now eases as you walk through hill meadows, with building ruins tucked into the brush on either side of the trail. Continue to Heritage Point, passing a sign warning about the cliff ahead. If hiking with children, now is a good time to rein them in, as the edge is covered in spots with loose rock.

At 0.75 miles arrive at Heritage Point, which sits upon a sandstone outcropping with views up and down the Bluestone River Gorge. Take a break and enjoy the view. The return trail reverses the same path for the first 0.2 miles and then breaks right. Follow the trail signs and exit the open area, moving along a flat trail in the woods. At 1.37 miles intersect the River Trail a second time; turn left here. The River Trail and Canyon Rim Trail ascend together for the next 0.2 miles. Reaching the original intersection of these two trails (encountered at the 0.3-mile mark), turn right and begin the steep ascent back to the original trailhead beside the Canyon Rim Center.

Looking upstream into the Bluestone River Gorge.

CANYON RIM TRAIL

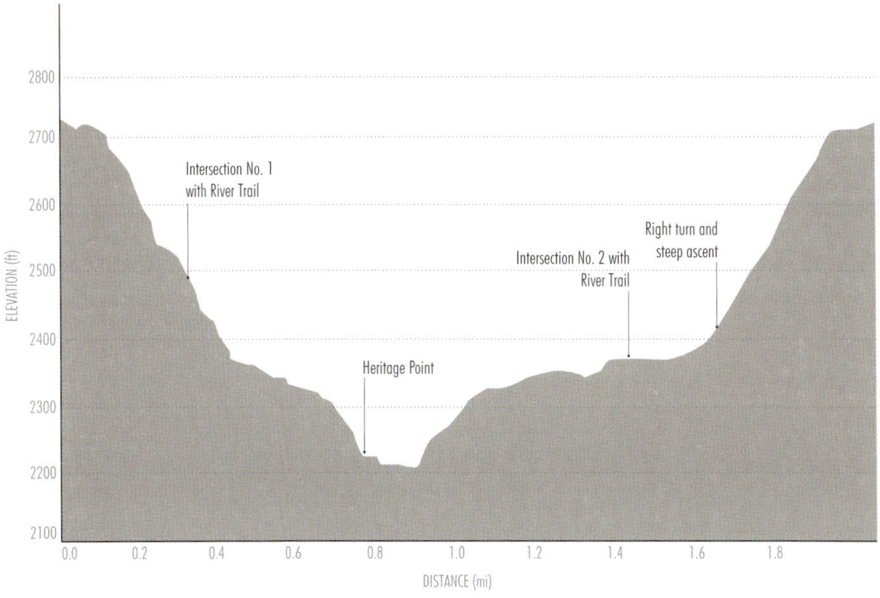

CANYON RIM TRAIL

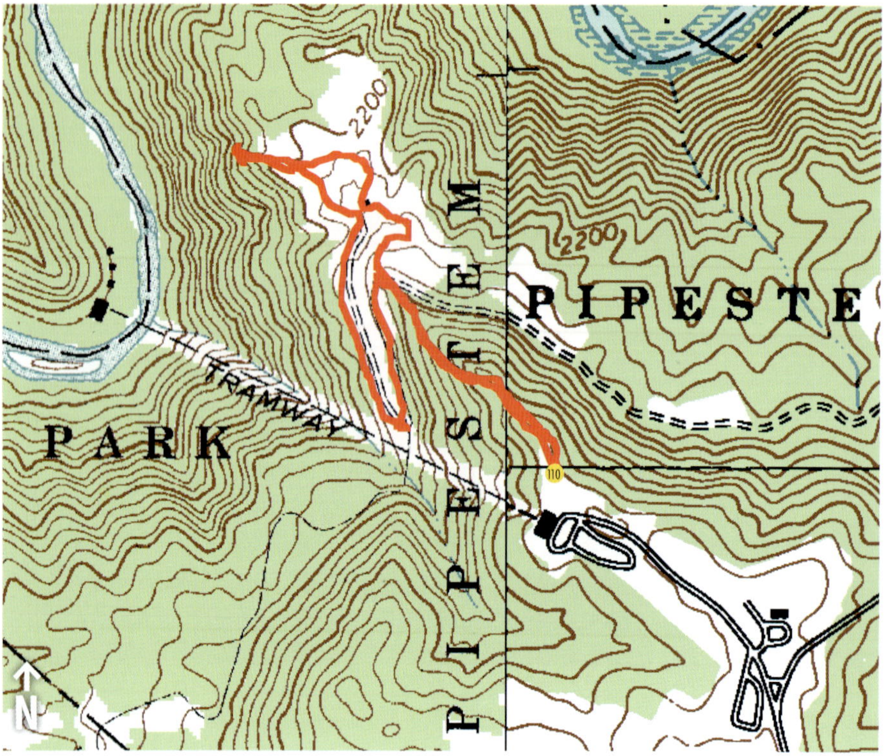

Trail Combinations/Options

After completing the Canyon Rim Trail, you can create a longer hike by combining it with the River Trail (Trail 114). At 1.37 miles intersect the River Trail the second time — turn right along the River Trail and hike to the river, crossing (if the water is low enough) and continuing to the Mountain Creek Lodge. Ride the tram back to the Canyon Rim Center or return via the same route. The one-way distance for this combination is 4.13 miles. If hiking this combination as a round-trip, be prepared for a long and continuous climb back to the trailhead.

You can also connect to the River Trail at this same intersection and access McKeever Lodge. Turn left at the 1.37-mile mark of the Canyon Rim Trail — the Canyon Rim Trail and the River Trail run along the same track for 0.2 miles in this direction. Rather than turning right at the 1.57-mile mark and ascending along the steep ridgeline to the original Canyon Rim trailhead, continue 1.2 miles along the River Trail to the lodge. This combination results in a 2.57-mile hike.

Additional Notes

Canyon Rim Center: This complex houses the upper station for the aerial tram that connects to the Mountain Creek Lodge below. It is also home to a gift shop and artisan shop that features work from local craftsmen. The aerial tram operates from May through October. As of press time (spring 2013) rates were $3 one-way, $6 round-trip, and an additional $4 for bike transport.

111 COUNTY LINE TRAIL

The County Line Trail is rugged and beautiful, moving through mature hardwood forests and rocky mountainside to a beautiful waterfall and intersection with the River Trail.

4 | 208 ft | 548 ft | 1.92 mi

Location: East of Interstate 77, northeast of Princeton, WV, off WV Route 20
Maps: USGS Flat Top quad 1:24,000, USGS Pipestem quad 1:24,000
Trail Options: Connects to the River Trail (Trail 114).
Facilities: Nature Center, picnic area, and parking for 26 vehicles.
Highlights: Indian Branch Falls, forest, wildlife.

Trail Milestones:

0.7 mi – Hemlock and pine grove (37°31.318 N, 080°59.956 W)
1.1 mi – Gravel road (37°31.282 N, 081°00.259 W)
1.2 mi – Indian Branch Falls (37°31.322 N, 081°00.349 W)
1.4 mi – Trail splits (37°31.467 N, 081°00.467 W)
1.92 mi – Intersection with River Trail (37°31.833 N, 081°00.544 W)

Finding the Trailhead

(37°31.495 N, 080°59.392 W)
From the park entrance drive 1.5 miles and turn left toward the Nature Center. The trailhead is located downhill and to the left of the center, between two buildings that are examples of early settler homes. A sign marks the trailhead for this trail and the Dogwood Trail (Trail 105).

Trail Description

Red Square Blaze
From the trailhead, follow the wide trail 100 meters before turning right onto a narrower track and descending along a sometimes-rocky path along the first 0.4 miles. At this point the trail levels off before ascending a short but steeper section. At 0.7 miles the trail winds through a grove of hemlock and pine then begins to descend gradually toward a road. Intersect this gravel road at 1.1 miles, and after another 0.1 miles reach the highlight of the trail, Indian Branch Falls. Move off the trail to the left and get a beautiful view of the 45-foot falls from an overlook.

After taking in the falls, return to the main trail and continue to 1.4 miles where the trail intersects an unnamed and unmaintained trail. Stay right here (a sign directs the way) and continue along the County Line Trail, now doublewide. Cross a small stream at 1.7 miles and intersect the River Trail at 1.92 miles, the trail's end.

Trail Combinations/Options

This trail connects with the River Trail (Trail 114) at its endpoint at 1.92 miles. If you turn left and hike the River Trail for 1.16 miles, you'll reach the Bluestone River; ford the river (if conditions allow) and continue another 0.9 miles to the Mountain Creek Lodge. It is possible to return by aerial tram from this point or reverse the same route.

At this same intersection at 1.92 miles, you can also turn right on the River Trail and hike 0.9 miles to its intersection with the Canyon Rim Trail before continuing a final 1.2 miles along the River Trail to McKeever Lodge.

COUNTY LINE TRAIL

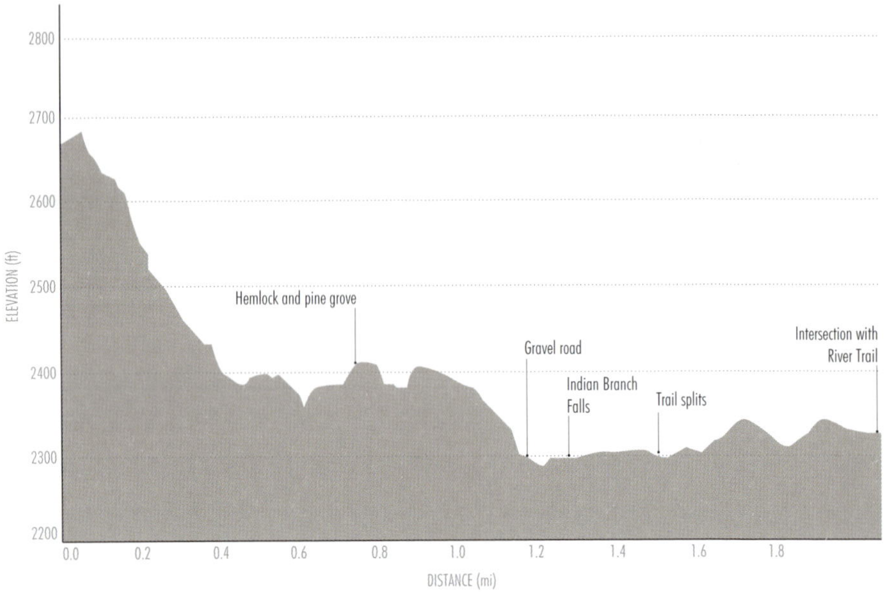

Equestrians touring Lake Shore Trail.

112 LAKE SHORE TRAIL

A beautiful and easy trail that circles Long Branch Lake and connects to a host of shorter branch trails.

1 | 363 ft | 306 ft | 2.48 mi

Location: East of Interstate 77, northeast of Princeton, WV, off WV Route 20
Maps: USGS Flat Top quad 1:24,000, USGS Pipestem quad 1:24,000
Trail Options: Connects to the Cottage Trail (Trail 99), Turkey Spur Trail (Trail 102), South Side Trail (Trail 104), Lake View Trail (Trail 106), Den Tree Trail (Trail 103), Law Hollow Trail (Trail 108), and Long Branch Trail (Trail 100).
Facilities: Small fishing dock, benches, and garbage receptacles.
Highlights: Lake views, mature forest, deer and turkey.

Trail Milestones:

0.5 mi – Intersection with Cottage Trail (37°32.108 N, 080°59.098 W)
0.9 mi – Intersection with Turkey Spur Trail (37°31.901 N, 080°59.225 W)
1.0 mi – Intersection with South Side Trail (37°31.875 N, 080°59.270 W)
1.3 mi – Intersection with Lake View Trail (37°31.927 N, 080°59.046 W)
2.1 mi – Intersection with Den Tree Trail (37°32.248 N, 080°58.750 W)
2.2 mi – Intersection with Law Hollow Trail (37°32.280 N, 080°58.786 W)
2.4 mi – Intersection with Long Branch Trail (37°32.245 N, 080°58.907 W)

Finding the Trailhead

(37°32.205 N, 080°58.987 W)
Note: The primary trailhead lies at the end of the Long Branch Lake Road. This is the primary access point for the disabled, closest to McKeever Lodge, and is the most often-described route for visitors.

To reach the trailhead, drive 3.1 miles from the park entrance along the main park road. You have two options for parking: McKeever Lodge has a large paved lot or there is a large gravel lot adjacent to the arboretum (the latter is closer). Hike the Long Branch Trail (Trail 100; see description) its entire 0.27 miles or hike 0.3 miles down the paved Long Branch Lake Road to the fishing dock and trailhead.

Trail Description

Blue Square Blaze
From the trailhead located beside the wooden fishing dock, turn right and proceed counterclockwise along the shores of Long Branch Lake. The forest here is a mix of evergreen and deciduous trees. Continue alongside the lake, bending in and out of hollows created by small seasonal streams. At 0.5 miles reach the intersection with Cottage Trail. Keep left here and continue along the lake until at 0.8 miles the trail veers to the right and away from the shore for a short time. After another 0.1 miles, intersect Turkey Spur Trail, encountering the South Side Trail soon after.

The trail now turns from its southerly course and begins to make its way to the side of the lake opposite the trailhead. At 1.3 miles intersect the Lake View Trail. Keep right, then left here to stay on the main trail; or alternatively, move to the left and get a close-up view of the lake and then return to the trail. At 1.6 miles the trail begins to climb high above the lake and deeper into the forest where it flattens for 0.1 miles before descending toward the dam. At 2.0 miles the trail moves into an open area and the dam comes into view to your left.

Intersect the Den Tree Trail in this field and continue straight, crossing a small stream below the dam. At 2.2 miles come to the intersection with Law Hollow Trail and ascend a steep bank before veering left toward the top of the dam. Take a moment to visit the dam (which is accessible) then continue along a paved road, passing a boat-rental building. At 2.4 miles intersect the Long Branch Trail

The blue-green waters of Long Branch Lake.

and turn left off the pavement for the last .08 miles to the trailhead.

Trail Combinations/Options

Lake Shore Trail links with seven other trails. None of these trails create an additional loop, but instead allow users to approach the Lake Shore Trail from different locations throughout the park. The trail description uses Long Branch Lake Road as the primary trailhead for two reasons: 1) It is the primary lake access for the disabled, and 2) It is the closest and most easily accessed point from McKeever Lodge.

LAKE SHORE TRAIL

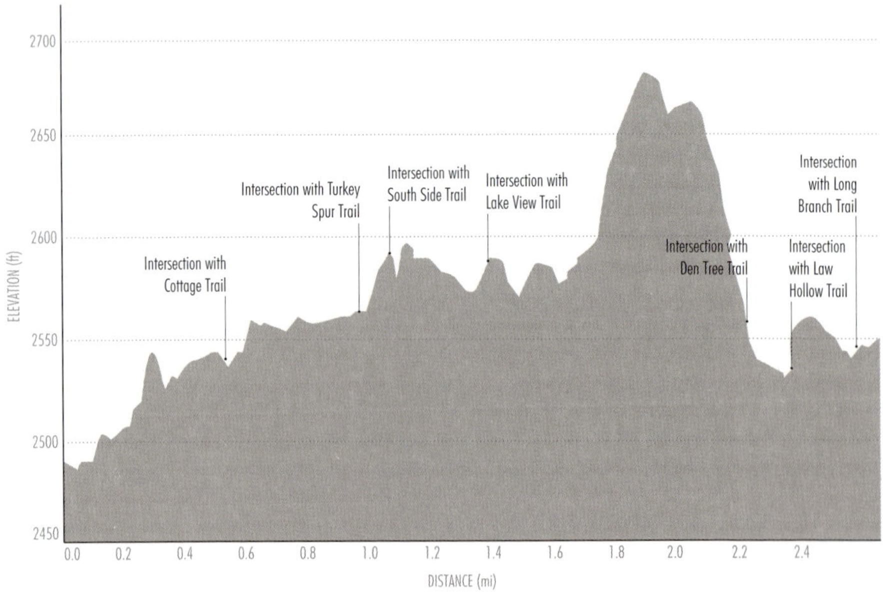

113 FARLEY LOOP TRAIL

An interesting and strenuous hike that climbs steeply past Raven Rock overlook and a patrol cabin before leveling off, passing an old family cemetery, and descending to the intersection with the Bluestone Turnpike Trail and River Trail.

5 | 786 ft | 849 ft | 2.55 mi

Location: East of Interstate 77, northeast of Princeton, WV, off WV Route 20
Maps: USGS Flat Top quad 1:24,000, USGS Pipestem quad 1:24,000
Trail Options: Connect with the Bluestone Turnpike Trail (Trail 98) and River Trail (Trail 114) at the trail's end.
Facilities: Mountain Creek Lodge and aerial tram.
Highlights: Raven Rock overlook, patrol cabin, old cemetery, and the Bluestone River.

Trail Milestones:

0.0 mi – Mountain Creek Lodge/tram (37°32.292 N, 081°00.533 W)
0.2 mi – Raven Rock overlook (37°32.313 N, 081°00.612 W)
0.6 mi – Patrol cabin (37°32.493 N, 081°00.877 W)
1.2 mi – Farley Family Cemetery (37°32.918 N, 081°00.690 W)
2.55 mi – Trail's end/Intersection with Bluestone Turnpike Trail and River Trail (37°32.734 N, 081°00.139 W)

Finding the Trailhead

(37°32.292 N, 081°05.533 W)
The trailhead is accessed via one of two methods: Take the aerial tram from the Canyon Rim Center and easily find the trailhead directly behind the lower tram station. If hiking the River Trail (Trail 114), walk to the Mountain Creek Lodge and climb the stairs between the two buildings to reach the trailhead — behind the tram station and marked by a sign.

Trail Description

White Square Blaze
From the tram-station trailhead climb steeply up the mountainside along poorly graded switchbacks, reaching a cliff line that resembles a ship's prow. Continue climbing steeply along the ridgeline and at 0.2 miles reach the Raven Rock overlook to the left. Take your time here to enjoy the fabulous views down valley.

Return to the trail and continue to climb another 0.3 miles before the trail levels off and enters a pine grove then moves into a meadow with a cabin. This "patrol cabin" has a fire pit, grill, picnic tables, and 12 metal-frame beds. The cabin also has an outhouse off to the left, but only the brave of heart should consider a visit! Speak with park staff regarding opportunities to spend the night here.

Continue past the cabin and reenter the forest above and behind it. The trail widens here and remains this way throughout the rest of hike. Move through sycamore, beech, and oak trees until reaching the Farley Family Cemetery at 1.2 miles. This cemetery is located 50 meters off the main trail, and is designated with a large yellow sign listing the interred and the date of their passing. Not long after, the trail begins to descend toward the river along a great number of well-graded switchbacks down Bearwallow Ridge. At 2.55 miles reach the trail's end and intersection with the Bluestone Turnpike Trail and River Trail.

FARLEY LOOP TRAIL

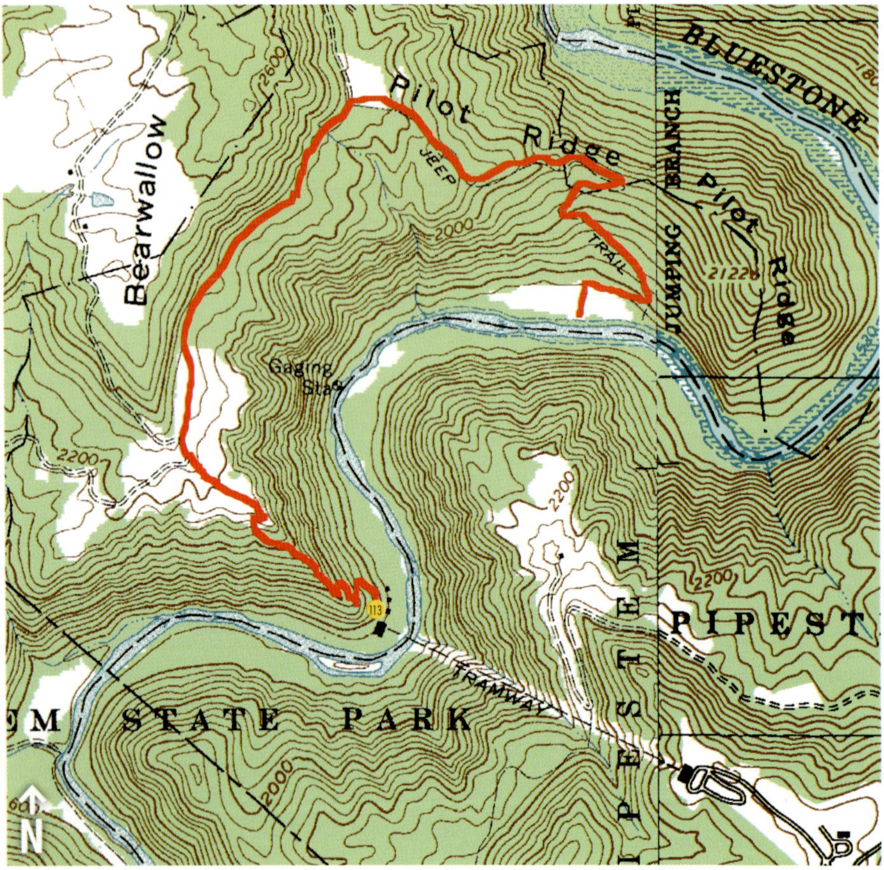

Trail Combinations/Options

Two trail combinations are available: The connection to the Bluestone Turnpike Trail (Trail 98 — turn left at trail's end) results in a 9.99-mile hike to Bluestone State Park. A better combination, and one often used by hikers, is to complete the Farley Loop Trail, intersect the River Trail (Trail 114), and then turn right to return to the aerial tram. This extension completes the Farley Loop Trail and creates a 3.45-mile hike.

Additional Notes

I keep seeing signs on the Farley Loop Trail about the Great Eastern Trail. What is this all about? The Great Eastern Trail is an effort by the Great Eastern Trail Association, local trail organizers, and the American Hiking Society to create a new long-distance trail in the eastern United States. Their goal is to create a trail that will eventually stretch from New York to Alabama.

FARLEY LOOP TRAIL

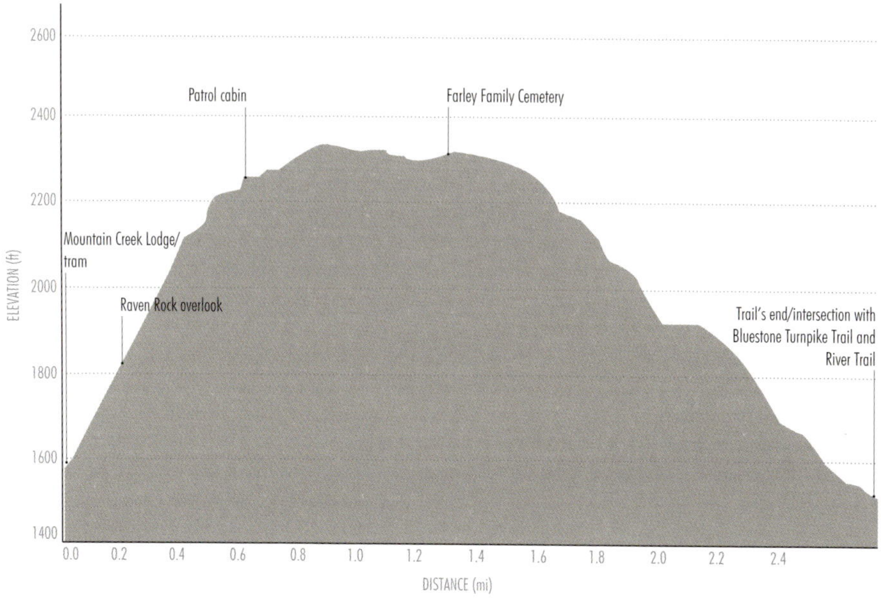

114 RIVER TRAIL

The park's longest and most adventurous trail journeys from McKeever Lodge atop the ridgeline to the depths of the gorge, crossing the Bluestone River and arriving at the intersection of the Farley Loop and Bluestone Turnpike trails.

Location: East of Interstate 77, northeast of Princeton, WV, off WV Route 20
Maps: USGS Flat Top quad 1:24,000, USGS Pipestem quad 1:24,000
Trail Options: Connects to Canyon Rim Trail (Trail 110), County Line Trail (Trail 111), Farley Loop Trail (Trail 113), and Bluestone Turnpike Trail (Trail 98).
Facilities: McKeever Lodge at trailhead, Mountain Creek Lodge at 4.16 miles.
Highlights: Bluestone River, wildlife, scenic views throughout.

Trail Milestones:

0.0 mi – McKeever Lodge/trailhead (37°32.463 N, 080°59.054 W)
0.9 mi – Power-line cut (37°32.194 N, 080°59.846 W)
1.2 mi – Intersection No. 1 with Canyon Rim Trail (37°32.294 N, 081°00.152 W)
1.4 mi – Intersection No. 2 with Canyon Rim Trail (37°32.144 N, 081°00.134 W)
2.1 mi – Intersection with County Line Trail (37°31.833 N, 081°00.544 W)
3.1 mi – Intersection with river, turn right (37°32.006 N, 081°01.098 W)
3.26 mi – Fording site (37°32.127 N, 081°01.108 W)
CROSS BLUESTONE RIVER
3.36 mi – Road intersection/waterfall above (37°32.199 N, 081°01.210 W)
4.16 mi – Mountain Creek Lodge (37°32.335 N, 081°00.514W)
5.06 mi – Intersection with Farley Loop Trail/Bluestone Turnpike Trail/trail's end (37°32.734 N, 081°00.139 W)

Finding the Trailhead

(37°32.463 N, 080°59.054 W)
From the park entrance drive 3.1 miles to McKeever Lodge and the arboretum. Parking is available in the arboretum's gravel lot to the right, or across the street in the paved area below the lodge. The trailhead is located just below the lodge, opposite the gravel lot at the arboretum. Multiple signs mark the trailhead.

Trail Description

Orange Square Blaze
Enter the forest and immediately descend along a wide and well-graded footpath. At 0.3 miles intersect an unmarked trail leading to a field to the right; keep straight and cross two small drainages over the next 0.4 miles. At 0.9 miles pass beneath a power-line cut and look right for views into the valley below.

At 1.2 miles intersect the Canyon Rim Trail the first time as it falls steeply from the right and crosses perpendicular to the trail. Continue along a wide path and angle downward toward the second intersection with the Canyon Rim Trail, at 1.4 miles. Just beyond, pass through a clearing and watch for passing trams as they make their way up and down the mountain. Deer often feed in this area, and you'll likely see one as you pass.

At 1.5 miles cross a cascading stream using well-placed stones. Continuing gradually downhill, intersect the County Line Trail at 2.1 miles to the left-hand side. Continue straight and right, passing through a field before reaching a portion of steep and rough trail that parallels a small stream. Cross two additional drainages at 2.6 miles, and at this point begin to hear the Bluestone River below.

Pass an unmarked trail that leads sharply right at 3.0 miles, and at 3.1 miles intersect the Bluestone River — the trail bends right almost 180 degrees and moves toward the fording site. Take extra care crossing the river, and NEVER cross without knowing its depth (see Additional Notes). People have drowned in the Bluestone River: Don't become a statistic and do not take the river lightly.

After successfully fording the river, arrive in a field at the other side. Stay straight, passing a picnic area to the right. At 3.36 miles intersect a gravel road and turn right along this road. Look up and to

the left to see a pretty waterfall tucked high above. Continue along the road, which parallels the river, for the next 0.8 miles until arriving at Mountain Creek Lodge. Many hikers end the journey here and return by tram, or stop and have lunch prior to continuing. Move past the lodge through an open field by the riverside and rejoin the trail into the forest at the end of the lodge building.

At 4.5 miles come across a cable car used by park staff to access the opposite side of the gorge. Attempting to use this crossing is prohibited. Continue another 0.56 miles to the end of the River Trail and the intersection with the Farley Loop and Bluestone Turnpike trails. Return to the lodge and use the tram to reach the Canyon Rim Center, or retrace your entire route back to McKeever Lodge.

Trail Combinations/Options

It is possible to connect with multiple trails throughout this hike.

Canyon Rim Trail Extension: To visit Heritage Point and take in its scenic vistas, turn right at the first intersection with Canyon Rim Trail (Trail 110), at 1.2 miles. Hike to the viewpoint and return farther down the River Trail (the 1.4-mile mark). Turn right to continue along the River Trail. This increases the total hike by 1.07 miles.

Farley Loop Trail Extension: At the end of the River Trail, turn left onto the Farley Loop Trail (Trail 113). Hike this trail its entire 2.55 miles in reverse of the guidebook description to arrive back at the Mountain Creek Lodge. This extension creates a 7.61-mile hike. The trail ends at the aerial tram station for a quick return to the Canyon Rim Center.

RIVER TRAIL: PART 1 & PART 2

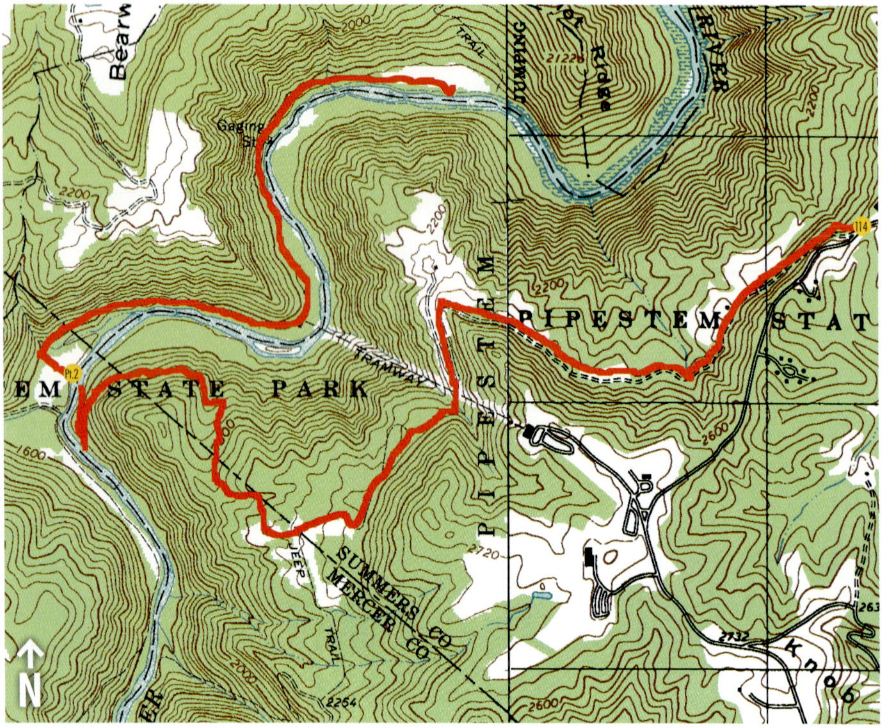

RIVER TRAIL: PART 1 (EAST)

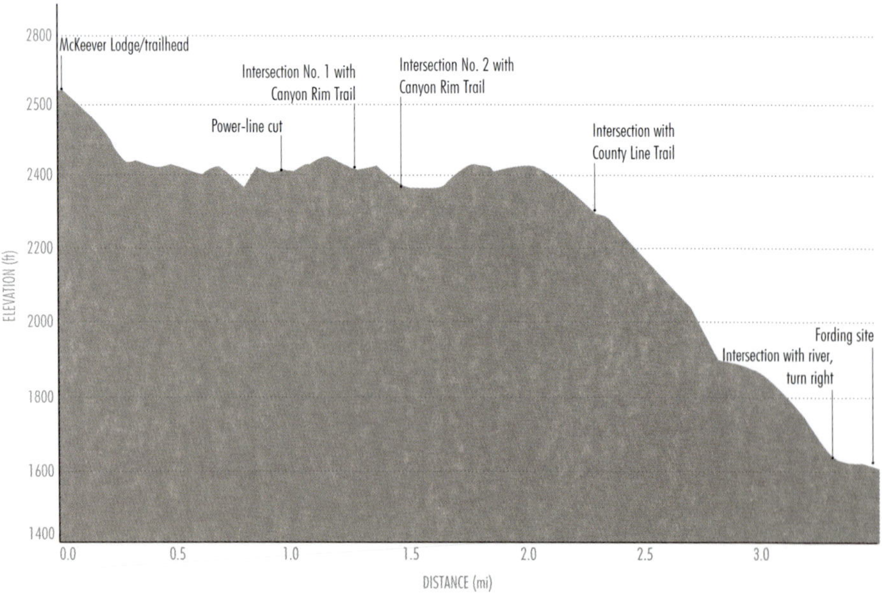

Bluestone Turnpike Trail Extension: The end of the River Trail links to the Bluestone Turnpike Trail (Trail 98). To extend the trail and arrive at Bluestone State Park, hike the entirety of this trail (7.44 miles) to create a 12.46-mile outing.

County Line Shortcut: Hike the River Trail to the intersection with County Line Trail (Trail 111) and turn left, forgoing the remainder of the River Trail and arriving at the Nature Center after hiking an additional 1.92 miles. This combination creates a 4.02-mile hike and does NOT return you to the original trailhead at McKeever Lodge. To reach the lodge, an additional hike of 1.6 miles is required using the main park road.

Additional Notes

Bluestone River Fording Information: In order to complete this trail, you must ford the Bluestone River. This generally is not difficult in summer when water levels are low, but every crossing should be taken seriously every time. Before attempting to ford the Bluestone River, please consult with employees at McKeever Lodge regarding current river levels and/or check with the US Army Corps of Engineers by calling (304) 466-0156 and listening to the recorded message regarding water levels at the "Bluestone River at Pipestem." It is also possible to see the river levels by checking the following websites:

- waterdata.usgs.gov/usa/nwis/uv?03179000
- water.weather.gov/ahps2/hydrograph.php?wfo=rnk&gage=pipw2

Aerial Tram: Please consult with park staff regarding the operational times for the aerial tram. The aerial tram generally operates from May through October. As of spring 2013, rates were $3 one-way, $6 round-trip, and an additional $4 for bike transport.

RIVER TRAIL: PART 2 (WEST)

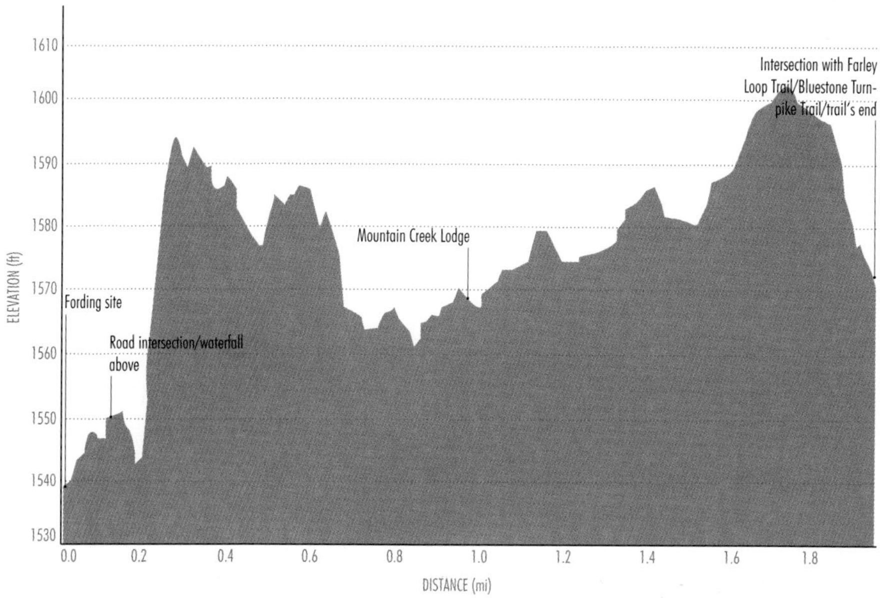

Mash Fork Falls at Camp Creek State Park.

19 OTHER TRAILS & OPPORTUNITIES IN SOUTHERN WEST VIRGINIA

Other Nearby West Virginia State Parks

The West Virginia State Park system comprises a wonderfully diverse group of parks throughout the state. While I've featured state-park hikes in the immediate New River Gorge region in chapters 12 through 18, a handful of other parks only a bit farther away also host great trails. I've included a short list of these parks below with information on location, trails, and contact listings.

Bluestone Wildlife Management Area

Location: From Interstate 64, exit 139, drive five miles south on WV Route 20. From Interstate 77, exit 14, drive north along WV Route 20 for 22 miles.

Trail Information: This area, a part of the West Virginia state park system, has seven trails open to hiking and two that allow mountain biking, for a total of 15.9 miles' worth of trail terrain. The two trails that allow mountain biking are the Red Sulphur Turnpike Trail and the Upper Shanklin's Ferry Trail.

Contact:
HC 65
Indian Mills, WV 24935
(304) 466-3398
bluestonewma.com

Camp Creek State Park and Forest

Location: Camp Creek State Park and Forest is conveniently located just 2.7 miles from Interstate 77. Take exit 20 (Camp Creek) and drive 0.5 miles south on US Route 19. Turn right onto Camp Creek Road and follow it 2.2 miles to the park entrance. The park headquarters is located on the right.

Trail Information: Here, you'll find 13 trails to enjoy. In addition to hiking, mountain biking, and horseback riding, there are also hunting and fishing opportunities. Please visit wolverinepublishing.com/nrg-trails-free for a free PDF download of these hikes.

Contact:
2390 Camp Creek Road
Camp Creek, WV 25820
(304) 425-9481
campcreekstatepark.com

Greenbrier River Trail

Location: The 78-mile Greenbrier River Trail is accessible from multiple locations — the most accessible, its southern terminus, is located just off Interstate 64. Take exit 175 (White Sulphur Springs) off the interstate and travel 2.7 miles west on US Route 60. Turn right onto Stonehouse Road (CR 38) and arrive at a gravel lot on the left.

Contact:
HC 82 Box 252
Marlinton, WV 24954
(304) 799-7416
greenbrierrailtrailstatepark.com

Trail Information: The Greenbrier Trail is a 78-mile trail that runs from its southern endpoint near Lewisburg, WV, to its northern endpoint near Cass, WV. It is a well-graded path that parallels the Greenbrier River, and is open to hikers, trail runners, cross-country skiers, and horseback riders.

Twin Falls State Park

Contact:
RR 97, PO Box 667
Mullens, WV 25882
(304) 294-4000
twinfallsresort.com

Location: From Interstate 64/77 (combined at this point) take exit 42 (Beckley/Robert C. Byrd Drive). Turn right onto WV Route 16/97 toward Sophia/Mullens and follow it 3.5 miles. At the intersection with WV Route 54 turn right and drive south 15 miles toward Mullens. At a town named Mabens, turn right onto WV Route 97 and travel 5.5 miles west. At this point turn left onto Bear Hole Road and drive 4.1 miles to the park.

Trail Information: This state park has 13 trails within its boundaries that range in length from 0.25 miles to four miles, with many options and combinations available. These trails are open to hiking and trail running.

Trails in Local Municipalities

Beckley, WV

Contact:
City of Beckley
Beckley, WV 25801
304-256-1747
beckley.org

Location: Easily accessible from Interstate 64, Interstate 77, and US Route 19.

Trail Information: *Beckley Rail Trail/Lewis McManus Memorial Honor Trail:* This trail, 3.6 miles in length, runs from Mabscott to the Cranberry Creek Crossing, with a spur to the New River Park. It is a 12-foot-wide paved trail equipped with lights and benches, and runs along what were originally the Piney River and Paint Creek Railroad Company tracks through Beckley, WV.

Lake Stephens, WV (Raleigh County)

Contact:
1400 Lake Stephens Road
Beckley, WV 25802
(304) 934-5323
lakestephenswv.com

Location: From Interstate 77, take exit 44 (Harper Road) and drive west along WV Route 3 for nine miles. Lake Stephens is located on the right.

Trail Information: Lake Stephens, operated by the Raleigh County Recreational Authority, is open May 1 through September 30 and offers 20 miles of hiking and biking trails.

Oak Hill, WV

Contact:
City of Oak Hill
100 Kelly Avenue
Oak Hill, WV 25901
(304) 469-9541
cityofoakhill.homestead.com

Location: From US Route 19, take the Oyler Avenue exit in Oak Hill, WV. Travel 100 meters and turn left onto Virginia Street (CR 61/28), driving 0.8 miles to the Oak Hill Train Depot and Bud Hill Memorial Trailhead. This is the easiest access point from US Route 19 and marks the midpoint of the White Oak Rail Trail.

Trail Information: *White Oak Rail Trail:* This trail is 7.5 miles long and occupies an abandoned line of the Norfolk Southern Railway. This trail, dedicated in June 2008, is the result of a dedicated group of community volunteers who worked diligently to acquire and repurpose this area for the enjoyment of everyone. A little more than four miles of the trail is paved, while its entire length is open to hiking and biking.

Trails on Private Property

ACE Adventure Resort Contact:
PO Box 1168
Oak Hill, WV 25901
(800) 787-3982
aceraft.com

Adventures on the Gorge Contact:
Ames Heights Road – PO Box 78
Lansing, WV 25862
(888) 650-1932
adventurewestvirginia.com

Wild Rock Contact:
Ames Heights Road
Lansing, WV 25862
(866) 929-9453
wildrockwv.com

The New River Gorge region also offers numerous trails developed on private property — all users should receive permission from the respective company and/or landowner prior to using these paths. The following companies have miles of trails open to guests:

ACE Adventure Resort: ACE has numerous trails within their 1,500-acre resort.

Adventures on the Gorge: Adventures on the Gorge, located within the Fayetteville, Lansing, and Kaymoor Region (page 36), has a system of trails that link into the New River Gorge.

Wild Rock: The community of Wild Rock has a well-developed system of trails that are outstanding for hiking, trail running, and mountain biking. These trails are well posted throughout thanks to the efforts of the developers, who have worked closely with the local non-profit New River Alliance of Climbers to signpost and allow access through the property to climbing areas within.

Young Virginia pines.

MADE WITH 100%
RIVER RUNNING
HIGH FLYING ROCK HOPPING
CAN'T STOP SMILING
WEST VIRGINA FLAVOR
NEW RIVER GORGE, WV
800-787-3982 • ACERAFT.COM
ACE
ADVENTURE RESORT

Future Trails/Trails in Progress

Trail growth in the New River Gorge National River and beyond has an exciting future. Below are some of the proposed trails that would allow users an even greater variety of outdoor experience:

New River Gorge National River

Brooklyn Miner's Connector Trail: This proposed 0.8-mile trail would connect the Brooklyn Mine Trail (Trail 28) with the Southside Trail (Trail 31) in the Cunard and Thurmond Region. It would also create a long all-trail hike or ride from Kaymoor Trail (Trail 14) to Rend Trail (Trail 30).

Garden Ground Stacked Loop Trail: This system, using a model similar to the Arrowhead Trail System's stacked loops, would create 33 miles of new single-track near the Terry Top Trail (Trail 38).

Hawk's Nest Connector Trail: This trail, not yet completed, will connect the Hawk's Nest Rail Trail (Trail 62) with Fayette Station Road. This trail is designed to be an intermediate-level trail for mountain biking or hiking, offering views of the New River.

Mud Turn Trail: This proposed trail would connect the gorge rim in the Grandview Region to the New River near the Glade Creek Region via a 2.8-mile path along Mill Creek on an abandoned road.

Panther Branch Connector Trail: This trail will originate at the northern trailhead of the Glade Creek Trail (Trail 43) and parallel the New River along an abandoned road and section of old railroad for 3.0 miles toward Panther Branch.

Other Local Trails Under Development

Meadow River Rail Trail: This proposed rail trail is a joint endeavor between Greenbrier and Fayette counties, with the support of the National Park Service. The trail will eventually run from Rainelle, WV, to Nallen, WV, and will be 16.7 miles long.

Meadow River Trail will occupy a line abandoned in 2008 by the CSX railroad company, coming to fruition thanks to $264,000 of federal stimulus money combined with contributions from Fayette and Greenbrier counties to purchase the right of way and assist in construction. (Originally built in 1907, the rail line once served the Meadow River Lumber Company, with multiple additional owners across the years.) The trail will cross the Meadow River at two points and take users through beautiful and isolated terrain. Primarily designed for hiking and biking, it will also feature access points for fishermen. A general access point for all users is planned for the town of Russellville (WV 41). Future considerations include a potential link to the Gauley River National Recreation Area or Babcock State Park.

Ice encrusts a spring along the Bear Wallow Trail, Camp Creek State Park.

Whipping through a turn in the Arrowhead Trail System.
Photo: Michael B. Boyes

20 NEW RIVER GORGE MOUNTAIN BIKING

Author's Note: A special thank you to Andy Forron of New River Bikes and Adam Stephens of Marathon Bicycles for their assistance in compiling this chapter. Their mountain biking expertise was invaluable.

Biking in the New River Gorge and Surrounding State Parks

The New River Gorge National River and surrounding state parks are an outstanding destination for mountain bike enthusiasts. The local community is made up of a motivated and talented group of riders dedicated to improving the experience and creating more opportunities for mountain bikers in the region.

For more information regarding trails, races, and other activities, check out the businesses and organizations listed at right.

How to Use This Chapter

This chapter is meant to add meaningful mountain bike information to each trail in this guidebook that permits riding — you'll find further information related to trail location, length, intersections, maps, and elevation changes within the main portion of the guide.

Rating System

The rating system for the mountain bike–accessible trails is based on a 1–5 scale similar to the hike rankings used throughout the guide. This modified system takes into account the technical and specific aspects of mountain biking within the *region only* — i.e., a trail ranked 5 on this scale would be the most difficult trail in the New River Gorge area, but not necessarily among the most difficult trails in the United States or world. As a comparison, using the "Trail Difficulty Rating System" developed by the International Mountain Bicycling Association (IMBA), trails in the New River region would fall between the Easiest (White Circle) to More Difficult (Blue Square) ratings.

Combination/Loop Rides

Within each section that follows I've listed a selection of combination and loop rides popular with local mountain bikers. The names for these combinations are listed from start point to end point, and include road link-ups. For example: Kaymoor Trail (Trail 14)/Cunard Access Road/Southside Trail (Trail 31)/Rend Trail (Trail 30).

Marathon Bicycle Company
marathonbikes.com
facebook.com/marathonbikes

New River Bicycle Union
nrbu.org
facebook.com/NewRiverBicycleUnion

New River Bikes
newriverbikes.com
facebook.com/pages/New-River-Bikes/67881882181

Raleigh County Cycle Club
rcccrides.com
facebook.com/pages/Raleigh-County-Cycle-Club/106177224983

West Virginia Mountain Bike Association
wvmba.com
facebook.com/groups/38594432567/members/

Road Cycling Information

As with mountain biking, road cycling in the New River Gorge is an exciting experience and the only method, outside of a motor vehicle, to legally cross the New River Gorge Bridge. There are too many possible routes to list, and the only limitation regarding road cycling in the area is your imagination!

7. Timber Ridge Trail: 2. A great link-up to the Fayetteville Trail. Pedal downhill from the trailhead to this link-up and then down to Wolf Creek. This area is inhabited by black bears, and a local rider recently unintentionally "raced" a bear through the woods.

8. Park Loop Trail: 2. This trail is a wonderful warm-up easily accessed from Fayetteville. It links to the Fayetteville Trail, allowing for long rides through the park and a connection to the Arrowhead Trail System.

10. Long Point Trail: 2. This trail provides a nice wide path to a fabulous viewpoint. Be careful of hikers, as it is an extremely popular route. The final 0.2 miles run along cliff line and are closed to biking. Future plans include a bike rack at the end of the mountain bike portion of the trail (0.2-mile point).

11. Craig Branch Trail: 3. This wide trail follows an old access road, is easy to follow, and makes for a fast downhill ride. Also, multiple connections to other trails are available, making this trail a portion of a longer ride. Pay special attention at the 1.3-mile mark and watch your speed as you enter the switchbacks. A mistake here can have serious consequences due to the steep surrounding terrain.

13. Fayetteville Trail: 5. Portions of this trail are among the trickiest and steepest in the region. Pay particular attention to the segment from the Long Point Trail (Trail 10) intersection to the Kaymoor Trail (Trail 14). At 3.3 miles encounter a set of stairs that require you to carry your bike. There are also several wooden bridges along the trail.

14. Kaymoor Trail: 3. A very nice flat trail that runs along an old mine-access road. The only tough section is the first 0.4 miles of climbing from the Fayette Station Road trailhead; this area is also difficult for the first-time rider on the return due to a narrowing of the trail and the steep surrounding terrain.

Combination/Loop Rides: Try this classic ride, which varies in difficulty and length depending on the trail number and direction chosen in the Arrowhead Trail System: Park Loop Trail (Trail 8)/Arrowhead Trail System/Craig Branch Trail (Trail 11)/Cunard Access Road/Southside Trail (Trail 31)/Rend Trail (Trail 30).

Chapter 6: Arrowhead Trail System

Notes: This stacked loop system is based on four trails, with all intersections marked by the letters A through O — the combinations and loops below are listed using these letters. Riding counterclockwise yields the fastest routes. Want to climb? Go clockwise for the full "mountain" experience.

15. Clovis Trail: 2. This trail is the best introduction to "actual" mountain biking in the region. Short, friendly, and on single-track for the new mountain biker, requiring some trail skills.

16. LeCroy Trail: 3. Great single-track connector to the Long Point/Timber Ridge parking area, for accessing those trails. From the end of LeCroy Trail, turn left onto a paved road then right onto Gatewood Road before taking another right onto Newton Road and arriving at the trailhead parking area (100 meters on left).

17. Adena Trail: 3. This trail has good flow throughout and adds some distance, as well as marks a nice step-up from the Clovis Trail. The connector from Adena to Dalton (G-M) includes a nice "roll-up" rock feature.

18. Dalton Trail: 4. This longest standalone trail within the system offers alternative lines along the route. The portion of trail between points M and N includes a very fun downhill ride.

Combination/Loop Rides: The Arrowhead Trail System is unique within the New River Gorge due to its lettered intersection markers, used below to describe four great loop combinations:

For the Young Rider: Arrowhead Parking-**C-D-E-**Arrowhead Parking

Easy Beginner Loop: Arrowhead Parking-**B-C-D-F-G-H-E-**Arrowhead Parking

Fun Loop: Arrowhead Parking-**A-C-J-K-L-M-N-H-I-H-E-D-F-G-H-E-**Arrowhead Parking

For the "Racer" in Each of Us: Arrowhead Parking-**B-C-J-K-L-M-N-H-G-F-D-E-H-A-**Arrowhead parking

Fayetteville's Original Bike Shop
NEW
BIKES
RIVER
www.New River Bikes.com
SALES
DEMOS
RENTALS
BICYCLE FITS
GUIDED TOURS
FULL SERVICE
CUSTOM WHEELS
NEWRIVERBIKES.COM
304.574.2453
Photo: M. Boyes

Biking along the upper portion of Old Sewell Road Trail toward Glade Creek Grist Mill. Photo: Michael B. Boyes

19. Town Loop Connector Trail: 2. This short connector trail allows access to the Nuttallburg Mine Complex for riders along the Keeneys Creek Rail Trail. There are a few curves, so stay heads-up for hikers.

20. Seldom Seen Trail: 1. A short single-track that leads to an abandoned community. At trail's end, make sure to dismount and check out the ruins.

22. Tipple Trail: 1. Mountain biking is permitted only along the first 0.3 miles, along the top of the coke furnaces. Once you reach the company store, you can either continue to the Seldom Seen Trail (Trail 20) or return by the same path.

24. Headhouse Trail: 4. This trail offers a steep descent and some technical riding through an area rutted by runoff. It leads steeply down to the Nuttallburg Mine headhouse and requires an almost continuous climb to return to the trailhead.

25. Keeneys Creek Rail Trail: 1. This gentle and well-graded (4 percent) rail trail follows an abandoned branch of the Chesapeake and Ohio (C&O) railway. This trail crosses four wooden trestle bridges.

25a. Keeneys Creek Road Return: 2. This road return connects the end of the Keeneys Creek Rail Trail to the original trailhead parking. The majority of the ride is paved and downhill, passing the many pools and cascades of Keeneys Creek. Using this road return creates a scenic round-trip ride.

Combination/Loop Rides: The only link-up available in this region is the following, which allows an in-depth look at the Nuttallburg Mine Complex and creates a 6.16-mile loop:

Keeneys Creek Rail Trail (Trail 25)/Town Loop Connector Trail (Trail 19)/Tipple Trail (Trail 22)/Seldom Seen Trail (Trail 20)/Tipple Trail/Town Loop Connector Trail/the remainder of Keeneys Creek Rail Trail/Keeneys Creek Road Return (Trail 25a).

Chapter 8: Cunard and Thurmond Region

26. Arbuckle Connector Trail: This trail is not an official mountain bike trail within the New River Gorge National River. However, I've included it here as a short connector trail/mandatory portage between the bike-friendly Southside (Trail 31) and Rend (Trail 30) trails.
28. Brooklyn Mine Trail: 3. This is a wide trail with a steady grade. It can be somewhat rough at times due to horse traffic and is not heavily used by local bikers.
29. Stone Cliff Trail: 3. A steady ride with some rocky areas throughout. This trail ends with a climb over the final 0.5 miles to the trail's end.
30. Rend Trail: 3. This trail has a steady grade, with numerous wooden trestle bridges that become extremely slick when wet, as well as a set of stairs that require a carry-around due to a detached spire that blocks the original rail-line route.
31. Southside Trail: 3. A relatively flat trail with only a few rises, but still a nice ride. As one local rider puts it: "Not your typical rails-to-trails ride." At 4.2 miles the trail narrows and it becomes necessary to climb up and over a small rise and rocky streambed. A great ride along the river, passing a number of former coal towns.
Combination/Loop Rides: The following combination creates a long ride that encompasses a number of intermediate-level trails in the region:
Kaymoor Trail (Trail 14)/Cunard Access Road/Southside Trail (Trail 31)/Arbuckle Connector Trail (Trail 26; portage)/Rend Trail (Trail 30). This one-way ride totals 19.2 miles of riding plus a 0.25-mile carry along the Arbuckle Connector Trail.

Chapter 9: Grandview Region

37a. Grandview Rim (road return only): 1. While the Grandview Rim Trail does not allow bicycle traffic, the road return for this trail, from Turkey Spur Overlook to the main overlook parking area at Grandview, is a popular and easy ride along paved roads. It offers nice views through the forest.
38. Terry Top Trail: 3. A wide and well-marked trail that begins with a long descent. While not frequented at this time, this trail could become part of a larger stacked loop system similar to the Arrowhead Trail System, but on a massive scale comprising 33 miles of looping single-track. Stay tuned for developments!
39. Little Laurel Trail: 5. The trail is wide and well graded throughout, with a few minor rough portions. Proceed with caution at the two-mile point, as a landslide has narrowed the trail significantly. While an easy ride to the river, the ride back to the gorge rim is a constant and grueling push for its entire length.
Combination/Loop Rides: No combinations available.

Chapter 10: Glade Creek Region

43. Glade Creek Trail: 3. From the northern terminus, this trail provides a steady climb to the southern trailhead for the entire 5.69-mile ride. Areas to note include the 0.8-mile mark, where one segment requires a carry up and over stone stairs; a bridge at 3.0 miles, which can be very slick (walk-across recommended); and at 5.3 miles, a landslide that requires walking your bike across a short section. April is a great time to visit, as wildflower blooms cover the surrounding area.
Combination/Loop Rides: No combinations available.

Chapter 12: Summersville Lake Wildlife Management Area

49. Salmon Run Spur Trail: 1. This short spur trail connects to the longer Salmon Run Trail 0.8 miles from the latter's upper trailhead. It is a wide and smooth path that connects in the middle of a tight downhill turn in the main Salmon Run Trail.
50. Long Point Trail: 2. A fun and straightforward ride that includes a fair amount of climbing, but is made worth it by the spectacular views at trail's end.
51. Salmon Run Trail: 3. Popular due to its abundance of tight single-track along a beautiful area.
51a. Salmon Run Road Return: 1. From the lower trailhead, follow this paved road back to the spur trail to

rejoin the main trail or ride all the way to the upper trailhead.

52. Battle Run Trail: 3. This trail begins along a wide, flat access road that borders the lake before climbing and, at 0.8 miles, entering the forest. From this point the trail follows an access road that is rutted in numerous places. Not popular with mountain bikers.

Combination/Loop Rides: The only available combination includes the links between the Salmon Run Trail (Trail 51), the Salmon Run Road Return (Trail 51a), and the Salmon Run Spur Trail (Trail 49).

Along Glade Creek.
Photo: Michael B. Boyes

Chapter 14: Hawk's Nest State Park

60. Cotton Hill to Hawk's Nest Dam Trail: 2. This trail is suitable for all ages and abilities up to its 0.5-mile point; from the junction with the single-track leading down and right, you'll want more advanced abilities and proper protective equipment to navigate the remaining 0.36 miles.

62. Hawk's Nest Rail Trail: 2. One of the area's most scenic trails, this is a mellow, wonderful ride on the descent but requires a constant climb to return.

Combination/Loop Rides: In the near future, the soon-to-be-completed Hawk's Nest Connector Trail will link the Hawk's Nest Rail Trail to the Fayette Station Road and the Fayetteville, Lansing, and Kaymoor Region trails.

Chapter 15: Babcock State Park

66. Triple Creek Trail: 2. A curvy ride along a lesser-used trail — keep your head up to follow the trail as it winds through the forest. Makes for a nice link-up with the Wilderness Trail (Trail 68).

67. Old Sewell Road Trail: 2. This wide and well-graded former rail line connects to the Narrow Gauge Trail (Trail 72) just before ending at a landslide. Makes for a fun descent or a steady climb, depending on the direction of travel.

68. Wilderness Trail: 2. A doublewide trail throughout its length that links to the Triple Creek Trail and creates a loop that is scenic but not challenging.

72. Narrow Gauge Trail: 3. A flat and fun ride, but watch out for the two "hike-a-bike" sections around sections of washed-out trail.

Combination/Loop Rides: Two combinations available:

- Narrow Gauge Trail (Trail 72)/Old Sewell Road Trail (Trail 67): a 4.11-mile one-way journey.
- Wilderness Trail (Trail 68)/Triple Creek Trail (Trail 66)/Park Road: a 3.51-mile loop.

Chapter 16: Little Beaver State Park

Note: Little Beaver State Park is home to the New's most technical riding and is a popular destination for riders. In wet weather, Little Beaver is the place to be, as it dries more quickly and drains better than many other locations. Many trails are short, but the connections are endless. The following descriptions are brief for that reason, as the nature of a ride is more dependent on the trail direction and combinations than on single-track technicality.

73. Hemlock Trail: 2. A short, steep connector from Nature Ridge Trail (Trail 88) to Beaver Creek Trail (Trail 82) that is not too technical but can be slick.

74. Drop Off Trail: 3. The name says it all. Be prepared to descend or climb, depending on the approach.

75. Turkey Spur Trail: 2. A nice alternative to the standard Rhododendron Run Trail route along a spur that then reconnects.

76. Creek Bed Trail: 4. This is a straight descent from ridgeline to creek along a doublewide but rocky trail.

77. Easy Street Trail: 2. Easy going as you wind along single-track through small hemlocks and pines.

78. Deer Trail: 2. A great connector between the park's two longest trails, Laurel Creek Trail (Trail 90) and Rhododendron Trail (Trail 89). A fun ride in and of itself.

79. Billy Goat's Gruff Trail: 5. Be prepared for technical and rocky going all along this short trail.

80. Topper's Ridge Trail: 4. This trail is similar to Billy Goat's Gruff Trail, but just a shade easier.

81. Black Bear Run Trail: 1. A fun ride along Little Beaver Creek. Keep an eye out for low-hanging rhododendron branches along the first 0.4 miles and the rocky stream crossing at trail's end.

82. Beaver Creek Trail: 1. An easy and straightforward ride along a popular trail. Watch for hikers and other mountain bikers approaching from the numerous intersections.

83. Stone Trough Trail: 5. One of the park's more technically difficult trails.

84. Crooked Rock Trail: 3. This trail connects Rhododendron Run Trail (Trail 89) with Stone Trough Trail (Trail 83). Watch for the curved wooden bridge at 0.2 miles.

85. Lake Front Trail: 1. The easiest trail in the park, this is a nice level ride with little technical difficulty. Take care crossing the bridge.

86. Weaver Way Trail: 3. Be prepared to "get on and off the gas" frequently as you make your way through the rhododendrons.

87. Railroad Grade Trail: 2. The right side (as you look upstream) is the much better portion of trail. The left side is cluttered with half-hidden stones that make for slow going.

88. Nature Ridge Trail: 3. One of the longer trails in the park, and should be included in any loop.

89. Rhododendron Run Trail: 4. Ride up or down Lilly Hill, a popular climb along this trail. At 1.2 miles watch for a log ramp.
90. Laurel Creek Trail: 4. Almost always included in a trip to the park, this trail is brilliant and easily combined with a number of other trails. Watch for the multiple bridges and the ramp at 0.2 miles. Some long, looping turns = great fun.
Combination/Loop Rides: The combinations available in this park are too numerous to list.

Chapter 17: Bluestone State Park and Bluestone National Scenic River

98. Bluestone Turnpike Trail: 2. This 7.44-mile trail follows the river, and is a little more difficult than your standard rail trail due to the uneven and often muddy surface. The segment nearest Bluestone State Park is wide but then narrows considerably toward the Pipestem end of the trail, with some areas requiring narrow single-track riding above steep grades.
Combination/Loop Rides: The only combination available is with the River Trail (Trail 114) in Pipestem Resort State Park. If riding from Bluestone State Park, intersect the River Trail at its lower terminus, riding past the Mountain Creek Lodge, fording the Bluestone River, and pedaling along a relentless uphill grade to the McKeever Lodge. This creates a 12.5-mile one-way trip.

Chapter 18: Pipestem Resort State Park

100. Long Branch Trail: 1. This short, paved route allows fast access downhill to the lake.
106. Lake View Trail: 2. A wide trail often used by horseback riders and that's thus often rutted, making for an unpleasant ride.
108. Law Hollow Trail: 2. This short trail leads to the main park road along an old access road; very muddy at the 0.3-mile mark.
112. Lake Shore Trail: 1. One of the park's more popular trails — with everybody. Expect to see many hikers and horseback riders.
114. River Trail: 4. A serious ride. Although the trail is wide along the majority of its length, pay special attention at 2.1 miles for a rutted section and at 3.1 miles at the Bluestone River.
Combination/Loop Rides: You can access the Lake Shore Trail from the Law Hollow Trail, the Lake View Trail, or the Long Branch Trail. The River Trail connects to the Bluestone Turnpike Trail.

Future Trails/Trails in Progress

Trail growth in the New River Gorge National River has an exciting future. Below are some of the proposed trails that would allow mountain bikers an even greater variety of experience:

Brooklyn Miner's Connector Trail: This proposed 0.8-mile trail would connect the Brooklyn Mine Trail (Trail 28) with the Southside Trail (Trail 31) in the Cunard and Thurmond Region. It would also create a long all-trail ride from Kaymoor Trail (Trail 14) to Rend Trail (Trail 30).
Garden Ground Stacked Loop Trail: This system, using a model similar to the Arrowhead Trail System's stacked loops, would create 33 miles of new single-track near the Terry Top Trail (Trail 38).
Hawk's Nest Connector Trail: This trail, not yet completed, will connect the Hawk's Nest Rail Trail (Trail 62) with Fayette Station Road. This trail is designed to be an intermediate-level trail for mountain biking or hiking, offering views of the New River.
Mud Turn Trail: This proposed trail would connect the gorge rim in the Grandview Region to the New River near the Glade Creek Region via a 2.8-mile path along Mill Creek on an abandoned road.
Panther Branch Connector Trail: This trail will originate at the northern trailhead of the Glade Creek Trail (Trail 43) and parallel the New River along an abandoned road and section of old railroad for 3.0 miles toward Panther Branch.

APPENDICES

A: LODGING

Fayetteville, WV: Fayetteville is the "adventure hub" of the region and an outstanding choice for lodging, as the town is located right on the New River Gorge, offering easy access to amazing trails and a variety of outdoor activities, including rafting, rock climbing, zip-lines, and other adventures. Fayetteville also allows easy access via US 19 to other areas that include Summersville to the north, and the interstates I-77 and I-64 to the south. All lodging options listed on this page lie within 30 miles of Fayetteville and the gorge.

Bed and Breakfast

The Historic Morris Harvey House
201 West Maple Avenue
Fayetteville, WV 25840
(304) 250-7090, (877) 253-0784
morrisharveyhouse.com

Hotels

Quality Inn
103 Elliotts Way
Fayetteville, WV 25840
(304) 574-3443

Camping

Camping is available at the following state parks in this book: Babcock State Park, Bluestone State Park, Little Beaver State Park, and Pipestem Resort State Park. You'll also find camping at all three "Adventure Resorts" in Appendix C (page 345) and at the two campgrounds below:

American Alpine Club – New River Gorge Campground
(Primitive camping – no RVs or trailers.)
55 Burma Road
Ames Heights, WV 25862
americanalpineclub.org/p/new-river-gorge-campground
facebook.com/AmericanAlpineClub?fref=ts

Chestnut Creek Campground (Primitive camping – no RVs or trailers.)
Lansing Road
Lansing, WV 25862
(304) 574-3136

Other Nearby Options

Oak Hill and Beckley, WV, located respectively along US Route 19 and interstates 64 and 77, also offer an abundance of lodging options within easy driving distance of the region's trails and other activities.

Cabin Rentals

Country Road Cabins
1508 Sunday Road
Hico, WV 25854
(888) 712-2246
wvcabins.com
facebook.com/CountryRoadCabins

Gorge Gateway Center
130 Laurel Creek Road
Fayetteville, WV 25840
(304) 574-1802
newrivergorgegatewaycenter.com

Hemlock Haven Cabins
Mallard Road
Hico, WV 25854
(304) 575-1260
hemlockhavenwv.com
facebook.com/hemlock.haven

Mill Creek Cabins
PO Box 148
Lansing, WV 25862
(800) 692-5005
millcreekcabins.com
facebook.com/pages/Mill-Creek-Cabins/142048502531494

New River Cabins
Smales Branch Road
Hico, WV 25854
(304) 640-7333
newrivercabinswv.com
facebook.com/pages/New-River-Cabins-Fayetteville-West-Virginia/155462794507378

Opossum Creek Retreat
Retreat Road
Lansing, WV 25862
(888) 488-4836
opossumcreek.com
facebook.com/cabinrentalswv

B: RESTAURANTS

The New River Gorge is home to a plentiful array of local restaurants sure to satisfy every appetite. From Pies and Pints, a Fayetteville restaurant that has won national acclaim and been featured on the Food Network and the Cooking Channel, to the standard American chain restaurants, your taste buds will be treated well during your visit.

Fayetteville and Surrounding Area

Burrito Bar at Breeze Hill
179 Oscar White Road
Lansing, WV 25862
(304) 574-2750
theburritobarwv.com
facebook.com/TheBurritoBar
Burritos, music, drinks, and far-off views at sunset.

Cathedral Café
134 South Court Street
Fayetteville, WV 25840
(304) 574-0202
facebook.com/pages/Cathedral-Cafe/208665849608?fref=ts
Whether you want breakfast, a great cup of joe, or to listen to a little music, this old Methodist church is just the place.

DiOGi's Mexican Grill
312 Court Street
Fayetteville, WV 25840
(304) 574-3647
diogismexicangrill.com
facebook.com/pages/DiOGis/69535519035
Why did they spell it like that? Have a great Mexican meal and find out why.

Dirty Ernie's Rib Pit
310 Keller Avenue
Fayetteville, WV 25840
(304) 574-4822
dirtyernies.com
facebook.com/pages/Dirty-Ernies-Rib-Pit/111717735530140?ref=ts
Eat meat and learn the interesting tale of Dirty Ernie, the man himself.

Don Patron's Mexican Grill
Route 19, Fayette Town Center
Fayetteville, WV 25840
(304) 574-2003
facebook.com/pages/Don-Patron-Mexican-Grill/244512855598521
Your full complement of Mexican favorites.

National Food Establishments in Fayetteville, WV:

Arby's
Bob Evan's
Dairy Queen
Gino's Pizza
Godfather's Pizza
Kentucky Fried Chicken
Long John Silver's
McDonald's
Subway
Taco Bell
Tudor's Biscuit World
Wendy's

The surrounding towns also offer a variety of local and chain restaurants to satisfy all tastes.

Gumbo's Cajun Restaurant
103 South Court Street
Fayetteville, WV 25840
(304) 574-4704
facebook.com/pages/Gumbos-Cajun-Restaurant/388127122424
Get your fill of low-country Cajun cuisine here in the high country of WV.

Pies & Pints
219 West Maple Avenue
Fayetteville, WV 25840
(304) 574-2200
piesandpints.net
facebook.com/piesandpints
Pizza and beer...better than you have ever had.

Secret Sandwich Society
103 Keller Avenue
Fayetteville, WV 25840
(304) 574-4777
secretsandwichsociety.com
facebook.com/SecretSandwichSociety
It's not a secret...their sandwiches are outstanding, and the deck is great too.

Swirl
117 South Court Street
Fayetteville, WV 25840
(304) 574-3005
swirlwv.com
facebook.com/swirlwv
Not your standard ice-cream shop!

Wild Flour Bakery
105 West Maple Avenue
Fayetteville, WV 25840
(304) 574-0001
facebook.com/wildflourbakerywv
Go here for baked delicacies!

C: ACTIVITIES, OUTFITTERS, GUIDES, & ADVENTURE COMPANIES

Not only does the New River Gorge have some of the best trails in the eastern United States, it is also an adventure-sports and outdoor-enthusiast wonderland. The following outfitters, guides, and adventure companies can help you make the most of your time in the area.

Adventure Resorts (Offering a Host of Activities)

Activities: ATV riding, fishing trips, flat-water kayaking, guided hiking, horseback riding, mountain biking, obstacle courses, paddleboarding, paintball, rafting, rappelling, rock climbing, skeet and trap shooting, spelunking, team building, water park, zip-lining
Companies: North American River Runners, Wildwater Expeditions

ACE Adventure Resort
PO Box 1168
Oak Hill, WV 25901
(800) 787-3982
aceraft.com
facebook.com/ACE.Adventure Resort.WestVirginiaVacations

Activities: ATV riding, fishing trips, flat-water kayaking, guided hiking, horseback riding, mountain biking, obstacle courses, paddleboarding, paintball, rafting, rappelling, rock climbing, swimming complex, team building, timber trek, zip-lining
Companies: Class VI, Mountain River, Rivermen, Songer Whitewater

Adventures on the Gorge
Ames Heights Road – PO Box 78
Lansing, WV 25862
(888) 650-1932
adventurewestvirginia.com
facebook.com/AdventuresOnTheGorge

Activities: ATV riding, fishing trips, float trips, guided hiking, horseback riding, mountain biking, paintball, rafting, rock climbing, zip-lining
Companies: Appalachian Wildwaters, Extreme Expeditions, USA Raft

River Expeditions
900 Broadway Avenue
Oak Hill, WV 25901
(800) 463-9873
raftinginfo.com
facebook.com/raftinginfo

Art (Learn More about Local Artisans)

Fayetteville Arts Coalition
PO Box 344
Fayetteville, WV 25840
(304) 541-9276
fayettevilleartscoalition.org
facebook.com/FayettevilleArtsCoalition?fref=ts

Studio B Art Boutique, Wine, and Beer Gallery
309 Keller Avenue
Fayetteville, WV 25840
(304) 574-9100
facebook.com/pages/Studio-B-Art-Boutique-Wine-Beer-Gallery/205270868720

Bike (Sales, Rentals, Repairs, and Tours)

Marathon Bicycle Company
104 East Maple Avenue
Fayetteville, WV 25840
(304) 574-2337
marathonbikes.com
facebook.com/marathonbikes

New River Bikes
221 North Court Street
Fayetteville, WV 25840
(304) 574-2453
newriverbikes.com
facebook.com/pages/New-River-Bikes/67881882181

Boat (Jetboat Rides on the New River)

New River Jetboats
49 Hawks Nest Park Road
Ansted, WV 25812
(304) 469-2525
newriverjetboats.com
facebook.com/pages/New-River-Jetboats/198581226822434

Climb (Guiding and Instruction)

Hard Rock Climbing
131 South Court Street
Fayetteville, WV 25840
(304) 574-0735
hardrockclimbing.com
facebook.com/pages/Hard-Rock-Climbing-Services/113399582026670

New River Mountain Guides
101 East Wiseman Avenue
Fayetteville, WV 25840
(304) 574-3872
newriverclimbing.com
facebook.com/NewRiverMountainGuides

Fish (Guiding and Instruction)

2FishWV – Freelance Fishing and Guiding Service
Court Street
Fayetteville, WV 25840
(304) 469-3272
2fishwv.com
facebook.com/pages/2fishwvcom/237594878370

Fly (Aerial Tours and Acrobatics)
Wild Blue Adventure Company
214 Hinkle Road
Fayetteville, WV 25840
(304) 574-1150
wildblueadventurecompany.com
facebook.com/pages/Wild-Blue-Adventure-Company/103810509671585

Gear (Gear, Maps, and Books)
ACE Adventure Gear
851 Fayette Station Road
Fayetteville, WV 25840
(304) 574-1900
aceadventuregear.com
facebook.com/pages/ACE-Adventure-Gear/106285982737574

Water Stone Outdoors
101 East Wiseman Avenue
Fayetteville, WV 25840
(304) 574-2425
waterstoneoutdoors.com
facebook.com/WaterStoneOutdoors

Golf (Golf, Driving Range, Pro Shop)
Bridge Haven Golf Club
Salem-Gatewood Road
Fayetteville, WV 25840
(304) 574-2120
wvweb.com/bridgehaven
facebook.com/pages/Bridge-Haven-Golf-Club/155964281107889?ref=ts

Raft (Enjoy the Rapids)
Offered by ACE Adventure Resort, Adventures on the Gorge, and River Expeditions. See "Adventure Resorts" (page 345) for contact information.
Other companies that offer raft trips include:
New and Gauley River Adventures
PO Box 44
Lansing, WV 25862
(800) 759-7238
gauley.com
facebook.com/pages/New-and-Gauley-RiverAdventures/231821576941?fref=ts

Ride (Horseback Rides and Tours)
New River Trail Rides
PO Box 67
Oak Hill, WV 25901
(888) 743-3982
ridewva.com
facebook.com/newrivertrailrides

Roll (Zorbing, aka Globe Riding, aka "Rolling Down a Hill in a Plastic Ball")
Orb the Gorge
88 Mountain State Campground Road
Lansing, WV 25862
(304) 250-4555
orbthegorge.com
facebook.com/pages/Orb-the-Gorge/198913693512709

Ski/Snowboard (Winter Fun)
Winterplace Ski Resort
100 Flat Top Road
Ghent, WV 25843
(800) 607-7669
winterplace.com
facebook.com/winterplaceskiresort?fref=ts

Walk (Tour the NRG Bridge by Catwalk)
Bridge Walk
PO Box 132
Lansing, WV 25862
(304) 574-1300
bridgewalk.com
facebook.com/newrivergorge-bridgewalk

Yoga
Kula Community Yoga Studio
128 South Court St.
Fayetteville, WV 25840
(304) 207-2988
wvkula.com

D: MAP RESOURCES

The United States Geological Survey (USGS) has a full complement of maps for the region. These maps are scaled at 1:24,000, with the most recent versions dated 2011. These maps are available online or at local retailers.

National Geographic has also produced a Trails Illustrated map of the area that includes the New River Gorge National River, Bluestone National Scenic River, Gauley River National Recreation Area, and some state parks. This map is scaled at 1:55,000 and is available online or at local retailers.

USGS Map Resources for the New River Gorge National River

Fayetteville, Lansing, and Kaymoor Region
- USGS Fayetteville quad 1:24,000

Arrowhead Trail System
- USGS Fayetteville quad 1:24,000

Nuttallburg Region
- USGS Fayetteville quad 1:24,000

Cunard and Thurmond Region
- USGS Fayetteville quad 1:24,000
- USGS Thurmond quad 1:24,000

Grandview Region
- USGS Prince quad 1:24,000

Glade Creek Region
- USGS Prince quad 1:24,000
- USGS Meadow Creek quad 1:24,000

Brooks and Sandstone Region
- USGS Meadow Creek quad 1:24,000
- USGS Hinton quad 1:24,000

USGS Map Resources for Nearby West Virginia State Parks

Summersville Lake Wildlife Management Area
- USGS Mount Nebo quad 1:24,000
- USGS Summersville quad 1:24,000

Carnifex Ferry Battlefield State Park
- USGS Summersville Dam quad 1:24,000

Hawk's Nest State Park
- USGS Ansted quad 1:24,000
- USGS Beckwith quad 1:24,000
- USGS Fayetteville quad 1:24,000

Babcock State Park
- USGS Danese quad 1:24,000
- USGS Thurmond quad 1:24,000

Little Beaver State Park
- USGS Prince quad 1:24,000
- USGS Shady Spring quad 1:24,000

Bluestone State Park and Bluestone National Scenic River
- USGS Flat Top quad 1:24,000
- USGS Hinton quad 1:24,000
- USGS Pipestem quad 1:24,000

Pipestem Resort State Park
- USGS Flat Top quad 1:24,000
- USGS Pipestem quad 1:24,000

E: NATIONAL AND STATE PARK CONTACT INFORMATION

Babcock State Park
486 Babcock Road
Danese, WV 25831
(304) 438-3004
babcocksp.com

Bluestone National Scenic River
Park Headquarters
P.O. Box 246
Glen Jean, WV 25846
(304) 465-0508
nps.gov/blue

Bluestone State Park
HC 78 Box 3
Hinton, WV 25951
(304) 466-2805
bluestonesp.com

Carnifex Ferry Battlefield State Park
1194 Carnifex Ferry Road
Summersville, WV 26651
(304) 872-0825
carnifexferrybattlefieldstatepark.com

Gauley River National Recreation Area
Park Headquarters
P.O. Box 246
Glen Jean, WV 25846
(304) 465-0508
nps.gov/gari

Hawk's Nest State Park
P.O. Box 857
49 Hawks Nest Park Road
Ansted, WV 25812
(304) 658-5212
hawksnestsp.com

Little Beaver State Park
1402 Grandview Road
Beaver, WV 25813
(304) 763-2494
littlebeaverstatepark.com

New River Gorge National River
Park Headquarters
P.O. Box 246
Glen Jean, WV 25846
(304) 465-0508
nps.gov/neri

Canyon Rim Visitor Center	(304) 574-2115
Grandview Visitor Center	(304) 763-3145
Sandstone Visitor Center	(304) 466-0417
Thurmond Depot Visitor Center	(304) 465-8550

Pipestem Resort State Park
P.O. Box 150
Pipestem, WV 25979
(304) 466-1800
pipestemresort.com

Summersville Lake Wildlife Management Area
West Virginia Division of Natural Resources (WVDNR)
Building 74
324 Fourth Avenue
South Charleston, WV 25303
(304) 558-2754

F: RECOMMENDED READING

The following books on the New River Gorge and surrounding area provide additional information on the region's history and recreation options.

Natural History

Amphibians & Reptiles in West Virginia
N. Bayard Green & Thomas K. Pauley
ISBN: 0822958023

Birds of West Virginia Field Guide
Stan Tekiela
ISBN: 1591930707

Flora of West Virginia
P. D. Strausbaugh and Earl L. Core
ISBN: 0890920109

Mushrooms of West Virginia and the Central Appalachians
William C. Roody
ISBN: 0813190398

The Butterflies of West Virginia and their Caterpillars
Thomas J. Allen
ISBN: 0822956578

Regional History

Coal, Class, and Color: Blacks in Southern West Virginia, 1915-32 (Blacks in the New World)
Joe William Trotter, Jr.
ISBN: 0252061195

Escape From Indian Captivity: The Story of Mary Draper Ingles and Son Thomas Ingles, As Told by John Ingles, Sr.
John Ingles Sr. (Edited by Roberta Ingles Steele)
ISBN: 0318036134

Life, Work, and Rebellion in the Coal Fields: The Southern West Virginia Miners, 1880-1922
David Corbin
ISBN: 0252008952

Lilly on the Bluestone
William R. Sanders
ISBN: 0962527300

September Blood: The Battle of Carnifex Ferry
Terry Lowry
ISBN: 1891852787

The Hawks Nest Tunnel: An Unabridged History
Patricia Spangler
ISBN: 098018620X

The Smokeless Coal Fields of West Virginia: A Brief History
W.P. Tams, Jr.
ISBN: 0937058556

Trans-Allegheny Pioneers
John P. Hale
ISBN: 096171462X

West Virginia: A History
John Alexander Williams
ISBN: 0937058564

West Virginia's Last Logging Railroad: Meadow River Lumber Company
Philip V. Bagdon
ISBN: 1883089808

West Virginia Narrow Gauge: Mann's Creek Railway
Ron Lane & Ted Schnepf
ISBN: 1883089360

Recreation

New River Gorge Rock Climbs
Mike Williams
ISBN: 098261540X

Whitewater Rafting on West Virginia's New and Gauley Rivers: Come on in, the Water's Weird
Jay Young
ISBN: 1609492463

G: TRAILS LISTED ALPHABETICALLY (INCLUDES HISTORIC TRAIL NAMES)

ABOUT THE AUTHOR

R. Bryan Simon, a native of West Virginia, is a graduate of the United States Military Academy at West Point and a former U.S. Army infantry officer and Army Ranger. After an injury in 2003, he left the military to pursue other goals.

Bryan is a partner in the firm Vertical Medicine Resources (vertical-medicine.com) and serves on the board of directors for the nonprofits Appalachian Mountain Rescue Team and the Appalachian Center for Wilderness Medicine; he writes on a variety of subjects related to wilderness and climbing medicine and adventure sports. Bryan met his wife, Deb, on Mount Kilimanjaro in Tanzania in 2001, and since that time they have climbed and trekked together around the world. When not on the road, trail, or rock, Bryan can be found at his home in the New River Gorge, WV.